Max Weber and Thomas Mann

Max Weber and Thomas Mann

Calling and the Shaping of the Self

Harvey Goldman

UNIVERSITY OF CALIFORNIA PRESS
Berkeley · Los Angeles · London

University of California Press
Berkeley and Los Angeles, California

University of California Press, Ltd.
London, England

© 1988 by
The Regents of the University of California

Library of Congress Cataloging-in-Publication Data
Goldman, Harvey, 1946–
    Max Weber and Thomas Mann: calling and the shaping of the self/
Harvey Goldman.
        p. cm.
    Bibliography: p.
    Includes index.
    ISBN 0–520–06279–5 (alk. paper)
    1. Vocation. 2. Personality. 3. National characteristics, German.
4. Weber, Max, 1864–1920. 5. Mann, Thomas, 1875–1955.
I. Title.
BV4740.G65   1988
126—dc19   88–1327
                                                                       CIP

Printed in the United States of America

1 2 3 4 5 6 7 8 9

To Elizabeth, Johanna, and Katherine

Contents

PART II.   PERSONALITY AND THE NEW MEN
OF THE CALLING

Preface

This book has its beginnings with a copy of Thomas Mann's *Doctor Faustus*, bought when I was a student in France and read in Heidelberg, Paris, and Lyon. I loved this novel like no other; I found it intellectually challenging and emotionally overpowering, but something about it and its artist searching for a "calling" troubled me, though I could not spell it out. When I reread Max Weber's lectures "Science as a Vocation" and "Politics as a Vocation," both of which strongly argued the need for a calling, my quandary deepened. Inspired by the parallels between these works, I have written this book, which is the outcome of my struggle, lasting many years, to understand what disturbed me about these writings of two men whose works I so admired. My quest led me to consider many other, and earlier, writings of Weber and Mann to uncover the foundations of their social thought, and these foundations are the subject of this book. In a future work I hope to provide an analysis of the three works that first provoked my interest and my puzzlement, works that reflect Weber's and Mann's mature political, social, and cultural understanding of Germany and of themselves.

The idea for the project first occurred to me in a course taught by Norman Jacobson at Berkeley, after I had been introduced to Max Weber's work by John Schaar and Robert Biller. Yet I would have been unable to carry it out had it not been for the people who taught me to read literature and political theory. My greatest intellectual and personal debt is to Herbert Josephs, who showed me things in literary works and about the self that I had never dreamed of. My teachers at Berkeley, Norman Jacobson, Michael Rogin, Hanna Pitkin, and John Schaar, created a unique atmosphere of intellectual inquiry open to diverse approaches to political thought as well as to the best works from other disciplines, literary, historical, sociological, and philosophical. This project officially began as a dissertation supervised by Norman Jacobson, Michael Rogin, and Wolfgang Sauer, and I am particularly indebted to them for their help.

I would like to thank the Bayerische Akademie der Wissenschaften, Munich, for access to its resources; the Institut für Soziologie at the University of Munich for use of its Max Weber Archiv and for space to work; and the Thomas Mann Archiv, Zurich, its director Hans Wysling, and the many talented people who work there for access to its extraordinary resources and for permitting me to read and write there in the summer of 1979.

Research for this project was supported by grants from the National Endowment for the Humanities; the Council on Research in the Social Sciences, Columbia University; and the Spencer Foundation, in a program administered by Teachers College, Columbia. The College of the University of Chicago gave me time off to do research in Europe; the Department of Political Science, Columbia, provided me research assistants. I would like to express my gratitude to all of them.

I received great personal help and professional support from Martin and Brigitte Riesebrodt and from Sabine Kudera, who are friends as well as colleagues. Several friends gave me the benefit of their knowledge and expertise and read all or parts of this manuscript. Two of them, Peter Breiner and George Shulman, have been my constant intellectual companions and community. I have discussed the issues of this work for many years with Peter Breiner, whose insight and support have been an enormous help. George Shulman read the manuscript with great sensitivity and helped me sharpen my ideas and vastly improve the work. Alan Milchman read the manuscript with knowledge and sympathetic understanding, and he gave me encouragement and advice. Friedrich Kratochwil lent to this work some of his exceptional intellectual rigor and was unstinting in his help and support. Jonathan Knudsen made numerous good suggestions drawing on his excellent historical sense. Marvin Cohen read the earliest version and pressed me to go further in asking questions and providing alternatives. Finally, Ken Jacobson taught me a great deal about good clear writing from his many years as an accomplished professional. To all of them I am profoundly indebted. I would also like to thank Jitka Slavik, Gail Kligman, Joyce Gutstein, Reinhart Koselleck, Lawrence Porter, Terry Lynn Karl, and David Landes, all of whom helped me at different stages of this project.

I wish to thank my fellow members of the social theory reading group at Harvard University in 1981–82, with whom I discussed Weber and many other issues: Alessandro Pizzorno, Thomas McCarthy, Jeff Weintraub, Jeffrey Herf, Don Black, Stephen Holmes, and Michael Donnelly. The Society of Fellows in the Humanities, Columbia, gave valuable responses to a talk I gave on some of this material in 1986. Some of it was also presented at the Sixth Max Weber Colloquium, William Patterson College, November 1986.

Finally, I would like to thank Naomi Schneider, my editor at the University of California Press, for her interest, her constant support, and her advice, and the others at the Press who have helped me so much, especially Mary Renaud and Sheila Levine.

The Problem of Work and Identity

Max Weber (1864–1920) is usually known as the man who made the idea of "disenchantment" or, more literally, "demagification" (*Entzauberung*) not merely an important theme for conceiving of modern life but perhaps its most essential aspect.[1] Thomas Mann (1875–1955), in contrast, was known to his children as "the magician" (*der Zauberer*), a man for whom a kind of magic was not only a fact of his life but also, in part, the object of his life, a man who could even conceive of "magic mountains" and find an audience ready to follow him there.[2] But the affinities between Weber and Mann are much greater than such simple oppositions might suggest. Indeed, though they probably met only twice,[3] Weber and Mann were engaged from early in their lives in remarkably similar enterprises. Their work was built on shared conceptions drawn from a common intellectual and national heritage. More important, the work of both men dealt with similar questions of personal identity and national self-understanding. Both sought to clarify the notions of self and work that underlay their own lives and the lives of their fellows, both strove to understand the connection between the inner life and the outer world, and both were more closely involved in magic than first appears. Still, if this book had been written in German, it could have been called *Der Zauberer und der Entzauberer*.

Early in their careers Max Weber and Thomas Mann discovered and analyzed those pieces of their social and spiritual inheritance that they thought remained valuable, strong, and significant. Each then sought to revitalize and give meaning to certain concepts of self and personality, of work and "service," drawn from the past but alive in the present, to guide their own lives and intellectual creation as well as politics and the life of the nation. This book is about a part of that common enterprise, the foundation of their understanding of the relation of self and work laid down in Weber's essays on religion and in Mann's pre–World War I writings. Our main concern is the structuring role of two key issues in their thinking, "calling" or "vocation" (*Beruf*) and "personality" (*Persönlichkeit*). Using these concepts, Weber and Mann eventually were able to analyze phenomena they took to be crucial for the development of the modern world, for their own nation, and for their personal lives. Indeed both men made use of them and the German "discourses" about them to work out profound problems of their own identity. Although the link between identity and work was an issue for many others in their time, nowhere was it analyzed as self-consciously or as well as in their writings. Ultimately they proposed their notions of the calling and personality to the world around them as the only hope for, and the only path to, living life with meaning in a time of failed social ideals, cultural disorientation, and despair. It is the encounter of these fundamental issues of self and work with the crisis of their culture that produced Weber's famous works on vocation and Mann's novels about European culture and about the devil's pact of Germany.

To both Weber and Mann the older German ideal of *Bildung*, or "cultivation"—which we can describe as a "spiritual discipline" for the shaping of character as well as a model for education—and the ideal of *Kultur*, or "culture," were no long able to shape individual development and social purpose effectively. They had been displaced, undermined, or, at the least, seriously challenged by the dictates of advancing "rationalization" and "civilization" as well as by new political and social realities: these new phenomena had transformed the ideals and reality of the class from which Weber and Mann came, the bourgeoisie, and posed a threat to German life generally and to the meaning of work and individual life particularly. Moreover, Weber and Mann believed, this threat to the individual and his identity was experienced most immediately in his relation to work and most critically in his confrontation with the problem of death: for each writer these experiences became the key to the meaning of life. Though they did not start out explicitly and consciously to solve such vast problems of modern culture, Weber and Mann were instinctively working toward the understanding of questions that later served them in their more deliberately prescriptive tasks. At the center of both men's responses to these problems was a reinterpretation and renewal of the concept of *Beruf* as the model relation to work and the basis of meaning and identity. Here *Beruf* is to be understood not in its ordinary everyday sense in contemporary industrial society in Germany, as "occupation" or "profession," but in its older, essentially religious, meaning, as "calling" or "vocation," a meaning that found its home in the ideals of certain sectors of the bourgeoisie after the Reformation. On the basis of service in such a calling, the "self-ideal" of the bourgeoisie—the "personality"—was once built.

Out of the struggle in nineteenth-century Germany between themselves as sons of the bourgeoisie and the legacy of their class and their parents, Max Weber and Thomas Mann were led to link identity, self-worth, and the calling in a new way. To them the identity of the self, confronting a social and cultural crisis of value, purpose, and meaning, could be established only by the self's "domination" and its mobilization in "service." Thus they tried to legitimate themselves by adopting a form of the relation to work that they found among their forebears. But the bourgeois forms of self-domination no longer had their former vitality. It was necessary, therefore, to revive the original form of the sanctified calling, grounded in the Reformation. At the same time they adapted the calling to kinds of work their forebears would never have considered legitimate. Furthermore, the issue of identity and its relation to what we can call "work considered as a 'service'" became for Weber and Mann an explanatory tool for understanding the crisis of their class and their nation, a point of entry and methodological foundation for conceiving of both history and the present age.

By analyzing the calling and personality as central aspects of Weber and Mann's intellectual project, we are taking a different approach to their thought than is customary. In Weber's thinking, for example, many writers focus on the central problem of rationalization. Yet we want to show ultimately that for Weber any credible individual response to rationalization must embody at least two aspects: first, a restored understanding of work as service—that is, the right understanding and the right use of the calling in the service of our chosen ideal or object, whether in politics, science, or social life generally—and, second, the resolution of the problem of identity and inner strength through the shaping of the self into the kind of personality that service in the "spiritual discipline" of the calling makes possible. In *The Protestant Ethic and the Spirit of Capitalism* (1904–5), Weber laid out analytically and historically the significance and power of the calling in the individual life of its adherents among the Puritan founders; he also described the consequences of this spiritual discipline for economic and political life in the West. The calling provided the believer a worldly means for justifying and fortifying himself and for dealing with the problems of meaning and death. But it also shaped a type of man whose appearance in the world, Weber argued, changed the destiny of the Occident. Weber's comparative analyses of religion then led him to a broader conception: the emergence and importance of what he called the "Occidental personality." This personality was a fashioning of the self achieved through the Reformation discipline of the calling as a service to God. The personality thus constructed transformed and fortified the self of the believer and made the "new" self capable of initiative, innovation, and strength of an unusual kind. For Weber the emergence of that new self had enormous significance, historically and personally.

Moreover, Weber became convinced of the capacity of the renewed ideal of personality—"discovered" in the Reformation but elaborated also in German intellectual traditions since Kant and Goethe—to fill the gap in the contemporary world left by the loss of older religious and cultural ideals of self, meaning, and character building. Furthermore, with his wartime recognition that the calling in essence was a form of service like the soldier's came Weber's realization that the issues that had been primarily of scholarly concern to him could be harnessed to address contemporary problems of identity and politics. In his last great lectures Weber attempted to modernize and secularize the notion of the calling and to revitalize the notion of personality as prescriptions for Germany's crisis of personal and spiritual direction, while criticizing the debased meanings these concepts had come to carry. First, in "Science as a Vocation" (1917) he tried to provide a path, for those capable of following it, to both individual meaning and to the reappropriation of a "disenchanted" world. Second, during and after the war he used the notion of the calling in "Politics as a Vocation" (1919) and his other political writings to provide a conception of political character and leadership that could aid in creating a politically capable elite, able to surmount the baser imperatives of a self controlled by personal interest and ambition. He strove in addition to shape the political culture of Germany and to create a politically educated nation that would know its own "vocation." Hence it is crucial to an understanding of Weber to lay out his discoveries of the calling and personality.

To Mann's work too there is a compelling traditional approach: many critics have discussed the dilemma of art and the artist and Mann's understanding of the artist's relation to life as the pivotal issues of his writing.

Yet we want to argue further that at the center of Mann's concerns was the resolution of the artist's problem of identity through a reappropriation of the notion of the calling. This led Mann to develop a "right understanding" of the calling or vocation comparable to Weber's: he used it to legitimate and fortify the self of the artist and later mobilized it as a response to the spiritual crisis of Germany generally. In *Tonio Kröger* (1903) Mann demonstrated what he believed to be the necessity of the right understanding of and adherence to a calling, basing his solution on the crisis and exhaustion of a certain segment of the bourgeoisie, first analyzed in *Buddenbrooks* (1901).

But after "solving" the problem of the artist's calling and portraying the reality of the called personality, Mann went through a crisis of his own. Feeling burdened by the obligation of producing good literature, fearing sterility and enclosure within his artistic self, Mann was unable to publish another good novel after *Buddenbrooks* for twenty-three years. In the meantime, however, he wrote one of his best works, the novella *Death in Venice* (1912), on sterility and the entrapment of the artist, in which he discovered the soldierly nature of the calling even before the experience of war. His creativity was eventually revitalized by his experience of the challenge to the meaning and existence of Germany posed by World War I, and he resolved this challenge through a reconsideration of the German cultural and national experience. The war brought Mann a new focus and subject, arising from his "discovery" of and identification with the German nation understood as the artist "writ large."

For a time Mann became a fervent nationalist and spokesman for an ideal of life and action he had seemed to question just before the war. But that kind of nationalism dissipated, and he incorporated his new understanding—which freed him for a new artistic project—and his new problematic in the achievement of *The Magic Mountain* (1924). Ultimately the later experience of National Socialism, which Mann lived through long after Weber had died, launched him into a new understanding of the nation and into an elaborate allegorical reinterpretation of Germany's misguided calling. Mann underwent many changes in the 1920s and 1930s. But in 1943, when he began to write *Doctor Faustus* (1947)—the great work of his maturity on art, Germany, the Nietzschean heritage, and the calling—he used terms and conceptions of self, personality, and the artist that derived principally from the earlier period of his work, from *Tonio Kröger* to *Death in Venice*. In *Doctor Faustus* he turned his back on nationalistic Germany and replaced it

with a higher conception, of which he made himself the "representative." Yet it is no accident that this great late work was based on ideas
first sketched out in his notebooks in 1905: hence the importance of that
earlier period for his development.

Though the elaboration and prescription of their solutions came
later, between 1897 and 1905 both Weber and Mann began to work out
and publish the principal elements of what were to be their analyses of
and responses to the cultural crisis of Germany and the personal crisis of
the self.[4] These underpinnings of their work have not been analyzed systematically before and deserve consideration. Indeed, these themes structure the meaning of many of their writings, often in problematical ways.
This analysis is intended to make clear a system of meaning—having to
do with self-justification, identity, and the need for a "redemptive" approach to work through a calling—that governs much of their thinking.
This system of meaning creates rich possibilities of understanding and
living, but it also precludes its authors from exploring other interpretations of self and world and other solutions to the problem of identity.
And, as we shall see, their own responses conceal elements that make
their "solutions" problematical.

The present study thus analyzes in two parts the basic understanding
of the calling and personality. In Part I we consider aspects of Weber's
and Mann's interpretations of the bourgeois class in Germany and in the
West, its strengths and its weaknesses, and in particular its grasp of the
meaning-giving potential of the traditional conception of "vocation."
This discussion will establish, principally from *The Protestant Ethic,*
Buddenbrooks, and *Tonio Kröger,* Weber's and Mann's understanding
of the inner crisis of the bourgeois class in Germany, the consequences of
this crisis for its more self-critical and "wayward" members, and the elements and significance of the calling in the older life of this class and in
the newer life of its heirs. In Part II we consider more directly the model
of self, personality, and identity that Weber and Mann develop and that
is founded on and shaped by their analyses and affirmation of the calling. This discussion appears in a systematic form mainly in Weber's
writings on religion. There he compares the emergence of a unique form
of personality in the West with the ideals of self and character-building
found elsewhere. This comparison leads him to define more clearly
what he takes to be the role of the calling generally in shaping the Occident. After Weber we will explore Mann's attempts to vindicate and
elaborate his conception of the calling and of the personality of the artist
first grounded in *Tonio Kröger.* These works culminate in the soldierly

ethos of *Death in Venice*. But in *Death in Venice* we begin to see the first evidence of the darker forces lurking in these ideals: the self that has been created and shaped confronts the danger of imprisonment behind walls of its own construction.

The culmination and real consequences of Weber's and Mann's understanding of calling and personality are found in Weber's political writings and lectures on vocation and in Mann's later cultural analyses and novels, works fraught with the language of fate, gods, devils, and devilish pacts. But the range and depth of these works are too great to cover in this book, and their analysis requires the understanding of prior terms. Here, therefore, we will provide the foundations of their use of calling and personality, foundations that form the basis of their understanding of self and culture. A future study will be needed to examine their social and political thought, that is, their application of these concepts and ideals to the social, cultural, and political problems of their time and the historical conditions that brought forth their responses. That study will raise serious questions about the models of self, personality, and work-as-service that they shared and elaborated, models that actually concealed, rather than truly resolved, the crucial dilemmas posed for identity by their experiences at the turn of the century.

Why do we treat Max Weber and Thomas Mann together, a social scientist and political thinker alongside a novelist and fiction writer, especially since our purpose is not intellectual history or *Germanistik* but the understanding of specific ideals, concepts, and problems? It is true that Weber provides the systematic thought about issues of self and work, whereas Mann provides more of the "inner history" of the same problems and experiences. Yet each tells not only part of the story of the time but also part of the story of the other, and thus they illuminate one another. Though they tell their stories from different disciplines and different angles, perhaps even opposite ones, their juxtaposition increases our understanding of the significance of such issues in the work of each man as well as in the time itself. In the convergence and parallelism of so many themes in their work, these men exemplify the self-understanding of their age and in addition cast a special light on problems of self, identity, and social life. They raised these issues neither in passing nor briefly. Though Mann died more than thirty years after Weber, both men thought and rethought these specific problems with intensity and power throughout their lives and work.

To perform our task it is necessary to overcome the way in which intellectual disciplines, especially social science and literature, are normally separated from one another in the domain of their problems and the nature and rigor of their method. Intellectual life has been divided into disciplines for the sake of convenience; unfortunately people have come to believe that the world itself is thus divided. But life and the world are not innately organized by discipline, and human dilemmas wander freely, ignoring the disciplinary boundaries we draw. We are accustomed to seeing the discourses of social science and of literature as quite distinct, concerned in different ways with different issues of "outer" world and "inner" world, the one focusing on explaining empirical "reality," the other on "fictional" explorations or representations of themes from that reality. But this distinction is unfortunate and artificial, especially for an approach to social science that is interpretive rather than causal in its orientation. Such an approach must rely on a broader range of cultural experience and expression and a wider set of themes to do its work.

This distinction is particularly problematical in discussing Weber and Mann. The importance and compelling nature of issues of self, work, and identity are dramatized by their appearance in the rich and complex works of two of the most original men of the century. Contrary to the stereotype of the empirical social scientist, Weber was fascinated with the images and notions of self and person and with the significance for action of conceptions of self linked to the "inward" relation to work. Not only are these notions central to his analysis of social reality, but they are also central to his attempt to resolve problems of action and identity in the political and social world in an age caught up in what he thought to be a crisis of meaning. He sought for truths wherever he could find them. It is no accident that Weber studied Husserl, or drew on Goethe's insights as a standard for human wisdom, or had frequent discussions of philosophy and aesthetics with Lukács, or planned to write a study of Tolstoy. Furthermore, even at the heart of his methodology, and clearly in *The Protestant Ethic*, Weber deploys a methodological device of "ideal types" that he himself calls a fiction. This image is not simply a metaphor, nor is it to be taken lightly, for in putting aside a "copy" theory of truth, Weber raises important questions about the means available to us for grasping the nature of existing forms of reality.

At the same time, Mann's fictional works do more than fill in the picture of the inner world Weber analyzes, for Mann was also engaged in a project to build explicit, though usually allegorical, links between the inner experience of the self and the outer and national experience of Germany. Contrary to the stereotype of the novelist, Mann formulated his own theories about self and nation and did not shy away from social and political engagements. Not surprisingly, Mann planned works on the life of Frederick the Great, was actively engaged in the political and social debates of the period during and after World War I, and read many studies of capitalism and the emergence of the bourgeois class.

Weber and Mann lived in a time and place that separated intellectual life by discipline considerably less than we do today. It was a time when the same intellectuals explored many different areas of expertise and knowledge and when intellectuals of all kinds were preoccupied with the nature, even the "cult," of the self and the relation between self and world. For our purposes the important thing is not just that both men wrote of politics and society or of religion and culture. Nor is it that capitalism, the bourgeois class, and the historical experiences of Germany were the common background to and initial focus of their analyses and self-reflections. It is that the preoccupations of both men converge in their problematical need for the calling and in their concern for the uncertain fate of personality and the future direction of Germany. As intellectuals in a European culture undergoing social transformation and a profound crisis of values, they were driven to a reconsideration of self, work, and identity. As members of the *Bildungsbürgertum,* their social, intellectual, and cultural inheritance linked them across disciplines and across time and space. As Germans their common concern was ultimately the spiritual and political fate of their nation and how to affect it.

Rather than interweave their lives and thought on every page, we discuss Weber and Mann in terms of their parallel development, a development that is itself remarkable. Generally we will unfold the key themes from interpretations of their writings to disclose immanently the meaning, role, and purpose of their categories. Although this process will involve some reconstruction of known texts from new points of view, it is meant to be not simply a rereading but rather a new reading. The introductions to the two parts of this work provide common points of reference culturally and conceptually. The conclusions provide syntheses, comparisons, differences, and common lessons and try to situate the broader meaning of Weber's and Mann's thought in the context of German experience. This book treats both Weber and Mann as thinkers and wishes to understand as fully as possible the meaning and especially the consequences of aspects of their work and thought. Its intention is to specify the power of their work along with the nature of their need and the need of the time to which they responded. It also hopes to reveal both their difference from their time and their difference from our time, while still recognizing how much they have to teach us—even if it is not exactly what they hoped to teach.

PART I

The Bourgeoisie and the Calling in Weber and Mann

I place some value on the finding that I perceived and discovered, through direct examination, completely on my own, without reading, the idea that the modern capitalist businessman [*Erwerbsmensch*], the bourgeois with his *ascetic* idea of duty in a calling [*Berufspflicht*], was a creation of the Protestant ethic, of Puritanism and Calvinism, and only afterward, recently, did I notice that it was thought and expressed at the same time by learned thinkers. Max Weber in Heidelberg and after him Ernst Troeltsch have treated "the Protestant ethic and the spirit of capitalism," and, carried to extremes, the same thought is found in Werner Sombart's work that appeared in 1913, *The Bourgeois*—which interprets the capitalist entrepreneur as a synthesis of hero, merchant, and burgher. That he is correct to a great degree is seen by the fact that I had given form to his teaching, as a novelist, twelve years before he had set it down.

> —*Thomas Mann, "Bürgerlichkeit," in*
> Reflections of an Unpolitical Man *(1918)*

Introduction to Part I

When we use the word *calling* or *vocation* today, we usually mean someone's work, occupation, or profession. We may mean that particular task or skill for which a person is especially gifted or talented, or we may mean the essence or "form" of an activity, as when Czeslaw Milosz says of the poet that he needs "to recover, at least for short moments, his true vocation—which is to contemplate Being." [1] We may even mean an activity for which someone has a special affinity or love, or toward which someone feels an impulsion or need, as when Sartre says of philosophy: "It became a vocation. I felt the need to do it." [2]

Reflections on the meaning of—and the self's relation to—work go back to the ancient world and have continued to appear recently, for example, in the writings of Hannah Arendt. [3] But *vocation* is a relatively recent concept, rooted in the Latin Middle Ages and fully developed only in the Reformation. The concept derives from the Reformation use of the Pauline notion of the religious "call" from God to salvation. [4] For a variety of religious and practical social reasons, however, the notion eventually became linked to the different "offices," "magistracies," or worldly occupations, understood to be ordained by God, that a person could occupy. We can characterize the calling as a mediator between worldly work and God's call. *Beruf*—and later, in a different way, Calvin's *vocation* and the English "calling"—became the vehicle of earthly orientation for the worldly life of the godly person, not only with respect to the religious call but also as labor in the service of godly purposes. [5]

As Michael Walzer and John Dunn demonstrate, the Reformation concept of the calling has been linked at different times to political thought and action and to action in society in general.[6] But over time the calling was gradually separated from its originally weighty spiritual content and adjusted to the needs and demands of the occupational structure in modern industrial society. In the nineteenth-century post-Hegelian German world "work was elevated to the position of being an end in itself," as Karl Löwith has suggested,[7] setting the stage for the later crisis in the meaning of work to which Weber and Mann responded. This crisis derived from the separation of work from the service of a higher and ultimate power and its immersion in a market-dominated bourgeois world whose values remained immanent. In Germany *Beruf* lost its sense of a higher and sanctified call. With the disappearance of the godly value, *Beruf*—originally an office or role sanctified and devoted to divine goals or purposes—eventually came to mean occupation. *Berufung*, which originally meant God's *act* of calling someone to a concrete *Beruf*, took over the older meaning.

Given these changes in meaning, it is striking to find the older term recovered, and so passionately, in the lectures Max Weber gave near the end of his life, "Science as a Vocation" and "Politics as a Vocation." What is so unusual is that Weber goes back to the older, Reformation, meaning of the concept, a meaning whose prehistory he had analyzed fifteen years earlier in *The Protestant Ethic and the Spirit of Capitalism*. Similarly it is provocative to find in Thomas Mann's major works on artists, from *Tonio Kröger* to *Death in Venice* and *Doctor Faustus*, the discourse of calling. Yet, like Weber, Mann provided part of the prehistory of the calling in his earlier novel about his forebears, *Buddenbrooks*. There we can see that the vitality of the calling was preserved after the Reformation in bourgeois attitudes toward work, identity, and the meaning of life. For both Weber and Mann it is not work simply understood that is at issue: it is work as a form of selfless service (*Dienst*) and submission or devotion (*Hingabe*) to a higher ideal, goal, or object. It is work as a calling, the submission to which and the discipline of which provide a source of self-justification and meaning to the man who feels himself called.

What could have led these extremely modern men to revive and renew the original power and significance of a term whose history had brought it to a routine, even ideological, use? Why did Weber and Mann actively seek and revive, and positively impose, the form of an ascetic ideal developed in the Reformation? Had the notion of calling retained a spiritual meaning all along, despite secularization and the superficial uses to which it had been put in the course of its history? Or did they seek to regain or restore a link with the past and to recover in modern work or *Beruf* a significance for "salvation" of some kind, a significance that had been lost and for which they hoped to create an equivalent in the secular world? How could a world in crisis over "ultimate values" and God, and how could two thinkers without God, hope to rely on the idea that service and devotion in a calling could provide "justification" or salvation?

The great early works of these two extraordinary men reveal the development of, and the significance they attributed to, the notion of calling. These works also show the separation of this term not only from the original religious spirit that gave it birth, but also to a great extent from the ideology of the members of the bourgeois class that were its later carriers and best exemplars. Part of the context for understanding Weber and Mann lies in the situation and nature of the class from which they came, the bourgeoisie, or *Bürgertum,* in Germany[8]—a class of which they were both self-proclaimed members, if somewhat uncomfortable ones—and also the subgroup of the *Bildungsbürgertum.*[9] Each man considered the bourgeoisie weak in different ways, and this weakness created grave dangers both for the nation and for the direction and identity of the children of this class.

To Weber this class, composed of the people of property and culture, held the hope of the German nation in its hands, although it was outwardly weak politically; indeed, Weber was critical of the German "big" bourgeoisie principally as a political class, not as an economic class. But the weakness was also inward and social: the bourgeoisie emulated the Junker nobility and its trappings, pursuing titles and estates and striving for membership in the reserve officer corps. This "feudalization of the bourgeoisie" revealed the bourgeoisie's weak attachment to its own native qualities and strengths.[10] In *The Protestant Ethic* Weber discovered the presence and strength of a "spirit" of capitalism in the Puritan countries of the past, a spirit that had once empowered earlier capitalist classes to turn away from the aristocracy as a social and political standard and to forge an identity of their own.[11] This spirit, he claimed, had also been the ancestor of the "duty to a calling" (*Berufspflicht*) characteristic of the work ethic of the modern capitalist order in general. But he believed that in the Puritans he had discovered as well a new form of "self," a unique product of the Reformation but not confined to it or to religious life, a self built on the calling. This new self had served as the foundation for the emergence of a new "aristocracy" of the spirit, a more than worthy successor to the aristocracy of blood.

While Weber was working on Puritanism and the bourgeoisie, Mann was dramatizing the inward defeat of the *Bürgertum,* unable to persist in the calling that had once made it strong and propelled it to power. As a social class the *Bürgertum,* even apart from its economic weaknesses, was failing particularly as an independent and reliable standard-bearer and a guide for ideals of identity, autonomy, and self-justification through work. Mann struggled in his youth to put his identity on a sure foundation and to establish himself in the highly competitive literary world. At the same time he chronicled the emergence of the bourgeois artist: this artist arose from the decline of one part of the bourgeoisie, to which he had belonged, vis-à-vis the rise of a new, more aggressive, and more economically astute part. In the process of defining himself against his own weaknesses, against the weaknesses of his class, and against what he considered weaknesses in the art of his times, Mann discovered a lack of engagement and belief in the men who had been the formerly staunch carriers of a calling. Their once-strong vocation had become a mere role that they felt forced rather than chosen to play and that undermined their once-secure personality. With *Tonio Kröger* Mann solved what for him was the problem of the weakness of the bourgeois inheritance to its sons: he discovered a way of emerging from the bourgeoisie with a revitalized form of the calling, yet free of a commitment to its older content, and with a renewed sense of personality outside traditional bourgeois circles.

Still, the bourgeois inheritance as it structured work and personality was the key for both men to the survival of its descendants and, they initially thought, to the survival of Germany. Thus for Weber and Mann, although in different ways, a central problem of both work and life was the relationship to the bourgeoisie of an alienated son: the son does not find in the class as presently constituted a pattern of action, an ethos of work, or a source of meaning to sustain his life. Nor is it clear what can enable the class itself to survive effectively, either individually or collectively, or what can equip it to fight vigorously for its ideals, economic, political, and cultural.

Weber and Mann believed that part of the solution to their personal dilemma and to their problematical relation to their origin was the reconstitution of the calling in a noneconomic sphere of life. They later strove to inject the calling "rightly understood"—and the notion of personality built on it—back into the lives of their fellows and their class to enable the class to confront the tasks and dilemmas that lay ahead. Whatever their critique of the bourgeoisie, they were both self-proclaimed members of it. The calling is in fact a profoundly bourgeois approach to work and life, though founded in a precapitalist age; at the same time it is an originally religious and profoundly spiritual one. The solution they found for themselves in the restoration of the calling connected them even more effectively to their class, though not through the normal range of bourgeois labor and bourgeois meanings. Ultimately, however, each man was to find a higher loyalty and a more significant sense of connection through his identification with the German nation, German culture, and the German future.

Weber and Mann forged a link between calling and personality. On the one hand, Weber did so analytically, descriptively, and explicitly both in his analyses of religion and in his prescriptions for the spiritual and political renewal of Germany in a time he thought to be without prophets or saviors. Mann, on the other hand, dramatized the "inner history" or experience of the men who lived out lives determined by these ideals. For each man these terms were both explanatory devices for understanding the world and devices for self-transformation and self-justification. In their hands these concepts ultimately became devices for the transformation of others as well.

CHAPTER ONE

Weber and the Puritan Calling

Controversy and argument have surrounded *The Protestant Ethic* since its publication.[1] In particular, much criticism has been leveled against the connection Weber makes between Calvinism and the spirit of capitalism. Yet a link between ascetic Protestantism and capitalism has been noted at least since the seventeenth century, well before the appearance of any modern scholarly work.[2] It will be our argument that the revolutionary contribution of Weber's *The Protestant Ethic* has less to do with the historical linkage of Calvinism and the spirit of capitalism than with the positing of the existence and action of a new type of "self" or "character" generated in the Reformation. This contribution is linked to the crucial role of *Beruf,* or "calling," in Weber's understanding of modern culture; it is also linked to the extraordinary powers with which, he claimed, the calling, as it emerged in early modern Europe, was able to endow what we can call "the first great entrepreneurs." These powers were the product of a character fortified in new, essentially religious, ways and in a form that made possible extraordinary feats of action and innovation carried on with great intensity and energy.

Indeed, it is not principally Calvinism but rather these first great entrepreneurs that are the real object of Weber's investigation—not the concrete and actual individuals but their *type*. Weber presumes that such individuals—able to overcome the resistance of tradition—were necessary and in fact present at the time of the birth of capitalism as a "system." They were the carriers of a special relation to work, and Weber scrutinized their ethos, habits, and beliefs for one purpose: to discover the sources of their strength. For *modern* capitalism to have developed as it did, Weber argued, a *new kind* of person must have existed, a person with special qualities and capacities for work, with a natural inclination for the new kind of rationalized labor that capitalism as a system brought with it. But, he argued, these new men possessed that inclination and capacity *before* capitalism was established as a system capable of imposing such labor through the pressure of its material demands, and they derived this strength from noneconomic—in this case, religious—sources. That new attitude and capacity for work, the product of the new kind of character, was precisely what Weber called the "spirit" of modern capitalism, and its "carriers" were the newly transformed men of the Calvinist Reformation.

In fact the "type" of the first great entrepreneur is essentially the same as the "type" of the figures who reappear as the politician, scientist, artist, and entrepreneur of Weber's later essays. Aloneness, an inclination to ascetic labor, devoted service to a god, self-denial and systematic self-control, a capacity to resist their own desires as well as the desires, pressures, or temptations of others—these are the qualities all of Weber's *Berufsmenschen* acquire through their submission in the discipline of the calling to an ultimate ideal or god. The key to their character lies, first, in the subjugation of the "natural" self and, second, in its transformation and fortification through the discipline of the calling as a unique relation of service to their ideal or god: the self is transformed into a personality in a process of formation that shapes it through a calling and equips it for a calling. For the Puritans the life in this calling, carrying out the actions that they believed served their god, became the source of certainty for religious men to the uncertainties of death and salvation. For secular men too, according to Weber in his later work, the life in a calling, fitted for the modern situation, holds out the only hope against the threat of purposelessness, directionlessness, and the meaninglessness of death in a civilization now unable to draw on more traditional solutions, dominated as it is by the advance of rationalization.

Trained in law and political economy, Weber was an extremely successful academic by the age of thirty. Before his nervous collapse in 1897–98 at the age of thirty-three, he had held professorships at Freiburg and Heidelberg and had done largely empirical social scientific and historical work examining the economic mechanisms of ancient and modern societies. These works were outstanding contributions, and they had an influence on and a place in his later social and political analyses. But the works he produced beginning with *The Protestant Ethic* reveal a set of

themes of even greater significance and value for the understanding of
German and Western history and of much wider resonance in the intellectual life of his time. It is with this work as well that his links with the
work of Thomas Mann are first established.

Other scholarly works had already taken up the subject of Protestantism and capitalism before Weber began to do so in 1897.[3] Moreover,
between the time of Weber's nervous collapse in 1897−98 and his recov-
ery in 1902−3, more works appeared that seemed either to confirm his
initial studies or to advance the analysis of the subject, even when he
himself disagreed with others' conclusions.[4] By the autumn of 1904 the
first part of *The Protestant Ethic* had appeared in the *Archiv für Sozialwissenschaft und Sozialpolitik*. After a trip to the St. Louis World's Fair
in late 1904, Weber completed the second part of his essay by the end of
March 1905, and it too was published in the *Archiv*.[5]

As a work *The Protestant Ethic* marked the beginning of a broad
comparative historical investigation into the economic ethics of the
world religions. Moreover, its concern with the three themes of tradition, charisma, and rationality and with what we can call the dialectic of
material conditions and culturally shaped actors foreshadows some of
the principal conceptual elements of Weber's more systematic treatise,
Economy and Society, begun before World War I but never completed.
Finally, in *The Protestant Ethic* Weber discovered and demonstrated
just how powerful the notion of practical "sanctification" through the
calling had been for the transformation and fortification of character
and for the release of energies turned toward innovation of a particularly rational kind in at least the historical development of capitalism.

But the calling and its power were no ordinary academic issue.
Weber's discovery was to underlie and inspire his own extraordinary reappropriation of the calling during and after World War I in his social
and political thought as a means for overcoming both the spiritual and
the political crises in Germany. Its importance can be seen partly in his
analysis of the origins of the capitalist spirit but also, and more important, in the working out and development of this issue over the remaining years of his life and in the significance and power he later attributed
to it.[6] Here we must reconsider the various themes and insights that appear in *The Protestant Ethic* as the setting for Weber's remarkable and
unusual discovery.

Weber's investigation of the calling was an attempt to discover the
origins of an element of modern culture that he believed had constitutive
significance for life in the world of capitalism. What he found was a new

self and a new attitude toward work: the self was transformed into a warrior in service to God, capable of undertaking "pious," rationalized, methodical action of an unusually disciplined and innovative kind. This transformation put life at the service of labor rather than labor at the service of life, for labor in the calling held the threads of life's meaning. It is the sources of Weber's way of posing the question of the calling and capitalism as well as the components of the calling itself that we want to uncover. In the process we will discover that for Weber the calling of self-denying service to an ultimate ideal is intimately linked to problems of historical innovation in general and to an understanding of the innovations that helped establish the capitalist world in particular. The role of Calvinism, in Weber's hands, was the provision of a character structure and a set of premiums for a kind of action that is typical of the "capitalist spirit" and that facilitated the birth of capitalism in the West.

The Discovery of the Calling in *The Protestant Ethic*

The Significance of the Calling

In 1902, in the midst of Weber's prolonged illness, his wife wrote to his mother that what tormented him the most was "the psychic pressure of the 'unworthy situation' of earning money and for the foreseeable future being able to accomplish nothing, along with the feeling that, to all of us, you and me and everyone, only the person with a *calling* [*Berufsmensch*] is considered a whole person [*für voll gälte*]."[7] The calling had always been for Weber the only meaningful mode of life he had allowed himself personally. According to Karl Löwith, in fact, "it is obvious that Weber's own sympathies were precisely with those Puritans to whom work in a calling and 'business' with its restless activity had become 'indispensable to life.'"[8]

In a letter of 1905 to Heinrich Rickert, Weber characterized *The Protestant Ethic* as "a sort of 'spiritualistic' construction of the modern economy," which revealed the "asceticism of Protestantism as the foundation of the modern *culture of vocation* [*Berufskultur*]."[9] As he wrote later, ascetic Protestantism "creates the appropriate 'soul' for capitalism, the soul of the 'man of vocation' [*Berufsmensch*]."[10]

How one defines what is unique to or characteristic of modern capitalism and "capitalist culture," what its "concept" is, will dictate what precisely one must explain and where precisely one must look for origins. It was neither modern capitalism simply understood nor its material foundations that Weber sought to explain in *The Protestant Ethic;* he sought, rather, the origins of the modern *Berufskultur,* which seemed to him still, in 1905, long after the contribution of Protestantism had been assimilated, the very basis of modern civilization. By 1913 he had made "rationalization" a central, and perhaps principal, category of his writings, and in 1920 the introduction to his collected writings on the sociology of religion made a certain form of rationalization the essence of Western civilization. But that conceptual emphasis had not yet appeared in 1905. At that time it was the idea "of *duty in a calling* [*Berufspflicht*]" that was "characteristic of the 'social ethic' of capitalist culture." This "peculiar" idea was "so familiar to us today," and yet it was not at all "self-evident." Further, this conception of duty was not merely important for the culture of capitalism: Weber maintained that it actually had "constitutive significance." Duty in a calling is "an obligation that the individual should and does feel toward the content of his 'vocational' activity [*berufliche Tätigkeit*]." Yet, Weber argued, it was not as if this idea "had appeared *only* on the ground of capitalism," for he took it as his task to show that it had appeared even earlier and quite independently.[11]

With this idea the contents of work impose a special obligation on the individual: he feels that he is obliged by his work, rather than being master of the work or being obliged simply by the need to earn a living. This new relation to work brings the "reversal of what we would call the 'natural' circumstances," and yet it is as "definitely a leitmotiv of capitalism as it is foreign to those people not affected by its touch." That it is also one of the constitutive elements of capitalist culture makes the inquiry into its origin and significance even more important.

> We will have to investigate whose spiritual child this concrete form of "rational" thought and life was, out of which this idea of "calling" and this devotion [*Sichhingeben*] to *labor* in a calling has grown, which we saw was so irrational from the standpoint of eudaemonistic self-interest, and which was and still is one of the characteristic constituents of our capitalist culture. What interests us here precisely is the origin of this *irrational* element that lies in this as in every concept of "calling."

But this question was not simply of historical interest. It had a contemporary importance that made its understanding urgent, for "the idea of 'duty in a calling' haunts our lives like the ghost of formerly religious beliefs." Indeed, for Weber the legacy of ascetic Protestantism and of capitalism is now an inescapable destiny. "The Puritan *wanted* to be a man of calling [*Berufsmensch*]—we *must* be."[12]

How does the notion of the calling fit into the picture of capitalism? Weber does not provide a more systematic discussion of the concept of capitalism or the unique features of modern capitalism as a system until his later works: part 1 of *Economy and Society,* the introduction to his collected essays on the sociology of religion, and his *General Economic History.* Yet *The Protestant Ethic* itself provides the material to make four distinctions crucial to understanding the uniqueness of capitalism: between capitalism in general and modern capitalism, between capitalism as an occasionally appearing "form" of enterprise and capitalism as a "system" or an economic order (precapitalist times versus capitalist times), between personal inclination toward work and an ethos that enjoins certain kinds of labor, and between two different spirits of enterprise, traditionalist and modern capitalist.

First, economic activities "by private entrepreneurs in the form of a turnover of capital (money or goods with money value) for profitable ends through the purchase of means of production and the sale of products" can be said unquestionably "to be conducted as 'capitalist enterprises.'" They may then be further qualified as more or less "rational," in the sense of relying more or less completely on careful calculation. But what is unique about *modern* capitalist enterprise is the appearance in the West of "a rational capitalist organization of industrial bourgeois labor" that arose in the development from the Middle Ages to modern times. The emergence of what Weber in his later work calls "(formally) free labor" and its integration into enterprise is the hallmark of specifically modern capitalism and the foundation of the highest forms of calculation, and hence of rationality, in enterprise. Second, modern capitalist enterprise is a new *form* of enterprise, or rather a development from the old form, once a number of social and political conditions have changed the situation of labor on the land. This distinction is at the heart of the difference between the capitalist epoch and the precapitalist: it is not primarily a distinction between forms of enterprise but between epochs in which capitalist enterprise is merely present and those in which it is actually dominant, that is, dictating the overall economic profile of society. In precapitalist times "the rational valorization of capital as an *enterprise* and the rational capitalist *labor* organization" had not yet become "ruling powers for the orientation of economic action."[13] Third, this development was the product of a transition more complicated than is normally thought, during which a new ethos of labor appeared not based on inclination, representing a new spirit of work and a new significance for work. Finally, this transition was actually mediated, according to Weber, by the emergence of the new spirit of

enterprise that overwhelmed tradition and that, when fused with capitalist forms of enterprise, led to the triumph of capitalism as a system.

The Spirit of Capitalism

Where and when the first scholarly discussions of a spirit of capitalism appeared is not certain.[14] By "spirit of capitalism" Weber denotes
a unique *attitude* toward work—not simply toward any kind of work,
but specifically toward the rational increase of capital. However much
some might claim that the spirit of capitalism must be identified with
greed or ceaseless acquisitiveness, Weber emphatically disagrees: greed
and acquisitiveness have been present and powerful since the dawn of
human history, most often in places where capitalism never took hold as
an economic system. Benjamin Franklin's approach to the increase of
capital, however, is unique and special. His ideal is the "*credit-worthy
honest man*," but above all

> the idea of the *obligation* of the individual toward the interest, assumed as an
> end in itself, in the increase of his capital. In reality: that here, not simply a
> technique of life, but a specific "ethic" is preached, whose violation is treated
> not as foolishness but as a kind of forgetfulness of duty; this above all be-
> longs to the essence of the matter. It is not *only* "business sense" that is
> taught . . . it is an *ethos* which is expressed, and in precisely *this* quality it
> interests us.

This contrast between "technique" as a set of specific means and "ethos"
as a guide to life more generally, and for which the means may be quite
variable, is an essential distinction of Weber's work. Such an ethos cannot be a product of mere training and habituation. Indeed, Franklin
goes so far as to ascribe his awareness of the utility of virtue to divine
revelation intended to bring him to virtue. Leaving aside the utilitarian
quality of Franklin's thought, Weber says that this revelation shows
something more at issue than the desire to "embellish" purely egocentric
maxims with moral decoration, in what would be an ideological and
apologetic fashion.[15]

Curiously, this ethos of striving to make more and more money is at
the same time linked with scrupulous avoidance of spontaneous enjoyment and of any other possible pleasure; making money in such an
ethos appears as an end in itself. Indeed, making money is the standard
by which life is measured; it is not measured by life needs that are recognized as prior and that then dictate the pursuit of gain to meet those
needs. "Man regards earning as the goal of his life, no longer earning as

the means toward the goal of satisfaction of his material life needs." To Weber this is a reversal of what one would have to call the natural state of affairs; but at the same time it is a leitmotiv of capitalism and an attitude closely connected to religious conceptions Franklin learned from his "strongly Calvinist father." Yet precisely here lies the connection between Franklin and the calling in capitalism. "The earning of money . . . within the modern economic order is the result and expression of fitness in the *calling*, and *this fitness* is . . . the real entirety of Franklin's morality." [16] Here again the difference between an ethos and a "morally neutral" inclination comes out. The attitude of a financier like Jacob Fugger, making money as long as he can, reflects daring and a "personal, morally indifferent, inclination" but not an "*ethically* colored maxim of life conduct." In Franklin "it is the 'spirit of capitalism' that speaks from him in characteristic manner," even though one would not maintain that "*everything* one can understand under this 'spirit' is contained there"; [17] "we use here provisionally the expression 'spirit of (modern) *capitalism*' for that conviction [*Gesinnung*] that seeks systematically and rationally *in the manner of a calling* for legitimate profit in the manner elucidated in the example of Benjamin Franklin." [18]

But to describe such a spirit is not yet to understand the value of it, or the need for it, or its difference from other "spirits," or its origin, or the effect it has on economic life. Obviously no explicit adherence to a set of ethical maxims of work is necessary for present-day capitalism to continue. The capitalist system is so well established, such a "vast cosmos," a seemingly "unalterable housing" (*unabänderliches Gehäuse*), that it can now force the individual to adapt to its rules. It "educates and creates" the economic subjects that it needs through a process of economic selection (*Auslese*). Thus a spirit of capitalism could be understood today, perhaps, as a product of adaptation (*Anpassung*), since the capitalist economic order needs "this submission to the 'calling' [*Hingabe an den 'Beruf'*] of earning money. . . . Whoever does not adapt himself in his life conduct to the conditions of capitalist success goes under or does not rise." [19]

But although the concepts of selection and adaptation are valuable when referring to the *re*production of an economic or social order already dominant, they cannot be used to describe a system in the process of establishing itself; instead we must examine the transformation, development, or movement from one system to another, for it is precisely the interstices between one economic order and another that are at issue. In this Weber agrees with Marx. [20] For Weber capitalism at its ear-

liest stages needed the pressure of more than material interests as a pre-
supposition to establish itself as a dominant system, though material interests and material reproduction are all it presently needs to continue.
Capitalism can now generate as well the attitudes and opinions best
suited to its own condition and continuation. But these were not enough
at the start of its history to overcome the enormous weight of what
Weber labels a traditionalist economic ethos. Indeed, for Weber "the
question about the driving forces of the expansion of modern capitalism
is not in the first place a question about the origin of the supplies of
money that were capitalistically valorizable but above all about the development of the capitalist spirit."[21]

The new work ethic here represents, we can say, a transformative influence, a helpful ally, and a component and inspiration of the new spirit
of capitalism. It is an agent of transformation or historical acceleration,
a catalytic element, *not* the creator of a new *system*. It is the embodiment of a new spirit of work that empowers its carriers [*Träger*] with a
capacity for initiation and persistence; it enables them to take the various elements of capitalist enterprise and turn them into a rationalized,
dominating economic order; it overwhelms old attitudes and patterns of
work by imposing the successful system, which then forces adherence
and change, even though the creation of such a system was not the intention of those who first developed the ethic. At its origin, Weber claims,
before capitalist enterprise was everywhere dominant, capitalism required a spiritual ally to help it become a system, or ruling economic
order, destroying old forms of enterprise, old economic attitudes, and
the old pace and intensity of life.[22]

But this new conception of duty in a calling, so important a part of
the capitalist spirit, does not appear only in capitalist conditions; Weber
argues that it actually preceded capitalism. In colonial Massachusetts,
for example, the spirit definitely preceded the establishment of the capitalist order. In New England, founded for religious reasons, there were
complaints of a specifically "profit-seeking calculation" as early as 1632;
and yet in the American South, established by big capitalists for purely
profit-making purposes, capitalism was always less developed than in
the North. Moreover, in Florence, the most highly developed capitalist
center of the fourteenth and fifteenth centuries, such a profit-seeking attitude was at best only tolerated; whereas in Franklin's eighteenth-century
Pennsylvania, with its petit bourgeois relations and a minimum of large
economic enterprises, this attitude was esteemed as "the content of a
morally commendable, even commanded, life conduct." Thus we can-

not speak here, with vulgar materialism, of "a 'reflection' of the 'material' conditions in the 'ideal superstructure,'"[23] however much such a reflection may be the dominant fact of capitalism and its material conditions today. Indeed, the possibility of finding such an ethos apart from the material conditions required for its fullest development will make possible and credible the examination of other cultures and societies for evidence of a similar ethos, even when the material conditions are not present.

The Significance of the "First Great Entrepreneurs"

The spirit of capitalism did not simply emerge on the scene and win the day; "it had to succeed in a hard struggle against a world of enemy powers," principally the force of tradition, not only in the outside world but within the individual as well. In particular the ethical attitude, socially and religiously grounded, that merely tolerated the widespread invasion (*Eindringen*) of the social group by free enterprise following the crumbling of tradition was one of the strongest "inner obstacles" (*innerlichen Hemmnisse*) to the adaptation of individuals to the demands of a capitalist economy.[24] And such an obstacle was not an easy thing to overcome: "The opponent with which the 'spirit' of capitalism, in the sense of a definite style of life bound by norms appearing in the cloak of an 'ethic,' had to struggle above all remained that kind of feeling and behavior that one can designate as 'traditionalism.'"[25]

That attitude, Weber argues, was not restricted to precapitalist enterprises, namely, handicrafts and primitive agriculture. Enterprises that are unquestionably capitalist may be carried on, he maintains, "in a strictly traditionalist spirit" or have "a 'traditionalist' character," from banks to export business to textile manufacturing using the putting-out system. A capitalist *form* can survive with a traditionalist *spirit*: even though form and spirit must have some kind of "adequate" relation to one another, there is no "relation of 'lawful' ['*gesetzlicher*'] dependence" between them. Thus the normal pattern, even "in the course of modern economic history," is a traditionalistically conducted enterprise "with continually recurring interruptions through ever newer and ever more powerful inroads [*Einbrüche*] of the 'capitalist spirit.'"[26]

This "wall of custom" was as strong among potential laborers as among those conducting business. "Man wants 'by nature' to earn not money and more money, but simply to live, to live as he is accustomed to living and to acquire as much as is necessary for it." Just as ethical

and traditional barriers to unlimited economic enterprise stood in the
way of entrepreneurs emerging who could conduct business intensely
and energetically in a capitalist spirit, so too, Weber argues, has this leitmotiv of labor in precapitalist times resisted the efforts of capitalist enterprise to increase productivity by increasing the intensity of labor and
to develop in laborers attention, initiative, responsibility, and freedom
from continual calculations of ease and short-term advantage. In both
cases the new attitude, when it appears, is not given by nature but is the
product of a long and difficult process of "education" (*Erziehung*) for
"capitalist culture." Indeed, for workers too labor has to be carried on
"as if it were an absolute end in itself—a 'calling.'" [27]

More than a spirit of acquisition was at work here. As Weber later
puts it, the obstacles and inhibitions of tradition "are not broken through
by the drive for acquisition as such." In other words, not unleashed desire but the *conquest* of desire—special ethical qualities combined with
restrained desire—was necessary. Indeed, for Weber ruthless acquisition, free of all ethical norms, has appeared everywhere in history, as
has the "inner attitude of the adventurer," free of all ethical restrictions.
The attitude of unscrupulous acquisition appears especially in countries
that are backward from a capitalist point of view. But it was neither the
unscrupulously greedy nor the great economic adventurers nor the commercial aristocrats, financial magnates, monopolists, state contractors,
state lenders, colonial entrepreneurs, or promoters who were bearers of
the new spirit, whatever other contributions they made to the expansion of the economy. It was the "*small* capitalist stratum," the "rising
strata of the industrial lower-middle class [*Mittelstand*], who were the
carriers of this attitude" and who created "what was *characteristic* of
Western capitalism," namely, "the bourgeois private economic organization of industrial labor." [28]

But Weber's description of the appearance and the effects of the spirit
of capitalism reveals far more than a new approach to business life. It
also shows the emergence neither of the old greed nor of a new kind of
desire but of a new kind of man and a new kind of power, a new character, a new self, and a new attitude toward work, whose qualities and
consequences, in Weber's view, were and are simply extraordinary. For
at some point, Weber says, the "ease" of the conduct of business ani-
mated by the traditionalist spirit was "suddenly disturbed," while generally there was no substantial change in the "*form* of organization" of
enterprise. Instead, a new "rationalization" appeared in business, with
increased rigor in the supervision of labor, new marketing methods, a

new willingness to adapt to the demands of different customers, large turnover and low prices, and reinvestment of profits in the business. These changes led to a bitter competitive struggle under whose pressure the old "idyllic" condition broke down, subjecting everyone to a new economic law: "whoever did not rise had to decline." This reversal was brought about not by new money but by the appearance of "the new *spirit,* indeed, the 'spirit of modern capitalism.'" Indeed, for Weber, the contribution of Protestant asceticism, which actually created the positive ethic, was the creation of "the 'soul'" that made it possible for "'spirit' and 'form' to be one." [29]

In his dramatic portrait of that appearance, Weber tells the essence of his story. The spirit's new powers, or, rather, the powers of those "with a calling," were visible precisely in the encounter with tradition.

> Its entry was not usually peaceful. A flood of mistrust, occasionally of hatred, above all of moral indignation, regularly opposed itself to the first of the new men; often—many such cases are known to me—there began an express creation of legends about mysterious shadows in his previous life. . . . only *an unusually firm character* could *save* precisely such a "new style" entrepreneur from the loss of his *temperate self-control* and from *moral as well as economic shipwreck* . . . beside clarity of vision and *energy,* it was still above all very specific and very distinct *"ethical" qualities* that, with such innovations, made it possible for him to *win* the simply indispensable *confidence* of the workers and to maintain his *vigor* for overcoming the *innumerable oppositions,* above all, however, the *endlessly more intensive rate of work* that henceforth was demanded from the entrepreneur and that is incompatible with a comfortable enjoyment of life—only indeed [these were] ethical qualities of a specifically different *kind* from those adequate to the traditionalism of the past. . . . they were . . . men grown up in the hard school of life, *poised and daring* at the same time, but above all *temperate and constant, rigorous* and *completely devoted to their object* [*völlig der Sache hingegeben*], with strictly bourgeois opinions and "principles." [30]

This description of the appearance of those new men bristles with electricity. Their effect on the world about them was dramatic. Their "unusually firm character," "ethical qualities," and "temperate self-control" saved them from "moral shipwreck"; this enabled them to "win confidence," gave them "vigor" for overcoming "opposition," and showed their "rigor" while they remained "devoted to their object." Obviously such qualities could not be the product of mere desire for acquisition or recognition or of new techniques. They had to be the product, in Weber's view, of a special relation to work, which must itself have been generated by much higher motivations; otherwise it could not have become such a world-conquering ethos so effectively. These special qualities of character allowed the new-style person to control the self, mobilize energies, act in new ways, and resist or command the obstacles that stood in his way, whether human or natural, while simultaneously preserving himself not only economically but also morally. Yet they are also the qualities of Weber's politician, scientist, and intellectual, all of whom are modeled on this archetypal innovator. Though such a person must struggle hard, he cannot be swayed. The entrepreneur "has nothing [from his vast productivity] for his own person—except: the irrational feeling of having 'fulfilled his calling' well [*guter 'Berufserfüllung'*]." This feeling, however, was precisely the source of his strength: the discipline of the calling and his capacity to devote himself to it, although its real strength derived from his service on behalf of a higher ideal and purpose than mere economic gain.[31]

It is precisely the nature and origin of the ideal entrepreneur that is the real object of Weber's attention in this work and actually carries the weight of the explanation. It cannot be stressed enough that the existence and nature of what we have called the first great entrepreneur, as portrayed in *The Protestant Ethic*, are issues *prior* to the argument that such entrepreneurs drew their strength from some variant of Calvinism. Arguing for a connection between Calvinism and the new entrepreneurs is almost straightforward compared to establishing the crucial historical necessity and *role* of a new type of *character* in innovating enterprise and transforming the social world. The idea that certain groups of Protestants played essential roles in the development of capitalism has a long history. Moreover, the significance of the calling in Protestant teaching and life has long been recognized. Suggesting that there were features of Calvinism itself that disposed individuals to become involved in capitalist enterprise, rather than some other field of action, was also not altogether new. But the key to the innovativeness of *The Protestant Ethic* and to the significance of the work within Weber's works more generally remains the "ideal type" of the entrepreneur; if we accept that such a figure was actually present historically in some form and was central to the development of the spirit of capitalism, then the problem simply becomes to discover what could have created and fortified such a man. If we accept Weber's mode of explanation, the central questions are these: Were there many possible sources of this character-transforming ethos, or only one? Is the religiously grounded calling the necessary prerequisite for understanding the appearance of the bearers of the capitalist spirit? Granted that a certain stance or attitude toward labor was necessary, could a *secular* ethic, perhaps, have had such an effect and provided such an exceptional capacity to withstand the recalcitrance of events and people?[32] If many sources were possible, why was it Calvinism that played this role in early modern Europe?[33]

Weber considered those who undertook this rationalization "new men" capable of standing against their time and of conducting this new mode of business despite opposition, resistance, and custom. What seems to have made these men new, if we follow Weber, was their calling, although the origin of that calling has yet to be explained. Weber's insight into the role of the calling and his conviction of the *need* for new-style men to undertake the tasks of rationalization launches and colors his whole investigation; this insight requires him to uncover the origin of *these* men and their power, which, since this power seems to reside in their relation to work, means a search for the origin "of the 'bourgeois' idea of the *calling*."[34] "How did a 'calling' in Benjamin Franklin's sense now arise from this at best ethically tolerated behavior? . . . From what circle of ideas did the arrangement of an activity under the category of 'calling' derive, oriented outwardly purely toward gain, toward which the individual feels himself *obliged*? Because it was this idea that gave the ethical foundation and support to the life conduct of the 'new-style' entrepreneur."[35]

Whatever the actual qualities of the new-style men, Weber specifies precisely *these* "measurements" of their personality and uniqueness and not others. It is one thing to speak, for example, of asceticism as bourgeois virtue; sects like the Quakers saved money in their temperate way as a result of religious motives and thus had income for investment and reinvestment. It is quite another thing when not only the qualities and injunctions of a sect are stressed, but the very structure of the self and the personality of the new entrepreneurs are made the central issue as well.

Weber's logic implies that it would have been impossible for anyone to initiate this process who had not already "surrendered completely to his object or task [*völlig der Sache hingegeben*]," that is, who was not living in an actual calling. The disposition toward economic, especially capitalist, activity of those with a calling has still to be explained. Yet for Weber those with such a disposition toward rationalistic activity at the origin of capitalism as a system *had to have a calling* of some kind. They could not have had the appropriate strength otherwise: neither interests alone nor a merely strong attachment to occupation could have impelled them in such a direction. For Weber their capacities could only have come from an unusual experience, particularly a profound relation to work, rooted in a religious ideal.

The need for innovation of this kind is due to the nature of tradition, as Weber understands it: "The further back we go, the more far-reaching is the manner of action, and especially also communal action [*Gemeinschaftshandeln*], determined exclusively through the adjustment to the 'customary' [*das 'Gewohnte'*] purely as such, [and] deviations from it appear extremely disquieting." But the adjustments of tradition are not only to the customary "outside" the self; they find a home within the person as well: "the inner spiritual 'adjustment' to these regularities contains in itself tangible 'inhibitions' [*Hemmungen*] against innovations." How is it possible that "the 'inertia' [*Trägheit*] of the customary" can ever be overcome in human social life? How can innovations ever appear, given the inwardly and outwardly accepted validity of the habitually done and the regular? Changes could come from conquest by or innovations borrowed from other cultures, of course. But the innovative powers within a culture generally derive from a different source: "according to all of the experiences of ethnology, the most important source of new orders [*Neuordnungen*] appears to be the influence of individuals who have specifically constituted 'abnormal' . . . experiences and through these are capable of conditional influences on others." [36]

Some unusual experience was necessary for the innovators of the capitalist order to find the strength for their actions. Any number of experiences were possible in principle. But in reality only religion provided such an experience for a broad range of people. No merely literary or intellectual theory, [37] indeed no secular ideal, could have mobilized enough people to undertake such tasks, even though isolated individuals may have been thus motivated. Something more pervasive, powerful, and compelling was necessary: the calling. In Weber's view this idea of the calling has remained in modern capitalist culture, shorn of whatever spiritual connections it once had; yet it is also a remnant of and a clue to its earlier history, with a powerful contemporary effect. Indeed, Weber finds this understanding of and attitude toward work almost a commonplace.

> The idea that modern work in a calling carries an ascetic stamp is, of course, also not new. That the restriction to specialized work [*Facharbeit*], with the renunciation of the Faustian universality of humankind that it requires, is generally in today's world the presupposition of valuable action, that also "deed" and "renunciation" inevitably condition one another today: this basic ascetic motif of the bourgeois life-style . . . is what Goethe wanted to

teach us, at the height of his wisdom about life, in the "Wanderjahre" and in the closing he gave to the life of his Faust. For him this knowledge meant a renunciative departure from a time of full and beautiful humanity.[38]

The continued presence of the idea of wise renunciation in German culture since Goethe—a sense Weber sees behind modern notions of labor—and Weber's personal sense of the powers that the calling could confer led him to search for the "Ur-calling" and for a prototypical representative of this work ethic at the time of the origin of capitalism.

A limited philosophy of history here announces itself in Weber, although not in the sense of an inversion of Marx's theory of history, which some interpreters of Weber have attributed to him. It is, rather, a paradigmatic model of innovation, a theory of how innovations and transformations are effected between radically different epochs or economic orders: they are mediated by a type of actor whose strength is rooted in a special kind of character building and whose appearance in history is not confined to the early days of capitalism. This is also the first form of Weber's use of the notion of "charisma" and its effect: a revolutionary power, embodied in individuals, transforms human relations in a specific realm, initiating changes, commanding and winning over followers, and resisting opposition.[39]

Thus the normal methods of criticism of Weber's argument do not go to the heart of the philosophy of history informing *The Protestant Ethic*. Critics have neither recognized the role of this conception of the new entrepreneur nor chosen to argue against his role and existence; they have accepted this aspect of Weber's model implicitly without clarifying its assumptions or exploring its limits. Their arguments have been directed largely against Weber's use of Puritanism as the background for the new entrepreneurs. Critics have sought to show, for example, that although Catholicism put restrictions on economic morality, capitalism and the capitalist spirit appeared first in Catholic countries (Fanfani), or that Weber misinterpreted Puritanism and the calling (Robertson, C. H. George and K. George, Samuelsson), or that the Puritans were mainly inclined toward the political transformation of the world, not the economic (Walzer), or that Nonconformists became actively involved in British economic life because of their exclusion from public affairs by the Clarendon Code at the start of the Restoration (Ogg, Wilson), or that capitalism actually developed earlier than Weber claims (Cohen, Nef), or that there simply is not enough evidence in Weber's work to support his claims (Marshall). None of these arguments, whatever their other value, goes to the heart of the question of the calling and spirit and the possibility of a new kind of character building that, Weber argues, emerged in the sixteenth and seventeenth centuries and provided a special element at "the birth of the modern economic man." Nor have critics considered the nature of Weber's explanation, which—to borrow words Paul Klee used to characterize modern art—does not "render the visible" but rather "makes visible."

It is particularly important that Weber works with an ideal type, rather than providing a single tangible example or illustration from an actual life; still, he refers generally to the "self-made parvenus of Manchester and Westphalia," principally in the putting-out business, and claims to know some examples of legends springing up about the new men. Weber has inferred the existence and importance of these men, or this type of man, but he does not provide details about them in *The Protestant Ethic*.[40] Yet this ideal-type construct became a paradigm of innovation and the innovative character in Weber's later work, despite the disclaimers in his own methodological writings about hypostatizing the types.[41] The type itself has become more than a tool of understanding. Through its dramatic role and its function in the explanation, it has become uniquely typological for all real innovative actors and personal innovative forces.

Weber understands such actors through his model of the strong self, and their presence in history is said to have been crucial for the development of the West. Weber's later work shows that he believed this type and model were archetypal for all who would bear the tasks of contemporary intellectual and political life. Weber does not believe that there are laws of history that govern the world or that allow one to predict events, but by severely restricting the conception of the kind of self that can act in new ways and by restricting the understanding of what enables the new self to become strong, Weber has made it nearly impossible within his scheme to conceive of a "strong self" that is not structured identically to the ascetic Puritan's. Setting aside the link between Protestantism and capitalism will not eliminate Weber's question of the need for and emergence of a new man of action at the birth of capitalism. It is the structure of Weber's understanding of historical innovation and innovators, and the "structure" of these innovators themselves, that must be understood. Indeed, these structures must be challenged by anyone who wishes to contest Weber's position effectively. They cannot be challenged easily without an alternative model of selfhood, action, innovation, and leadership; one would need a model not based on ascetic devotion to an ideal served in a discipline like the calling, Weber's model of the strong self and its action.[42] It may seem that empirical criticisms of his work could cast into doubt the basis of his thinking about Calvinism, since that basis led him to ascetic Protestantism as the crucial factor in the development of the spirit of capitalism. But all such criticism has led only to the search for other sources for the same developments and innovators. Conversely, whatever empirical defense might be made of Weber's understanding, his explanation of the origins of the capitalist spirit rests principally *not* on Protestantism but on the necessity of the ideal type of the new-style entrepreneur.

The notion of the new man—the special character type that contains within itself the seeds of innovation, rational methodical action, and a new self—thus becomes, if unintentionally, a permanent hypothesis in Weber's work. It also serves him as an entry point for examining why a capitalist spirit did not emerge anywhere else, what the nature of charismatic leadership is, and what the ethos, model, and pattern should be for meaningful work in a Germany reeling from spiritual, social, and political problems. The new man and the structure of the new self were the beginning of Weber's quest to understand the unique forms of autonomy and independence he found in the West. It is a quest of enormous significance for his own work and for social science and culture generally. We must now consider what Weber took to be the sources of that new person who took the stage in the seventeenth century.

The Origin of the Calling

The source of the "relationship of man to his 'calling' as a task [*Aufgabe*], as capitalism needs it,"[43] is the object of inquiry, and the logical place for Weber to begin, given his other observations, is with the origin of the notion of the calling in the Reformation.[44] Yet, according to Richard Douglas, by the start of the sixteenth century and before the Reformation there were already a number of different vocabularies of "self-knowledge and secular vocation." Douglas calls them theories of "individuation," deriving from different traditions and prominent, or at least debated, in humanist circles; all these theories focused in some form on the relation of the individual to his appropriate "task."[45] There was, first, the biblical theory, codified by many, including Aquinas, in which human "inclinations" toward one sphere of activity or another were regarded as gifts of grace within a human society divided into estates, whose spheres were themselves intended by Providence. Second, there was the pre-Christian theory, rooted in the classics, codified by Cicero in *De officiis,* and shared by humanists like Petrarch, Erasmus, and Vives, which emphasized particularly the discovery of one's own native character and talent (*ingenium*) as well as the cultivation of one's aptitude within different disciplines. Third, there was the Greek or Hellenistic theory, vaguely medical and psychological, derived from Plato, Aristotle, Hippocrates, and Galen, codified by Ficino, focusing, like the humanist theory, on the inclination of individuals rather than on the distribution of talents into estates.

The most important pre-Reformation theory was the humanist theory to which Erasmus subscribed, whose ideas show the greatest contrast with the Lutheran and Calvinist notions of *Beruf;* they also point up the contrast between the two principal and different "vocabularies" that Douglas describes, the classical and the biblical. In describing how one finds a career, Erasmus claims that there must be a deliberate human choice of a particular way of life (*genus vitae*) and above all the private determination of career consistent with one's nature, aptitude, and constitution. In other words, we choose what best suits us or what we enjoy. Indeed, our happiness depends on applying ourselves to what we are naturally fitted for. In defending his personal choice to repudiate holy vows and follow his own "nature," Erasmus follows Cicero and the Stoics, as well as humanist generations before him, in arguing that we should weigh our own traits and estimate our natural ability to decide who we wish to be and what *genus vitae* is right for us. As Douglas says: "The humanist belief that history is in some measure man-made, and that society is the achievement of human labor, contributed toward the idealization of work long before the Reformation." [46]

With the Reformation, however, there were profound changes that began when Luther separated the notion of vocation from the humanist ethic by arguing that both the "temporal calling" and the religious call were from God. Our vocation was hence *commanded*, not *selected*. As Weber puts it:

> Now it is unmistakable that already in the German *word* "*Beruf*" exactly as, in perhaps a still more meaningful way, in the English "calling," a religious conception—a *task* set by God—at least resonates. . . . it appears chiefly that the predominantly Catholic peoples know an expression of similar coloring for that which we call "calling" (in the sense of a position in life [*Lebensstellung*], a definite area of work) as little as does classical antiquity, while it exists among *all* predominantly Protestant peoples. [47]

As Weber later wrote in *Economy and Society,* early Christianity lacked any notion of a specific "dignity" of work. Work became honorable only much later in the monasteries of Catholicism as a principal means to asceticism. The monk, indeed, was the first "man of the calling" (*Berufsmensch*).[48] Thus although the notion of *vocatio* existed among Catholics, it was not a discipline for all believers. It meant specifically the call to the *religious* vocation for the monk and the priest called into God's service and had no relation to any *worldly* tasks. As Vontobel writes, those who worked in the world performed a service but not a calling with any significance for salvation.[49] Nevertheless, for Catholicism "works," if not "work," could have an effect on salvation.

But beginning with Luther's translation of the Bible, according to Weber, the calling developed from this obviously separate, specifically religious task to something worldly, bearing a special sanctification. Luther translated two different Greek concepts with *Beruf*, the Pauline *klēsis*, in the sense of the call to salvation, a purely religious concept, and also the words *ponos* and *ergon*, which mean work; he thus connected the religious call to the concrete tasks in the world that everyone performs as work.[50] At the same time, with the conception of *sola fide* Luther rejected the possibilities in Catholicism of winning salvation through works and of attempting to excel worldly morality by withdrawing into the purely religious life of the monastery, represented by the Catholic division between *praecepta* and *consilia*. Luther believed that only through the fulfillment of one's worldly duties could one live acceptably to God.

As Douglas argues, Luther posited a twofold call, the spiritual or invisible vocation available to all, *vocatio generalis*, experienced through baptism, and the external and visible vocation, the concrete office an individual occupied, the *vocatio specialis*. For Luther no calling is to be taken up by choice but only as the result of a command or call. God's "act of calling" (*Berufung*) the human being to a concrete office or vocation (*Beruf*) is mediated by a "calling through man"; yet although it comes *through* man, it is still ordained *by* God. The vocation is hence not chosen by or produced from the *self*. Both the spiritual vocation and the temporal calling come from *outside* the person, through baptism or the *mandatum Dei*.[51] For Weber the crucial innovation is this:

> the valuation of fulfillment of duty within the worldly callings as the highest content that the ethical activity of the self could generally receive. This is what the idea of the religious significance of everyday worldly work had as an undeniable consequence and what first generated the concept of calling in this sense.[52]

Luther's moral emphasis on a religious justification of organized worldly labor in a calling was an extraordinarily significant product of the Reformation.[53] Yet this radical concept nonetheless remained "traditional," according to Weber, for Luther's emotionalist faith, which experienced salvation in a feeling of refuge in God, could not generate antitraditionalist or rational patterns of conduct. Moreover, Luther's faith in Providence led him to identify obedience to God with acceptance of everything as it is, and he saw the calling as a lot ordained by God in which one must remain and labor, for God has no interest in achievements, but only in obedience. For Luther, one serves God *in vocatione*, not *per vocationem*. This "coloring drowned out the other idea also present, that work in the calling is a, or rather *the*, task set by God."[54]

Thus in Weber's view Lutheranism lacks that restless and relentless drive to control rationally or to transform the world that we see in Calvinism. Luther could not have established a new connection between religious principles and work in the calling of the kind that led to the conception of duty in a calling as modern capitalism and the spirit of capitalism know it. For though Lutheranism did provide psychological "motives" or incentives (*Antriebe*) for a specific conduct of life, these incentives could not lead adherents to rationalize enterprise, as the spirit of capitalism did. Perseverance, yes; rationalization and innovation, no. This is not to say that *any* of the religious reformers was ever motivated by an ethical regard for the pursuit of worldly goods as an end. Their purposes were strictly oriented to the salvation of the soul. For Weber it is not the dogmas or religious ideas themselves that are at issue; it is, rather, the potential psychological consequences of faith for believers and the modes of action undertaken to deal with those consequences, whether to displace certain feelings or to induce them through specific activities.[55]

Luther's sense of the calling is thus of problematical value for Weber's specific inquiry. Although the legacy of Luther's concept remains of great importance, "without Calvinism his work still would not have been of outward permanence."[56]

Calvinism and the Calling

Weber locates the modern idea of the calling in Calvinism and the other principal sects of ascetic Protestantism—Pietism, Methodism, and Baptism (including the Mennonites and the Quakers). This idea formed one of the components of the spirit of capitalism, and of these sects Calvinism was the most important. It was the faith, says Weber, over which the great political and cultural struggles of the sixteenth and seventeenth centuries were fought in the most developed countries of Europe: England, the Netherlands, and France.[57]

For Calvin too there was a general spiritual calling and a particular temporal one. The *vocatio* is from God, mediated through men, according to God's will. But unlike Erasmus's *genus vitae*, it is set *against* one's own nature and inclination; yet, as a divine command it is at once irresistible and *imposed* on our nature. God works *in spite of* our natural inclinations. This shows the difference between the choice and the call, between choosing and being called, between *eligere* and *vocari*. Vocation is the office or station in which God places us for his employment, not for our enjoyment; it is a special burden taken on as our only spiritual hope and purpose, not for personal fulfillment. Moreover, it is unlawful to transgress the bounds of the assigned vocation or to desert the station in which God has placed us.[58]

Weber argues that certain other features of Calvinism in general colored the notion of the calling and made it available for different purposes and possibilities than Lutheranism allowed. It was this, he said, coupled with the transformation of the religion in succeeding generations as pastors strove to deal with new problems among their flocks, that allowed the calling to become the source of very special powers and inclinations. Weber takes as the most characteristic idea of Calvinism the doctrine of predestination, following from and yet profoundly affecting the concern for the afterlife. Reflected in this dogma is the notion of God's absolute freedom to choose to save or not, beyond the power of human merit or guilt to change it. Luther too believed in predestination, deriving it from Paul; yet because predestination for Calvin was also "conceived" (*erdacht*), not merely "experienced" (*erlebt*), his conception of it was more rigorous, relentless, and cold. Not only were works no longer of value for salvation, but faith itself could not win grace.[59]

> In its pathetic inhumanity, this teaching must have had one consequence above all for the mood [*Stimmung*] of a generation that surrendered itself to its overwhelming consistency: a feeling of unheard of inner *isolation of the single individual*. In what was for the men of the Reformation period the most decisive matter of life, eternal salvation, man was banished to follow his road alone to meet a destiny fixed from eternity. No one could help him. No priest. . . . No sacrament. . . . No church. . . . Finally also: no God, for Christ too only died for the elect.[60]

The consequence of this faith was also the completion of the evolution of Western religions in the direction of "rationalization" and the elimination of magic (*Entzauberung*) from their spiritual practice and from life as a whole.

> That great process in the history of religion, the elimination of magic from the world, which set in with old Jewish prophecy and, in association with Hellenic scientific thought, rejected all *magical* means of seeking salvation as superstition and sacrilege found here its conclusion. . . . There was not only no magical means but no means at all to bestow God's grace on one to whom God had decided to deny it.[61]

Yet even this was not all: while condemning desire and the impulses of the flesh, Calvinism also eliminated the confessional, denying to believers any means for discharging the emotional *sense* of sin. Moreover, by focusing completely on exclusive trust in God, some Calvinist pastors were even led to warn against any trust in the aid or friendship of other human beings. Bailey exhorted believers to imagine each morning before going out that they were going "into a wild forest full of dangers," and to pray God for "'the cloak of foresight and righteousness,'"[62] thus further isolating the believer from the comfort of others.

The elimination of means, especially magical ones, to win salvation, the stress on the enormous dangers to the believer of desire and other impulses of the self, the denial of a means to "work off" the feeling of sin, and the caution against putting trust in anyone but God—these led, in Weber's view, to the psychological "impulses" (*Antriebe*) of Calvinism that moved the believer to seek counsel about how to make himself feel secure in his call. These doctrines taken together must have had the effect, says Weber, of cutting people off from any human or purely religious sources of support apart from trust in God, of making them fear any "outbursts" of self, and of creating that anxiety among the generations after the confident founders that would lead them to displace their fear into worldly activity of a special kind—and to make the vocation what it came to be. Moreover, action and purpose had to be dictated purely by devotion and submission to God's purposes and for God's glory. This orientation to act *in majorem gloriam Dei* was the principal characteristic of "work in a *calling*," even when serving the interests of the collectivity. And it is in the consideration of charity that the true nature of work and action is revealed:

> "Charity" [*Nächstenliebe*] expresses itself—since it may be only service in the glory of *God*, not of the *creature*—in the *first* place in fulfillment of the tasks of the *calling* [*Berufsaufgaben*] given by the *lex naturae*, and it receives thereby a peculiarly objective-*im*personal character: that of a service of the rational formation of our surrounding social cosmos. For the wonder-

fully purposeful formation and arrangement of this cosmos, which, following the revelation of the Bible as well as natural insight, is evidently cut to serve the "usefulness" of humankind, allows work in the service of this impersonal social usefulness to be recognized as furthering God's glory and therefore as God-willed. The complete elimination . . . of all those questions about the "meaning" of the world and of life . . . was completely a matter of course for the Puritan.[63]

Here we have one of the great gifts of the calling in Puritanism: the elimination for the believer of the problem of the meaning of life and the world. This gift is so intimately attached to the essence of the discipline of the calling that we can see it accompanying all Weber's uses and deployments of the calling, even in a secular world that must find its ultimate ideals elsewhere than in God. It is part of the great bequest of Puritanism and the Reformation to the West.

The Subjugation of Self and Work

For Weber the first principal result of the adherence to Calvinism and the acceptance of its religious imperatives was a transformed self, inevitably the product of the question of whether the individual was one of the elect or not. Calvin himself believed in an "invisible" church and rejected the notion that one could learn a person's state of grace from behavior. But in succeeding generations pastors faced the disappointment of many believers with the answer that one should be satisfied that God has chosen and put one's complete trust in Christ. According to Douglas, moreover, a more secular idiom of self-knowledge and vocation began to penetrate the early orthodoxy of Luther and Calvin, and thus the basic doctrine of the founders survived intact for only two generations. Yet Weber considers the search for *certainty* of salvation of utmost importance, for out of this sprang "all the psychological drives of purely *religious* character."[64] First, believers were urged to consider themselves chosen and to combat all doubts as the temptations of the devil, since lack of self-confidence could only be a result of insufficient faith and hence of imperfect grace. One therefore had a duty to attain certainty of one's own election and justification in the daily struggles of life, to "make fast" one's own "call" (*Berufung*). But, following from this, the second form of pastoral advice was the most decisive: "To *attain* this certainty of self, *restless work in a calling* was enjoined as the most outstanding means. It and it alone drives off religious doubt and gives the security of the state of grace." The self can find assurance, then, only through its overcoming and subjection in a calling. Or as Douglas puts it: "Self-knowledge and vocation are inseparably bound to the knowledge of God and of God's intention: the whole meaning of vocation is to be found in abnegation of the self." [65]

The significance that work in a calling thus came to bear derived from the limited means available to believers to experience their own state of grace in the here and now. According to Weber, the only possibilities of feeling oneself assured of grace in religions of salvation are to experience oneself as "the vessel *or* as the tool of godly power." The mystical path of the first alternative produces a kind of unity with God and thus a form of rest in the godly bosom, but the opposite is the case for the second, ascetic, path. Since God is absolutely transcendent for the Reformed Churches, only the second path is open to them. To feel communion with God, Puritan believers had to feel "that God *worked* [*wirkte*] ('operatur') in them, and that they were conscious of it—that therefore their *action* sprang from the faith worked [*gewirkt*] through God's grace, and this faith was in turn legitimated through the quality of that action as worked through God." Only when one's conduct was not only God-willed but "worked" by God could one attain the certainty of grace, see signs of one's election, and lose the fear for one's salvation. [66]

Weber's picture implies that the godly person of Calvinism was not a self-sufficient actor but an *agent* of godly purposes, that his "self" created no barrier to godly intent because that self had been transformed into a transparent medium of godly action. This subjection of the self to God's imperatives gave to every action of life in a calling a potential religious significance. Indeed, according to Charles and Katherine George, the calling became "a kind, and an absolutely essential kind, of Christian worship." [67] Moreover, with Calvin's mistrust of all feelings and moods as potentially deceptive, the believer was forced to prove his faith through its objective effects (*Wirkungen*), rather than its subjective experience, for the *certitudo salutis* to be able to serve as a sure foundation for life. But actions and works could not be considered singly or in isolation, for the believer needed the accumulated and consistent evidence of God's "effect" at every point of his life, permeating life totally. Hence it was not merely regulation of life and self that were necessary, but "a systematic regulation of one's own life," "*systematic* self-*control*," and "a systematic rational formation of ethical life as a whole." [68] This quality distinguishes Calvinism from both Catholicism, whose "method" aims only at the religiously called, and Lutheranism. It is also the origin of the Western conception of what Weber calls "personality," the taming and unification of the self through the systematic overcoming of feeling and desire in the service of higher purposes: "The God of Calvinism demanded from his own not single 'good works,' but a sanctification of works raised into a *system*. . . . The ethical praxis of everyday man was thus stripped of its planlessness and systemlessness and shaped into a consistent *method* for the whole of life conduct." Puritan asceticism worked, along with every "rational" asceticism, to enable man "to maintain and bring to bear his 'constant motives' . . . against the 'affects'— thereby educating him into a 'personality' therefore, in *this* formal-psychological sense of the word." [69] This overcoming of "affect" by "motive," this subjection of feeling and the heart to method and system, this transformation of the self and the "powerful deepening [*Verinner-lichung*] of the personality" brought by Puritanism [70] are the core of what we can call the "rationalized" personality.

Such an approach to systematic rational asceticism was certainly known in the West before the Reformation. Indeed, monasticism had raised the ascetic supervision and rational mastery of life to a high level to educate the monk, through the systematic "domination of self," into "a worker in the service of God's kingdom." [71] Thus Puritanism was not completely original in its modes of systematic self-control. But it was original both in its elimination of "magic" and the discharge of sin and in the range of its application, for unlike Catholicism it extended the imperative for this methodical asceticism to all believers. The Catholic layman was not absolutely enjoined to transform his life into a systematically supervised ethical whole. Despite the biblical ideal that the whole man be changed, transformed, and reborn by the experience of grace, organized Catholicism did not drive the layman to such a rationalized system; in dogma, rather, it treated the performance of "good works" as a succession of individual actions, the worth of each one determined by its intention. The believer's experience of confession and absolution—the institutional dispensation of grace—weakened in practice precisely the imperative toward and the possibility of this overall transformation by allowing pent-up feelings of sin and damnation to be released. Through the abolition of confession and absolution, of the Church as mediator, and of the higher status of the *consilia evangelica*, the Calvinists removed the barrier to the planful penetration of life with asceticism. Like the monks of the Middle Ages, the Calvinists oriented themselves only toward the transcendental goal of salvation and in the process rationalized the world of work. Yet they not only lived an ascetic life, but were also taught to seek "the *proof of faith* in worldly life in the calling" and were thus provided with "the *positive impulse* to asceticism."[72] The search for proof thus led to a rational formation and "methodical control" of the whole of one's life in accordance with God's plan.[73]

Apart from Pietism and Methodism, which despite their undoubted asceticism had an "emotional" quality that made them "secondary movements" in Weber's investigation, there were two independent sources of ascetic Protestantism besides Calvinism: first, Baptism, and, second, the sects that came from it—the Mennonites and the Quakers—for none of which predestination was a crucial religious fact. In these cases religion was nonetheless still freed from any reliance on "magical means" to salvation and was thus rationalized along with the world: "The radical demagification of the world [*Entzauberung der Welt*] did not allow inwardly another path than inner-worldly asceticism. For communities that did not want to deal with the political powers and their doings there also followed the outward streaming of these ascetic virtues into work in the calling." Relying on the role and importance of a Christian conscience, refusing any political callings, and opposed to the aristocratic way of life, the approach to the calling of the Baptists and the Quakers had "enormous significance for the unfolding of important sides of the capitalist spirit," specifically in their policy of rigorous honesty. Yet Calvinism was more directly responsible for the "liberation of the private economic energy of acquisition." Above all, it was not from the social institutions and the ethical influences of the Calvinist sects themselves that such a "release of individual powers" was derived; in their supervisory and "inquisitorial" role the churches could even inhibit such a development. Rather, it was exclusively "the *subjective* acquisition of ascetic religiosity," "the ascetic striving for methodical acquisition of salvation," that worked these effects.[74]

Life in the calling means self-regulation and control based on the concern for salvation. Higher purposes must be imposed on the unruly self: it must be watched constantly and protected from its inclination to favor the "flesh" and to trust in the needs and purposes of other human beings lest it break out and stray from the only path acceptable to God. The struggle for certainty was the motive force for this subjection of the self and for the devotion to the service of a higher purpose in the discipline of the calling, as well as for the systematic and methodical supervision of life through rationalized discipline: "Precisely in everyday life the grace and election of the religiously qualified proved themselves—certainly not in everyday life as it was, but in everyday action methodically *rationalized* in the service of God. Rational everyday action, raised into a vocation, became the proof of salvation." This relation of the self to work clearly reveals the consequences for economic life—and for the larger culture of capitalism—of the Calvinist conception of the calling. "For there has perhaps never been a more intensive form of the religious valuation of ethical *action* than that which Calvinism produced in its adherents." [75]

The Calvinist calling is a *command* of God's to work for his glory, not a *fate* (*Schickung*), as in Lutheranism, that one must submit to and be satisfied with and in which one is automatically serving God's purposes. The believer must labor toward impersonal godly purposes, and his submission takes the form of active *service* on God's behalf rather than mere obedience. The Christian believes that God "must have willed the *objectively purposeful* as a means for the exaltation of his glory." Thus inner-worldly asceticism "first asks after 'tasks,' and in regard to these it organizes temperately and systematically." Good works as the fruit of the calling are a means of getting rid of the fear of damnation rather than of attaining salvation; it is through the calling alone that the believer "proves" himself as called to salvation before God as well as before himself. "For only in a fundamental change of the meaning of the whole of life in every hour and every act could the effect of grace as a removal from the *status naturae* into the *status gratiae* be proved." [76] Weber even speaks later of asceticism "in its rational form" as "taming the corrupted creature through work in the worldy 'calling.'" [77] The replacement or conquest of nature and of one's own nature by the self transformed through grace—which is thus no longer the old self—is the achievement of the new man of Calvinism.

The Breeding of Capitalist Individuals

According to Weber the spirit of ascetic religion unintentionally gave rise to economic rationalism "because it placed a premium on the decisive thing: the ascetically determined rational impulses." The calling, as the "highest ascetic means" and surest proof of rebirth, was the most powerful aid to the "expansion" of that conception of life, economic rationalism, that Weber calls the spirit of capitalism. "One of the constitutive components of the modern capitalist spirit, and not only of this, but of all modern culture, rational conduct of life on the basis of the *idea of calling*, was born—that is what this presentation meant to prove—from the spirit of *Christian asceticism*." [78]

Given that religious influences were present, "in what direction" did they work? Such influences can only be understood, Weber later argues, if we keep conceptually distinct the two key structural elements of capitalism, the capitalist spirit and the specific nature of "modern everyday capitalism, bureaucratized 'according to the calling.'" The "ethic of calling" developed out of the Protestant form of asceticism, and "certain economically relevant components of the modern life-style" developed "out of the 'ethic of calling.'" The capitalist spirit in the Weberian sense represented the development "from the romanticism of economic adventure to the rational economic method of life," while contributing to the development of an economic system from what had been merely opportunities for profit; it was the Puritans who were carriers of this ethos rather than, for example, the Jews, who stood on the side of political and speculative adventurers' capitalism. The differences between the two types of capitalist attitude "went hand in hand with religious differences." [79]

How did the Puritan conception of the calling and the demands of the ascetic life "*directly* [influence] the development of the capitalist style of life?" In the first place, Protestant asceticism sought the sign of election in the fruits of labor in the calling. Though the usefulness of the calling and its pleasingness to God were found first in ethical measurements, and second in the importance of production for the community, there was also "as a third and naturally in practice most important point of view: private economic 'profitability.'" This concern for the fruits of the calling meant that "in its psychological effect" asceticism freed the acquisition of goods from the "restraints" of traditionalist economic ethics. Since the fruits of enterprise were measured in profits, success in the calling led to acquisition, but not as its goal. In the second place, this acquisition led to accumulation and investment (*Anlagekapital*) in enterprise, because asceticism prohibited the spontaneous enjoyment of possessions as an indulgence of the "desires of the flesh" and as a danger to the demand for constant activity, which was threatened by idleness. Wealth was condemned only when pursued as a goal, with the intention of living a rich life, as a temptation to idleness and sinful indulgence. But as the "fruit of work in a calling" or as the result of "performing the duty of the calling" it was not simply tolerated; it was commanded. [80] "And if we now hold *together* that tying up of consumption with this unchaining of the striving for acquisition, then the external result is near at hand: *formation of capital* through *ascetic compulsion to save*." [81]

The consequences were apparent, however, in the effects not only on entrepreneurs and businessmen but on laborers as well. "The treatment of labor as a 'calling' became for the modern worker just as characteristic as the corresponding conception of acquisition for the entrepreneur." Religious asceticism provided the businessman with "temperate, conscientious workers, unusually able to work and clinging to their work as a life purpose willed by God." These qualities could not have been evoked simply by manipulating the wage level. Only labor performed as "an absolute end in itself—a 'calling,'" produces what is required, and such an attitude is not "given by nature." The "productivity" of labor, then, could be increased powerfully by laborers subject to an asceticism in which the striving for God's kingdom could be done "*exclusively* through the fulfillment of duty in work as a calling."[82]

There were ideological consequences as well: "only the methodical life of the ascetic sects could legitimate and transfigure the economically 'individualistic' impulses" of the modern "bourgeois-capitalist *ethos.*"[83] Moreover, ascetic faith provided the assurance that "the unequal distribution of the goods of this world" was a product of Providence. The seventeenth-century religious transformation left to its "utilitarian" heirs an "extraordinarily good conscience" in the acquisition of money. This particular form of the ascetic style of life made for an easy transition to the normal mode of bourgeois self-justification, in which profit and property are seen not as ends in themselves but as "measurements of one's own ability." Richard Douglas maintains that already in seventeenth-century discussions of the calling increasing attention was paid to issues of "inclination" or "preference" in the choice of vocation; it was described more and more with reference to the profit and advantage of individuals rather than to the benefit of the community. In principle the general call and its imperatives were meant to limit the particular calling and were supposed to serve as a guide apart from success. But from the seventeenth century on, even within Puritan debates, the issue of one's *particular* calling in the world received more attention than the subject of one's *general* call to salvation. The emphasis on the benefits to the individual led to the view that vocation "is in one sense imposed, but in another it is chosen according to one's gifts."[84] Finally, under the sway of such purposes Puritanism and Calvinism stood against the non-rational, self-indulgent habits of the feudal classes. Thus when the Puritans esteemed agriculture, it was the practices of farmers and rational cultivators that they approved, not the habits of landlords and squires; when they made money, they invested it not in land or in feudal habits of life but back into business,[85] offering a contrast to the less inwardly fortified and less self-confident bourgeois classes of modern Germany.

It is thus not surprising that Weber could later write: "Such a powerful, unconsciously refined arrangement for the breeding of capitalist individuals has existed in no other church or religion, and in relation to this everything that even the Renaissance did for capitalism shrivels up."[86] This "breeding" and production of capitalist individuals, innovative entrepreneurs and dutiful, obedient workmen—"new men"—is the real contribution to capitalism of Calvinism and of its sanctification of work through the calling, in a time before material power itself could create or "socialize" so effectively.

Beyond capital accumulation and the religious defense of the exploitation of labor, Protestant asceticism furthered "the tendency toward a bourgeois, economically *rational* conduct of life," because it was "its most essential and above all: its single consistent carrier [*Träger*]." Thus "it stood at the cradle of the modern 'economic man.'" As Weber later writes, apart from its creation, nurturing, and glorification of the "man with a calling," Protestant asceticism furthered "the rational objectification and socialization [*Versachlichung und Vergesellschaftung*] of social relations"; indeed, "the contents of life were above all oriented not to persons but to 'objective' [*sachliche*] rational goals,"[87] which were impersonal and dictated imperatives to the persons who hoped to serve and to fulfill them.

Yet for Weber the calling is not just a feature of the past: it is *our* "fate" as well. The "providential interpretation" of profit once "ethically transfigured" the Puritan businessman. But all that is left today is "the enjoining of the ascetic significance of the firm calling," which "ethically transfigures the modern *specialists* [*Fachmenschentum*]." The Puritans were motivated by the glory of God to live life in a calling serving higher purposes; what is left today is "only the duty to the 'calling,'" the "methodical proof of a calling in the life of acquisition." Whereas the Puritan "*wanted* to be a man of calling [*Berufsmensch*]— we *must* be it," though without any higher justification. For the union of the spirit of capitalism and the form of enterprise created the system of capitalism that governs life today and compels our obedience. At the same time the search for the kingdom of God was replaced simply by "temperate virtue in a calling," and the religious supports for acquisition disappeared and were replaced by "utilitarian worldliness." No religious powers are needed any longer to support capitalist undertakings. Whereas Puritans regarded material wealth as secondary to higher purposes, the modern material world has become a "steel-hard housing" (*stahlhartes Gehäuse*)—usually translated as "iron cage"—not a surprising result of the actions of the "steel-hard Puritan merchants" (*stahlharten puritanischen Kaufleuten*).[88]

The Lesson of the Calling

The purpose of this detailed treatment of the calling in Weber's early career is to discover neither the more general social effects of the calling nor even its specific economic consequences for the development of capitalism; it is, rather, to see the creation of a new kind of person, modern "economic man," "the man with a calling," the "carrier" of a new spirit. We want to understand the origin of the capacities of this new man and new character, formed and educated by ascetic Protestantism, which inclined him toward systematic rational conduct and supervision of his life in the calling. Though Weber's emphasis in his later work is principally on "sociologically" understood relationships, he retained precisely this interest in and emphasis on the formation of "new men" through adherence to the calling, as "Science as a Vocation" and "Politics as a Vocation" both demonstrate.

Though Weber's understanding of the context in which social action takes place shifted during his career, his awareness of the need for the shaping of character for modern tasks, political and intellectual, remained clear and strong. This awareness brought with it a conviction about the need to return to the "individualism" of life in the calling as a response to the collapse of a shared, or "collective," sense of meaning in life. For in Puritan times there were "inner tensions between 'calling,' 'life,' 'ethic' . . . [and] today we live in the middle of renewed tensions."[89] The calling in Weber's later prescriptive work is a secular revival and reappropriation of an historical and inherited conception, analyzed in his analytical work and rooted in the Reformation; but it is revived for a world deprived not only of its former stability but also of the original motivation toward such a form of inner-worldly asceticism, namely, the search for proof of one's salvation.

> The idea of "duty in a calling" goes around in our lives like a ghost of formerly religious beliefs. Where the "fulfillment of the calling" cannot be placed directly in relation to the highest spiritual values of culture—or where, not conversely, it must also be felt subjectively as mere economic compulsion—there the individual today mostly renounces its interpretation altogether.[90]

But this is a renunciation of interpretation that Weber sought to undo, both for himself and for Germany.

When Weber characterizes Calvinism as having foregone all reliance on magical means, however, he is only partially correct. Magical means were dispensed with in religious practice and observance, and grace could not be won through either faith or works; yet the practical outcome of these conditions and pressures in the development of the idea of the calling restored a kind of magical means, a means of psychological magic, to the life of the believer. Indeed, in *Economy and Society* Weber himself suggests that in religions where faith alone served as the means to salvation, faith could even give "a kind of surrogate for magical powers."[91] The calling could not win one salvation, but it could provide an inner conviction or "proof" of election, calm the anxiety that comes from meditating on God's vast scheme and on the prospect that one might be consigned to hell, and prevent the emergence of doubts about the meaning of life and of the universe. Its magic, moreover—and more important for Weber's own intellectual development—transformed "old" men into "new" men, men who were reborn for a new set of tasks. It gave them powers that had not been seen in everyday life before: a capacity to fortify the self through self-denial; a special strength to pursue goals against resistance and to win obedience to one's will, otherwise known only among "charismatic" leaders; and a capacity and disposition for systematic rational action. This is the magic of its power and the source of its attractiveness to Weber.

The Protestant Ethic is the scene of Weber's first great encounter with the calling and with the conquest of self that it both demanded and made possible. The paradigmatic type of the first great entrepreneur was the most brilliant of Weber's early theoretical insights into the origins of capitalism, and it became an explanatory device of enormous power, but with serious problems, in his understanding of culture generally. Apart from its nearly mythic power and its value for our understanding of both capitalism and the West, *The Protestant Ethic* is the foundation of Weber's later search for a viable, compelling, and effective ideal of the person in both private and public life, the outcome of which was only clear in the experience of World War I.

While Weber was establishing the origins and power of the calling in *The Protestant Ethic*, Thomas Mann was engaged in a comparable enterprise, though in a purely literary form. He drew a dramatic portrait of the calling of the artist who emerges from bourgeois origins and of the relation of this calling to that of his bourgeois forebears and to the life of his fellows in society. What Mann had worked out in his writings by 1903, although not in systematic form, were discoveries similar to Weber's. They became for him too the key to resolving early dilemmas of identity, meaning, and self-justification, though in ways different from Weber; they also became a foundation for much of his future work, even though they left him with dilemmas he was unable to solve until his picture of the world expanded through his identification with Germany in World War I.

Mann's work yields a fuller, more concrete portrait of the "rebirth" brought by the calling and provides us with a more rounded picture of what must be seen as the cost of a life lived in disciplined service to an ideal, a service that plays the role, even in a modern life, of salvation and justification of the self. For Mann too life in the calling is a paradigm with enormous prescriptive power and explanatory value. It sets off its devotee from others who only seem to be engaged in the same enterprise but who in fact lack qualities crucial to the calling: not only qualities of strength and "hardness," which the called man can find nowhere else but in his calling, but also qualities of "softness" and indulgence. These qualities still make him a warrior, but one who fights on a different battlefield and has a weakness for what others take to be his natural and appropriate enemy. It is to Mann's early discoveries and to the origin of the artist as "servant" that we now turn.

CHAPTER TWO

Mann and the Calling of the Artist

By the time he was fifty years old Thomas Mann was an institution in German letters. He won the Nobel Prize in 1929 at the age of fifty-four, and well before the beginning of World War II he had become a "representative" figure in German life and letters both by his own design and by others' efforts. His career began in earnest with his emergence as the best-selling author of *Buddenbrooks* and continued through a series of literary works before World War I, during which time he was also haunted by self-doubts and the fear that he would never again write anything as good as his first novel. During World War I he set aside *The Magic Mountain* and turned to essayistic and didactic writing, emerging as a defender of the German cause and, more than that, of the spiritual and political condition of Germany more generally. Yet with the end of the war, and despite his continued conviction that his wartime *Reflections of a Nonpolitical Man* remained a truthful portrait of the spiritual mission of Germany and of his own art, Mann became a defender of Weimar democracy. Later, after his initial reluctance in exile to denounce Hitler, he emerged as a champion of the anti-Nazi cause.

His artistic production took him from the portrayal of the crisis of a bourgeois family to an intense consideration and identification of the artist and the artist's calling, and thence to a wider and more explicit treatment of the competing intellectual and cultural currents of German life before and after World War I in *The Magic Mountain,* his first explicitly allegorical treatment of the German "condition." In 1943 Mann began to write *Doctor Faustus,* an allegory of German decline told through the story of an artist, his isolation, and his madness. These details point up a crucial fact: the artist's life and calling became an allegory of Germany in Mann's work from at least World War I to 1947. His understanding of the artist's calling was worked out most fully in *Tonio Kröger* in 1903, dramatized by contrast in *Death in Venice* in 1912, and finally made most explicit in a portrait of its dangers in *Doctor Faustus* in 1947. With the calling we grasp not only Mann's concept of the artist and his self-understanding, but also his understanding of Germany.

As a young man Mann experienced his life in art as virtually illicit, and he felt constant pressure to prove himself to society at large, both by the spiritual value of his art and by its material success. He also experienced his art as imposing coldness, isolation, and distance on his feelings and his life, an experience that led him to characterize literature as "death." There is, of course, an evolution in Mann's conception of the artist. His obsession with the artist's illicitness and virtual criminality, his experience of self-hatred and estrangement, and the intensity of his experience of art as the death of lived life all abated over time, appearing eventually as the objects of analysis rather than of inner torment. Yet from his earliest formulations in 1903 to his death in 1955 Mann remained convinced of the necessity of a right understanding of the artist's calling lest he be destroyed by the misfortune of violating its demands or be undermined by the compromises demanded by society.

Alongside his fictional treatments of this theme and throughout his career, Mann reflected on the identity and calling of the artist in the most recent stage of Western society. These observations increasingly reflected on German fate and German politics, particularly in the attempt to understand two of the most crucial and most deadly experiences of this century, World War I and National Socialism. Yet his work is part of a long tradition of reflection on the artist and society. The split within the artist between feeling and observation, his estrangement from life, his feelings of being an outsider and a threat to society—whatever their basis in Mann's personal experience—were also subjects of concern to artists before him throughout Europe and in Germany in his own time, and Mann read and learned from them.[1] That reflection begins with Schiller at the end of the eighteenth century and includes Flaubert and later the decadents. Yet only in Mann does the artist come to stand so completely as a symbol of the society to which he belongs. Thus when W. H. Auden, Mann's one-time son-in-law, wrote that Mann's work was too limited because of its preoccupation with the artist—someone who,

Auden argued, shared very little with the life of others in society—he showed how little he understood the significance of Mann's work on the nature of the calling. For it is precisely in Mann's treatment of the artist's calling, the structure of the artistic self or "personality," and its symbolic relation to German life that Mann speaks most compellingly. Moreover, it is not only the demonic artist of Mann's later work that has symbolic significance, but also the artist and the artist's calling as they appear from the start of his career. Indeed, Mann interprets the waywardness of Germany in departing from its earlier cultural promise in the same terms as the waywardness of the artist in departing from the more balanced view of art enunciated in *Tonio Kröger*: Germany's departure from the path that *its* calling, properly understood, would have laid out for it is at the root of Germany's "devil's pact" with Hitler. In his concept of the artist's calling "rightly understood," Mann adheres to a conception of service, commitment, and vocation that is intimately related to the demonic path of his last artist and thus of Germany itself.

This chapter and Chapter 5 show the development of that conception before World War I, when its foundations were laid. By demonstrating the relation of Mann's conception of calling to Weber's, and by using Mann's dramatization of the issue to reveal its inner history, we will be in a better position to assess the historical significance of the calling in German thought and self-understanding and the role in shaping German, and modern, identity that both men ultimately wished it to play.

The Intellectual Artist Without a Calling: "The Joker"

French literary developments of the late nineteenth century had an enormous influence on Mann's early stories and on German literature generally. The period 1870–80 saw the rise of naturalism, whose great champion, Émile Zola, published the first volume of his Rougon-Macquart series in 1871. The emergence of naturalism was a symptom of the power, perhaps even the victory, of the scientific outlook in literature. It took nature as its general principle and provided a set of empiricist criteria for the dissection not of reality as a whole but of social life in its particular detail. Its earliest manifestos try to reconcile an enthusiasm for science with a devotion to ethical ideals. But naturalism was only briefly in vogue, for by the end of the 1880s it was torn by internal divisions and challenged by newcomers, leading to a decline of its reforming zeal. According to Roy Pascal, however, naturalism, particularly in Germany, "opens an era that may be called that of the bourgeoisie with the bad conscience," and the new self-criticism of the bourgeoisie is "perhaps the most signal feature of the culture of the post-1880 period."[2]

Impressionism succeeded naturalism and involved the realistic analysis of the psyche, feelings, dreams, and sensations, instead of social reality. One could even say that the new psychological novels of Bourget, Barrès, and Huysmans resulted from naturalism applied to the psyche. Impressionism, however, was passive and contemplative, resigned, uninterested in social reform, and concerned with the representation of passing moods and sensations; it was a genuine aestheticism, with no consideration for the world outside. In its rejection of bourgeois life and of the reforming social concerns of naturalism, impressionism renounced involvement in "life," as given in bourgeois society, for "art," thus setting up a dichotomy Mann was to use later. It even sought to "justify" life by art, viewing art as the only real compensation for the disappointments and limitations of life. The impressionists saw artistic works as self-reflective and autonomous, produced only for other artists; art became the subject of art, and the aesthete strove to "turn his life into a work of art." Impressionism gave birth to the "dilettante" as the new focus of literary attention: free of concern for anything outside himself and his own sensations, priding himself on his superfluousness and uselessness, rejecting the ideal of naturalness for that of artificiality, and striving to make himself independent of nature. Nature was now considered ugly, no longer a standard of judgment, and it was constrasted with the prized and positive artificiality and beauty of culture. In this new aesthetic life appeared monotonous and boring, dominated by a bourgeois discipline and routine considered destructive; but by driving the sensitive into withdrawal, it produced an efflorescence of consciousness and intellectualism, which were now given pride of place in artistic creation.[3]

"Decadence" is the name given to the more general phenomenon at work, and it is of particular interest for German developments and for the young Mann, as he wrote much later:

The word *decadence*, which Nietzsche wielded with so much psychological virtuosity, had penetrated the intellectual jargon of the times; a German novelistic genre-picture at that time, today forgotten, was called "novel of decadence"; tired, aestheticising overripeness and decay formed the themes and cadences of the lyric from Hofmannsthal to Trakl; and whatever may have been meant by the catchword *fin de siècle* which spread all over Europe, whether neo-Catholicism, Satanism, intellectual crime, or the brittle refinement of nervous excitation—it was, in any event, a formula of decline, an all-too-modish and somewhat foppish formula for the feeling of the end, of the end of an age, the bourgeois age.[4]

The obsession with feelings of crisis, doom, and the end of civilization sets off decadence from other aspects of aestheticism. Although the term had only a short vogue in Europe, Jean Pierrot argues that decadence was the "common denominator" of all literary trends of the last two decades of the nineteenth century in France, the country from which much of the influential literary work flowed. The phenomenon of decadence was a major stage in the developments that derived from romanticism. It was a reaction to naturalism based on a pessimistic conception of human existence, often with the strong conviction of the power of a fateful determinism, of heredity, and of the subjection of all nature, including love, to mechanistic laws and control. The whole of French literature at the end of the nineteenth century was pervaded by this pessimism, melancholy, and disillusion. The decadents longed to escape from nature and society. They desired to shut themselves off in their inner world to escape, through refinements of feeling and sensation, the boredom and banality of everyday life, to make imagination into a power that could transform reality. They strove "to feel that they had dethroned life and put art in its place," thus rendering life bearable.[5]

The principal figure associated with decadence and its formulation as a model for life and literature was a French writer of enormous importance for German literary developments. This man was Paul Bourget, whom Nietzsche praised, to whom Thomas Mann's brother Heinrich dedicated his first novel, and whom Thomas read at least by 1895—even before he read Nietzsche. Accepting decadence as a grave spiritual crisis for the collective life of humankind, Bourget nonetheless asserted its literary and spiritual value. In 1876 he wrote: "We accept, without humility as without pride, this terrible word *decadence*." In an essay on Baudelaire entitled "Theory of Decadence," in *Essais de psychologie contemporaine*—which Pierrot calls "the first true manifesto of the decadent esthetic"—Bourget argues that the appearance of decadence foreshadowed coming disaster and dissolution on the collective level. But when internalized, when "the individual life has been exaggerated under the influence of acquired well-being and heredity," decadence can accentuate the individuality of artists, leading to a flowering of great works. Incapable of normal work or reproduction, the decadents were "very superior as artists of the interior of their soul," and "the abundance of delicate sensations and the exquisiteness of rare sentiments have made of them virtuosi, sterile but refined, of pleasures and of sadnesses."

For the decadents desire and reality are in persistent imbalance and disharmony, Bourget maintained, because of the physical and nervous exhaustion of civilization: the human species, having reached an age of decline, now longs for past "ages of untamed energy or deep faith." But this imbalance is also a product of the exercise of thought: reflection, anticipating pleasure, undermines spontaneity and empties pleasure of substance, thus exhausting the organism. This exaggeration of the life of consciousness, this *dédoublement* of the psyche—where one part thinks and acts while the other observes and judges—destroys the soul and undermines the capacity to live, but it is nevertheless the modern fate. Moreover, the influence of science has depoeticized reality and destroyed religious faith, causing widespread nihilism. Disillusionment leads to sadness, despair, and pessimism for the decadent and to the artist's desire to escape completely from reality into art. Life is lived in imbalance, in the obsession with neurosis and the need to live on one's "nerves," and it becomes the vogue to be suffering from and agitated by a nervous disorder. Still, despite these untoward consequences Bourget follows Baudelaire in affirming decadence; in a chilling remark he says that, in comparison with the bourgeois, the decadent "represents a richer treasure of human acquisition. . . . Let us therefore delight in the singularities of our ideals and form, and pay the price of imprisonment in a solitude without visitors."[6]

These developments are the setting for Mann's first important work about the calling, "The Joker" ("Der Bajazzo"), a first-person narrative and confession told by a character *missing* a calling and filled with disgust (*Ekel*) at his existence.[7] In letters of 1895 Mann spoke of the main character as a "useless decadent" and an "unhappy dilettante and Eichendorf-like good-for-nothing, translated into the modern."[8] His "outer life," led in a "mechanical, well-regulated and calm manner," contrasts starkly with "the ugly process of dissolution" of his "inner life," and this situation leads him to consider suicide. Mann denied, of course, that he was in any way affected by or dependent on the developments of literature among his *fin-de-siècle* contemporaries in Europe.[9] But this claim is certainly untrue, especially for the early writings; the problematic Mann shared with others is one for which his work provided what he thought was a solution. The plight of "The Joker" is fully overcome only in the resolution of *Tonio Kröger*.

"The Joker" begins with a description of a childhood similar to Mann's own (and to those of his later fictional characters Hanno Buddenbrook and Tonio Kröger) in an old, probably northern, town whose principal business is trade. His father is a merchant, his mother a somewhat abstracted lover of music and piano playing. Drawn to his mother's music and to the arts, and given to mimicry and constant clowning in school, he invokes the profound disapproval of his father, who wants him to go into business and who sees his son's artistic talents—drawing, playing with a favorite puppet theater, his schooltime triflings—as "talent for buffoonery" (*Bajazzobegabung*), clowning, and *blague*. Having embarked halfheartedly on a business career, the narrator soon reveals his true attitude toward the world, an attitude that will come to haunt him. Charming and comfortable among his youthful acquaintances, he says nevertheless, "I began to despise, from instinct, all of these people, who were dry and unimaginative."

> For the present it had its attraction to move, strange, superior, and calm, among these relatives and acquaintances whose narrowness I mocked, while I met them with skillful charm out of a desire to please, and I basked pleasantly in the confused respect that all of these people exhibited before my being and essence, for they suspected with uncertainty something oppositional and extravagant in it.[10]

Disinclined to lead an everyday bourgeois life, still absorbed as an adult in his childhood fascination with theater and music, though without the inclination to pursue the arts actively except as a consumer and observer of culture, the narrator takes up residence in the south of Germany. He is relatively secure, with a small inheritance from his late parents, but lacks the means to frequent the well-to-do bourgeois circles he had been used to in his youth. He has no work of any kind and no desire to pursue his artistic interests as a creator, and he has chosen to arrange his life in this way for maximum personal freedom and enjoyment. From the start of his new life, he experiences feelings of aversion, anxiety, and foreboding, assuaged only by walking the streets and looking at "the working people [*Berufs- und Arbeitsleute*] who are spiritually and materially too unendowed for leisure and enjoyment." The narrator has "broken with 'society,'" refused "to serve it in any way"—for service is what any relation to society would entail, he believes—and chosen to go his own way. But since he lacks wealth, this choice means that "there is no specific social circle" to which he "obviously . . . belongs[s]" that would allow him to identify himself with it, either through status or work.[11]

Without work, without the wealth that would put him in better society, and with only contempt for "the Bohème" of artists and intellectuals he sees as a crowd discussing anarchism at "tables sticky with absinthe"—an image of bohemia drawn directly from Bourget's *Edel*— the narrator has nowhere to go but back to his room; there he stimulates his nerves in a predictable way, given his inclinations, through reading "a great art work, one of those monstrous and cruel creations" produced by "a dilettantism of genius." Yet although this experience stirs in him a desire "to express, to communicate, to show" these feelings, " 'to make something of them,' " his desire is stillborn. Though he recalls his real talents, he sees their only purpose in the winning of success, reputation, recognition, praise, envy, and love from those whom he despises.[12] After his failure to make contact with a woman who attracts him, he is convinced that all attempts to break out of his condition are doomed; this resignation leads him to see himself as a victim of his own vanity, "unable to see myself with other eyes than those of 'people,' and I am perishing of a bad conscience."

> Ach, I was not justified, I the least, to hold myself apart and to ignore "society," I, I who am too vain to bear its disdain and disregard, I who am unable to do without it and its approval. But it is not a matter of justification? Rather of necessity? And my useless buffoonery [*Bajazzotum*], could it not be worth any social position? Now, indeed, it is just this buffoonery through which I must in any case perish.[13]

Klaus Schröter describes the figure of the joker as the first of those artist figures with a strong intellectuality that Mann dealt with so often and in some of the best works of his career. These are Tonio Kröger, Gustav von Aschenbach, Adrian Leverkühn, and Felix Krull. The buffoon himself exemplifies the dilettantism that Schröter defines as "an attitude of observing indecision, a self-control continually critically awake, which is able to obstruct every impulse of the will."[14] Though critics have seen a number of autobiographical elements in this story, and even elements from the life of Mann's brother Heinrich, it is clear that this condition of dilettantism, a product of *fin-de-siècle* decadence, is something Mann analyzes, rather than affirms, and for which he later attempts to provide an antidote.[15]

What is the true condition of the narrator of this story? He is a man of bourgeois origins who wants to live a bourgeois life in idleness but lacks the necessary work or wealth; he is thus cut off from "society" by his economic condition, by his self-consciousness, and by his sense of not having an identity. Moreover, he holds the world in contempt, expressed as a feeling of superiority, though he admits his enormous desire for recognition and admiration. He has artistic talents but at the same time disdains artists and his potential audience, especially if that audience is composed of ordinary people. The critic Helmut Haug asks, "What does the buffoon lack to become the artist?" It is not talent; "he is lacking ultimately only one thing: the 'will to the work' ['*Willen zum Werk*']," that is, the will to create from his experience a delimited work with concentration and form—"endowment, gifts are not solely a given but are to a high degree a fact of the will, which chooses its goal in original freedom." [16]

Interesting though Haug's remarks are, this is not all that is missing from the joker. Haug partly admits as much when he describes the father's understanding of his son's indifference. The father recognizes that the son has talent, though perhaps not the gift of a focused will, but he recognizes too that the son is indifferent "toward any 'other,' namely, specialized, specific, limited, and limiting activity." This, then, is what the joker is truly missing: the capacity to find an identity through a delimited sphere of work and through belief in the "validity" or value of work, particularly in art. This would allow him to mobilize his talents and shape his experience, while taking the risk of the failure and lack of applause that is always inherent in such work. The one gift he lacks is *not* the will but the calling. Haug's simplistic notions of "original freedom" and of the will's capacities ignore the realities of social experience and the importance of cultural inheritance. The buffoon does not inherit the one thing Mann believed could support him even if he chose to refuse a normal bourgeois occupation: an orientation to work in the form of the calling, which justifies, legitimates, and gives identity to its adherent. Moreover, as Mann later attempted to show in *Tonio Kröger,* adherence to this calling makes it possible to overcome, if only a little, the estrangement from the world experienced by the man of bourgeois origins who cannot legitimate himself to himself as a bourgeois. It enables him to obtain recognition, even if he can never gain acceptance, from the "children of light."

For Mann the commitment to the personal solution of the calling is the answer to a dilettantism born of decadence; it is not, as for Bourget, the social solution of family, nation, and church. For Mann the calling provides an approach to the bourgeois world, or at least a position in relation to what he believes are the contradictory worlds of the bourgeoisie and the *bohème*—the *bohème* representing in an undifferentiated way the normal world of art. The called man estranged from the bourgeoisie is between two worlds with a foot in each—not, like the buffoon, outside both of them. The aesthete-buffoon can only redeem himself and break through to the world with a real calling, borrowed in form from bourgeois life but filled with the content of art. According to Schröter the two early stories, "Enttäuschung" and "Der Bajazzo," take as their main theme "the search of the 'dilettante' after 'experience' [*Erlebnis*], which for once would lay claim to him totally, to his senses and his feelings. He does not find it; and when he believes he has found it, it is only illusion that deceives him." [17] This search for experience that would grasp the self totally was as much a problem among youth at the turn of the century as it was at the end of World War I, when Weber observed it in his demand for the revival of the calling in "Science as a Vocation." To both Mann and Weber this condition can only be overcome through a right understanding of, and a life in, a calling: the calling alone leads to "conquest" of the world, either through winning an audience for one's work or through involvement in and mastery of the rationalized spheres of the world. Only self-fortification through a calling and entry into the battle for the world promises to overcome estrangement—an overcoming, however, through domination both of self and of others.

It is evident that to Mann only a shift in one's understanding of the world and its people, a diminution of the sense of superiority, and an acceptance of the desire to be acknowledged and acclaimed by others can eventually make possible the effective relation to the world that the calling allows. One could even say that what the joker lacks most is the will to break through his isolation and to put himself in relation to "people," to overcome his disdain and to recognize his need; this breakthrough might make it possible to fulfill his deep desire for acknowledgment, whatever he chooses to do with his life. The problem of work is thus intimately related, for Mann, to the problem of identity and of one's regard for and need for the world. Whereas for Weber the Puritan calling makes it possible to resist tradition and the self in order to work, thus separating the person from "life," for Mann the calling puts one back in touch with life and the world, even if in a form more limited than one might otherwise desire.

The Failure of the Calling: *Buddenbrooks*

The joker emerged from a family whose last "normal" male bourgeois representative was his father. Whatever the joker needed to make a life of work for himself, whether in business or in art, was not passed on, despite the artistic inclinations he acquired. Dilettantism and will-lessness were shown to be possible outcomes of such an upbringing, a theme echoed in contemporary French and English literature. But Mann revealed another possible failed outcome of bourgeois life: not just the crippling of its sons' capacity for normal life—its daughters, as we will see, are never at issue in the same way—or the crippling of the capacity for work, which is closely related, but total defeat and death. Invited by his publisher in 1897 to submit a long manuscript, Mann turned to por-tray the figure of "the sensitive latecomer Hanno,"[18] the protoartist, more sensitive than the joker and without mockery. Unable to find any support in his family or social environment or to insulate himself from his sense of rejection by life through any false feelings of superiority and disdain, Hanno is fated to die. Yet while planning this novel, Mann was drawn to a more detailed examination of the past that produced this ill-fated boy, to give the complete prehistory of an emergence that was the product of decline (*Verfall*). Indeed, in T. J. Reed's view the full history of the decline was always present in Mann's plan, since from the begin-ning Mann saw the whole story from the point of view of the ending: Hanno's inadequacy to face life somehow compensated for by the devel-opment of his unusual sensitivity.[19]

But *Buddenbrooks* is not just, as Mann says, "a social novel in the guise of a family saga." It is Mann's "own prehistory as well as Hanno's."[20] For as Fritz Kaufmann remarks, this is no mere bourgeois novel: "What takes place here, under the guise of telling a story about a Lübeck family, is a bringing forth, through a selection of autobiographi-cal material, of the conditions of the artist's existence."[21] Mann himself makes this point plain: "In order to portray a human essence doomed to die [*todverfallenes*], incapable of life [*lebesunfähiges*], a poet needs only to portray himself—leaving out the creative gift."[22]

In *Buddenbrooks*, subtitled *Verfall einer Familie* (*Decline of a Fam-ily*), Mann draws on many details of his own family history to show how the worldly calling of one bourgeois family ceases to exercise its hold; this loss leads to the development of more "sensitive," though crippled, individuals—not far from Bourget's formula for decadence—and leaves no alternatives within the terms of that family's understand-ing of itself and of the world. In the novel we witness the collapse of traditional bourgeois self-denial and holy devotion to work and success among those embarked on a bourgeois career, and the indulgence in-stead of impulses of escape and concealment, which lead first to economic decline and finally to the end of life. Though the bourgeois calling may once have been an aid to the spirit of capitalism and to the later breeding of "capitalist individuals," in *Buddenbrooks* it becomes merely the background to a new transformation: the collapse of the calling within the world of one bourgeois family of *Erwerbsmenschen* and the emergence of the artistic but powerless soul. This decline took its first form in the dilettantish aesthete of "The Joker"; in *Buddenbrooks* the decline appears in the defeat of will and of the calling, not only in the death of the family's offspring but through the decline of the sensitive, yet bourgeois, father, Thomas Buddenbrook. Mann later writes that the "morality of pessimism," or "Schopenhauer's musical pessimism," and Nietzsche's "psychology of decline [*Verfall*]" were among the elements that shaped the novel. In terms strongly reminiscent of Bourget, Mann says that he set out to portray "the psychology of wearying life, the refinements of soul and aesthetic transfigurations that accompany biological decline [*Niedergang*]." [23] Only in *Tonio Kröger* are the resolution and antidote found to the corrosive effects of bourgeois decline in the reappropriation, rebirth, and rejuvenation of the calling among the offspring of the bourgeoisie, but in the form of the artist's life.

It was Bourget, according to Schröter, who awakened the "bad bourgeois conscience" in Mann, and that conscience was strengthened through his reading of nineteenth-century literature and, more important, Schopenhauer and Nietzsche. For the young Heinrich and Thomas Mann, the *Bürgertum*, or bourgeoisie, was the fundament of all social, political, and cultural order and the source of *Bildung*—education, cultivation, or character formation. Yet their further intellectual development and reading, especially of the early Nietzsche, heightened their criticism of the bourgeoisie. [24] Still, as Reed says, "for all his problematic relations with *Bürgertum*, Thomas Mann remained proud of his origins and deeply influenced by their ethos, as he was aware." [25] The condition of the bourgeoisie and the process of decline in one family are the context for understanding the state of the calling as Mann found it.

Wolfgang Martens says that *Buddenbrooks* reflects the economic changes the merchant class underwent in Wilhelmine Germany. [26] But, contrary to Martens, it is clear from Mann's inquiries and the external evidence that these changes were underway well before Wilhelm II's accession to the throne. *Buddenbrooks*, which takes place from 1835 to 1875, takes the Lübeck of that time of transition and economic change as its setting. The development of the Prussian Customs Union, the revolution of 1848, the Prussian wars of the 1860s, conflicts with Denmark, and the vagaries of the grain trade as cheap American and Russian grain flooded the market in the 1870s—all of these added up to precisely the kind of economic decline that the old merchant city and the old privileged grain-trading burgher families like the Buddenbrooks (members of an exclusive oligarchy) confronted.[27] Still, the recognition of these hard facts does not prevent the principal character of the novel, Thomas Buddenbrook, from taking the contractions and eclipse of Lübeck's merchant prosperity as a sign of his own personal failure and of the failure of his calling. He links his external fate to his inner capacity, or lack of it, to command the world through adherence to a firm calling.

The Significance of the Bourgeois Father

Thomas Buddenbrook was based on Mann's father, though Mann's father apparently had more success in business. Mann stressed his father's significance in shaping the person he himself became: "How often in life have I confirmed with a smile, *caught* myself frankly in doing so, that it is still actually the personality of my dead father that, as a secret model, determines my conduct."[28] Recalling the hundredth anniversary of his father's firm, which he had attended as a fifteen-year-old, Mann described how he saw his father "prudently representing a century of bourgeois proficiency [*bürgerlicher Tüchtigkeit*], and my heart was anxious. . . . I knew then that I was not the successor of my father and of my ancestors, at least not in the form that one tacitly expected of me, and that I would not lead the old firm further into the future."[29]

The continuities and the discontinuities between father and son, portrayed in the novel and experienced between Mann and his father, are central for understanding the transition from the calling of the *Bürger* for business to the calling of the not traditionally bourgeois artist—yet bourgeois nonetheless—for art. Mann pointed to his father's distinctive yet *bürgerliche* features as well as to the lessons he took from his father and from his father's life. His father was "not robust, but nervous and susceptible to suffering, yet a man of self-control and of success." Mann said that his father had taught him and his brother Heinrich

"the serious conduct of life," the ethical, that converges with the bourgeois [*Bürgerliche*] to so high a degree. For the ethical, in contrast to the purely aesthetic . . . is quite properly the bourgeois nature of life [*Lebensbürgerlichkeit*], the sense for duties in life, without which the drive toward achievement, toward the productive contribution to life and to development, is lacking; this, which encourages an artist not to perceive art as an absolute dispensation from the human, to found a house, a family, to give his spiritual [*geistigen*] life, which is often adventurous enough, a firm, respectable—I can again find only this word—bourgeois foundation [*bürgerliche Grundlage*]. If I have acted and lived in this way, so there is no doubt that the example of my father contributed decisively.[30]

It is therefore not surprising that Mann could say of the character Thomas that he was "the mystical form related threefold to me, as the father, offspring, and double," based on his father, yet his own creation, and, in truth, ultimately his double.[31]

The Calling and Its Crisis

Buddenbrooks is the story of the decline in fortunes of a merchant family in an unnamed northern German trading city; but it is not so much about the outward decline of the family in wealth and power as it is about the change in the inner life, and therefore the disposition to and capacities for outer life, of the family members. They develop over generations from blithe self-confidence, to the religious sanctification and strengthening of work, to self-doubt and inner conflict, and finally to outright rejection of life in any form and the longing for death. Mann later reported the generally held, and accurate, popular view that it was a novel whose subject was "the process of de-bourgeoisification [*Entbürgerlichung*], of the biological loss of proficiency [*Enttüchtung*] through differentiation, through the increase of sensibility."[32] Rilke, the same age as Mann, wrote a review of the novel when it first appeared:

> The story shows the calm, unself-conscious life of an older generation and the nervous, self-observing haste of its descendants. . . . It is shown with particular subtlety how the decadence of the family manifests itself above all in the fact that the individual members have changed the direction of their lives, as it were: no longer is it natural for them to live . . . toward the exterior world; rather, the tendency toward introversion becomes more and more apparent.[33]

The founding generation of the family, building its business in the Napoleonic period, displays worldly confidence and is aggressive and commanding in business. Thomas's grandfather, old Johann Buddenbrook, admires Napoleon, hates false scientific ideas, laughs at things religious, and makes fun of his granddaughter's difficulties in reciting her Lutheran catechism. He is a free-thinking deist, more Enlightenment

figure (*aufgeklärter Mann*) than religious Protestant.[34] He is especially
critical of the way the obsession with technical education and making
money has displaced traditional ideals of classical education and Enlightenment values. His open and enlightened attitude toward how one
ought to live, how the "personality" should develop, and what model
the shaping of the self ought to follow is captured in his advice to his
granddaughter: "One person is not the pattern for all. Everyone after
his own fashion" (15).

Thomas's father, Johann the Consul, inherits from his father the traditional commitment to business, but it has combined in him with a
piety drawn from his extremely religious mother. He was "the first of
his stock, with his fanatical love of God and the Crucified One, who
knew and cherished non-everyday, unbourgeois [*unbürgerliche*], and
differentiated feelings" (259). Religious piety in the younger Johann
seems to represent not an original inspiration to labor but almost a falling away from what are understood to be purely bourgeois inclinations
in others. Here the mother's influence as a pattern for the children out-
weighs the father's, a pattern that holds true for all the generations of
the Buddenbrooks.

Beyond his defense of the German Customs Union, French constitu-
tionalism, and whatever else favors the practical life, Johann's motto is
"Work, pray, and save" (176). Like the Puritan ascetics of the seventeenth century whom Weber described, he believes in applying oneself
to practical tasks above all:[35] he is critical of the study of Greek and
Latin because "there are so many serious and important things that are
necessary to the preparation for the practical life" (98). In him religious
sanctification of work and duty becomes clearly visible, signaling the revival of a pre-Enlightenment view. The life of business is no longer just
an occupation or an expression of the strength, inclinations, or talent of
the self and personality, consistent with one's nature. It has instead become a calling in the Calvinist sense, an obligation even against one's
nature and a call higher than anything toward which mere nature di-
rects us. The calling of Johann the Consul has more than a worldly significance: it is also a source of strength for the self, providing a sense of
unique inner value and nourishing the confidence of the man who sees
his success as the expression of God's will and of his own holy life. But it
punishes the failure, as the wayward, with crushing self-doubt.

Yet as Erich Heller observes, it is Johann the Consul, not his son
Thomas, whose own judgments (though not in business) first falter and
who first begins to dwell on problems of decline and doom.[36] His most

important failure comes in pressing for the marriage of his daughter Tony to a repulsive man who, it soon turns out, has tricked the wealthy Buddenbrooks to rescue himself from bankruptcy. Johann's insistence on the marriage of his daughter to a person of the right class—who turns out nevertheless to be a failure—and his inability to foresee the swindle despite his investigation reveal, according to Nachman and Braverman, the "irony of his apparent worldliness and practicality." For his acting on "blindly accepted imperatives upon which he was utterly dependent" results in a "major financial disaster, while, incidentally, destroying his daughter's life."[37] Johann's sense of doom emerges in a discussion of the previous owners of the house the Buddenbrooks move into at the beginning of the novel. He speaks not of the business mistakes leading to the bankruptcy of the former residents but of the owner, who was "as if lamed," who must have felt that everything "was moving irresistibly to an end": "This firm had been ruined, this old family was *passé*." Their head had made a terrible choice of a business partner with whom "his destiny would be fulfilled. . . . He must have acted under the pressure of an inexorable necessity." He was almost certainly aware of the problems in the firm and those created by his associate. "But he was paralyzed." Enough, says his father; "that is just one of your *idées*" (24–25). Yet this is a premonition of the fate of the Buddenbrooks, for it is Johann's eldest son, Thomas, who will in fact take in a partner and live out just such a paralysis and end, and whose death, followed shortly by the death of his own unworldly son, will bring an end to the Buddenbrook family.

In Johann the Consul's children what we can call the "signs" of decay become embodiments of it: among them the calling for business, grasped only by Thomas, cannot be sustained. The novel is principally the story of Thomas and of his son, the ill-fated Hanno, who dies in adolescence. Even before he entered his father's firm at sixteen, Thomas "looked forward to his calling with seriousness and eagerness." Once he had begun, he "was at his task with devotion [*mit Hingebung bei der Sache*] and imitated the quiet and tenacious diligence of his father" (77), and he "settled into the business with talent" (81). Yet Tom also is inclined to wander, however temporarily, from the paths of duty. He has an affair with a shopgirl whom he loves but leaves to follow the dictates of business and family fortune, becoming a consul like his father. He marries another woman whom he loves, who is even musical, although quite cold; yet she is also wealthy, for "if Consul Buddenbrook's first law was 'to keep up the *dehors*,' he showed himself in this relationship imbued with the *Weltanschauung* of his fellow citizens [*Mitbürger*]" (313). Standing over the body of a dead uncle, estranged from the family many years before by marrying for love rather than money, Tom imagines talking to the dead man: "You learned too late to make concessions, to show consideration. . . . But that is necessary. . . . If I had been like you, I would already have married a shopgirl years ago. . . . Keep up the *dehors*. . . . Although you were proud . . . you also possessed no ambition" (276–77). Tom's caution is well founded, for in his society revealing one's weaknesses or showing unacceptable attitudes, impulses, or tendencies brings community censure to the offender, just as Tom is severe toward his uncle. The preoccupation with appearances, which regularly brings him back to the straight and narrow, coupled with the community's subtly coercive but extreme judgmentalism, eventually form the prison, both inside and outside, from which he cannot escape.

Tom takes over the family business at his father's death and prospers. "The longing for action, conquest, and power, the desire to force fortune to its knees, flamed up quickly and vigorously in his eyes. He felt the gaze of the whole world directed at him" (257). To this point he seems entirely in control of his fortunes and his destiny. Indeed, he has turned his back, or so it seems, on those of his sides he thinks inappropriate to his calling and origins, especially his tendency toward self-reflection and examination. To his sister Tony he remarks: "I have myself frequently reflected on this nervous, vain, and curious occupation with oneself, for I was likewise inclined to it earlier. But I noticed that it makes one confused, incompetent, and unsteady . . . and self-control [*Haltung*], equilibrium, is to me the most important thing for my part. . . . Ach, we should sit down, devil take it, and accomplish something, as our forefathers accomplished something" (265–66).

This choice has evidently been successful, for "it was soon noticeable that, since Thomas Buddenbrook held the reins in his hands, a more brilliant, a fresher, and a more entrepreneurial spirit ruled the enterprise" (267). He takes a new partner; still, "the 'personality' in the business, however, about which there was no doubt, was the younger of both partners . . . who . . . loved above all to insert his own person into the daily struggle for success" (268). As he says to a friend, "It takes personality. . . . I always have the need to direct the course of things when current, with a look, word, and gesture . . . to control it with the immediate influence of my will, my talent, my fortune" (269).

Yet at the height of his success, after the birth of his son, his election to the town senate, and the building of a new and stunning house for his family, he begins to reveal the dark inner side of his outward experience. Only at this point, at the moment of inner difficulty in the midst of outer success, does he begin to speculate about the nature of work and success in his calling. To begin with, "the demands which he himself and other people were placing on his talent and his strengths were growing," and this begins to wear him out (418):

> Just now I feel myself older than I am. I have business cares. . . . It seems to me as if something were beginning to slip away, as if I were no longer holding this uncertainty so firmly in my hands as before. . . . What is success? A secret, indescribable strength, circumspection, preparedness . . . the consciousness of exerting a pressure on the movements of life around me through my mere existence. . . . The belief in the adaptability of life to my favor. . . . Fortune and success are in us. We must hold them: firm, deep. As soon as something here inside begins to yield, to relax itself, to become tired, immediately everything becomes free around us, resists, rebels, withdraws from our influence. . . . Then one thing follows another, blow follows blow, and one is finished. . . . it still does not exactly need to be death. But the decline . . . the descent . . . the beginning of the end . . . (430–31)

In these words Thomas reveals not only his weariness but also the distance he has traveled from his forefathers' approach to work and success and the power and importance of his understanding of vocation. For his grandfather, confidence and inner strength, enlightenment reason, and business acuity and courage were the sources of success. For his father, Johann the Consul, success and fortune derived from God, although practical ideals and practical education, coupled with honesty, were instrumental in that success. But Thomas is without the direct confidence and exuberance of his grandfather and no longer sees success as God-given, as his Puritan father had. The bourgeois vocation in business, as he sees it, must rely purely on the strength and confidence of the inner man, the self, for its sense of achievement. The ordering and domination of the soul and the restraint of all that threatens to tear loose within are the source of worldly fortune. Inner strength alone controls the world, and failure to control is a failure of the self. In Thomas's vision the real threat to success in the vocation lies not in the recalcitrant world but within—the real enemy is oneself. The feeling of election is a sign and token of election. Any sense of flagging inner strength brings forth visions of chaos and failure in the world outside; any doubt or feeling of weakness or weariness is taken as a sign of decline and leads to terror. When confidence in his capacity to dominate men and the world and to turn them to his own advantage begins to fail, we see how weary and pressed the inner man is—already holding at bay his own chaos and rebelliousness—to hold the chaotic and rebellious world at bay as well. To Thomas no external success can truly persuade the inner man of his own strength. Indeed, there may be an inverse relation between inner and outer, for Thomas even believes that "often the outer, visible, and tangible signs and symbols of fortune and ascent first appear if in truth everything is already declining" (431). Thomas has not yet had any real failure in his life or business; he merely begins to doubt, to notice his strength for certain struggles failing, and then he can only watch as his confidence slips away. In such a man the strong vocation in the world can survive only as long as he can control the life within. The Puritans had the service of their God as an inspiration and reassurance. Thomas has only the feeling of strength to inspire him.

There are two major sources of his doubt. The first is in the visible world: not failure of a normal kind, but the failure of things to go as planned. In the midst of an argument with his mother over giving money to the widowed husband of his dead youngest sister, he reflects:

> Nothing yielded any more! Nothing went any longer according to his will!. . . Events went their way without him! But it seemed to him that it could not have happened earlier, that it would not have *dared* to happen earlier. It was a new shock to his belief in his fortune, his power, his future. . . . And it was nothing but his inner weakness and despair that broke out before his mother and sister during this scene. (435)

Although his failure to persuade his mother results in financial loss to his firm, what makes him angry and despondent is that, having shaped himself in his calling for the control of self and world, he finds that the world no longer bends to his will, even in his own house. He reads the signs of this rebellion in only one way: his inner strength must not be as great as before. What once gave him the capacity to master the world was the "grace" and certainty he experienced in his firm acceptance of the calling. Submission and success at "making fast one's call" fortify the conviction of personal worth and strength. But Thomas has lost this sense of grace in a hostile social world. Without the calling's fortifying power and its assurance of "certainty" through submission, and without a supportive social world or religious context to reinforce and give meaning to the calling and its value, he can no longer harness his will to satisfy his purposes and to master the world. With this loss doubt begins to grow in Thomas; the outer world is even less responsive, and real crisis is around the corner.

Not that he had become to a smaller degree than before an important and indispensable personality there outside. . . . He was a rich man, and none of the losses he had suffered, not even excepting the hard one of the year '66, had placed the existence of the firm seriously in question. But . . . the idea that his fortune and success were gone, this idea that was more an inner truth than one based on outer facts, put him in a condition of . . . suspicious despondency. . . . There was nothing more to perceive of that new and fresh spirit with which the young Thomas Buddenbrook once enlivened the enterprise. (468–69)

Yet the lack of vigor in the business and the resistance of the world are only part of the problem. The second source of doubt and sign of weakness lies, in his opinion, in his own scruples, misgivings about the life of business, and doubts about the meaning of his activity. Noting that he can no longer blithely act out the part of a ruthless businessman, Tom takes this too as a sign of failure to live up to the ideals of his ancestors and of his calling. Having lost money in the grain trade as a result of the Austro-Prussian War of 1866, he experienced how harsh the world of business was, how "the cruel brutality of the business life" drove out all kind sentiments and enthroned "a raw, naked, and dominating instinct of self-preservation." When one experiences misfortune, even one's best friends greet one with " 'suspicion,' cold, negative suspicion."

Had he not known that? Was he called [*berufen*] to be surprised about that? How much he had later been ashamed of himself about it in better and stronger hours, that he had been scandalized in the sleepless nights of those times, that he had rebelled, full of disgust and incurably wounded, against the ugly and shameless harshness of life. (469–70)

Failure suggests to the community something almost criminal, and its censure can be warded off only by success. Yet this once-acceptable aspect of business is harder and harder to bear. The only way to counteract doubt and scruple is through self-confinement and an even firmer devotion to the calling. "A man who stands firm and without doubt in his calling recognizes only this, knows only about this, values only this," he tells himself (472). If this calling can once again be made firm it will be possible to return to his former "self"—or, rather, to his self refashioned in the calling—and to accept the hardness of the world as an unlamented given. But even his speculations are signs to him of wavering faith and of his limited capacity to bear the calling's demands, and hence of the beginning of failure. In his view, only by adhering to those demands completely, to what we might call (following a later usage of

Weber's) the "laws" of the calling, can he once again find hope. Without the firm calling the result can only be worthlessness and powerlessness, for failure in business is failure in life.

Yet his case is not so simple. "Was he a practical man or a tender dreamer? . . . he was too shrewd and honest not to have to admit the truth that he was a mixture of both" (470). Having struggled all his life to keep his feelings in line, "would he never completely learn" that life "was hard, and the life of business, in its ruthless and unsentimental course, was an image of the whole of life?" (469). Even after teasing someone, he feels that what he has done is low and mean.

> With resistance he felt it to be so, with that desperate resistance that he had to oppose every day in practical life to his sensitive nature, if he still could not grasp it, could not get over it, how it was possible to recognize a situation, to see through it, and yet still to take advantage of it without feelings of shame. . . . But to take advantage of the situation without feelings of shame, he said to himself, that is ability for life. (628)

Thomas's way of asking about awareness or knowledge versus unselfconscious "life" will follow many of Mann's characters: how to have knowledge of the harshness of everyday life, have insight into its severe or even corrupt nature, and yet still act without inhibition, with naïveté, innocence, and spontaneity.[38] And all Mann's artists will manifest Thomas's inward divisions.

Thomas searches in genuine Protestant fashion for a visible sign of grace, a sign that the world will still bend to his will. Presented with a grain deal he thinks shady, he overcomes his "scruples"—unfortunately overcoming his rationality and his better business judgment as well—and goes ahead. He can no longer distinguish the doubts of good judgment from the doubts of inner weakness.

> Yes, it was a pointer, a sign to raise himself up! It was a question of a beginning, a first stroke, and the risk that was bound up with it amounted to one more refutation of all moral scruples. If it succeeded, then he was revived, then he would venture again, then he would hold fortune and power again with these inner elastic clamps. (474)

When this deal fails, his paralysis is confirmed. Having ignored his external success as a sign of inner strength, he now lets an external failure confirm the self-doubt and fear deeply planted within him. Thereafter his doubts overcome him.

Decline and the Loss of the Calling

Thomas sinks into a weary attempt to put on a correct exterior while concealing from everyone his total inner collapse.

> The imaginative vivacity, the lively idealism of his youth were gone. In play to work, and with work to play, to strive after goals with a half serious, half playfully meant ambition on which one conferred only an allegorical value—to such brightly skeptical compromises and brilliant superficialities there belong much vigor, humor, and good spirit; but Thomas Buddenbrook felt himself inexpressibly tired and morose. What there was for him to have reached, he had reached. (610)

This lack of dynamism or hope in his affairs gives the final blow to his calling. Failure alone does not produce so deep a sense of defeat; it is the recognition that all his strength, energy, and purposes must be marshaled merely to prevent any slipping or decline of fortunes that cannot improve. He is left to imagine a desperate hanging on in which new accomplishments and advances are impossible. Having "served" the old firm with enthusiasm—indeed, having lived this life playfully and even symbolically, in certain ways like an artist—he is now "lamed through suffered misfortune and inner exhaustion" (611).

Moreover, as a member of the town senate he has advanced as far in public and community affairs as he can. More "cultured" than his fellows, he entered business at the age of sixteen and remained a "mere" merchant. He cannot now go further—become mayor, for example—given the standards of the *Bildungsbürgertum* and the traditions of the city, because he did not go to a *Gymnasium* (at least) to study the humanist and classical curriculum. This self-decorative obtaining of diplomas was the external mark of culture in a society that took as its standards not the inner life but the outer signs of social esteem, even for the relatively unrelated positions of local officialdom and leadership. By every measure this is a class whose standards Thomas can no longer meet.

Thus a man to whom the validating signs of existence were the ability to realize great plans and to overcome the "petty reality" of the present is reduced, in both business and public life, to a holding action in a detestable present. This is the final defeat: "He was empty within, and he saw no plan and no enthralling work to which he could devote himself [*sich hingeben*] with joy and satisfaction" (612). Without the support and conviction needed to make his calling "effective," his pursuit has no meaning. He can see no way to respond to his condition except through concealment: concealing this reality from everyone, even his family, and performing his "role," however mechanically. At this point he begins to long for the end.

Knowing that the society and community of which he is a part is judgmental, severe, and subtly coercive, he still takes great caution to preserve "the *dehors*." To reveal his weakness or his inclinations and reservations would lay him open to merciless criticism and, worse, to mockery, and thus to a public defeat that would reflect his private humiliation. Though his brother faces such hostility every day because of his preference for actresses and his other idiosyncrasies, Thomas has remained a part of that community where the foundations of life are credit, civic responsibility, reputation, and economic success. He believes only in that society, and he knows and recognizes no other. Thus his life in society becomes (if it is not already) an elaborate performance.

> All his life he had presented himself to people as a practical man; but, so far as he correctly counted as one, was it not . . . due to conscious consideration? He had formerly had successes to record . . . but had they not resulted from the enthusiasm, the momentum, that he owed to reflection? And if he was now laid low, since his strengths . . . seemed exhausted: was it not the necessary consequence of this untenable condition, of this unnatural and exhausting conflict inside him? . . . his father, his grandfather, his great-grandfather . . . had been practical men . . . fuller, more whole, stronger, more uninhibited, more natural . . . than he. (470)

In this conflict the only acceptable resolution would be for his practical side to defeat his more sensitive and doubting side. There is no room in society, as he understands it, for the rejection of business life. Nor is there room in his inner world for self-acceptance. To be divided within himself is to be as much outside society as one who openly rejects it, for neither society nor the traditions and standards within the self will tolerate doubts about or forms of behavior that go against accepted social pursuits. Only the clear adherence to the calling of business, pursued with devotion and shrewdness, can make life bearable. For Thomas, having lost his inner strength and consequently his self-esteem, a failure in his own eyes, the last possibility is at least to conceal this decay from the prying eyes of the world. He is unable to find comfort even at home. His wife is reserved and cold; he suspects her of having an affair with a military officer besides. His son and only child is a constant disappointment to him, even more disinclined to the practical life than he is. So he tries to recover some small part of satisfaction through pretence, to keep disapproval at bay. He resorts to a meticulous preparation in front of the mirror before every public appearance, even before dinner with his family, hoping to induce in himself a sense of "freshness, calm, and intactness" (613). All these preparations create in him "the feeling of satisfaction and readiness with which an actor who has put on his makeup, finished in all details, takes to the stage."

> Truly! Thomas Buddenbrook's existence was no different from that of an actor—one, however, whose whole life down to the smallest and most everyday triviality has become one constant production, a production that, with the exception of a few small hours of solitude and relaxation, constantly lays claim to and consumes all strength. . . . the impoverishment and desolation of his inner self . . . [was] coupled with an inexorable inner obligation and dogged determination, at any price, to represent worthily, to conceal his frailty with every means, and to preserve the *dehors*. (614)

This is the reality of the decline. Not only does the narrator observe this decline, but Hanno, Thomas's son, discovers it as well, seeing through the sham of his father's life to the empty, ceaseless striving and the agony. This desire "to represent worthily" and to conceal the truth of inner failure turns Thomas into a Sisyphus. Without a purposeful calling his life becomes constant playacting, a skillful but destructive attempt to deliver the image he would like to present both to the world and to himself. He is not deceived about who he is: he never confuses the man he feels himself to be with the man the world sees, except at certain moments of public speaking. Playing his part with determination, if not with conviction, and unable to conceal the truth from himself, Thomas ceases completely to live a real life. "Only this gave him the feeling of separation and security, that blind intoxication of self-production in which he attained his success. . . . it was much harder for him to attain domination over himself in sitting quietly inactive. Then the tiredness and weariness rose up within him" (615). Thomas is the slave of a performance in which he can at best induce the feeling of being his old self, if only briefly. The world is now controlled not by the force of his will mobilized in the calling but by the force of his acting in a carefully contrived setting with all the makeup in place.

Thomas is reluctant to celebrate the jubilee of his firm because he no longer feels at one with his ancestors. He is not "born" to this life, as Mann would later say of Nietzsche, but "called" to it, yet with what can only be seen as an ineffective faith. The calling is not according to his "nature" but is a product of "culture." Whatever the underpinnings of the business life were for his forebears, these underpinnings are now gone, and only the shell of the calling remains, the form without the inner support and content. Neither pure economic struggle for its own sake nor the religiously sanctified obligation to work and prosper are alive in Thomas's life. The rationale of the calling has vanished. He struggles against the limits of the practical life without the benefit of the justifications and unself-consciousness that might have inspired him to persevere despite scruples. His ancestors did not struggle against their calling, but Thomas does not have their option. As the critic Jochen Vogt observes: "Where Johann Buddenbrook wanted still to trust in 'God's grace,' his son sets up 'composure' [*Haltung*] and 'accomplishment' (*Leistung*], 'risk,' 'struggle,' and 'success'—concepts that altogether betray rather a soldierly than a Christian ethos." [39] Vogt recognizes here the quality that makes Thomas a direct forebear of that soldier of art Gustav von Aschenbach. Yet Vogt does not adequately reveal the extent to which the Puritan calling, which is clearly the Buddenbrook model, is in its very nature a soldierly ethos, an ethos of self-command, of domination of the world, of battles within the self and with the outside world. It is not that Thomas's model of the soul is more soldierly than Christian but rather that such a soldierly existence acquires sanctification from the devotion to and enlistment on behalf of a higher value, ideal, or god, which alone sanctifies struggle and gives meaning to life. Unable to be a Christian soldier or a man with the natural taste for battle, Thomas is in a war with no purpose; yet war is the only life he knows. He has disciplined and shaped his soul for struggle only to find that the motive for the tremendous military discipline he originally imposed on himself cannot be sustained simply by his former desire for success or by the vanity of seeing its effect on and power in the world. The calling, originally both soldierly and Christian, has lost its justification and thus cannot serve as a justification for the man who follows it.

Thomas has no place in society to retreat to when this model of behavior and personality becomes untenable. The calling for business remains his ideal from a time in which it had meaning in the scheme of things. Lacking religious support or a carefree attitude toward labor, Thomas dwells in his calling as in a prison in which the prisoner must act as if he were free. [40] Feeling imprisoned and hopeless, weary and defeated, Thomas's thoughts turn toward death. The Pietist Protestantism that nourished his ancestors had never consoled him. He had even flirted with Catholicism as a boy. Now, going back to his Protestant roots, he finds no cause for hope.

No, in the highest and ultimate things there was no aid from outside, no mediation, absolution, soothing and consolation! All alone, independent, and from one's own strengths one must unravel the riddle and obtain clear readiness in intense and assiduous work, or depart in despair. (653)

The Protestant teaching that motivated Weber's entrepreneur to face life with resolution and energy, and that once motivated Thomas's father, is now a confirmation of doom, precisely the feeling that the calling was intended to dispel. A Protestant without a calling in life is lost, even in facing death.

Decadence and Death

In the depth of his despair Thomas happens to read, of all things, Schopenhauer's *The World as Will and Representation* and is particularly affected by its chapter entitled "On Death and Its Relation to the Indestructibility of Our Essence in Itself." Schopenhauer is the one modern Western philosopher who could express for him the unutterable agony of his life and the long-sought peace of death.[41] Schopenhauer was already a pivotal thinker for the decadents of late nineteenth-century France, and his book echoes the weary longings for death common to both the decadents and Mann's hero. Far from being Mann's personal interest alone, Schopenhauer was a central figure in mediating the reception of the concept of "life" into German letters. If not a household name, Schopenhauer was part of the ordinary intellectual currency of the end of the nineteenth century.[42]

But it is neither mere chance nor for pure literary effect that Thomas happens on this work, for Mann himself read the book halfway through the writing of *Buddenbrooks,* was himself "under . . . its fresh impression, the twenty-three- or twenty-four-year-old author," and did not wish to keep it to himself.

To him, the suffering hero of my *Bürger* novel, I gave the dear experience . . . and allowed him to find life in death, salvation from the bonds of his tired individuality, liberation from a role in life that he had taken symbolically and represented with bravery and intelligence, but that had never satisfied his spirit, his longing for the world, and was a hindrance to him, to being something other and better.[43]

In Schopenhauer Thomas finds confirmation of his own negative experience and the impossibility of its being otherwise. Schopenhauer "seizes hold of life, this life so strong, cruel, and scornful, in order to

defeat and condemn it." Having concealed and felt guilty about his sufferings "before the coldness and hardness of life," Thomas now receives
"from the hand of a great and wise man the fundamental and solemn
right to suffer in the world" (654).[44]

For some moments Thomas finds his consolation here, even though
he does not fully understand what he has read. He is able to turn the
world's judgments back upon it, to negate his self-blame, and to forgive
himself for the inner strife and what he takes to be the outward failure
of his life. The only replacement for his lost calling is portrayed here as
the negation of the world and the longing for death. Indeed, he begins to
feel that "death [is] a happiness . . . the return from an unspeakably
painful wandering," but, more than that, "the liberation from the most
adverse bands and barriers" (656). That is, death is the means of overcoming the isolation and restraint he experiences in life: he can unite
with "being," become reconciled to a life that judges him, and escape
the deeper isolation in which he has sought protection. "Through the
barred window of his individuality the person stares hopelessly at the
circular walls of external circumstances, until death comes and calls him
to return home to freedom" (657).

For this person who has felt himself failing at what the world demands and has felt inwardly divided between his natural impulses and
the demands of his calling, life is a prison and death a liberation and
fulfillment. But we must remark that this desperate state arises only
when it is impossible to envisage *living* differently, only when life as it
is seems absolute, unrelenting, and without an alternative within its
bounds. Bourgeois society leaves Thomas with no other path once he
has found himself incapable of pursuing his calling. He has no acceptable way to renounce the past or the present and live toward a different
future, for society dwells within him as well: it takes the form of harsh
judgments of his most sensitive, hence most "wayward," characteristics—wayward in that they cannot be used to carry out the principles or
live the values of bourgeois society, at least not yet. He is unable to find
another path, another calling, perhaps less traditionally bourgeois but
still within the bourgeois world that he is constitutionally incapable of
leaving. Hence he must seek his freedom in death, a fate and a choice
shared by his son, who will choose it well before he enters bourgeois
society as a working adult. Indeed, as part of his renunciation of life
Thomas inwardly renounces his son even more completely than before,
and he dismisses any desire to live on in that son, "a still more anxious,

weaker, more unsteady personality. . . . I do not need a son!" (657). Yet "somewhere in the world a boy is growing up," he thinks, "well endowed and successful, gifted to develop his abilities, already grown and untroubled, pure, hard, and vigorous. . . . That is my son. That is I, soon . . . soon . . ." (658). This inward identification with a better son and self—which looks toward the future and the world—shows that the desire to renounce life is in truth the desire for a different life.

Thus Thomas does not long remain a Schopenhauerian world-rejecter, as Erich Heller observes,[45] though Thomas himself does not realize this, for he concludes: "Have I ever hated life, this pure, hard and strong life? Foolishness and misunderstanding! I have only hated myself, for I could not bear it. But I love you . . . I love you all, you happy ones" (658). A true understanding and agreement with Schopenhauer should have led Thomas to a rejection of willing and a rejection of life for its suffering; for the only things that Schopenhauer affirms, apart from death, are detached contemplation of this vale of tears, as in philosophy and art, and the asceticism of the saint. Thus when Thomas arrives at a simple affirmation of life through his philosophic wanderings, it is less a Schopenhauerian rejection than a vaguely Nietzschean affirmation of life, or at least an affirmation influenced by the vogue of *Lebensphilosophie* so prominent at the end of the nineteenth century.[46] Indeed, within a day of his "conversion" by Schopenhauer, Thomas loses his newfound resignation and dies shortly thereafter. This forgetting indicates that insights won through philosophizing and "mere" thought are never able to overcome the experience and traditions of a lifetime—a theme repeated throughout Mann's literary career. The patterns of life and work have been reinforced by a bourgeois society hostile to impulses that hesitate before it, question it, or doubt it. Thomas's son, Hanno, will have even less to keep him alive.

Hanno: The Artist with No Calling

One reason for the enormous sense of failure Thomas feels is the failure of Hanno, his only child, to display any interest in or aptitude for the practical life of his father. Indeed, Hanno is continually oppressed by his father, who subjects him to merciless scrutiny and interrogation hoping to find evidence of practical inclinations and capacity. Hanno is a dreamy, gentle child, almost feminine, closer to his mother and inclined to love music as she does. Nothing could more disappoint his father, who, like the joker's father, is anxious that the masculine virtues of a male-centered business life be transmitted to his son, ensuring a future for the firm of the Buddenbrooks.

From an early age Hanno shows musical gifts that distinguish him from the other Buddenbrooks and that in another society, another class, or perhaps another family might be recognized for their value. He is pictured playing as a boy of four, unpressured, without obligation, "without the world yet demanding service from us . . . where the impatience of those whom we still want to love does not yet torment us for signs and first proof that we will be able to accomplish this service with proficiency" (437). But this time does not last. His father demands a display of the qualities and knowledge appropriate to mastering the difficulties of practical life, and whenever their discussions begin to take on the form of an examination of the boy's knowledge, "his mood [sinks] to zero, his power of resistance [breaks] down completely" (511). Thomas sees in him one more instance of the weakness of his own capacity for practical life: he has been unable to engender in his son a taste for the worldly vocation as it is normally understood in society. Indeed, it is clear that his hostility toward his son is actually an expression of hostility toward himself, for the boy turns away from a bourgeois role that Thomas himself cannot sustain. He crushes in the boy precisely those impulses to stray from the normal bourgeois path that he has tried to crush in himself, but that have instead crushed him.

Music and art are not recognized in this society as legitimate objects of a calling for males; it is no accident that the only adult male to show an aptitude for music, apart from the organ master in the church, is the army officer who plays duets with Thomas's wife Gerda and whom Thomas suspects of having an affair with her. He is therefore a man who, although a soldier and hence "male," seems to bring along with his potentially unacceptable musical interest a threat to bourgeois society in the form of illicit love and adultery. The only possible support for Hanno's musical inclinations could have come from his mother, who is an admirer of the "new music," meaning Wagner. Indeed, she is always disputing what she takes to be Thomas's pedestrian musical judgment, but she can impart little strength to the young Hanno, for she resides in a distance, coldness, and reserve so profound that she is a kind of absence at home and shows warmth for little apart from her music.

The role of mothers, and of women generally, in *Buddenbrooks* is curious, for they are clearly more decisive than the fathers in the novel for the development of the attitude toward work and bourgeois society in all the generations—more decisive than the novel itself acknowledges or explains. Johann the Consul, Thomas's father, may be a dedicated businessman, but his whole view of life comes from his mother's intense piety; his father's carefree business pursuits, humanistic tastes, and irreverent enlightenment spirit are far from his own temperament. Thomas inherits the family business and the mantle and form of the business calling from his father, but he has neither his father's piety nor his absolute commitment to that calling. He has inherited the male role but not the crucial tone of male business society, for his mother, from whom he has inherited most of his sensibility, has neither piety while her husband is alive nor an ordinary bourgeois background. Hanno in turn, despite pressure from his father to be "male" in his response to the calling for business, inherits his mother's abstracted quality and musical gifts and tastes and shows no fitness for the practical life.

Thus though the *form* of the calling for business is inherited by the son from the father, who is the bearer of this form, the specific *ethic* of work that the son inherits comes from the mother. Something crucial, therefore, is lacking in the paternal inheritance, for the father cannot pass on the *spirit* with which he works, and thus the son's relation to the mother is more decisive, whether the mother is pious, aristocratically detached from bourgeois pursuits, or artistically detached from bourgeois life. But if the mother does not reinforce the vocation, it finds little internal support from the model and actions of the father alone.

The case of Hanno shows even more, however. Society, as portrayed in the novel, is male in its demands and opposed to what it takes to be the female nature of artistic interest. Bourgeois society here fuses social identity and capacity for work with sexual identity. This is an issue that Tonio Kröger, the hero of Mann's great artist novella, will also experience painfully and personally. It is taken to be unmanly and potentially illicit to choose art over practical life, for such a choice reveals an ambiguous sexual identity in the male artist or an identity that threatens the social order, as the army officer does. Indeed, the hero of *Death in Venice* will take the problem of this ambiguity to its end point. Thus it is not surprising that Mann, for whom the problem of ambiguous bourgeois identity is crucial, also takes as a related theme the nature of ambiguous gender identity in the artist. In his work these ambiguities are linked and heightened particularly in the artist who has to prove the bourgeois and "male" value of this female side of his character by achieving male success, especially financial, in the pursuit of his calling. But for Hanno, though music is the province of the feminine, his own mother is too cold to help him sustain a strength that could fortify him against the extreme pressure and degradation coming from his father, from bourgeois society, and even from the everyday demands of schooling.[47]

Hanno has long seen and understood even better than his father what the life of business has done to Thomas. He has seen how hard this life is, seen the mask descend over his father's face when he does business, seen "a conscious and artificial exertion in which, instead of sincere and simple inner participation, a terribly difficult and exhausting virtuosity had to compensate for composure and backbone" (627). In such a relationship, Hanno and his father share little. Their closest moment happens around an experience of suffering. Thomas stands stricken one day on a balcony above the entryway to the sitting room where Gerda sits all day with the young officer. Hanno stands by his side, equally troubled by the situation.

> One thing was certain, however, and they both felt it, that in these seconds during which their gazes rested on one another, every strangeness and coldness, every pressure and every misunderstanding between them sank away, that Thomas Buddenbrook could be certain of the loyalty and devotion of his son, as here, so everywhere where it concerned not energy, ability, and bright-eyed freshness, but rather fear and pain. (650)

Yet though the sufferer is understood by his son, he passes on suffering without being aware of the torment he creates. Losing his inner call, Thomas presses Hanno relentlessly for signs of its presence in him. But Hanno can manage none of it. Persecuted by his teachers in school and by his father at home, he escapes into the refuge of his music but finds no support for his identity and his differentness. Hence, he is dominated by others. Because music is unacceptable as a calling for a Buddenbrook, he can find no relief from his sense of inadequacy, worthlessness, failure, and defeat. Finally he cannot resist the authority and pressure of male parent and society, can marshal no resources on his own behalf. The sources of male legitimation, the worldly calling and performance in expected roles, are out of Hanno's reach, and his feminine detachment from the worldly, which is his essence, is no match for the demand that he display male virtues in a bourgeois calling. The attraction to art, stigmatized as unmanly, is also understood by the novel (and perhaps by society) as a form of decadence and melancholy, an understanding that portrays decadence as a feminine falling away by a male from the masculine world, to which the male is not, or is no longer, attracted.

Yet we can also say that, unable to find support in his environment, Hanno also fails to find "his" philosopher, the philosopher of the proto-artist, as Tonio Kröger, the artist, will find Nietzsche. Hanno needs a philosopher who can legitimate him, justify his own nature to him and his relation to the dominant society, make him understood to himself, and fortify him to act on that nature. Schopenhauer may be the perfect philosopher for the crisis and defeat of the wayward bourgeoisie, but Hanno needs a thinker for the bourgeois who cannot stray because he cannot enter the lists of the calling for practical life in the first place. Still, Fritz Kaufmann argues that Hanno "perishes of weakness. . . . He lacks the vital energies for real work. Only with the strength of life can art grow beyond it." He maintains further that in *Buddenbrooks* "Hanno's end is still interpreted in Schopenhauer's terms, namely as the spirit's withdrawal from life's summons."[48] Yet the lack of energy for work cannot be the decisive issue, for the same could be said of the joker, who at least survives. Hanno lacks not just the energy for work but the energy for *life,* not just the calling but the capacity to survive in a bourgeois world with which he cannot identify and that cannot grant him any of its energy and confidence, not even enough to keep him alive.

In the midst of a terrifying day at the *Gymnasium,* a day like a night-mare, yet which the narrator tells us is typical, Hanno confides to his closest friend:

> I would like to sleep and not know anymore. I would like to die, Kai! . . . No, nothing matters to me. I can will nothing. I don't even want to be fa-mous. I'm afraid of it, exactly as if there were something wrong with it! Nothing can come of me, be sure. . . . One should just give up on me. I'd be so grateful for it! . . . I have so many worries, and everything is so hard for me. (743)

Shortly thereafter Hanno dies, signaling the death of the protoartist un-able to survive without a calling.

The Failure of the Calling

Buddenbrooks's real story is a tale of the weakness of a social and personality ideal, the failure of the worldly vocation of capitalist busi-ness life to support Thomas and Hanno. It chronicles the collapse of that form of self-denial and devotion to work and accumulation that were once crucial to the life of business and the indulgence of impulses that lead to economic decline and ultimately death. At the same time

both Thomas and Hanno experience their failure in their practical vocation as unacceptable: society demands the calling, and the individual
believes only in it. Thus they have no ground on which to rebel.[49] When
they fail, the only possible responses that the novel reveals, and that the
novelist has discovered thus far, are to remain a mere actor as long as
possible and simply to wait for death, or to succumb more openly, explicitly, and quickly. As yet, there is no acceptable alternative for anyone
but unworldly women, no sanction to give up the demands of everyday
practical life to find another path.

Thomas's nature should have led him to marry his first love, the
"flower" girl. But when he turns his back on her—on the alternative
of rejecting the "appropriate" bourgeois choice and isolating himself
from bourgeois society—he clamps himself in the irons of the bourgeois
life that will destroy him, that forces him to be totally what he is only
partially. Gerda, who brings a whiff of the Latin, musical, and unbourgeois into the high-bourgeois life, is never for him what the flower
girl could have been. Even when he chooses in an unbourgeois fashion,
Thomas chooses only halfway, with an artistic but cold and detached
woman.

Even though the bourgeois mode is the standard of judgment and de-
partures from it are considered straying, it is the bourgeois choice, the
bourgeois calling, that is the straying and waywardness for Thomas. It is
disloyalty to a part of himself, a straying from his nonbourgeois impulses, impulses he sees only as weakness and failure. He stands between these two alternatives, where a total choice for either would spell
disaster; it is of little moment which choice he actually makes.[50]

Bourgeois life in its decline, as portrayed in Mann's work, thus far
provides us with two failed outcomes for its sons: the decadence and
will-lessness of the joker, who survives the bourgeois family, and the defeat and death of Hanno, who does not. It provides as well a portrait of
the decay within the bourgeois individual who finds himself lost in mid-
course. Only in *Tonio Kröger* is a cure provided for this disease of the
bourgeois calling, a resolution that was in fact Mann's own: the failed
bourgeois son survives the bourgeois family to grow up and reattach
himself to bourgeois life, partly through his "love" of it, though at a
distance, and partly through his reappropriation for art of the form of
the bourgeois calling. The calling's demands in the artistic life will be as
great as those in the practical life. Tonio alone will be able to overcome
his inward divisions and integrate his "feminine" artistic side, although
only as an expression of love for and "impotence" in "male" life. He

will elevate his art to a calling and turn his artistic soul effectively to the purposes of art, bearing its burden but winning its redemption, redemption from the estrangement, weariness, and will-lessness that might otherwise have been his fate.

The Artist with a Bourgeois Identity: *Tonio Kröger*

Tonio Kröger (1903), already in preparation during the writing of *Buddenbrooks,*[51] is Mann's fullest description of the meaning of vocation. It is a story in which the plight of Hanno and of the joker are overcome by the acceptance for art of the form of the bourgeois calling. It is also Mann's solution to problems of artistic identity that had haunted writers since Flaubert, who propounded an ascetic "religion" of art in which life was lived for art's sake and who was the first "to practice writing as a systematic bourgeois calling."[52] Tonio overcomes self-doubt and the paralysis of self-consciousness through service to a calling that is formally an inheritance from bourgeois society. It is linked to a simultaneous recognition of the darker side of "life" that tempers an otherwise unqualified blind acceptance of whatever life dictates or demands. Tonio sees himself serving life through his calling, yet he also serves the understanding of life, and that means serving powers that penetrate life and reveal its truth and its lies; these powers represent the "darkness" to what Tonio calls "the children of light," those who live unself-consciously, without the need to understand. Yet Tonio does not lapse into "negation" or what he takes to be the nihilistic attitude of the blind opponents of bourgeois society: he loves that life despite its flaws and despite his knowledge and understanding of it, and he believes that this love is the source of his capacity to serve life. The demands of the calling are severe enough, however, and the dangers of "excess" great enough that this resolution cannot serve everyone. Still, as Erich Heller observes, Tonio's experience will henceforth play a central role in all of Mann's future work on artists.[53]

Mann himself achieved great success, literary and economic, with *Buddenbrooks,* attaining social legitimacy and overcoming his feeling of being without identity and without worth.[54] Tonio Kröger does the same, though more through his worked-out understanding of the calling than through financial success, and Mann used Tonio's achievement to measure all artists whose problematical callings lead them to ruin. In *Tonio Kröger* the artistic soul turns the circumstances and contingencies of his character into fate and necessity; his feelings and sensitivity, his estrangement from bourgeois life, and his vanity are transformed through the calling into important and necessary conditions for *all* life in art. By an elaborate ruse he finds a way to forgive himself and to win an identity that he can accept and have acknowledged by the world without having to give in totally to the world's demand that he live the practical life. He is the first, and perhaps the last, of Mann's artists with a proper vocation. A personality like his will appear as a necessity for art, and this necessity will replace his sense of personal culpability in falling out of bourgeois life and cleaving to art. Tonio, that is, finds the "ultimate ideal" his personality can serve and then claims that only a personality like his can serve art properly. But this acceptance of and reconciliation with his condition through giving himself to the calling— though it mobilizes the will and makes possible the transformation of sensitivity into artistic form—exacts its own price, a price that it takes the artist somewhat longer to accept.

The Emergence of Art as a Vocation

Mann's first effort at reconciliation between the artist and society was "The Hungry," the story of a brief episode in the life of a young artist named Detlef, whom Peter de Mendelssohn describes as "a pure self-portrait" of the author.[55] According to Hans Vaget, Mann strove in "The Hungry" to find "an alternative philosophical resolution for the fundamental art-life antinomy" at a time when he was having difficulties completing *Tonio Kröger*.[56] It is a story of the artist's longing for revenge against a life that excludes him, an artist who longs for reconciliation with life but for whom "mind" (*Geist*) is "playing hatred" and art is "formative longing."[57]

> You are after all mine, he felt, and I am above you! Do I not see through your simple souls with a smile? . . . Is not the power of the word and of irony in me aroused in view of your unconscious activities, so that my heart beats with desire and lustful feeling of power, to reshape you playfully and in the light of my art to expose to the world your foolish happiness of feeling? (266–67)

Mind is dangerous to Mann and his artists as a tool of revenge and a form of spiritual domination. Art understood as mind and knowledge can revenge itself by reshaping, exposing, and making over "merely" real creatures from a position of superiority in order to discredit what cannot be possessed. "The Hungry" portrays an artist torn by these longings. He is filled with hatred of the life he longs for, but even when he recognizes that hatred, he can see himself only as an outcast looking in on society. He cannot work out an acceptable reconciliation with his calling.

Mann provides a more successful resolution in *Tonio Kröger,* Mann's "Portrait of the Artist as a Young Man." Unlike Joyce, however, who solved the problem of the artist's identity for himself once and for all, Mann frequently reverted to this theme long after *Tonio Kröger* was published, for the subject continued to hold a key both to his self-understanding and to his later understanding of Germany. *Tonio Kröger* shows the struggle of the young artist to overcome the weakness of the model of the practical calling provided by the bourgeois class and ethos. It shows as well how a "wayward" male offspring of this class is able to find a way back to the form of the calling while changing the field of its deployment from economic competition to art. In the process the artist rejects the cult of the artist-as-genius, rooted in both the classical and romantic traditions, and overcomes decadence, Schopenhauerian pessimism, and the preoccupation with death and decay, the latest form of this cult.[58] This rejection is carried out from the point of view not of art but of bourgeois society, whose perspective is reincorporated in an important respect into the stance of the artist. This perspective is justified by the argument that no art can really live without close and essentially affectionate contact with life—understood, of course, as bourgeois life. At the same time art is upheld as a unique form of knowledge, a unique expression of mind, spirit, or *Geist,* which also acts as a mediator between spirit and life.

The discipline that mediates between bourgeois life and the artistic life is the calling, rightly understood. Life becomes the love object of art. But this new infusion of *Lebensphilosophie* is not enough, by itself, to make the life in art serviceable: the calling (*Beruf*) is the form in which this new content must be served. A bourgeois mode and discipline of work—and their manner of channeling and validating the self of the artist who works this way—become the tangible link to the bourgeoisie. At the same time life is treated more critically and ironically, since a "true" calling for art is understood to demand distance. The calling *tames* intellect, mind, and spirit—which Nietzsche and Mann both saw as possible threats to life—and makes them available for service and devotion to life (*Dienst* and *Hingebung*). Moreover, the calling draws on and is vivified by "life," since it embodies bourgeois life in the form of the bourgeoisie's attitude to work, quality, and service.

Tonio Kröger shows Mann's one genuinely successful alternative to the decadence of the bourgeois family: the overcoming of mockery and impotence in life and of the sense of weakness, defeat, and death. Yet this alternative is a successful path only because it provides the *bourgeois manqué* with a bourgeois path of deviance as well as a way to remain the legatee of the exhausted burgher. If *Buddenbrooks* is a story of "de-bourgeoisification" (*Entbürgerlichung*), *Tonio Kröger* is based on what we can call the "bourgeoisification" of the artistic calling: the artist remains a loyal son of the bourgeoisie but in a way that limits the identification with his class home.[59] Those who trespass the limits of this calling by moving too close to the class (the "established" Gustav von Aschenbach) or too far from it (the bohemian and virtually nihilistic Adrian Leverkühn) will be destroyed. Note that they do not simply fail as artists; on the contrary, they are both artistic successes. But they are destroyed. For Mann the refusal to be limited by the right understanding of the calling may not be the undoing of art; but it will certainly have an effect on art, and it may be the undoing of the artist and of life itself.

Tonio Kröger grows up in a household like Hanno's and the joker's, and he has the same relations with his parents as those young men had. He is mediocre in school and is chastised by his father—correctly, he thinks, for he judges himself and what he considers his disreputable performance by the standards of his father and of society. He pursues confident and unself-conscious youngsters as friends but never has the success with them that he desires. The blond, blue-eyed Hans Hansens and Ingeborg Holms of this world seem to lead uncluttered, playful lives, without fear, loved by all. Tonio yearns for their acceptance and acknowledgment and can only feel ashamed of himself by comparison with them.[60] Yet he feels superior to the people of his hometown and is scornful of the "crude and mean" life they lead (289).

Feeling himself called to the life of intellect, or spirit, Tonio becomes a writer.

> He surrendered himself completely to the power that seemed to him the most exalted on earth, to whose service he felt himself called [*zu deren Dienst er sich berufen fühlte*] and which promised him high rank [*Hoheit*] and honors, the power of intellect [*Geist*] and word, which is enthroned smiling above unconscious and mute life. (289–90)

His hard work in a calling is aimed self-consciously at fame. It is the path to recognition, the reward promised by his vocation: what he cannot obtain for himself as a human being he can obtain as an artist.

He worked, not like someone who works in order to live but rather like one who wants nothing other than to work, because he esteems himself for nothing as a living human being, wishes to be considered only as a creative man and for the rest goes about gray and inconspicuous, like an actor without makeup, who is nothing as long as he has nothing to portray. (291)

He lives his life only to be of service to the calling that can win him acknowledgment. Out of the struggle between his desire for life and his capacity for work are born unusual creations, and when he is not working he is waiting, he "is nothing."

Thomas Buddenbrook became an actor only when his capacity to sustain the calling weakened; he had adopted a mask or role to compensate for the lack of purpose, inner drive, and strength needed to pursue the calling in a situation where no possibility of giving up this calling existed. For Tonio, the calling is itself a role; he takes it as the norm that his own life and feelings are of no consequence and must be lived only for the sake of this role. His calling is, precisely, not living; it is the mobilization of life for the sole purpose of the performance of his task, as a result of which he hopes to be recognized. He takes for granted that his role alone has importance to the artist and that his life must serve it.[61]

Naturally there are benefits to this service: "It rewarded him with all it had to give . . . it sharpened his gaze . . . it opened to him the souls of humankind as well as his own . . . and it showed him the inside of the world and everything that is ultimately behind words and deeds." But it also has a price: "it took from him pitilessly everything it was accustomed to taking as payment" (290). Tonio sees this situation not as an accident but rather as the natural condition of all art and all artists. Indeed, he has contempt for those "little men" who aim to be happy and who do not realize "that good works originate only under the pressure of a wretched life, that whoever lives does not work, and that one must *die* in order to be wholly a creator" (291–92, my italics). The calling is like Christian redemption: it demands that the called person die to life, to be reborn as artist and creator. Tonio becomes as harsh a judge of · frivolity, self-indulgence, and mere happiness as his father before him. His attitude toward work is a strictly traditional continuation of his bourgeois past, justifying to himself the misery of his world and of his feelings of separation, loneliness, coldness, and monstrosity. He performs his work as an obligation to art, bearing hardship like the Protestants of old, who devoted themselves to the severities of ascetic labor in a practical calling. We are never told how art became important enough to demand such a total sacrifice of life. Nor are we told of any reward or "grace" revealed through service to art that is higher or more transcendental than worldly fame. But Tonio lives his calling like an enormous burden of guilt, like Cain, "for he could not bear it in the circles of the innocent with their happy, dark understanding, and the mark on his brow disturbed them" (290). Is it really for the sake of art and intellect that he suffers as he does? In fact this burden of the calling is borne for quite different reasons.

The Conflict of Life and Calling

In a moment of frustration Tonio talks to a Russian woman who has emigrated to Germany, a painter, another artist, but one free of the conception of calling that Tonio defends and to whom Tonio may freely express himself. "Literature is not a calling at all, but rather a curse. . . . An artist, a real one, [is] not one whose bourgeois calling [*bürgerlicher Beruf*] is art, but rather one predestined and condemned [*verdammt*]" (297). Art is death and damnation, an inescapable negative sentence for those who are called in which one's predestination, hell, and condemnation are experienced in life. One need no longer await one's punishment in the beyond. Art is an affliction, a curse that swallows up life, and the artist is a victim.[62]

> You begin, marked out, to feel yourself in a mysterious contrast to the others, the ordinary, the respectable; the abyss of irony, unbelief, opposition, knowledge, feeling that separates you from human beings gapes deeper and deeper, you are alone and henceforth there is no more communication. What a fate! (297)

The extraordinary dilemma of the artist is that he can no longer communicate with ordinary people. He seems irrevocably sundered from those who share nothing of his insight or interest. The artist could in theory seek out the company of like-minded people. But in fact it is people like himself, artists and worshipers of art, whom Tonio wishes to avoid, for despite his contempt for the everyday world he craves to speak to the ordinary and even to live like them. Tonio longs not for "the extraordinary and the demonic as the ideal . . . a vision of bloody greatness and wild beauty," but for "life as the eternal contrast to intellect [*Geist*] and art . . . life in its seductive banality . . . for the innocent, the simple, and the lively . . . for the bliss of the commonplace."[63] Yet those who are drawn to art and artists like himself are not worshipers of life but rather those "to whom poetry is a mild revenge on life—always only suffering ones and yearning ones and poor ones." What Tonio wants, however, is "someone of the others, the blue-eyed . . . who have no need of intellect" (302–3). He might have added, "who have no need of me."

Tonio claims that the true artist's relation to life is one of love, not revenge, though Mann, like Detlef in "The Hungry," confesses this revenge in his essays.[64] But Tonio reveals here his truly divided nature: while opposing the desire for revenge on life in general, he insists that he must negate his own life in particular for the sake of his art. He desires to have a life like "the innocent," which would allow him to live without hostility toward his life; yet his own life and service in art are a form of revenge, a refusal to accept life, despite his claim "I love life" (302): he loves "life," but not *his* life. The only life that should be loved is the life of the ordinary bourgeois, not the life of the artist. This is part of his misery: although he loves life, the only ones who appreciate his work and hence "want" him are those he believes to be crippled and vengeful, the victims of life. His true home, much to his horror, is with the outcasts. Yet this realization does not cause him to wonder whether there is something to be prized about outcasts like himself over the bourgeois lives he extols and the bourgeois society in which they live. Nor is he led to understand how vengeful he is toward his own life because of his disappointments. His awareness ought to cause him to reevaluate the whole basis and foundation of an art based on the "innocent" attractiveness of the bourgeoisie or to question more deeply his vision of art and its origin. Yet Tonio is never led to question deeply a world that he feels rejects him, a world in which sensitivity, art, and knowledge are visible only among the defeated of bourgeois society.

Naturally there is strong social support for Tonio's estrangement.[65] Though the prestige of the man of letters generally grew during the nineteenth century in Germany, with the unification of the German Reich the prestige of writers declined within ruling circles and in society as a whole. The novelist Theodor Fontane attributed this suspicion of writers to their penetration of truth and their appearance of being unessential; in a society that valued the officer and the bureaucratic official as models, writers went unacknowledged by the state. Only writers with public positions gained prestige: those who had passed examinations, received degrees, held offices, titles, medals—in short, anyone with a token of state power. This was so even though the writer was generally no longer a bohemian or an aesthete, and rarely had been.[66]

Art had had an unusually exalted position in German thought since

Schiller's time. But whatever the significance of the writer in theory, the practical isolation and separation he actually experienced was difficult to reconcile with the exalted role of cultural reformer he was supposed to fulfill, especially if one took seriously the other widespread countervailing image of the artist as mad or criminal. The sense of estrangement and illegitimacy that Mann in particular felt also had a legal basis, for the efforts of the German state to censor and forbid the distribution or production of literary and theatrical works it considered subversive of state or religion increased dramatically after 1890. The criminal code was used more and more to prosecute artists, academics, and politicians. In France too Flaubert, Baudelaire, and the Goncourts were prosecuted, without success, for offenses against morality.[67] It is little wonder that an artist still attached to the bourgeois society that prosecuted him might experience himself and his activity as illegitimate and, through his identification with bourgeois and state authority, might see society and the ruling powers as justifiably mistrustful of him and of his work.

Tonio observes that the growing sense of the artist's differentness from others changes the personality profoundly. "Your self-consciousness flames up, because you are aware of and feel the mark on your brow . . . which escapes no one." No matter how much pain one takes to disguise this separateness in order to seem like an ordinary bourgeois, it is instantly apparent, "and everyone will know that you are not a human being, but something strange, alien, other." Even Thomas Buddenbrook has more success in his deception. The artist lacks a "good conscience and solidly grounded feeling of self" (297–98), for he "knows" that "an honest, healthy, decent human being does not write, act, compose at all" (296).

The calling of art requires not only that one give up living; it requires that one give up feeling as well: "[He] is a dabbler who believes a creator may feel. . . . Feeling, warm heartfelt feeling, is always banal and unusable, and only the irritations and cold ecstasies of our depraved, our artistic, nervous systems are artistic" (295). Indeed, "it is necessary that one be something outside the human and inhuman, that one stand in a strangely remote and unsharing relation to the human" if one is to be an artist. The capacity for "style, form, and expression" presupposes "a certain human impoverishment and desolation. . . . it is over with the artist as soon as he becomes human and begins to feel" (296). The calling for art means supporting the triumph of form over content, the triumph of artistic shape over "the indifferent material," for "place too much on what you have to say, let your heart pound too warmly for it, then you can be sure of a complete fiasco" (295).

Here Tonio finds a rationale and a value for his own coldness, detachment, and lack of feeling: it is not that his personal qualities are unfortunate but unchangeable—no, to be an artist one *must* be cold, he suggests; to be an artist one must be like him. He sees himself as a representative and a type, not just an individual with an idiosyncratic or even a unique constitution. To be a "consummate artist" one *must* be "an impoverished man" (297). Tonio's reflections on art even at this point do not represent mere observations of his personal situation and fate; they are meant to be a philosophy of the artist and of art itself and, given his understanding of the relation of art and life, a philosophy of life as well. They are an attempt to generalize his own experience and his feelings, to question any art and any artists that do not partake of them, and to justify his mistrust of those who are drawn to art. He defends his undermining of his own life and at the same time defends the society that has led him to become an enemy of his life and to feel an outcast. Only the elevation of his personal dilemma into a fact, not about himself but about the nature of artists everywhere, can allow Tonio to accept, if only in part, his qualities and situation. His art must be validated by a higher principle for his service to it to have a chance of being bearable.[68] His self must be sacrificed in service as his ancestors' lives were before him so that he may win the recognition and acceptance that only art can bring to him, redeeming, finally, his hideous life. The estrangement of the artist is permanent, Tonio insists, and rooted in the nature of things.

Yet even when he has established himself as an artist, bourgeois society still shuns him: only the nonnormal esteem him. There seems to be no way out of this, for though the artist wishes it were different, his condition cannot easily change.

> I tell you that I am often sick to death of it, portraying the human without sharing in the human. . . . Is the artist a man at all? Let one ask "Woman" about it! It seems to me we artists all share a little the fate of those prepared papal singers. . . . Our singing is quite touchingly beautiful. However . . . (296–97)

In this view the artist is one of the *castrati*, irrevocably deprived of what he requires to lead a normal life. It is no coincidence that when he talks about artists he speaks only of males and that the metaphors of the artist Tonio deploys revolve around the masculine-unmasculine distinction. Nor is it coincidence that Tonio ignores that he is speaking with a female artist, an emotional Russian one at that, who experiences life differently—for women in this society are not condemned to be like Tonio.

They have no "maleness" to lose by giving up traditional bourgeois callings and analyzing life from a distance. They are permitted to be artistic and remote from everyday bourgeois concerns, even cold, like Gerda Buddenbrook, yet they are still capable of "normal" life.

The masculine metaphors indicate the connection of normality with the male-dominated world of presumedly unself-conscious labor; to Tonio burdensome self-consciousness—triggered by estrangement from society—and distance from "life" and from the proper path marked out for men are particularly unmale and part of the curse of art and of the calling for it. Women lack this paralyzing self-consciousness because they do not fall short of societal norms in tending toward art (though even Gerda seems unusual and distant to the citizens of her adopted town). Having lost the conviction of his calling, Thomas Buddenbrook envied the spontaneity of his ancestors, who experienced no distance from society and its demands and carried out their calling according to their nature. Their maleness, we might add, was secure, since maleness can be found only in the community of men with a calling.

For Tonio too being apart and following a path different from the normal bring self-consciousness and the feeling of monstrosity, here identified with castration and loss of masculinity. But women are not obliged to justify themselves in this way before the tribunal of society outside or before the tribunal within the self, and, like Lisaweta, they need not have the potency associated with men. Women are not obliged to measure up to a standard of vocational normality and male identity; properly speaking, they have no calling in bourgeois society, but only a role to play; and society not only approves of this, it stands for it. For women art can be accepted as indulgence and freedom without the cost that the male artist must bear. For a male in the world of *Buddenbrooks* to become an artist is to run the risk of extreme censure. In Tonio's world, society, in the persons of his father and the "innocent," still censure, avoid, disapprove of, or are indifferent to him, even though he survives childhood and is a moderately successful artist. Yet to become an artist in his world is to run the risk of becoming unmanned, or feminized, or icy cold, giving up everything human, "healthy," and based on feeling.

From the perspective of the "healthy" and "normal," says Tonio, art is an enormous threat, and therefore Tonio the artist must himself be a threat. "And will you really take a stand for this cold and vain charlatan?" In the hands of the *Literat*—the dismissive name Tonio uses for those whose approach to art is different from his—who cannot attain the heights of true art (as can the *Künstler* or *Dichter*), art is the embodiment of unmitigated knowledge and insight, he says, and it seeks to set itself up as superior to life, judging and dismissing it. Because art wishes to give expression to everything, even the ineffable, and hence to freeze it, reduce it, and capture the essence of what is otherwise "mere" living feeling, the world must be careful. "What is expressed, so runs [the artist's] creed, is disposed of. When the whole world is expressed, so it will be disposed of, redeemed, dismissed" (301–2). As a position, this unusual view of art and its power is possible only after Nietzsche's critique of the elevation of truth over life and his demonstration of the service of truth as a new asceticism concealing a hostility to life and undermining the will to power. But it is also an expression of the power of art to "disenchant" (using Weber's language) and to remove mystery. Yet Tonio is not convinced that this is the only possibility for art: "Still, I am no nihilist . . . with regard to living feeling. You see, the *Literat* does not basically grasp that life prefers to continue, to live, that it is not ashamed of it, even after it has been expressed and 'disposed of.' . . . all action is sinful in the eyes of the intellect [*Geist*]" (302).

This is Tonio's version of *Lebensphilosophie*,[69] and his observations on the conflict of life and art, of knowledge and feeling, are revealing, though also a product of attitudes more widely shared in his time. However much German social developments played a role in shaping Mann's conception of the relation of artist and society, Nietzsche was the greatest spiritual influence, at least from the time of *Tonio Kröger*. Nietzsche's antinomy of life and art and his notion of the isolation of the artist and the intellectual in society were influential everywhere in Europe at the end of the century, especially on those artists seeking to overcome decadence.[70] With its defense of life and critique of Schopenhauer's life-denying ideals, Nietzsche's work was read as a denunciation of the decadent attitude and an appeal for "reconciliation" with life and action.[71] For Tonio too life is beyond critique, judgment, and standards of justice and injustice. Indeed, he agrees with those who claim that it may be predicated on injustice, as Nietzsche suggests: no matter what the world of judgment, mind, and intellect may claim to know, life takes priority over all judgment against it. Life does not have clean hands.

Mann's vision implies that this world of *Geist*, once given sway, undermines in at least two ways not only the regard for life but also the capacity to act. First, by making it seem that life is wrong in some way, it undermines the confidence of those who must live and act, who must pursue unjust paths. They become weary of struggling against their own scruples, like Thomas Buddenbrook, and become incapable of carrying on in their calling. These doubts based on knowledge and moral critique undermine commitment. Second, to Tonio the artist's expression of feeling in the rigorous form of art undermines spontaneous, simple, and innocent feeling through "disenchantment." When an artist feels, he is immediately led to get to the "truth" of the feeling, that is, he can no longer let himself feel in an unself-conscious manner. He has understood what stands behind the feeling and will now experience it as nothing but the mask for an underlying truth or reality. The implication is that self-consciousness and understanding remove the spontaneity and innocence one would feel if one had not subjected feeling to scrutiny: one should let feeling emerge, be experienced, and inspire action without analyzing or penetrating its "meaning."[72]

The condition of the divided self is not limited to Tonio. "This affliction specific to the writer was often deplored during the decadent period," according to Jean Pierrot. In their pursuit of new elements of reality for analysis, the decadents focused on sensations and feelings, analyzing every emotion of self and others, seeking their hidden mechanisms. This led them to feel that all spontaneity in themselves had been destroyed, that they were fated to be torn between the two sides of their nature. One side experienced and felt; the other, which coldly observed and analyzed, was judgmental and disillusioned. In Maupassant, whom Mann read, the writer laments "the second sight that is simultaneously the strength and the whole wretchedness of writers." For Maupassant everything becomes a subject not for experience but for observation. Everything is analyzed endlessly: as soon as he sees something, he must know why it is so. Thus writers can never be actors in the world, like the "good and simple folk are who live life unaware." A writer is "a sort of dual personality," suffering from an affliction "that makes him into a terrifyingly contrived and complicated creature."[73]

Thus, says Pierrot, the decadent artist became an unbalanced being with excessively refined sensibilities and an overdeveloped critical intelligence. The consequence was the destruction of will and the desire to act followed by skepticism and relativism. These in turn had further consequences. First, dilettantism developed, marked by a refusal and an incapacity to take up any definitive moral or intellectual stance, what Pierrot calls "a sort of Don Juanism of the intellect." Second, the artist felt himself to be without roots, unable to integrate into any social whole. In the midst of the indifference and futility these experiences generated, the decadent artist felt "cut off from society around him; he shrank from contact with his fellow men, and, out of aristocratic disdain for vulgar ambition, shut himself away, retired to his own inner world."[74]

For Tonio too insight is a disease, because "the empire of art is growing, and health and innocence are dwindling on earth. One should conserve most carefully what is still left over . . . and one should not want to seduce people to poetry!" (303). For Weber the realm of art is a rare haven for spontaneity and feeling against the encroachments of rationality; for Tonio, surprisingly, art itself is the principal demystifier and danger to life. When art is taken to be the domain of intellect and critique, it is a threat to every free impulse as well as to the "innocent" devotion to calling still present in bourgeois society. Unmanning its more sensitive male practitioners and forcing them to dwell in a frozen realm far from the vitality of life, exposing the secret in the heart and inhibiting feeling ever after, art as intellect threatens to cripple life.

But, while Tonio describes his own experience of feeling and writing as the nature and the danger of art and therefore sees himself acting as life's enemy, he nonetheless deplores this condition and himself as unnatural. "There is something I call disgust with knowledge [*Erkenntnisekel*], Lisaweta: the condition in which it is enough for a man to see through a thing for him to feel already disgusted to death (and not reconciled through it)—the case of Hamlet, of the Dane, of this typical *Literat*" (300). Knowledge is Tonio's curse.[75] Yet, though he "loves feeling," he has contempt for those who feel, and he retains "the full consciousness of ethical superiority over the abominable invention of being." He can justify and use these faculties, which he deplores, only in the calling for art, where they are not a disadvantage but rather a *sine qua non* for art as he understands it. Yet that art, which has already eaten away at him, threatens to eat away at all life as well. Is it possible to win back feeling? Is it possible to discover another way to live life in art? Is it possible to be an artist yet reduce the threat that art poses to life? For the moment the calling is death, both for the artist and possibly for life; but for the artist it is all there is. But Lisaweta remarks, in her analysis of Tonio's discourse, that Tonio is "quite simply a *Bürger* . . . a *Bürger* on the wrong path . . . a *Bürger* gone astray" (305). As Tonio finds out, this is not far from the truth.

The Artist with a Bourgeois Identity

Tonio has now put the case for art and its needs as well as for life and its mistrust of art.[76] But however well clarified, his identity and condition cause him suffering and conflict. Called to literature, which justifies and strengthens him, Tonio feels called to knowledge and insight, for literature to him means knowledge. How appropriate that Tonio, who, following Nietzsche, has seen himself as Hamlet, should travel to Elsinore in Denmark, as Mann himself did in 1899. Knowledge that destroys the knower, knowledge that he cannot avoid: Tonio voyages to the seat of the ancient court of Denmark and finds there a knowledge that reveals the heart of his self-torturing calling.

In the Danish resort where he lodges, he sees a couple he recognizes as the two loves of his youth, Hans Hansen and Ingeborg Holm—or, rather, a couple so similar in race and type that it might as well be them, since we know that he longs for them more as types in bourgeois society than as individuals. Peering through a glass door into the dining room where everyone is dancing, Tonio has a revelation.

> Had I forgotten you? he asked. No, never!. . . It was you for whom I worked, and if I heard applause, I secretly looked around me [to see] whether you had shared in it. . . . You should not make your bright eyes cloudy and dreamily stupid from staring into verses and melancholy. . . . To be like you! To begin once again, grow up like you, decent, happy, and simple . . . at peace with God and the world, loved by the innocent and happy, to marry you, Ingeborg Holm, and have a son like you, Hans Hansen—free of the curse of knowledge and the creative torment, to live, love, and praise in blessed ordinariness! (332)

Tonio's true project and purpose are here revealed: to write in a way that would win him the approval and adulation of the ordinary people whose love he craves, just as he craved it and tried to win it as a child, and whom, indeed, he desires to resemble.[77] His purpose in writing all along has been to win over the ordinary, those who care not at all for what he does. His deepest desire is to be like them, for they care only for those like themselves, loved by "the innocent and the happy." It is his repeated failure that each time sends him back to his dreams, to his wistful observation of those he loves who do not love him, and that laid the foundation for the hatred of his own life, a hatred that consumes him. He dreams of being other than he is so that he might have the love of those who love others. Giving his life for art could never win him this love, of course, although he hates his life enough to sacrifice it. The unloved self would be easy to part with, if doing so could, paradoxically, win the loved other. Even here, in what Mann makes Tonio's epiphany, Tonio reaffirms his vision of himself as the monster he feels himself to be, recalling a time he danced the wrong part as a youth and provoked Inge's laughter.

And would you also laugh again today, now that I have become something like a famous man? Yes, you would, and you would be right to do it three times over! And if I had produced, all alone, the nine symphonies, "The World as Will and Idea," and "The Last Judgment"—you would be eternally right to laugh. (334)

But Tonio now sees that this laughter is aimed not at him personally but at the irrelevance and life-denying nature of art, of which he is merely an accidental embodiment. To be able to do nothing as an artist, no matter how great, that would win Inge's love and erase the painful memory of her laughter—only now does Tonio recognize how impossible it was to win her all along. To discover not only the impossibility of one's love but also the fact about oneself that, one is convinced, makes one unloved, and to discover the impossibility of winning love no matter what the achievements: this is the truth of his situation, and Tonio re-affirms here his unworthiness, not a simple personal unworthiness but a rejection based on the clear-sighted avoidance of art and the artist by the "normal." Only a person who could be all the things he is not—not simply himself, only better—could obtain the woman he desires. But his desires must remain impotent; for innocence knows to avoid him, and he is left driven by the inner demand that he work, create, and give shape to insight and experience, all devoted to the secret agenda of winning love from an impossible object. Even in the form of an impersonal fate rooted in the nature of art, his situation gives him no rest.

> To long to be able to live simply and fully in one's feelings, without the obligation to come to activity and to dance, sweetly and idly resting in oneself—and yet still to [have to] dance, nimbly and alertly to have to perform the difficult, difficult and dangerous, knife dance of art, without completely forgetting the humiliating absurdity that lies within having to dance while one loves. (334–35)

Reflecting back on his life, Tonio sees a vision of bleakness: his heart was alive, but the past showed him only "numbness; desolation; ice; and intellect [*Geist*]! and art!" And, we should add, guilt.

> He saw himself eaten up by irony and intellect, laid waste and paralyzed by knowledge, half worn out by the fevers and chills of creation . . . refined, impoverished, exhausted by cold and artificially acquired ecstasies, lost, devastated, tormented, sick—and he sobbed with remorse and homesickness. (336)

Out of the bleakness of this picture of himself as a decadent, Tonio arrives finally at what he believes to be its overcoming, and he composes a self-defense for the eyes of his painter friend back in Munich. He re-affirms her insight that he is a bourgeois lost in art, the product of a father who was "correct from Puritanism and inclined to melancholy" and a mother who was exotic, passionate, and impulsive. He is "a bur-gher who has gone astray into art, a bohemian with nostalgia for his good upbringing, an artist with a bad conscience," who says of himself: "I stand between two worlds, am at home in neither." [78]

> For it is my bourgeois conscience that lets me see in all artistry, all excep-tionalness, and all genius something deeply ambiguous, deeply disreputable, deeply doubtful. . . . I admire the proud and cold ones who venture on the paths of great, of demonic, beauty and despise humankind,—but I do not envy them. For if there is anything capable of making a poet [*Dichter*] out of a *Literat,* then it is this burgher love of mine for the human, the living, and the ordinary. (337–38)

Tonio accepts as his own the bourgeois world's opinion of the cult of the genius and of the exceptional value of art, a cult spawned in Schil-ler's time, strengthened by the romantics, and twisted by the decadents. Tonio accepts the dubious character of his art and of the artist in rela-tion to bourgeois society. At the same time he rejects the positive image of the artist as redeemer and defends bourgeois society against the nega-tive artist who rejects and despises humankind: both the naturalist art-ist, who is an enemy of and rebel against bourgeois society, and the decadent writer, who is a detached genius creating in a cold, aestheticist realm.

Only his bourgeois love of ordinary bourgeois life, he claims, saves him from these extremes and makes possible his development from a *Literat* into a true writer, a *Dichter.* That this should be a necessary step for every writer seeking to be a *Dichter* is by no means certain. The im-portant thing is that Tonio *must* see it this way: he must believe that this is the truth of the artist, the fundamental quality of the genuine *Dichter.* Tonio must look to the suprapersonal demands of *Dichtung* and *Kunst* to legitimate and justify the mixture of feelings, impulses, and condi-tions within him. Having spoken of his admiration for other kinds of lonely artists, he can now dismiss them as models for himself, not on the grounds that the house of art has many mansions or that his personality is simply different and must take another path, but on the grounds that true art demands from the true artist the differentness that is within *him.* In this defense of his art, Tonio defends himself as the true artist. [79]

In Tonio's philosophy of art his personality serves a higher purpose; its coldness, detachment, and sacrifice of life are no longer merely inclinations, idiosyncrasies, or simple facts. They are not merely useful to *his* art, but necessary for *all* art. It is not just that a man with his personality can find a home in art; it is that art must find a personality like his to be realized. He is the right tool of art. As an embodiment of the true artist, and only as such, are he and his relation to the world vindicated, his cold nature redeemed, and the emptying out of his life justified by destiny. His artistry is a result of fate (337). By making his life a service to a higher principle in the calling, to an art that is coldly intellectual yet loves life, Tonio finds the strength to defend and explain himself to others, to accept his own nature, and to limit the threat that art, especially his art, can pose to life in society. He is finally able to be an artist, although he mistrusts art; yet he can remain a bourgeois in his loves, preferences, and prejudices and in his approach to work itself, although he believes he mistrusts the bourgeoisie as well.

Feeling worthless, inclined by fate to ironic knowledge and artistic creation, Tonio turns his character and person into a possession of art even with the consequent pain, an art that he insists must be understood as he understands it, an art between two worlds. He *must* give himself to these demands and this discipline, for art demands it of everyone who will be an artist. In this elevation of what he is into a fact not of his own nature but of the nature of all artistry, he finds relief. To thus affirm his condition requires that he also endlessly affirm his bargain, his "pact" with art; he must accept the limits on his life while remaining attached to life through his unfulfilled and unfulfillable longing for it: creativity in exchange for life and feeling. Tonio was originally driven to this conception of his work to achieve self-acceptance and to gain the recognition as an artist that he could not get as a man. But at the end of the story, when art has become a genuine calling, not just an occupation, craft, or simple object of his love, Tonio finally gives it an almost magical power to govern his life: it makes his sacrifices necessary and justifies him against those who argue for a different view of the artist.[80] In so doing, and despite the strength he gains, Tonio makes it impossible to reach a deeper understanding of the estrangement, compulsion, hostility, and love that he feels or of the society that has spawned him and yet does not prize him or his art.[81]

In Tonio's hands the calling is magic: it is mixed with a love of bourgeois life and draws on bourgeois society's approach to work, but it is tempered by a more critical regard for the defects of that society and rescues Tonio from the joker's fate as well as from the hopelessness of Thomas and Hanno Buddenbrook. It gives him an impulse for work al-

most as compelling as that of the original Calvinist vocation. But though
it strengthens his character and gives him the power to go on, it costs
him the continuation of a set of relations both to himself and to his society that remain painful and conceal the sources of insecurity, fear, and
ascetic renunciation of life.[82]

Mann and the Calling for Art

Tonio comes to his solution only through a lengthy struggle to understand his relation to his burgher past. Mann himself declared much later
that in *Tonio Kröger* he portrayed a "spiritual form of life" and that he
himself was "a *bürgerliche* storyteller, who actually tells only *one* story
his whole life long: the story of the loss of one's burgher nature [*Entbürgerlichung*]—not [then transformed] into the bourgeois or into the
Marxist, but into the artist, into irony and freedom of art ready to wander and escape."[83] With the overcoming of the *Bürger*—the old estate-
like patriciate—and the resolution of society into the two opposing
classes of the bourgeoisie with capital and the working class without it,
Mann takes a third path, unallied. Not surprisingly, Paul Weigand says
that *Tonio Kröger* provides "evidence of Thomas Mann's efforts to construct an apology for his nature."[84] In 1917 Mann quoted approvingly,
though "with irony," from an earlier autobiographical sketch:

> Those who have leafed through my writings will recall that I always opposed
> the form of life of the artist, the writer, with the most extreme distrust. . . . I
> know what a writer is, for as confirmation I myself am one. A writer is . . .
> one who is definitely useless in all areas of serious activity . . . not only not
> useful to the state, but a rebelliously minded fellow . . . for the rest an in-
> wardly childish charlatan, tending to dissipation, and in every respect dis-
> reputable, who should have nothing other to expect from society . . . than
> silent contempt.[85]

Mann's personal path to reconciliation with the calling was not easy,
and his commitment to literature did not end or even definitively resolve
his problems with the meaning of and confidence in his life and his calling. Naturally his great success with *Buddenbrooks* brought him enormous financial and popular success and partly stilled his sense of the
illegitimacy of art as a calling.[86] But although Mann continued to defend
his calling and himself in the face of what he took to be societal mistrust
and doubt, it was more than the burden of social judgment that he found
difficult: like Tonio, he recognized that the calling itself made demands
that were hateful, and his own experience has important parallels with

Tonio's. In 1901, shortly after the acceptance of *Buddenbrooks,* Mann, then nearly twenty-six years old, wrote to his brother Heinrich in the midst of his intimate friendship with Paul Ehrenburg.

> Are you well? With me very mixed. When spring comes, I will have behind a tremendously rough winter for me inwardly. Depressions of a truly dreadful kind with quite seriously meant plans for self-elimination have alternated with an indescribable, pure, and unexpected inner joy, with experiences that cannot be told and whose intimation would act like boasting. But they have proved one thing to me, however, these very unliterary, very simple and vital experiences: namely, that there is in me still something sincere, warm, and good, and not purely "irony," that in me after all everything is not yet desolated, overrefined, and corroded by accursed literature. Ah, literature is death! I will never grasp how one can be dominated by it *without* bitterly hating it. The ultimate and best thing that it is able to teach me is this: to understand death as a possibility of succeeding to its opposite, to life. I dread the day, and it is not far off, when I will be shut up alone again with it, and I fear that the egoistic desolation and overrefinement will then make rapid progress.[87]

"Literature is death": hardly the description of a life task in the practice of which the artist feels his own nature fulfilled. In describing the relief he feels in his "adolescent infatuation" with Paul Ehrenburg,[88] Mann reveals that the calling, once accepted, is as much a burden and a curse as any judgment or criticism from society; it is not a blissful fulfillment or an easy escape into freedom from an unreasonable order of things. It "dominates" its person, and Mann struggles hard to discover in himself whether there are human qualities left in him other than those devoted to the calling, qualities that the calling seems not only to displace but to destroy. The vocation uses up his life for its purposes and leaves the life nothing. But Mann knows no approach to living other than service in the calling. As he says in a later letter to Heinrich, "Happiness is a service [*Dienst*]. . . . I have not made it easier for myself. Happiness, *my* happiness . . . is too little akin to peace and too close to suffering."[89] Though society may accept the language and form of the calling, now transported into realms it had not normally sanctioned, the artist still feels himself used up by his art. So far, the means of reconciliation with art, or at least its acceptance, do not lie in the calling itself but only in love. "Actually, I negate and ironize only out of old habit at the writing table; for the rest, however, I praise, love, and live."[90] Doubts about his calling beset Mann in the ensuing years, and further successes were elusive. Even love does not redeem one from the struggle for success in the calling.

The reliance on love as salvation expresses itself as well in the court-ship of his future wife, Katia, dramatized in his novel *Royal Highness.*

> You know that I could not develop myself personally, humanly, like other young people, that a [talent] can act like a vampire: bloodsucking, absorb-ing; you know what a cold, impoverished, purely presentational, purely rep-resentational existence I have led for many years; know that for years, *im-portant* years, I regarded myself for nothing as a person and wanted to be considered only as an artist. . . . A cure for the representative-artistic that clings to me, for the lack of innocent trust in my personal-human side, is possible through one thing: through happiness, through *you.*[91]

Again Mann suggests that his life is destroyed by art, has been a sacrifice to art, and has undermined his ability to approach confidently the people he loves. As he puts it elsewhere, "to the greatest, the most insatiable, their talent is the sharpest scourge."[92] Only love, he believes, can free him from the permanent imprisonment of the soul that his calling de-mands. Thus what he seeks is society's acceptance of him as an artist, which comes through *Buddenbrooks,* and Katia's acceptance of him as a human being.

But even this is not enough: Mann seeks not just acceptance of him-self as artist, but acceptance of his view and interpretation of art and the artist and of the artist's necessary relation to society. He defines a con-ception of the calling of the artist that will justify his own detached na-ture and isolated condition; this conception shows his nature to be not exceptional and unfortunate but typical and representative, not only personally unavoidable as his own fate but also necessary to the pursuit of any calling for art. This conception is worked out in *Tonio Kröger,* and it serves both as self-justification and as the standard for judging the calling of other artists, including his brother and the artists whom he later creates. He even speaks explicitly of this calling as an "*ethos* of personal devotion [*Hingabe*] (which is quite akin to love)."[93]

Like Mann,[94] Tonio turns himself into an institution, not a man, with an ideology of art and the artist that fortifies him in a secure role in so-ciety. But for both the author and his creation this ideology limits the range of questioning and stands in the way of a deeper understanding of the artist's calling and self and the character of bourgeois society. It be-queaths to artists and critics of the future a picture of the necessary qualities of the artist that will set as inviolable a pattern for others as the image of the "normal" life of the "innocent" set for Tonio.[95] Tonio is the bourgeois in the artistic life—he has some critical distance from bourgeois society, even a measure of contempt and a feeling of superiority—and only after World War I did Mann begin to question his earlier understanding of the social world. In the meantime he continued to dwell on the nature and condition of the artist as a type, but his best work between *Tonio Kröger* and *The Magic Mountain* was a story of the disaster of an artist who diverges from the pattern of the calling discovered in *Tonio Kröger*, the disaster of Gustav von Aschenbach in *Death in Venice*.

The Appropriation of the Bourgeois Calling

Fritz Kaufmann writes of Mann's early work, principally of the collapse of Thomas Buddenbrook, that "at the bottom of his heart man cannot rest content with a 'calling' which no longer presses on towards any ultimate goal, but ensnares him in a network of means." For Kaufmann the calling of the artist is the successor to the collapse of the bourgeois subject. "After its eclipse in the mechanization of industrial life, the concept of work as a test of man's higher vocation had, as it were, its last refuge in the experience of the artist and his productivity." But this refuge does not guarantee hopeful results, for "when the faith in a universe of divine creation is lost, artistic creativeness will become utopian, and inspiration will die away." Still, Kaufmann says, Mann's position follows from "the Christian mystic and Protestant tradition" and supports a conception of work as "an 'ethical symbol of life,'" not, as in Flaubert, as "self-mortification for the sake of art." To Mann "work is still holy . . . as an expression of man's need and guilt and a struggle to justify his life, and as a means, perhaps *the* means, of personal self-realization, a religious egomania in acceptance of his calling." [96]

But there is more to the calling than Kaufmann admits. Thomas Buddenbrook commits himself originally to a calling that is the expression of his powers and imagination. Yet whatever goals he attains, he can find no satisfaction or rest, driven on endlessly by projects to realize his will. Determined to dominate self and impulse, which he sees as the source of all victory, he finds himself wearied by having to strive beyond his external and internal limits. Thomas's real problem goes beyond his inability to pursue a calling based purely on a "naturalistic ethics" [97] without divine purpose or devotion to a social or religious whole outside himself: once he finds that calling inadequate, he is incapable of changing. He is not allowed, or does not allow himself, to reorient his life, question what its purposes have been, and give up what he has been doing in order to follow a different star. He cannot give it up because, first, he knows no other way than the bourgeois calling for practical life and, incapable of pursuing it, he believes himself a failure and a weakling in life generally. Second, he experiences his society as hostile to scruples, weakness, and doubt and even to the unconventional, and so it is; but so is he, both toward himself and toward Hanno. Third, he has no love in his life that he can acknowledge, or any refuge in the family, either because love is turned elsewhere, as with Gerda, or because he does not open himself to it, as with Hanno.

This problem derives not from the loss of a more "divine" purpose and goal of the calling—though this may be a convenient interpretation for him—but from an important crisis in the meaningful social world and in the psyche, a crisis both in this novel and in society at large. Yet neither Mann nor Weber acknowledges that these personal experiences of meaninglessness and confusion are expressions of estrangement rooted in social life: the experience of failure in society, isolation from others, and pressure and judgments from within and without. They both see the problem instead as the loss of a "god." In Mann's work, as in Weber's, rather than recognizing this tangible state of things, the "heroes" are driven once more to find a "holy" purpose to justify their sacrifice and self-domination. If that goal or cause or task or god cannot be found in religion or in ordinary bourgeois satisfaction in work, then a new goal must be elevated and sanctified, given ideal power and made an ultimate purpose. Such a god is given the power to justify the most extreme denial of life, the overcoming of the hated self, and the repression of life' conflicts. If such a goal, purpose, and animating force cannot be found at all, then the result will be the dilettantism of the joker, the defeat of Thomas, or the total hopelessness and death of Hanno. Or so they imagine.

The discovery of the new god of art, which itself serves both life and *Geist,* is the alternative Tonio develops for himself and for the artist. He justifies his willingness, even desire, to sacrifice his life to art by developing a calling that can justify and sanctify in no other way than this. In the calling to art one may devote oneself and gain strength, redemption, and justification. Even in a society that does not and should not value art too highly, there is still the possibility of success and a form of acceptance. This possibility is closed to those whose devotion to art is linked to a critique of bourgeois society unmitigated by "love." They must wander forever in icy realms, perhaps justified by their own critical cause or goal but never able to gain that reconciliation with society that allows Tonio to empty his life almost cheerfully on behalf of art. To allow oneself to be unmanned by a society that feminizes and excludes the artist becomes bearable in Tonio's world only when it is done in the name of impersonal service. Personal rejection and loss are transformed into impersonal and sanctified sacrifice, and one may accept one's empty life, defend it before others, and still preserve a fantasy of connectedness to society.[98] The calling can fortify the "wayward" bourgeois in pursuing his not-quite-licit path by demanding the same self-sacrifice and denial that it demanded of his bourgeois father; but can it give him inspiration and the themes and substance of art? His detachment and isolation from society and its problems threaten to leave him absorbed in narrow problems of self, although the crucial problem of self and identity—reconciliation with the calling—has apparently been solved. For Mann a new problem soon emerged, that of the emptiness of the artistic self and the lack of theme, the loss of inspiration, linked with the excessive attachment to literary form. It took him nine years to give this problem form.

Mann plunged into his family history to uncover the roots of decadence and dilettantism in "Der Bajazzo," and in *Buddenbrooks* he drew even more from his own background. *Tonio Kröger* is the culmination of Mann's search for a full understanding of the artist's calling, but it is the beginning of an artistic enterprise that had great difficulty generating a subject beyond ever narrower reworkings of the artist theme. With the completion of *Tonio Kröger* Mann had, in many ways, exhausted his store of material; he had reached the limits of analyzing the artist who remained self-absorbed and cut off from social involvement and social understanding until the crisis of the cultural and social world entered his work in *The Magic Mountain*. Between these two works he could not find a great inspiration until the themes of exhaustion and sterility led him to Gustav von Aschenbach and *Death in Venice*, a story about the inner life and dilemma of an artist who, like Mann, seems to be at the end of his creative rope.

A sophisticated and compelling portrayal of the artistic calling is the major intellectual attainment of Mann's work to 1903. In some form this attainment remains central to Mann's later intellectual and artistic development, even to his attempt to understand the origin and meaning of Nazi Germany. This conception haunts Mann's heroes even when he believes he himself has given it up. Moreover, it is a conception intimately related to the analysis of calling in Max Weber, in which only the commitment to an ultimate cause within the discipline of the calling can give life meaning, justify action, and fortify character for otherwise impossible tasks. The notion of the calling is an integral part of both men's understanding of the social world and of their explanation of the bourgeois class, its failures, and its successes.

Conclusion to Part I:
The Nature of the Calling

For Weber and Mann the calling is not just an approach to work; it is an entry point for the most profound issues that they raise about themselves and about self, person, and identity in general. It is also their entry point for understanding the identity and spiritual condition of their nation and its culture during a "crisis of value." This crisis had been an explicit concern in European, and especially German, intellectual life at least since what Karl Löwith has called the "self-dissolution of Protestant theology" and the critique of religion by the Young Hegelian D. F. Strauss, and it found its greatest analyst in Nietzsche.[1] But whereas Nietzsche aimed his attack at asceticism, Weber and Mann restore an ascetic source of meaning and value.

The calling is a mode of justification of the self through a relation of ascetic service to impersonal ideals and ends. In the hands of Weber and Mann it is a magical device for creating in the person a sense of "grace" and purpose, of significance and personal value, through the devotion to ideals, the service of which "sanctifies" the self. In the discourse of the calling, value is located neither in the self and its development nor in the discovery of what the self is or contains nor in what it creates; it lies, rather, in the capacity to discipline oneself in work for the ideals on behalf of which one becomes a tool and a servant. These ideals sanctify the person through work, provide an opportunity to sacrifice the "natural" self, and allow its transformation into something higher and more valuable. Without these things, life and the self have no meaning.

What Weber and Mann hope to do in their adherence to the calling is to return, in a "nonpolitical" and nonreligious time, to a conception of justification of the self in and through work and practical sanctification. Neither man is under the illusion that all questions of the private or public realm can be resolved purely on this basis; for each the goal and meaning of activity is found only in the ideal that is served. But the attainment of identity and strength through a unique relation to and discipline in work has a history in Western, and especially German, thought that they strove to link to human achievements in the contemporary world in both the political and the inward and intellectual realms.

In a time when work no longer has a place in a system of sanctification derived from an established belief system or an accepted path to otherworldly salvation, this renewed sanctification of self and work lifts work out of the routine world of everyday existence and gives it spiritual significance. Mann and Weber link the notion of work not only to the distant past, to the world of the Puritan saints, but to the recent past as well, to the habits and practices of the bourgeois class from which they come and whose uncomfortable heirs they are. They also link it to the present of the nation and to the spiritual and social crisis of their time. It is only as a calling—in a secular time but still carrying much of the religious baggage of a time gone by—that the nature and meaning of work appear to them. The calling is the measure of their relation to life, to self, and to inner and outer worlds. The calling is not primarily a source of self-satisfaction or of the satisfaction of craftsmanly desires, nor is it seen as the fulfillment of talents or of satisfying involvement with an activity that they love. Instead, it serves the needs of self-definition, self-justification, and identity through devotion to a higher ideal through service. The calling is both real and a symbolic form, and in their revived and newly deployed notion of it, Weber and Mann find sources of strength for both the self and, they believe, the world. But whereas Weber elaborates principally the strength of what we can call "the self in the calling," Mann portrays the dark side of the calling along with the strength, though he does not always realize or understand the real darkness or the real significance of the darkness he does see.

In their obsession with the notion of the calling, Weber and Mann reveal the first clue to their problematical relation to self and society. Though they both explore the calling at the same time, Mann is the first to lay out an ethos of the calling for himself in explicit terms, though in fictional form. However implicitly Weber understands the calling as an ethos and however thoroughly he analyzes its emergence in history, he does not formulate it as an explicit ethos for himself and the contemporary world until 1917, and even then he does so in the setting of helping others, especially youth, to understand the need for and the path to their calling. Nevertheless, until the war, which revived them, both were hampered by inner inhibitions, hesitations, or paralysis.

Weber and Mann made the calling as they understood it the bridge to and the foundation of a conception of self and meaning. Their ideas of calling and service were made more urgent later by the experience of war and by their need to defend their most cherished ideals against attack from without and loss of conviction from within the nation. The significance of these ideas was enormous for all aspects of German life, they thought, and determined the intellectual options available for the "wayward sons" of the bourgeoisie looking for models of purpose, identity, and work. With the calling thus grounded personally, historically, and socially, the experience and analysis of lives lived in the service prescribed by this spiritual discipline became the object of Weber and Mann's increasing attention.

Weber was convinced that the Reformation had brought, as part of its contribution to Western culture, a new organization of the self and person—the "personality." But he was also sensitive to the philosophical and literary tradition that had nurtured and sharpened the understanding of this object of German striving and character building. He followed *The Protestant Ethic* with the analysis of economic ethics in the world religions to discover the shape, modes, and consequences of the self formed in different cultures and along different paths to salvation. The "Occidental self," formed in the crucible of Christian Europe, ascetically shaped in the Reformation, and secularized in German idealism, was markedly different, he believed, from the self produced elsewhere. And if that were true, it might be possible to recover the original meaning of that self from within the tradition, the kernel of the personality formed through the calling; once its antiquarian elements had been stripped away, it might then be possible to mobilize that conception of self for contemporary purposes.

In a parallel fashion, convinced of the importance of the calling not just to his bourgeois ancestors but to his own life as an artist, Mann analyzed other aspects of that life, as well as the crises, difficulties, and problems that such a life brought with it. As his experience of life in the calling deepened, Mann discovered other aspects of the ethic of the artist's life and added them to his artistic ideology. He was also fascinated with "wrong turns," with the dead ends and problematical resolutions of the dilemmas of artistic existence in bourgeois society. Such outcomes were always possible even for a successful artist, thanks to the nature of art itself, when he could not feel himself a part of the society in which he lived. He reworked the special pathos discovered in the burden of the artist's personality until it found its most heightened expression in the suffering of *Death in Venice*. Thereafter he had to find another path to the artistic analysis of his experience of the life of service, mediation, and "knowledge."

With the first understanding of the meaning of the calling in place, we must now add the component of personality. In a sense personality is another form of the same theme: it is the consequence of the shaping of the self through the calling and a product of discovering the right relation to work. The notion of the calling does not disappear from Weber's and Mann's work or from our analysis. Indeed, the two terms belong together, because Weber and Mann forged the link between them. The calling thus takes on an even greater significance in Part II as its implications and consequences further come to light.

PART II

Personality and the New Men of the Calling

Introduction to Part II

In Part I we analyzed the calling as a spiritual discipline and a means to justification and sanctification through service to an ultimate ideal. In Part II, we discuss personality as the most important personal and social creation of this discipline. We will consider as well the tradition of German thinking on personality and analyze Weber's and Mann's treatment of the nature, significance, and problems of the personality created in the calling, whose value they consciously affirm within the German tradition of discourse.

Traditions of shaping or "overcoming" the self have a long history throughout the world. All of the world's religions can be said to have given imperatives in some form to the "natural" self they found in the world. All diagnosed in their own way what they took to be the failings or limitations of the self, gave special guidance to that self, and provided prescriptions to the believer based on the promises of salvation that they brought: from the need for obedience to law to tame the self prone to wander, to the conquest of the self for the service of God, to the complete renunciation of self and desire, to the search for harmony between the self and the powers of the universe, to a reconciliation of the self with dharma and one's place in the divine order. In their different diagnoses, paths to salvation, and remedies for earthly suffering, these religions and cultures have recommended forms of character shaping on a mass scale.

In Weber and Mann's time, this nearly universal concern with character shaping and the transformation of the self continued to be a problem, a priority, and even an obsession; but this concern was limited by the lack of an established shared diagnosis of the problem of the self and of the means to transform, overcome, or accept it. Indeed precisely because religion in its traditional form ceased to have so compelling and powerful a hold—and because material interests began to dominate life and to set an ideological and cultural agenda of their own—the interest in identity and the shaping of character or the soul intensified in the West. A secular tradition of thinking about the self had already emerged in Germany in the late-eighteenth-century conception of *Bildung,* "self-cultivation." Like the earlier ideal of the calling, *Bildung* was a discipline that shaped the self, but it was oriented toward development of the self, not toward its domination on behalf of service. Still, the ideal of *Bildung* was disputed even in its own time and was finally undermined in the crisis of the late nineteenth and early twentieth centuries. Whatever the value of *Bildung* as an ideal, the German middle classes were forced to search again for some stable point on which to ground identity and to shape ethical action, to find a guide to lead the self toward meaning and toward an appropriate relation to work and one's role in the world. They found this stable point in the more demanding ideal of personality. The obsession with self and identity was not confined to Germany, however, nor was the narrower concern with personality, despite its greater importance there. The attraction of the religious writings of Kierkegaard, rediscovered in Europe before World War I,[1] the sociological writings of Durkheim, which were contemporary with those of Weber,[2] and the literary work of the French decadents and the German intellectual elite reveal similar concerns.[3] Our interest, however, is not with the whole tradition of spiritual disciplines or even with the narrower range of contemporary writings but principally with the outcome of one such discipline in Germany, the notion of personality as the product of life in the calling.

What is personality in this sense? Weber attributed the origin of the type of the first great entrepreneur to the experience and efforts of ascetic Protestantism. But Puritanism was also the source of what Weber called personality. In its doctrine of the calling and its devotion to the purposes of God, Puritanism transformed the self of the Puritan believer into a personality: a subjugation of the natural self and its unification from within through devotion, shaped by a life in "wakeful" and systematic service to its ultimate ideal, God. But the concept of personality as an Occidental model of the self has a long and varied history in the languages and cultures of Europe. The German discourse of personality derives primarily from, and has its most important actual uses in, the epoch and work of Kant and the writings of the *Sturm und Drang* period of German culture, especially in Goethe. It is also important, though less central, in Humboldt, the great theorist of *Bildung*.

Despite its changes through the romantic period and its later political misappropriation by the *völkisch* movement, the concept of personality was revitalized and given an important role and presence in the history, philosophy, and social movements of Weber and Mann's time, for example, in the historical writings of Treitschke and Meinecke, in the work of Nietzsche,[4] and in the popular concerns of the youth movement.[5] But it was especially prominent and important in the work of the neo-Kantians—in particular in Wilhelm Windelband's histories of philosophy—and in the discourse of late-nineteenth-century Protestant theologians confronting the issue of social reform, among whom was Weber's friend Ernst Troeltsch. These discussions went on principally in and around the Evangelisch-Soziale Kongress, of which Weber was a member and an important participant.

Weber referred to Kant and Goethe as the models for his understanding of duty and self in *The Protestant Ethic,* whereas Mann was inspired by the conception of the artist's self in Goethe and Schiller. Between Weber and Mann, it is Weber who works out the meaning of the concept of personality most explicitly. He derived its role and importance neither from religious precepts and fundamentals, as did the Puritans, nor from philosophical presuppositions, as did Kant. Rather, he first experienced its importance in his own development—shaped by Pietism, by the traditions of *Bildung* among his class, and by the crisis over the meaning of his own calling during his breakdown. This personal stake was coupled with his encounter with the concept of personality in the world: in the history of philosophy and literature since the eighteenth century, in the influential discourse of *Bildung,* and in the revival of the concept in his own time. Armed with this inherited conceptual apparatus and the refinements of contemporary reflection, Weber's historical examination of the spirit of capitalism led him not only to attribute the creation of personality in the modern sense to the Puritans but also to measure its significance for action outside the purely religious realm and eventually to advocate a revitalized form of it as a response to the problems of self and identity in contemporary Germany.

Though the war brought Weber to reconsider and focus more sharply on the main themes of his life work, the sociological works of the war period and after extended and confirmed his earlier analyses of the significance of the calling and the shaping of the self. Weber believed that the ideals of *Bildung* and broad self-development were no longer adequate for equipping the self to meet the demands of a world dominated by rationalization and disenchantment. Only the transformation of the self into a personality and its unification for the undertaking of service could meet contemporary needs for meaning and make possible the mastery of the rationalized orders. Thus Weber wanted to go back to the original form of the Reformation discipline of the calling, to make it suitable for a secular time, and to apply it to life today. The calling was the only form of self-shaping that could lead even in secular conditions to the creation of personality.

For Mann, who had seen the workings and the failings of the calling for business among the *Bürgertum*, it was possible that the calling, "rightly understood," could still solve the problems of identity and work for those who came after the bourgeoisie. But whereas Weber was working out the triumphs of personality in the Occident, Mann had already chronicled the unraveling of the bourgeois personality in the character of Thomas Buddenbrook; even so, he revived that form of personality as an ideal in *Tonio Kröger*. In later works he vindicated that ideal negatively against what he took to be its enemies among artists and positively in an allegory of the artist in the guise of a prince. But, more important, Mann fortified his concept of personality with an "ethos of suffering" that he himself experienced, recognized, and then linked to his ideology of the artist who creates in a life-and-death struggle with his time and himself. Yet the artistic calling and personality finally began to show the burden of the same fatal flaws Mann had found in the bourgeois calling and personality, a burden dramatized in *Death in Venice*. For Mann World War I brought a major crisis in and reorientation of his work, and it interrupted his literary productivity for a number of years. He struggled initially to preserve and defend certain traditional German ideals and the spiritual inheritance of *Bildung*; but he too was led to see their impracticality in a world whose essence was no longer "culture," but "civilization." It was the ideals of calling and personality that guided his approach to self and identity.

As Part I demonstrates, the issue of the calling was not limited to the Reformation and the analysis of the Puritans or to certain sectors of the bourgeoisie. For Weber and Mann it was of much greater significance: historically in the origin of the capitalist spirit and the legacy of duty in the modern world, and personally in the ideals of work, meaning, and personality found among the descendants of the bourgeoisie. Before we can understand how Weber and Mann mobilized their ideals of the calling and personality for a Germany in crisis during World War I and after, we must consider the strengths and weaknesses of the ideal of personality portrayed in Weber's analyses of the Occidental self and in Mann's explorations of the consequences of the personality created by life in the calling. And not only its weaknesses: we will also see its dangers. For the ideal of personality presents enormous problems when allowed to develop to its ultimate conclusion.

CHAPTER THREE

The Discourse
of Personality

Two main traditions of thinking about personality emerged in the late eighteenth and early nineteenth centuries in Germany and are important for Weber's and Mann's use of the term.[1] One derives from the reflections of Kant on reason as the creator of the moral personality. The other is found in Goethe and Humboldt, among others, and concerns the development of the whole self, with the harmonious integration of the experiential, sensual, and reasonable parts of the person into a unity created by the formation (*Bildung*) of the self. Like Humboldt, Goethe began as an advocate of the harmonization and flowering of the self rather than with the Kantian project to dominate the self through the hegemony of pure practical reason. Nevertheless, he moved closer to Kant in his later concern with duty and with the need for notions of self and identity other than those of mere self-development. Humboldt, the defender of the ideal of all-sided *Bildung,* was also forced to reckon with the importance of duty and self-limitation. But his ideal of *Bildung* remained more an ethical category linked to personality than a force for shaping the concept of personality itself. Kant and Goethe were principally decisive for Weber's use and Mann's fictional portrayal of personality.

At the beginning of the tradition of *Bildung,* in the great period of classicism, idealism, and neohumanism, there were arguments not only between thinkers but within thinkers about the source and nature of personality. The need for self-shaping and the formation of the personality were universally acknowledged. The question was whether these goals could be achieved by *Bildung* (where the powers of the self were integrated and formed into a totality in which the variety of the world was incorporated), by deliberate specialization, by submission to the duty imposed by a single ultimate task and ideal, or by submission to the laws of reason. Even Goethe's answer was not totally unambiguous. This is the debate that Weber and Mann ultimately entered.

The Transcendence of the Natural Self: Kant

The principal philosophical source of the German idea and use of personality is Kant, who came close to formulating the concept that Weber thought the Puritans had achieved and to the form that Weber later made his own. Indeed, Kant's achievement is hardly surprising, for Weber notes in *The Protestant Ethic* that Kant was partly of Scottish ancestry and strongly influenced by Pietism and that, moreover, "many of his formulations are directly connected to ideas of ascetic Protestantism."[2] According to Kant humankind belongs to "two worlds," the sensible and the intelligible; its being in relation to the second, higher, "determination" (*Bestimmung*) and the laws of that intelligible world should be the guide to human aspiration. In the *Critique of Practical Reason,* first published in 1788, Kant questions the source of duty that provides the law the mind reveres even when the person does not obey it.

> It can be nothing less than what lifts man above himself (as a part of the world of sense). . . . It is nothing other than *personality,* i.e., the freedom and independence from the mechanism of the whole of nature, at the same time regarded as a capacity of a being [*Wesen*] whose particularity is namely pure practical laws given by its own reason; the person therefore, as belonging to the world of sense, is subject to his own personality, as far as he belongs at the same time to the intelligible world.

Personality is therefore the capacity of humankind to overcome dependence on the sense world and its mechanical laws. A being attains or is elevated to personality when it gives itself its own pure practical laws based on reason, moral laws revealed to us by the categorical imperative. Only by obedience to such laws are human beings able to overcome both the world of sense and their "dependence on their so far very pathologically affected nature," a human nature that interferes with self-overcoming or self-transformation.[3]

Personality in the *Critique,* therefore, is in the "disposition" of everyone—more precisely, in the disposition of all rational beings—through the power of reason alone. Nature and the world of desire interfere with the subjugation of the natural self to this other world and disposition, the personality. The moral law within "begins with my unseen self, my personality," "elevating my worth, as an *intelligence*, endlessly, through my personality, in which the moral law reveals a life independent of animality and even of the whole world of sense."[4] Thus personality falls in the set of what Kant calls "categories of freedom," which determine the "free faculty of choice" (*freie Willkür*), as opposed to the "categories of nature."[5] But independence is not all that personality provides.

> [Its] inner comfort is . . . purely negative, with respect to all that may make life happy. . . . It is the effect of a respect for something quite different from life, in comparison and contrast with which life, with all of its enjoyment, has rather no worth at all. He still lives only out of duty, not because he finds the least taste for life.[6]

This remarkable statement shows us the affinity of the Kantian conception of personality—and of the means required to shape it—with ascetic Protestantism, whose sense and object of duty put the imperatives of life and its enjoyment far in the background or even specifically demean and reject them. Kant's formulation suggests that the regard for personality and duty is a response to an experience that has made life seem senseless and valueless; living "out of duty" provides the means for living despite the loss of a "taste" for life. Thus the Kantian conceptions of personality and duty echo in secular form an originally religious experience of self, duty, and life and provide a secular ideal of strength and obligation.

Indeed, Kant's *Religion within the Limits of Reason Alone* (1793) provides a more literal connection to his ascetic Protestantism. There Kant focuses not on individual acts and obedience to maxims in particular cases but on the issue of the "conviction" or "disposition" (*Gesinnung*) of the whole personality, which is the "ultimate subjective ground for the adoption of maxims."[7] Kant says that the original "tendency" or "predisposition" (*Anlage*) toward good in humankind can be divided into three classes, "as elements of the determination [*Bestimmung*] of men." The first is the predisposition toward "animality" (*Tierheit*), the human being taken merely as a living being, which does not require the exercise of reason. This predisposition includes the drives for self-preservation, for the propagation of the species, and for social contact with others. Kant classifies all of these under the category of "physical and purely mechanical self-love." The second element is the predisposition toward "humanity" (*Menschheit*), the human being taken as a rational being, which bases itself on practical reason and which serves nonanimal motives. This predisposition includes the inclination to acquire worth in the opinion of others, originally a drive to get one's due and to be seen as equal but which can also become a striving for superiority. Kant says that nature uses this rivalry as a spur to the creation of culture (*Kultur*). He classifies this second predisposition under the category of "physical self-love, but which nonetheless compares," that is, is based on comparing the self with others. The third element is the crucial one: the predisposition toward personality. Only personality "alone for itself has as its root practical reason, i.e., reason giving laws unconditionally." As personality humankind is rational and "capable of accountability," that is, responsibility; it has "respect for the moral law as for itself a sufficient motive for the faculty of choice [*Willkür*]." A being with such a faculty of choice has "good character," which no one is born with but which "can only be acquired." Indeed, the idea of the moral law is not a "predisposition to personality; it is the personality itself." [8]

Reflecting on the restoration of the predisposition toward good in someone who is an evildoer, Kant distinguishes between being legally good and being morally good, between changing one's practices (*eine Änderung der Sitten*) and changing one's heart (*eine Herzensänderung*), between virtue as empirical (*phaenomenon*) and practical and virtue as intelligible (*noumenon*) and done from duty alone. Such moral good

> cannot be effected through gradual *reform* . . . but must be effected through a *revolution* in the conviction or disposition [*Gesinnung*] in the man (a going over to the maxim of the holiness of the conviction); and he can become a new man only through a kind of rebirth, exactly as through a new creation . . . and a change of heart. . . . From this it follows that the moral education [*Bildung*] of man must begin not from the improvement of practices [*Sitten*], but from the transformation of his way of thought [*Denkungsart*] and from the grounding of a character.[9]

It is no accident that Kant then refers to John 3:5 and Genesis 1:2 on new creations. He is also describing the equivalent of what Paul called justification by faith over works (Romans 3:21, 27, 28), the renewing of the mind (Romans 12:2), the rebirth of the creature (Galatians 6:15), and the transformation of the heart, favoring them over mere conformity to stipulated practices and the "law." [10] Kant provides here a secular formulation of "rebirth," for what had originally been a Christian religious understanding whose significance was renewed in the Reformation. Focusing on the whole man, on the unity of the personality,

Kant suggests that the personality is obedient to duty as its ultimate principle rather than to individual acts, practices, and mere conformity to given works and rules. Weber argued that just such a conception was at the heart of the Puritan personality.

Following Augustine in *The City of God,* Kant criticizes the Stoics and their notion that undisciplined "natural inclinations" are the cause of human beings' "sin" or their failure to fulfill their duty.[11] For Kant the natural inclinations are, "considered in themselves, good" and not to be extinguished. Rather, "one must . . . tame them so that they do not clash with one another, but can be brought to a harmony [*Zusammenstimmung*] in a whole called happiness." Inclinations are not the danger; it is the "wickedness (of the human heart) . . . which secretly undermines the conviction [*Gesinnung*] with soul-destroying principles" and which is the real enemy of the morally good.[12] One must make the "good principle" (*Prinzip*) sovereign over man to overcome this wickedness and elevate the person into a personality. It is not sensuousness (*Sinnlichkeit*) but a "self-incurred perversity," a "corruption" (*Verderbtheit*) that works against the "most heartfelt adoption of true moral principles into the disposition [*Gesinnung*]." Yet corruption is not an ordinary defect; it is a great threat to the highest good. Stripping away what he calls the "mystical veil," Kant argues that apart from the adoption of true moral principles "there exists no salvation [*Heil*] for men"! Nor can such a salvation, such a "good grounded in self-activity," be found "*superstitiously* through expiations, which presuppose no changes of mind [*Sinnesänderungen*], or *fanatically* [*schwärmerisch*] through supposed (purely passive) inner illuminations."[13] In pure Protestant fashion Kant suggests that no discipline of works, no institutional patterns of forgiveness demanding expiations, and no mystical illumination can be relied on or be the source of the elevation of the good principle to sovereignty or be the source of personality. Only the principle of the good itself—the moral law that is the "self-legislation of the spirit" and that corresponds to the lessons of scripture[14]—can create personality; it unifies the self under a first principle, makes the self capable of responsibility and the imputation of accountability, and allows it to recognize in others the same quality and principle.[15]

The Kantian model is formally similar to what Weber later defends as the "true" structure of personality, and Kant's model draws from the same original inspiration in Paul that fortified the Puritans. But in Kant's case the source of personality and its strength derive from the principles of reason and are based on the moral law derived from the categorical imperative. For Weber, however, reason cannot provide such a guide, and the self must find a different source for and relation to its "principle," a source more like the source of the original pattern of Puritan faith. For Mann duty and responsibility as the support of the person create dangers in isolation from feeling and compassion and from the direct experience of and engagement with reality. Despite their differences with Kant, however, Weber and Mann sympathize with the strength and power of his conception of personality in its relation to the natural self. Yet their interest is not in doing the morally good; rather, they use Kant's conception for the sake of "justification" and "salvation" of the self through the service of any higher good, cause, or object with self-denying discipline, devotion, and commitment, whether the cause be science, the nation, or art. Only through a comparable elevation of the self above the person given in nature—by way of service in a calling—can human beings aspire to the goal of personality, though no one can say who will ultimately reach it.

Bildung and Personality: Humboldt

There is a tradition that competes with Kant's notion of personality. Wilhelm von Humboldt developed more generally the ideals of self-formation, or *Bildung,* and along with them an ideal of the all-sided development of the self and a competing notion of personality. According to Hans Rosenberg:

> *Bildung,* as conceived by the German neohumanists in the age of Lessing, Herder, Winckelmann, Goethe, Schiller, Kant, Fichte, and Humboldt, meant much more than advanced school training, general and vocational. *Bildung,* no doubt, called for trained minds and for more and better knowledge, but no less for character and personality development. *Bildung* implied supreme emphasis on inwardness and tenderness of the heart. It invited man to seek happiness within himself by orienting his total life toward the harmonious blending of spiritual elevation, emotional refinement, and individualized mental and moral perfection.[16]

Though his views changed during his lifetime,[17] for Humboldt, the "true goal of man" remained "the highest and most harmonious formation [*proportionierlichste Bildung*] of his strengths [*Kräfte*] into a whole."[18] *Bildung* is "the process of self-becoming [*Selbstwerdung*] of the individual, who embodies in himself a true and ethical world,"[19] and for whom the path to fulfillment is the "improvement of our inner selves." Thus *Bildung* means "education" in the sense of *self*-cultivation or self-formation rather than in the sense of training or learning.[20]

With an educational and cultural agenda clearly different from Kant's moral one, Humboldt was the first to make *Bildung* a goal and a program. For him true morality consisted in the motto first "form [*bilde*] yourself" and only then "affect [*wirke*] others through what you are." The state must limit itself to creating conditions for *Bildung,* never dictating its goals, for "the formation of human beings" means precisely "not educating them toward external goals." Instead, "all *Bildung* has its origin alone in the interior of the soul and through external institutions can only be called forth, never brought forth." The goal of the human being must be "to form himself in himself," which must never be a mere means toward any other result. The ultimate purpose of the person should be to strive for "the unity of his whole being, which alone gives the person true value."[21] This unity is not attained, however, by reason's command to the natural self to tame desire, inclination, impulse, and whatever else is native to it but by the imperative to form and to develop oneself according to the "law" of one's own self.

Humboldt's proposal was not initially aimed at external accomplishment or achievement (*Leistung*). The growth of individuality and the highest development of human powers into a totality were the true purposes of the human being. A person's worth depends on what he *is,* not on what he *does.* Yet this self-cultivation or -formation does not exclude the absorption or internalization of culture or immersion in the products of human creativity. As Humboldt wrote to his wife, "He who can say to himself when he dies: 'I have grasped and made into a part of my humanity as much of the world as I could,' that man has reached fulfillment. . . . In the higher sense of the word, he has really lived."[22] Thus *Bildung,* in its original sense in Humboldt, focused on "being," on the struggle for liberation from goals and imperatives set from outside the self, and on the absorption of the highest examples of human culture into one's own "humanity," all of which make a person whole.

Bildung also takes as its "highest good" the "unfolding of the personality,"[23] but personality in a sense different from Kant's. For Humboldt the self must follow an "inward" pattern, and it must flourish and unfold, unbound by laws prescribed by abstract reason to overcome the world of nature and the flesh. This inner pattern or form determines the personality and allows the self to develop and harmonize all its faculties, making it a whole but not a unified servant of the higher laws of practical reason and morality. This process encourages natural development rather than demanding the imposition of moral or religious imperatives that hold the self to a higher standard than it could provide from within. Thus the metaphor in Humboldt is organic and sculptural rather than moral: unfolding and shaping rather than elevating and taming.

Humboldt was influenced, perhaps, by his reading of the Scottish Enlightenment figures Smith and Ferguson and by a concern for the increasing division of labor and specialization in society. Thus he focused on individual particularity and spontaneity, trying to combine into a totality those human mental powers that threatened to be fragmented in a society that prized the one-sided development of the self and its capacities.[24] Yet Humboldt did not stop with the "pursuit of harmonious and fully developed faculties." After a period of personal inactivity and private cultivation of the self, and possibly under the influence of Goethe and Schiller, Humboldt became interested in concentration on the accomplishment of concrete tasks. He wrote to his wife: "A man must give himself up to *one* limited definite objective and lose himself, at least for a time, in its pursuit."[25] Sounding like Thomas Buddenbrook, Humboldt wrote: "The truly great person . . . the man who is truly cultivated in the intellectual and moral sense, exerts by these qualities alone more influence than all others, simply because such a man exists among men, or has existed."[26] For Humboldt this "idea of the primacy of the will" to shape things outside, produced by the formation of the self, is actually the "very essence" of *Bildung*.[27] The capacity of the will is developed not through technical training or practical experience but through self-formation mediated by immersion in scholarship, which results in forcefulness and influence. Yet despite his renewed interest in applying himself to a task and his new career as the minister of culture in the Prussian government,[28] Humboldt still maintained that the self could grow only from within. It must be nurtured by its learning, not from engagement with the powers and forces of the world. Thus it is necessary to cultivate a detachment from the world, rooted in the wholeness of one's inner self, which must remain disengaged and grow according to its own law. "One must have a world of one's own within, over which the waves of life roll on, while it quietly grows unseen."[29]

In the course of its evolution and particularly through the collaboration of Schiller and Goethe, *Bildung* developed into an "ethical category alongside personality [*Persönlichkeit*]."[30] Humboldt remained concerned with what Roy Pascal calls "the division in the psyche, the personality, caused by the one-sidedness of man."[31] Although he became more convinced of the need for one-sidedness and for the application of the self to a narrower field of action, he did not abandon his desire for the absorption of the world into inner experience.

Duty and Personality: Goethe

It was left to Goethe to find a path between all-around development of the personality and specialization, to support self-development while at the same time subjecting the self to obligations. Goethe poses the problem of personality in an effort to understand the difference between the nobility and the bourgeoisie, the *Bürgertum*,[32] in the famous letter of Wilhelm to Werner in book 5, chapter 3, of *Wilhelm Meisters Lehrjahre* (1794–96). The *Lehrjahre* concerns Wilhelm's search for self-fulfillment, for the cultivation (*Ausbildung*) of personality on the part of a *Bürger* living in a world dominated by the nobility. As Wilhelm writes:

> In Germany a certain universal, if I may say so, personal education [*Ausbildung*] is possible only for the nobleman. A *Bürger* can earn profit and cultivate [*ausbilden*] his spirit to the highest necessity; his personality, however, is lost, whatever he may do. . . . He may not ask "What are you?" but only "What have you? what intelligence, what knowledge, what capacity, how much ability?" If the nobleman gives everything through the exhibition [*Darstellung*] of his person, so the *Bürger* gives nothing through his personality, and should give nothing.[33]

Thus Wilhelm thinks the *Bürger* is unable to attain the unity of being the nobleman may attain, a unity equivalent to personality. Through his birth into a class confined in German society to a life of acquisition, the *Bürger* can only "have," even if that having amounts to a great number of separate and fine qualities. The aristocrat "should do and effect," but the bourgeois "should accomplish and create" within a specialized area. He "should cultivate individual talents in order to be useful, and it is already assumed that in his essence no harmony is or may be, because he must neglect everything else in order to be useful in *one* way." For this dilemma of the bourgeoisie Wilhelm does not blame the individual classes but rather blames "the constitution of society." Yet he says: "[I have] an irresistible inclination" to the "harmonious cultivation of my nature, which my birth has denied me."[34]

Goethe, however, shows Wilhelm's aim to be an illusion when pursued in so bald a form, and he reveals both the need for specialization and the setting of bounds to one's strivings—although still determined from within by the personality itself—and the need for activity within a real community. Specialization within the community leads to the "building up of personality and self-knowledge." Goethe thus links Wilhelm's early search for beauty and the harmonious totality of existence to his later appreciation of systematic and skillful work.[35] What Manfred Riedel calls the "'bourgeois' idea of the connection between work and cultivation [*Bildung*]"[36] is given its definitive expression in this work and in the much later *Wilhelm Meisters Wanderjahre*. In *The Protestant Ethic* Weber says of the *Wanderjahre*, a product of the old Goethe, that it provides a parallel to the Calvinist single-minded devotion to duty and to one's task, creating through work the conviction of salvation.

The tradition of *Bildung* underwent a change not only during Humboldt's career but also during Goethe's. Before Goethe had finished *Faust* and his *Wanderjahre* he had begun to stress the value of self-limitation, renunciation, and the importance of duty. Weber, for example, quotes an exemplary saying of Goethe's: "How can one get to know oneself? Through contemplation never, but certainly through action. Try to do your duty, and you know immediately what is in you. But what is your duty? The demand of the day."[37] Yet Goethe does not adhere to Kant's fundamental maxims, dictated by reason, as the source of duty; rather, he adheres to a picture of self-development in which the dynamism within the self confronts, masters, and even adjusts to the obstacles and givens without. Indeed, Georg Lukács says that *Wilhelm Meisters Lehrjahre* is actually a great polemic against Kant, revealing a contempt for moral codes imposed on individuals by "a unitary system of rules," whatever it may derive from. Moreover, says Lukács, the systems of Kant and Fichte actually stood in the way of the development of personality. For Goethe human beings should become sociable "by virtue of free, organic spontaneity and bring the manifold development of their individuality into agreement with the happiness and interests of their fellow-men." The educators in his novel, then, "constantly stress contempt for moral 'imperatives,'" that is, for the imposition of uniform codes on every personality. Goethe's answer to Kantian uniformity is, rather, the conception of the "beautiful soul" in book 6 of the *Lehrjahre*, borrowed and refined from Schiller.[38]

Thus for Goethe the unitary personality reveals itself in work and activity, in conformity with what it takes to be its duty and the "demand of the day," and fulfills itself both through self-limitation and through involvement with all the powers available to it. In this sense Goethe is

not satisfied with Kant's abstract moral maxims, although he preserves
a conception of duty, work, and fulfillment similar to the features of the
structure of personality that Kant defends.[39]

Yet even in Goethe there remains an ambiguity. Goethe's work recognized "the necessity of 'Einseitigkeit' [one-sidedness] and the definition
of 'Bildung' in terms of this necessity," accepting the inevitability of specialization and seeing it, "if freely chosen, as a necessary means to the
fulfillment of the personality." Consequently Goethe defends a notion of
personality based on renunciation, duty, and specialization within a
larger social world, a notion later attractive to Weber and Mann. Moreover, according to Roy Pascal, Goethe's characters are not really harmonious; each lacks certain strengths. For Goethe, with his great sense of
the importance of the social world, totality is "something to be achieved
only by a community as a whole, not by an individual in himself."[40] As
Bruford observes, "Goethe in *Wilhelm Meister* did not mean his hero to
become finally a man of harmonious all-round culture such as Humboldt had envisaged." Though Goethe was at times attracted to such an
ideal, he believed that it had been attainable only by the ancients. Thus,
according to Kurt May, Goethe abandoned "the modern humanistic
ideal of harmonious 'Bildung,'" and his novel "ends with the recognition that a man of his day could not develop the full harmony of his
nature and would do better to aim at being, and to have himself educated as, a fragment, a single part."[41]

Still, Roy Pascal argues that in Goethe's *Wilhelm Meister,* despite the
final resoluteness of Goethe's Wilhelm, the hero "remains remarkably
indeterminate to the end," indicating a "conflict between Goethe's pre-
cept and its 'hero,' and as such a conflict between ethical principle and
artistic realization." Hence the work shows a discrepancy between intention and artistic truth, revealing Goethe's own "spontaneous and in-
voluntary resistance to the doctrine he himself is affirming, his protest
on behalf of 'Bildung' of the free personality, against the social and practical necessity of one-sidedness."[42] This tension between specialization
and development, unresolved even by Goethe, remained an issue into
the twentieth century, when the discourse of self and personality, nature
and freedom, instinctual chaos and unity of purpose was reborn in
Weber and Mann's time.

CHAPTER FOUR

Weber, the Occidental Self, and the Creation of Personality

Weber provides the elements of a more systematic account of the nature and formation of personality in a variety of contexts, but he does not synthesize these elements in any one place.[1] Inspired as much, perhaps, by his immersion in the philosophical and literary traditions of Germany as by the empirical evidence, Weber concluded that ascetic Protestantism was at the origin of the Western conception of personality. This special result that ascetic Protestantism brought for the self and for action in the world distinguished it from all other religions, Western and Eastern, as well as from the nonreligious valuations of self found in premodern aristocratic and "noble" cultures. As a consequence, ascetic Protestantism played a crucial role in shaping Western culture.

Weber's crucial innovation was to forge a link between the concepts and phenomena of calling and personality and to give these concepts a strengthened and altered content and power by going back to their origins. Although the Calvinists and Puritans did not actually use "personality," Weber fitted the idea, developed in its modern form by Kant, to the Puritan achievement. He then refined it through an analysis of other religions and their "culture-carriers" (*Kulturträger*) and by a comparison of the different ideals of self, character building, and work in each culture. Weber took the term out of the primarily religious debates of his time and divorced it from its romanticized and mystified uses in heroic, *völkisch,* and national history in order to link it to economic action and social innovation in the past. He then recommended personality in a revived form as a secular ideal for his own time, both in politics and in

intellectual life, with "ultimate values" substituted for its former center-
ing in God. Yet he still linked it to the older, religiously generated, need
for the calling and its discipline. The higher values served in the calling
help to create personality, which, both he and Ernst Troeltsch argued,
no one is born with and which all must earn and achieve in their own
lonely fashion.

The fullest consequences of Weber's application of personality are
seen in his lectures on vocation and his late writings on method. But the
foundation of that application lies principally in his examination of religious cultures. To understand the prominence of the preoccupation with
personality in Weber's time and to grasp the context of Weber's innovative revival of the concept and its significance in the debates of his
time, we must consider the use of the term in some of the discussions of
Weber's contemporaries. Then we will turn principally to Weber's studies of religion to see the centrality of the concept of the Occidental personality in his analytical work.

The Idea of Personality Among
Weber's Contemporaries

The enormous influence of Kant and Goethe, apart from that of the Reformation itself, on the notions of self, personality, and work was a result of the continued and widespread attention these men received in
German intellectual and practical life and of the consistency of their
conceptions with the religious and cultural heritage of Germany generally. Their conceptions even obtained a different kind of vitality, though
a problematical one, in the appropriation of the concept of personality
for chauvinist and nationalist purposes.[2] These notions made a more
positive contribution at the end of the nineteenth century, first, in the
revival of Kantianism in the universities and, second, in the debates
among Protestant theologians over a modern Christian ethics that would
allow the believer to retain an orientation to Protestant "inwardness"
while confronting the problems of a changing industrial society and
economy. In politics, philosophy, and religion at the turn of the twentieth century, the nature, sources, and importance of personality were
central issues.

Windelband and the History of Personality

Among Weber's near contemporaries the principal influence on
the systematic revival of the conception of personality were the neo-

Kantians, normally considered for their profound influence on the development of Weber's methodology rather than for any other, more substantive, influence. The key figure is Wilhelm Windelband (1848–1915).[3] In his *Lehrbuch der Geschichte der Philosophie,* first published in 1891, Windelband gives the history of the concept of personality an unusual prominence in academic philosophical discourse, even though it first became important as an explicit concept only in the late eighteenth century. By historicizing the conception of personality and showing its roots in a variety of traditions, both classical and Christian, Windelband reinforced the ethical and personal legacy of Kant.

The first features in the development of personality in Windelband's account lie in the Stoic notions of unity and independence of the self. For Windelband, following Kant, it was with the Stoics in their conception of the rule of the soul by its leading principle, the *hegemonikon,* that "*the problem of the personality*" first emerged; they were the first to maintain "the intrinsic value of the moral personality." For them too "the *personality* first becomes a determinative principle," since they emphasized the "unity and independence" of the individual soul, "as contrasted with its particular states and activities." But although this regard for "the heightened significance of the *personality*" continued in Hellenistic and Neoplatonic philosophy, it was Christianity, according to Windelband, that made "the concept of personality as spiritual inwardness [*Innerlichkeit*]" part of the permanent inheritance of the West: the "spirit" was taken to be "the actual essence of individual (as well as divine) *personality.*" Christianity shows a deeper acceptance of the diverse but essential constituents of selfhood as well as a developed ethical point of view. It recognizes that free will and creative action are possible but makes the self dependent on a higher creative principle, which, in Christian perspective, is the "personality of God."[4] Ultimately, according to Windelband, Augustine provided the foundation for the Christian achievement. "The soul is for him . . . the living whole of *personality,* whose life is a unity, and which, by self-consciousness, is certain of its own reality as the surest truth."[5] This "discovery of the personality" was solidified by the Augustinian influence on medieval philosophy and on the Protestant Reformation, which made such ideals widely pervasive and significant in a new way.[6]

In one of his nonhistorical writings Windelband argued that the "enduring will" [*dauernde . . . Wollen*], under the control of the "constant motives," forms the essence of "personality." Weber absorbed these terms directly into his analysis of Puritan personality. Though both the "constant will" and the "immediate will" determine human choice for

Windelband, "freedom of choice resides . . . in this ability of the personality to realize itself or its character decisively [*sich selbst oder ihren Charakter . . . zur entscheidenden Geltung zu bringen*] against circumstances."[7] Thus for Windelband the personality fulfills itself or its goals in action, guided by its constant motives, empowered by its permanent will. This element is part of the enduring legacy of reformed Christianity.

To Windelband, then, the history of philosophy, particularly in its Christian period, shows the significance and centrality of the conception of personality as unity within the multiplicity of the self, dependent for its ultimate purpose on the divine principle. This conception gained special significance after the Reformation, linked to the practical imperatives of the discipline of the calling, and it must certainly have influenced Kant, probably through his Pietist upbringing. Finally, Windelband underscores the constancy of will and motive as the essence of personality in its effort to accomplish its purposes against the resistance of the world and the pressures of the desires acted on by the "immediate will." Windelband's views contributed a systematic understanding of the concept of personality to contemporary discussion, at least for Weber.

Protestant Theology and the Debate over Personality

The conception of personality produced in the Reformation and "completed" by Kant also influenced the thinking of late-nineteenth-century German Protestant theology. Weber was a participant in this world of debate through the Evangelisch-Soziale Kongress, founded in 1890, and through his involvement with its principal publication, *Christliche Welt*. Nearly all the theologians of the period believed in the "cult of personality" and in the identification of Christian existence with "the moral personality"; they wanted to focus religious feeling directly on immediate religious experience and its rootedness in the transformed self, the personality. But the struggle over what a genuine Christian "social ethic" was or should be brought new dimensions to the discussions of personality in religious debate. Theologians were confronted from many sides with the demand for organized action and intervention on the "social question"—the question of the condition and needs of the working classes and the growing socialist movement—and they were divided over how Protestants should deal with it. There was a more liberal wing, based in the Evangelisch-Soziale Kongress and strongly inspired by Weber's friend Friedrich Naumann, and a conservative wing, which split from the Kongress in 1895–96 to follow Adolph Stöcker into the

Freie Kirchlich-Soziale Konferenz. But theologians split even within the liberal wing over the possibility of applying the personal inspiration of the autonomous individual within the Christian faith to new conditions: to the dilemmas posed by the rise of socialism and other mass movements and to a social world no longer governed by personal relations of authority and domination but instead governed by the impersonal relations and forces that modern society had brought in its train.[8]

Personality was central to the ethical discussions of all wings of the Lutheran and Pietist liberal theologians. There was a first group that resisted any notion of an implicit obligation of the individual to obey social principles derived directly from the revelations simply given in the Bible. They defended the idea that any social ethics should be seen as "a theory of the forms of realization of the religious personality ideal": social ethics could not be discovered as the independent product of religious revelation or principles alone but must always be related first to the needs and motives of the "single person's service of God."[9] Others among this group were concerned to preserve the social order that defended their own privileges; they wished to maintain both private property and social stratification by profession as supports of personal freedom, of individual independence, and of the atmosphere necessary for nurturing Protestantism and the autonomous personality it founded. They protested against any practices that might force the person to give up his material well-being. Such practices seemed to reduce the person to a mere "means," even if that means were toward the betterment of the social condition of humankind: "The spiritual-ethical personality may never be sacrificed to the economic growth of the whole." Despite opposition,[10] these views made it difficult if not impossible to develop a social theory from what came to be called *Kulturprotestantismus.* This left Christian ethical theory with only "the culture of personality" as its object of interest. Manfred Schick describes this defense of the autonomous individual as the "defensive ideology of a social stratum," namely, the *Bildungsbürgertum,* which saw "its human ideal in the educated, well-balanced personality, reconciled with social conditions."[11]

A second group was more actively engaged in the shaping of a social ethics. It tried to overcome the dualisms of individualism versus socialism and of personal ethics versus impersonal relations, dualisms that plagued the debates over Christian social action. A principal event in the debate over these dualisms and the serviceability of "the ideal of personality" came in 1894 in the discussions at the Kongress over the situation of the East Elbian agricultural laborers, discussions in which Weber played a major role.[12] The situation of the laborers presented a special dilemma for Christian social ethics: any examination of the transformation of agriculture in the east of Germany revealed the disappearance of personal relations of domination as the central fact of peasant life and their replacement by class conflict and class domination. This transformation created not only a new social and political climate in the east but also a new problem for Christian ethics: an ethics founded purely on personal relations and "respect" for others became untenable.

This changing social situation created new conditions for ethical reflection, especially among the pastors who had concerned themselves with relations between individuals, regulatable by personal ethical imperatives and rules. The new situation depended purely on the *impersonal* relations of market forces, class relations and conflicts, and mass movements. It led to serious questioning, by those still concerned with personality, about the "transferability of this most inward personality ethic" into modern life. Friedrich Naumann, at the time a close associate of Weber's, retained for many years the serious hope of bringing to the lower classes (*Unterschichten*) what had been an essentially bourgeois concern with personality. It was to be in the form of an ideal of the "thoroughly educated individual in the midst of the division of labor, mass organization, and legality: the highest happiness of the children of the earth is still the personality."[13] He hoped to show that the personal message of the New Testament was still valuable for a world of impersonal mass movements and could be used as a social political text and a "guidebook on worker's rights." But the impossibility of simply transferring these ethical precepts became obvious, for Christianity was confronted with "spheres of reality that resisted above all any ethical judgment." It was widely recognized that these spheres—for example, the political and the economic—were essentially governed by laws of their own, by an "immanent lawfulness" (*Eigengesetzlichkeit*), which independently dictated the direction of their development and provided imperatives on the basis of impersonal yet decisive rules and needs.[14] As a consequence it was difficult to imagine the potential role of personality and the ethics appropriate to it in such a "rationalized" context. Weber later made the dilemma of impersonality raised in religious debates a central aspect of his analysis of rationalization and pointed to the *Eigengesetzlichkeit* of the rationalized spheres of the world as the heart of the problem of the personality confronting the modern world.

Finally, a third group of theologians, in reaction to contemporary intellectual developments and challenges, found a haven in the idea of personality as a refuge from the increasing inroads made by empirical science into many of the areas of dogmatic reflection. They sought escape to an inward and personal realm in which technical issues and the imperatives and laws of the natural sciences would have no special validity and in which the realistic and empirical temper of the times could make no advances. This separation of realms was a part of what Kant had intended when he spoke of the two realms of human life and the freedom from the merely natural that was to be found in personality, though Kant's purposes were not escape but reconciliation. Since Kant was seen by many Protestants as the "completer" of the Reformation and even the continuer of Luther's work in a new form, this theological reliance on the Kantian ethos—whose origin was in reason and was hence purely secular—caused no difficulty for the theologians but rather strengthened their position.[15]

Thus the ethical debates among Protestant theologians, in which Weber played a part as an early critic of German social developments, forcefully raised the issue of personality. They challenged the situation of the modern believer in a social world no longer governable by traditional ethical conceptions based on respect for the personality as actor and subject, respect rooted in the experience and privileges of the *Bildungsbürgertum*.

Troeltsch and the Elaboration of Personality

Within the theological tradition there were others who kept the concept of personality from degenerating into an empty ideal. The most important of these was Ernst Troeltsch (1865–1923).[16] He was the most interesting of Weber's contemporaries for whom the notion of personality was of great importance, and he was both an active participant in the debates among the theologians and a close associate of Weber. Troeltsch played an important role in framing the debate over the social ethics of Christianity, the question of the positing and creating of values in the modern world, and the nature, meaning, origin, and importance of personality. He debated theologians over the significance of history for the study of religion and for the meaning and significance of modern theology, and he wrote an extraordinary historical work, *The Social Teaching of the Christian Churches and Groups* (1911), a response to the ethical debates of the theologians. In it Troeltsch maintains that the social theories and social policies of the modern churches must follow the path opened up by Calvinism, for Calvinism showed to all "that the

ethico-religious values of the Christian idea of personality and love are
just as closely bound up with the general assumption of the economic-
political-legal substructure as are all other spiritual and ethical values in
general."[17] Troeltsch relies on the Reformation inheritance, continued
by Kant, to defend a notion of personality that, he suggests, is both historically rooted and still vital.

Apart from social ethics, the consideration of Christianity is important for other reasons: "the cause of freedom and personality" is the key
to the modern world, and this brand of "individualism" was a Christian
legacy, as was the idea of the calling, not the product of the secular
world of the Renaissance.

> It is based . . . on the idea which is essentially Christian, of the destination of
> man to acquire perfected personality through the ascent to God as the source
> both of all personal life and also of the world. . . . It is the metaphysic, herein
> implied, of absolute personality, which directly, or indirectly, permeates our
> whole world and gives to the thought of freedom of personality, of the autono-
> mous self, a metaphysical background, which has its influence even when it is
> contested or denied. This spiritual temper was founded by Christianity and
> Israelite prophecy.[18]

For Troeltsch the permanent attainment of individuality, the creation of
"the spiritual individual of the autonomous personality, filled with objective values, and therefore representing an actual value of its own,"
was a result of the Reformation. Indeed, it was even an effect "not
wholly . . . but still very largely, of medieval Christianity," which in-
cluded elements of both Stoicism and Neoplatonism. The individual
sects and the Reformation ultimately broke through what Troeltsch
calls "the Catholic shell," although such a theory of social life and civilization, "founded upon the values of free personality in union with God,
and of universal human fellowship, was only established with the greatest
difficulty." Thus personality has its roots in the medieval world.[19]

For Troeltsch, a believing Christian, the modern age must look to the
Christian ethos and its "conviction of personality" for a source of
strength and individual heroism: we live "in a general spiritual situation, in which the emotional life is infinitely deepened and refined, and
in which the natural motives for heroism are altogether lost, or else the
attempt is made to try to reawaken them on the side of brutal instinct."
The Christian personality is achieved through "a union of will and the
depths of being with God," and once attained it rises above nature and
the natural self and is the only sure support for individualism in the
Western world. Moreover, the Christian ethos recognizes social differ-

entiation and inequality and yet, "by the inner building up of the personality" and the sense of obligation, transforms this world into "an ethical cosmos." Finally, of course, it provides a goal beyond the relativities of earthly life.[20]

For Troeltsch the idea of personality is at the heart of all moral action. Action based on an "ethical conviction" (*ethische Gesinnung*) is the product of a "unified working through of the complete personality."[21] Conversely the true end of moral action is the "attainment and defense of a free personality, which has its foundations in itself and possesses a certain unity of its own."

> Out of the flux and confusion of the life of the instincts, the unity and compactness of personality has first to be created and acquired. . . . No man is born a personality; everyone has first to make himself into a personality by obedience towards another instinct, which leads to unity and homogeneity. Freedom and creation constitute the secret of personality. . . . It is a creation which takes place in obedience and in devotion to an attraction towards emancipation from merely natural and accidental determination—an attraction to the imperative "ought." . . . So far it is a purely formal aim of independence from mere fate, and of self-determination from within, through the ideal of an internal unity and clarity of our being, which ought to be, and obliges us.[22]

For Troeltsch this picture accurately describes the ethos prevailing in the "literarily educated upper strata" of the modern German world, with their focus on the development of personality and their desire to bind humankind one to another. This ethos is "the Kantian formula, but also at the same time the spirit of Protestantism, indeed of Christianity under the influence of a fully internalized foundation and a this-sided immanent sphere of activity above all."[23] The morality of conscience "originates in the aim of achieving the dignity and unity of the personality, and is therefore purely formal . . . outside time or history." The question of the particular concrete ends or "cultural values" that one must strive toward is a separate and later question.[24]

In *The Social Teaching*, therefore, Troeltsch proposes to raise, among other things, "the question of the inward influence of Christianity upon the sense of personality"; for the "basic idea of the worth of personality and of the unconditioned fellowship of love" was integral to Pauline teaching. Like Kant and Windelband, Troeltsch finds the beginnings of the idea of personality in the later Stoics: they argued for the duty of the will to discern the law of nature and "through this knowledge to achieve the control of the external desires of sense, and also the inward dignity and purity of harmony between the will of man and the ordering of providence, and thus through knowledge to attain the personality which is hidden in God."[25] This overarching Stoic principle was a vehicle of self-transformation, or, better, of self-taming: it imposed harmony and unity on a potentially disharmonious self and put the self into a comfortable relation with Providence. Yet for Troeltsch it is only with the collapse of the militaristic, polytheistic, nationalistic conquering states of antiquity and the rise of the religions of the Middle East that ancient "life values" were transformed and that a new ideal of humanity was developed. "The emphasis on the independence of personality in individuals and the universal idea of humanity is due to Monotheism."[26]

The next stage of this development came in the Reformation. Troeltsch makes a distinction between the Lutheran and Calvinist orientations toward action and faith, as Weber did. Yet for Troeltsch both Luther and Calvin provided an understanding of personality, however different their results. Luther emphasized freedom and personality, the priesthood of all believers, and the preservation of faith and the state of grace. He fostered "the cultivation of the emotional life of the individual . . . the maintenance of the sense of an unmerited happiness." The Lutheran's main sentiment "is one of loving self-surrender to God and a loving self-giving to his neighbor." In the Lutheran ecclesiastical ideal, the central importance of practical achievement was replaced by "the supreme decisive power of a personal 'heart-faith' in the forgiveness of sins."[27]

But Calvin refused to emphasize this emotional side of the relation to God and dismissed the constant preoccupation with personal moods and feelings as unnecessary. Indeed, it was Calvin's intention to place God in the foreground, directing attention away from the self toward concrete aims and purposes. The Calvinist was "alone with God and his own soul," feeling within himself the "grace of election," and the effect of this experience on the mind of the Calvinist differed greatly from the Lutheran experience. To Calvin the chief point was not "the self-centred personal salvation of the creature, and the universality of the divine will of love, but it was, rather, the glory of God." Thus, as an elect person, "the individual has no value of his own; as an instrument to be used for the tasks of the Kingdom of God, his value is immense." Hence justification by faith does not lead to an *unio mystica* and a quietistic repose of a Lutheran kind but is the source of a method of activity and a spur to action. "The will, with which the soul has to do, is active." The Calvinist "is filled with a deep consciousness of his own value as a person, with the high sense of a divine mission to the world, of being mercifully privileged."

The Calvinist elect struggle to become independent of all that is "creaturely" through a severe self-control attained by "ascribing all individual personality and its achievement to the working out of predestination," for "this idea of personality . . . arises out of the idea of predestination." All that is secular is reduced to a means through rigorous disciplining of the instinctive life, the destruction of instinctual feeling, and the placing of limits on sensual life in general. Though the most severe self-condemnation is the foundation of this experience, the elect experience themselves as part of a spiritual aristocracy, detached and aloof from all that is secular and creaturely. Moreover, despite the focus on action and acquiring distance from feeling, the value of moral achievement in Calvinism does not lie in the doing of particular actions and deeds "but in the spirit in the whole personality, generated by faith, in the total change of heart effected by conversion," a notion similar to the secular formulation Kant gave to this phenomenon.

Still, Calvinism views existing conditions as divine ordinances to which all must submit and in which a spiritual minority of the holiest must rule. "Within these limits, however, Calvinism gives a value to the personality of the elect soul which is thoroughly in harmony with the idea of Kant, while in this respect Luther tends to remain within the range of ideas controlled by mysticism." Calvin's own mind was "characterized by the highest sense of duty towards an objective task in life, a sense of duty which does not consider the feelings and inclinations of the individual but which concentrates entirely upon work for God"— another link with Kant.[28] The Calvinist ethos, then, has led historically to a "strong emphasis upon personality" and to an "intensification of the sense of personality," rather than to an altogether unique conception.[29]

In Troeltsch's analyses, then, we find a thorough recognition of the power of personality and of its continued value in the modern world— rooted, however, in an originally religious experience. Personality is constructed *against* a natural self of desire, built around service to an impersonal task and hence serving an impersonal higher power. This service takes the form of asceticism, involving active self-denial within one's calling and allowing the overcoming both of "natural man" and of the devil. A stronger agreement with Weber could not be found.

In the discourse of Weber's contemporaries, therefore, following from the tradition of the Reformation, from Kant, and from Goethe, we find the importance of personality expressed in a variety of forms and contexts. This discourse of self and personality both within the older tradition and the contemporary debates forms the background to Weber's analyses of personality in the setting of his methodological reflections and religious sociology.

The Concept of Personality in Weber's Sociology of Religion

Personality and the Occidental Self

While he was working on *The Protestant Ethic,* Weber provided his earliest discussion of personality and of the ideal type of the rational self in his methodological essay on Roscher and Knies.[30] In considering the nature of the free actor and of free action, Weber draws on the Kantian distinction between the realm of personality and the realm of nature. For Weber freedom resides in a situation where the "decision" for an action is based on grounds of the actor's "own . . . *deliberations,*" not disturbed by "'external' constraint or irresistible 'affect.'" This means that an actor is free when he is unimpeded by inner feeling or external limits and relies on a rational analysis of means and ends in his deliberation or in performing his action. Furthermore, the more free a person's action is, and thus the more a person's "constant will" is at work—to borrow Windelband's terminology—the less action has the character of a "natural event," and the more appropriate it is to use the concept of personality for such an actor. "Personality" is a concept "that finds its 'essence' in the constancy of its inner relation to specific ultimate 'values' and life 'meanings,' which it stamps into purposes in its activities and thus translates into teleological-rational action." Ultimate values, an "inner" relation to these values, constant will, and rational action are thus the hallmarks of personality. Weber sets this conception against the "romantic-naturalistic" notion of personality maintained, for example, by the *völkisch* thinkers. They find the essence of personality not in freedom but in nature, in the "vegetative 'underground' of personal life," in the "irrationality" of forces affecting temperament and the development of mood and feeling. Their notion is ultimately psychophysical[31] and inverts the proper sense of personality, seeking its essence in a kind of inner "necessity" rather than in the freedom of rational "submission" to what is highest.

Weber here lays out a Kantian version of the personality in which it is opposed to, or rather lifted above, nature and merely natural determinations. It translates higher values into rational action; yet it is constrained by factors in the social world dictating the limits and possibilities of such action. Unlike Kant, however, for whom the dictates of pure practical reason determine the self as personality, Weber states that the "innermost elements" of personality—"the highest and ultimate value judgments, which determine our action and give to our life meaning and significance"—determine the self. Indeed, it is not reason and obedience to reason's laws in the first instance that are the hallmark of personality; rather, "the worth of 'personality' lies settled surely in the fact that for it there are values to which it connects its own life." These values cannot be ascertained or derived by reason but are developed in the "struggle against the difficulties of life." Further, "to *judge* the *validity* of such values is a matter of *belief*," not of reason, pure or otherwise, or of scientific judgment,[32] though philosophy and other efforts at the interpretation of life need not give up the search for meaning. Weber effectively adopts this understanding of personality, though not yet the Goethean stress on duty and renunciation; moreover, he has shorn the concept of any Kantian conviction concerning the possibility of giving oneself the moral law based on pure practical reason and the categorical imperative. It is not clear here whether his original inspiration stemmed from the Puritans or not.

In *The Protestant Ethic,* contemporaneous with these methodological reflections, Weber draws on Windelband, giving the beginnings of a historical account of the effect on the shaping of the self of the Calvinist ethos rooted in predestination and realized in the calling.

> The Puritan—like every "rational"—asceticism worked to enable man to maintain and realize [*zur Geltung zu bringen*] his "constant motives," especially those that it itself "trained" [*einübte*] in him against the "affects": thereby educating [*erziehen*] him, therefore, into a "personality" in *this* formal-psychological sense of the word.[33]

Though the Puritans did not use the concept, they nonetheless achieved its "essence." Personality is, by this account, a product of creating within the person and then strengthening one or a set of "constant motives" or purposes, or, in Weber's later formulation, "serving" ultimate values. These values are mobilized against feeling and the life of sense and desire, and the person not only supports or upholds them but actively works to realize them. This concept stresses conscious but impersonal purposes and ideals over feeling and the "natural" self, as well as action and realization of ideals in impersonal service. It opposes all forms of contemplation and self-absorption as well as all forms of action to realize purposes derived purely from the natural self. All Occidental forms of personality are, for Weber, essentially ascetic, built on conquest of the affective self and oriented toward fulfillment in the world through service of the ideals or motives that have gained hegemony within the person. Thus it is not surprising that Weber stresses the importance of the "primacy of the will." Internal hegemony becomes the foundation for the attempt to make the motives externally hegemonic in the world.

The merely formal sense of personality must be given concrete content by the specific ideals, values, or motives that the person makes the object of his action and interest, whether derived from religion and its promise of salvation or from any other more secular source. Whatever the value or object or law one adopts, personality lies in subjecting the self to it and taming desire, feelings, inclination, vanity, and the natural self—that is, subjugating the "person," who is otherwise subject to the senses. For Weber, as for Calvin and Kant,[34] the task and the submission to *its* "law" are the source of personality and of the elevation of the self above the chaos and heteronomy of the conflicting value spheres "below." The "objective task" is an ultimate task set by God or chosen by oneself. The law of that task is the set of imperatives prescribed by one's ideal or goal and served systematically in the calling. For Calvin work for God alone provides that objective task. For Kant it is the pure practical laws of reason prescribed to itself. For Weber it is the laws derived from one's ultimate ideal. But in all three cases the structure of personality is the same. Thus Weber's view, like that of Reformation Christianity and idealist philosophers, is that humankind dwells in two spheres. Misunderstandings of personality must be combatted, for they deflect people from a correct understanding of the proper object and prevent them from transcending the world below for the "higher" realm, whatever it may be.

This formal notion of personality, given its original form, special power, and orientation by ascetic Protestantism, makes up the core of what we can call the Occidental self. By the time of his studies on religion in *Economy and Society* (1910–11) and in the *Economic Ethics of the World Religions* (1915–19), Weber had a more systematic understanding of the nature and significance of personality, and he used it to explore its distinctive Western sense. Rooted originally in religious experience, personality involves for the self "a systematization from within, and moving outward from a center, that the individual has himself achieved." It means that the person becomes a "systematic unity," "a whole," not just "a combination of useful particular qualities"; nor are his actions merely "a series of occurrences." In one place Weber says that "this striving toward unity from within [*von innen heraus*]" is what "we associate with the concept of 'personality,'" whereas in a later work he adds that the "unified systematization of life conduct" is "usually described as 'ethical personality.'" Being a personality means, in general, having an "an 'inner core' [*einer 'von Innen heraus'*], an altogether regulated unity of life conduct, deriving from some central point of view [*Stellungnahme*] of one's own." [35]

Though Weber speaks occasionally of the possibility of the existence of personality outside the West, specifically in Asia, it is the notion of the ethical personality that is distinctively Western. It has been uniquely effective, for the "Occidental ideal of actively acting 'personality,' based . . . on a center, be it religious concerning the beyond, be it inner-worldly," is unknown to and would be disapproved of by all the religions of Asia. "At the foundation of all specifically Occidental meaning of 'personality'" is the idea that "through simple action according to 'the demand of the day'" one may achieve the right "relation to the real world." But Weber goes on to add another dimension: we cannot find elsewhere in the world "the effort according to the Occidental manner to pull oneself out of the swamp by the forelock and to make oneself into a 'personality,' through the hunt after what exactly, and to this individual only, is specific and unique, in contrast to all others." Personality is normally identified with a structure of self potentially universal, which transcends the particularity of human desires, needs, and wants; transcendence is on behalf of something taken to be true for all humankind—in the case of the commands of God—or is based on a trait and endowment common to all rational beings, as in the case of pure reason. But here personality is linked to the capacity for individuation through the discovery of what is unique to the self, a capacity, he is convinced, that Asian religious culture does not provide. This capacity for differentiation is linked to the individualization derived from the Reformation legacy of the personal relationship to God, as Troeltsch described it; it is also mirrored in Weber's secularization of that legacy in the capacity of the individual to choose his ultimate ideal and serve it with all his being. The implication of this other element is that Asian religions do not permit, among other things, a differentiation of the self from the mass of human beings. That must be why Weber can say that a "rational practical ethic" and an "'inner-worldly' autonomous life methodology

of Occidental character," both of which flow from the achievement of
"ethical personality," is the unique achievement of the West and was not
possible anywhere else for a variety of reasons.[36]

Though many groups throughout the world, religious and secular,
were "'wakeful' and always in hand, ever restrained and steady ['*Wach*'
und immer bei sich, stets behersscht und gleichmässig]," Puritan "wakeful restraint" had a different foundation from the wakefulness of other
groups. It derived from "the necessity of the subjugation of the creaturely under rational order and methodicalness in the interest of one's
own certainty of salvation."[37] As a consequence Weber concludes that
significant practical influence of a religious search for salvation is most
likely when it derives from the "creation of a 'life-conduct,' specifically
determined religiously, held together through a central meaning or a
positive goal . . . a systematization of practical action in the form of its
orientation toward unified values."[38] The specifically Puritan influence
is related to the dogmatically articulated experience of predestination
and its effect on the creation of an "ethical total personality" oriented to
ascetic action; it is also related to the calling as the vehicle of this asceticism and of the search for salvation.

Belief in providence and predestination is specifically an experience
of the religions of Asia Minor and the West, particularly Islam and Calvinism, and is radically opposed to all notions of magic that hope to
influence God's choice. The particular importance of predestination, to
Weber, is that it can give the believer the highest possible sense of certainty of salvation, provided the believer can assure himself of belonging
among the elect, whom Weber calls the "aristocracy of salvation." Their
election is only ascertainable by the presence of indications or symp-
toms of the appropriate "charisma," that is, the God-derived power of
action in the world, which assures the believer that he is God's "tool"
in the fulfillment of divine purposes in a "continuous and methodical"
way. The sanctification experienced by the Puritan believer was the
product of "the consciousness of a central unitary relation of this his
short life to the supramundane God and his will. . . . Only the life lived
according to firm principles, regulated from a unitary center, could
count as God-willed." Thus Puritanism placed a tremendous premium
precisely on the transformation of the self into a unified personality. But
the specific and exceptional fact about this capacity for the service of
God's will is the role of the personality: it is as a whole, expressed in
action, that the individual is saved or condemned, not through the sin-
fulness of particular actions or the holiness of particular "good works."
What is important are not

individual offences—which happen to the predestinated person as a creature like all sinners—but the knowledge that it is not these offences that give assurance of salvation and of the persistance of grace, but the God-willed action flowing out of the actual inner relation to God, established through the mysterious relation to grace, therefore, through the central and constant quality of the personality.[39]

"Total behavior" was thus the central concern of Puritan ethics,[40] not the individual moments or deeds of that behavior, whether good or bad—though of course no amount of ethical behavior could win salvation. Evidently the path to integration and systematization of total behavior for the Puritans had to proceed through the "total personality."

For under all circumstances, the determinism of predestination was a means of the most intensive conceivable systematic centralization of the "ethic of conviction" [Gesinnungsethik]. The "total personality," as we would say today, has been provided with the accent of eternal value through "divine election," not through any individual action.[41]

In his discussion of other Christian paths to salvation, specifically salvation through the believer's "social achievements"—good works—Weber attempts to clarify the meaning of the Puritan Gesinnungsethik, even though Calvinism ignores good works and relies on salvation from an outside and higher agency. There are, he suggests, two forms of the systematization of an ethic of good works. In the first form the particular actions of individuals, whether good or evil, are "evaluated singly and are credited positively or negatively to the one needing salvation . . . whose religious destiny depends on his actual achievements in their relation to one another." This standpoint is found in Zoroastrianism, Hinduism, and popular Judaism, and a form of this ethos appears in Roman Catholicism and the Oriental Christian churches. In Catholicism, which looks to intention as the source of the ethical evaluation of action, "the intentio . . . is not a unitary quality of personality, whose expression is action," but rather the "thought [Meinung] behind the concrete individual action." For Catholicism, then, conduct of life "remains an ethically unmethodical one-after-another of individual actions." The notion of rebirth in the Puritan meaning—rebirth in this life through faith—"in the strict sense of an ethic of conviction [Gesinnungsethik]," cannot, therefore, be the consequence of an approach like the Catholic one, despite the original Pauline stress on rebirth.[42]

The second form of systematization is oriented not to winning salvation but to winning a sense of certainty. It includes the ascetic religious response of Calvinism and considers the "essence" of the person, treat-

ing individual achievement only "as symptom and expression of a corresponding ethical total personality that is manifested therein." The ethical action of such a person is derived

> "from the totality of his essence," as we would express it. Religiously ap-
> plied, it means: in place of formal sanctification by works through external
> individual achievements, there comes here . . . the value of the personal total
> pattern [*Gesamthabitus*]. . . . In any case, however, the manner of the indi-
> vidual action then matters ultimately only as far as it has truly "sympto-
> matic" character, but not if it is a product of "accident."

This is the foundation of all forms of *Gesinnungsethik,* which Roth and
Wittich translate as "ethic of inwardness" and which is "generally the
specific form of ethical rigorism." It leads to, or may derive from, a "rational *methodical* direction of the whole of life conduct." Yet it makes
the social-ethical significance of action of secondary importance, for it
implies that the religious effort centered on the *person* is of utmost importance: works are a means of "self-perfection" broadly understood,
not of salvation.[43]

Thus it is not really the self as constituted or as given in nature that is
elevated here to a position of value in its own terms; rather, that self is
taken as the object, or raw material, of the believer's work and efforts.
Salvation is achieved through the transformation of the self, either by its
unification with the deity in a mystic sense (which is possible in some
religions) or its availability as an "instrument" for godly purposes in an
ascetic sense (which is the Calvinist possibility). Thus actions and rational methodical life conduct, oriented toward the "perfection of self,"
can become a "method of salvation", but only in the sense, for Calvinism, of expressing the grace of God and carrying out his tasks.

For Weber, despite the many forms of self-shaping manifested in the
various religious cultures of the world, the Puritan "transformation of
self" was unique in its capacity to structure a special kind of personality, or, as he sometimes suggests, the *only* kind of personality: formed
from the subjugation and unification of self under the dominance of a
higher value, usually sacred or divine. Yet it is not only this unity that is
notable for Weber but also its mobilization in the direction of sanctified
or "pious" action undertaken as the fruits of a rational methodical service of the higher value. Historically this mobilization has been able to
initiate change and overcome the weight and resistance of tradition in
economics and politics. Though there are individual examples of such
action throughout history, such an ethos is only possible in a wide-

spread, sustained, and consistent way, in Weber's view, in the modern Western world, that is, the world after the Reformation. This ethos contrasts not only with the ethos of Catholicism and the other Western religions but also with the ethos of the now-displaced aristocracy in its greater concern with "being" than with "doing," an ethos we will discuss later.

What accounts for the uniqueness of Puritanism in the shaping of the self into personality? Why is the situation of self-transformation in other religious cultures so different? To answer these questions we must consider how the salvation religions generally have shaped the self toward purposes of both the beyond and the here and now, and specifically how the differences between the religions of the Occident and Orient have produced such different consequences. We must discover how this kind of ascetic religious virtuosity, channeled into calling and rooted in personality, could have emerged in the West alone, whereas the "selves" of the East took a different form and had a different effect and power.

Occidental and Oriental Religious Culture

The Occidental personality can be understood only by examining a number of details: first, the structures of Occidental religions as opposed to those of the Orient;[44] second, the distinctive ways Christianity distinguished itself from both Islam and Judaism; and third, the way ascetic Protestantism was able to extend the field of asceticism—thus distinguishing itself from the rest of Christianity—while heightening the need to transform the self into an instrument for unified methodical service of godly purposes. Only ascetic Protestantism created generalized motivations to seek salvation through exertion (*Bemühung*) in the calling and sanctified inner-worldly ascetic and profitable work. For Weber only this unifying discipline actually produces personality in the truest sense; and only these personalities, perfected by and acting through the calling, ever helped on a substantial scale to create the "spirit of capitalism." No such personalities and no such spirit could have emerged from the "adaptation to the world" of Confucianism, the "rejection of the world" of Buddhism, the "magic garden" and traditional vocational ethic of Hinduism, the "rule of the world" and feudal enjoyment of Islam, the hopes and economic law of a "pariah" people like the Jews, or the institutional grace and double ethic of Catholicism.[45] The principal factors that account for the emergence of personality out of ascetic Protestantism in Weber's work are, first, faith in a transcendental God; second, the power and persuasiveness of an "ethical" or emissary prophecy that permitted the unification of life conduct in subservience to a single supreme and holy ideal; third, the lack of "institutional grace," which forces the believer to seek salvation in domination and mastery of the self; and fourth, the stress on active asceticism as the only way to "prove" one's faith or salvation.

The primary difference in historical consequence between the salvation religions of the West and of the East is that the former eventuated generally in asceticism and the latter in contemplation. In Christianity, in particular, there was an "inner selection of motives" leading toward active conduct, usually of an ascetic kind; these tendencies were present from the start, not just from the advent of ascetic Protestantism. In these motives lie the original sources of what was later to become personality. Weber stresses five features in accounting for the difference between East and West.[46] The first and most important is "the conception of a transcendental, absolutely all-powerful God"—a "personal" God, which arose in Asia Minor alone and was imposed on the West—coupled with the "creatureliness" of the world created by him out of nothing. The distance between this God and his creation put a limit on the possibility of mystical possession of the deity or self-deification. All salvation, therefore, had to have the character of "an ethical 'justification' [*Rechtfertigung*] before that God, which was to be accomplished and proved only through some sort of active conduct." The second feature, parallel but in contrast to the first, is that Eastern religions in general were "pure religions of intellectuals," with either an impersonal God or one that stood within the world. This intellectual stratum strove to make the world "meaningful" (*Sinnhaftig*); human intellectual mastery could lead to a grasp of the world's nature and of God, in a universe where nature and God reflect one another and are in harmony. This path was impossible for the West, for a perfect God was understood to have created an imperfect world, and nothing in that imperfect world could so grasp the deity or his creation. Hence meaning could never be the direct focus of religious pursuit.[47] Third, the existence of rational Roman law in the West, carried over into the religious sphere, made it possible to describe one's relation to the personal God as "a kind of legally definable relation of subjection [*Untertanenverhältnis*]" with bonds of duty and obligation, something not possible in the East, where piety took a pantheistic form. Fourth, both Rome in its opposition to the cults of the

Greeks and Judaism in its opposition to Mediterranean cults opposed "ecstasy" as a path to salvation; this led to an emphasis on practical rationalism, later confirmed in the development of rationalism within monasticism and of work as the principal means to asceticism. Fifth and finally, the existence of a terrestrial, "monarchical" head of the church in the West, with a centralized control of piety, made the Western development of rational approaches to work unique. "Only in the Occident did the other-worldly asceticism of the monks, where they became the disciplined troops of a rational bureaucracy of office, become systematized increasingly into a methodology of active rational life conduct." Ultimately, Weber notes, ascetic Protestantism took the last step of bringing this rational asceticism into the world. Thus we can say that Protestantism generalized the possibility of personality achieved and fulfilled through sanctified action.

The "tension" (*Spannung*) between a supramundane or transcendental God and his will, on the one hand, and the "orders" of the world, on the other, leads to an active and ascetic "specialized" approach to life in the world; it also leads to an "ethic of calling," where the believer acquires the qualities that God demands and makes himself into a focused instrument or tool (*Werkzeug*) of godly purposes.[48] This tension is crucial for the creation of personality, for it motivates the conquest of self and world. The worldly ascetic produced by such tension becomes a systematic rationalist. He not only rejects the ethically irrational, aesthetic, or emotional, which are attractive to the natural self: his goal is above all "'wakeful' [*wache*] methodical control [*Beherrschung*] of his own life conduct." He seeks "triumph" not only over the world but, more important, over the self and the "temptations with which he has always and again to struggle actively." For the ascetic "the certainty of his salvation always proves itself in rational action, clear-cut in meaning, means, and end, according to principles and rules." According to Weber, inner-worldly asceticism reached its peak in the experience of Calvinism and the remoteness and inexplicability of the Calvinist God. But in Calvinism the believer is more than a "tool" of God; he becomes a "warrior for God" (*Gotteskämpfer*), a soldier engaged in battle, and his battlefield is as much the natural self as it is the world. For the religious man of vocation, as for the soldier, the question of meaning is moot.

> The inner-worldly ascetic is thereby the acknowledged [*gegebene*] "man of vocation," who does not ask or need to ask after the meaning of the concrete practice of his calling within the *whole* world—for which not he, but his

God carries the responsibility. . . . for him the consciousness is enough to execute in his personal rational action in this world what is for him in its ultimate meaning the unsearchable will of God.[49]

Yet the ascetic heart of the new personality is not attainable by everyone. It is possible only for those capable of transcending and mastering given human nature and the natural self in a consistent, systematic, and enduring way. "Methodologies of sanctification" tend to separate those who are religiously "qualified"—capable of ethical justification before God—from those who are unqualified, that is, unable to maintain the constancy of motive, inner purpose, and service that alone allows salvation to be provable. Hence what Weber calls "religious virtuosi" become a status group within the community of the faithful, and the methodical doctrine of sanctification becomes an ethic only of these virtuosi, the new "aristocrats" of the faith. The qualified ascetic may be able to master the world, unify and dominate the self, and maintain a constant calling, but he cannot "raise the religious endowment" of the average person, enabling him to be more capable of sanctification.[50] The "warriors of God" are an exclusive group; not all can be of their number. Hence both religious asceticism and the personality that it makes possible through disciplined service in the calling are possible not as mass solutions but only as a path for an unusual and capable elite. There can be no guarantee that ascetic pursuits and disciplined behavior will be consistently and fully possible for others.

But what is the source of the religious promises, the goals of salvation, the ultimate ideals around which the ascetics of the spirit, the new personalities, have generally organized and subdued the self? In the history of religion, Weber says, that source has been prophecy. Indeed, it is precisely the disappearance of prophecy in the modern world that will make it so difficult for the new "aristocrats of the spirit" of Weber's time to find the ultimate organizing values and discipline that will allow their own transformation into personalities and "soldiers" of a new faith. Only in the Near East did there emerge the type of prophecy that gave the self the ethical focus that could empower it both for action and for self-domination.[51] This is the "ethical" or "emissary" prophet, who announced a divine mission or ethical duty of obedience and who is different from the "exemplary" prophets of Asia, who demonstrated the way to salvation by personal example. Speaking of prophecy in general, Weber says: "A true prophecy creates a systematic orientation of life conduct toward *one* measure of value from within [*von innen heraus*], over against which the 'world' serves as material to be formed ethically according to the norm."[52] Prophecy of either kind involves for both the prophet and his followers "a unified configuration of life, won through a consciously *unified, meaningful* position toward it." It means "orientation of life conduct toward the striving after a sacred value [*Heilsgut*]." The life of man and of the world are given "a specific systematic unified 'meaning,'" and human life "must be oriented to it and through the relation to it must be unifiably, meaningfully formed." This always means "an attempt at the systematization of all manifestations of life," with the intention of organizing practical life into a *"life direction [Lebensführung]."* This systematization leads to the tensions both in the "inner conduct of life" and between the individual and the world.[53]

These, then, are the elements we can extract from Weber's account, and they constitute the nature of personality for him: first, unification and systematization of life on the basis of an ultimate and sacred value, usually provided by prophecy; second, ascetic conduct, built on the subjugation of the natural self that faith in the value makes necessary but only strength of character makes possible; third, an orientation toward the realization or service of the value in practical action and the making over of the world, embodied in fighting as a soldier of God on the battlefields of self and world; and fourth, a channeling of human energies and purposes through the discipline of the calling.

Models of Self and Personality in the Orient

Weber sets this unique Occidental development of personality against models of self and meaning within other religious cultures and within the world of the aristocracy. The other models are not invariably judged to be failures or "negative" when compared to the modern West; still, their "shortcomings" vis-à-vis the Occidental personality and its power and possibilities are manifest everywhere in Weber's work, especially from the point of view of the strength with which they endow adherents for action in the world. Weber's examination of the world religions, of course, was undertaken for the purpose of discovering what role these religions played in encouraging or preventing the emergence of capitalist development; it offered him a comparative test of his thesis concerning the role of Protestantism in the development of the spirit of capitalism. But in this examination Weber provides the raw material for a deeper appreciation of the nature and role of personality in general. We have noted already the general differences between Western and Eastern religions. A more detailed review of these other religions and models highlights the importance of the conception of the modern Occidental personality to Weber's analyses of social action and development.

According to Weber, although Confucianism, the most important religion of China, does develop the personality, it does so in a way entirely different from the West. Confucianism was originally the "status ethic" of a group of officials, possessors of feudal prebends, who were essentially secular and rationalistic. Their ideal was the "gentleman" educated in aesthetics and literature who devoted his life to the study of the classics. Chinese religious development, according to Weber, was determined in China by the lack of a supramundane God and of a tradition of ethical prophecy. "A tension against the 'world' never emerged, because an ethical prophecy of a supramundane God posing ethical *demands* was fully missing, as far back as memory serves." Nor did the appearance of "spirits" raising demands substitute for this lack, for they always raised specific demands, "never the inner formation of the personality *as such* and its life conduct." "*Never* has the Chinese 'soul' been revolutionized through a prophet." There was, hence, no tension between God and the natural world, between ethical demand and human failing; thus there was no leverage for influencing conduct through the generation of "*inner* forces that were not purely traditionally and conventionally bound." Confucian duties always consisted of expressions of piety toward living or dead relatives and ancestors, "never toward a supramundane God and *therefore* never toward a holy 'object' [*Sache*] or 'idea.'" Thus the central foundation of Occidental personality was missing. "The Confucian was lacking the central rational methodology of life of the classical Puritan, religiously determined from within."

The Confucian, on the one hand, used philosophical-literary education as the means to his goal: self-perfection through adaptation to the eternal order, wakeful self-control, and the repression of whatever irrational passions might shake inner harmony. These means were used to preserve the "propriety" that molds the gentleman into a personality. The Puritan, on the other hand, strove "to master the influences and impressions of the world as much as himself through a definite and one-sidedly oriented rational will"; the Confucian did not. "The narrowing and repression of the natural life of desire [*Trieblebens*], which the strict volitional ethical rationalization brought with it and which was bred into the Puritan, was alien to the Confucian." The Confucian individual ideal was "the shaping of the self to an all-sided harmoniously balanced personality"—not unlike the eighteenth-century ideal of *Bildung* in

Germany. Only in a bureaucratic office, free to immerse himself in the wisdom of the classics, could the Confucian pursue the "perfection of personality" to which he was devoted: striving for universality [*Allseitigkeit*] or well-roundedness, not for specialized service in a calling. This goal was quite clearly opposed to the ethos of the Occidental ascetic. The refined man, or gentleman, was absolutely not a tool or a means for any useful purpose specified by God or a prophet; he was, rather, an "end in himself [*ein letzter Selbstzweck*]." Further, in China the value and worth of personality derived not from working out one's task and salvation alone but from proving oneself within a group of similarly qualified associates. Thus what we can call the "witness" to one's conduct and self was completely different, and decisive for the difference, from Puritanism. "For the supramundane all-knowing God observed the central inner disposition [*Habitus*], whereas the world, on the contrary, to which the Confucian adapted himself observed only the graceful gesture." Consequently the Confucian personality, unlike the Puritan, was not shaped from the "inside" standing against the world but from the "outside," not from a unified core but as an "adaptation" to the world. The Confucian is missing precisely such an inner core, a central and autonomous value that dictates life conduct.

> An optimally adapted man, rationalizing in his life conduct *only* in the measure required for adaptation, is . . . no systematic unity but a combination of useful particular qualities. . . . Where all reaching beyond this world is lacking, so must all independent weight against the world be wanting. Domestication of the masses and good conduct of the gentleman could thereby emerge. But the style that [Confucianism] lent to life conduct must remain characterized through essentially negative elements and could not let arise any striving toward unity from within [*von innen heraus*], which we connect with the concept of "personality." Life remained a series of occurrences, not a whole placed methodically under a transcendental goal.[54]

In specifying these facts, Weber is implying an interesting and problematical theory of social innovation. When he says, "Where all reaching beyond this world is lacking, so must all independent weight against the world be wanting," he is indicating his conviction that one cannot ground individual strength within the world alone, even in alliance with associates. If one desires to generate the strength and force needed to overcome the resistance of the world, one must find a "transcendental" ideal that goes beyond the immanent. Or, at the least, one must find a relation to one's ideal that can draw on the same power or leverage that the striving after other-worldly ideals has provided in the past.

Occidental personality is thus associated with a "positive" ethos: the striving for unity created "from within" allows for the subjugation of the natural self in a methodical manner under the domination of a higher goal. Despite the fact that he has noted the Confucian effort to dominate all passion that might ruffle serenity, one element of "ethical personality," Weber suggests that Confucian personality is still "negative": it does not permit unity or striving of the Occidental type but leaves the personality in the form of a disconnected "series" of acts and events striving only to adapt to the world as it is. What makes Confucian personality structure essentially negative in Weber's view is, first, its lack of an overarching transcendental goal, which alone can inspire the individual toward self-transformation "from within"; second, the lack of an ethical tension with the world to motivate the self to conquer itself and the world; and, finally, the presence of an ethos that calls for self-perfection and sees the self as an "end in itself." Whatever else Confucianism could accomplish, it could never, according to Weber, lead to a transformation of the social order or allow the development of an inner strength to make possible the overcoming of the weight of the world and its traditions on behalf of goals posited or defended from within. We can say that Confucianism was, in this sense, an ethos of readers, not innovators; of beautiful gestures, not actors; of gentlemen, not real personalities.

In South Asia too there were obstacles to the emergence of an ethos and of a personality of the modern Occidental kind. Buddhism, for example, was originally the religion of a group of contemplative mendicant monks with their own religious "technology" who rejected life within the orders of the world, lived a life of migration, and treated all other followers of their beliefs as laymen. A creation of intellectuals based on the teachings of an exemplary prophet who rejected the world as unworthy of one's engagement, Buddhism rejected rational purposive activity, for it led away from salvation. Indeed, according to Weber, all of the mass religions of Asia accepted the world as eternally given as it was; there was thus no "tension," and hence no motive, to transform the world in accordance with any divine commands. In Buddhism there is no deity, no savior, no prayer, no religious grace, no eternal life, and no predestination. The field of attention is focused exclusively on the individual and his psychic state. Buddhism seeks wakeful self-control of all natural drives and the achievement of a psychic state remote from any activity or proof through work and entirely free from passion or desire. All passion is on an equal, and negative, footing: thus hatred is no more a threat to salvation than love, and "the passionately active devotion to ideals" is as much an obstacle to salvation as malice. In Buddhism, as in Puritanism, salvation is a purely personal act of the single individual, unconnected to any of the status obligations and possibilities offered by, say, Confucianism. Because it accepts the doctrine of *karma,* which Weber defines as "the universal causality of ethical recompense," Buddhism maintains that one forges one's ultimate destiny through the consequences of one's own conduct. Most important, according to Weber, "it is not the 'personality' but the meaning and value of the *single* act" on which the karma doctrine bases itself: "no single world-bound action can get lost in the cosmic causality that comes out ethically meaningful, but completely impersonal." [55] Thus the essential feature of Occidental personality—an inner core or center from which all acts flow—is missing in Buddhism. Despite its asceticism and its subjugation of the self through the overcoming of desire, the theodicy of Buddhism is concerned with individual acts rather than with the unified unique personality as a whole. Once again the leverage over the world and the self that comes from an ethical prophecy with its demands is missing, though there have been few disciplines for the overcoming of the natural self more demanding than Buddhism.

Hinduism's "carriers," according to Weber, were originally a hereditary caste of genteel and cultured literati, the Brahmans, whose magical charisma, like the Confucians', rested on their possession of sacred knowledge; later non-Brahmanic ascetic sects gained influence in India, followed by the appearance of a sacramental savior religion. Hindu philosophy and religion depend on a belief in the soul and on two other beliefs: the transmigration of souls (*samsara*) and the certainty of ethical compensation (karma). For Hinduism, as for Buddhism, there is an automatic functioning of the ethical process, and no consequences of actions are ever "lost" or unexperienced. But Hinduism makes ritualistic purity its central demand. Once again there is no election by divine grace of any kind, and each individual creates his own destiny exclusively. According to Weber, Hinduism actually provides choice among a variety of possible holy ends toward which a believer may strive, and the means appropriate for the religious life depend on which end is sought. Ultimately, however, knowledge, whether mystical or literary, is the path to the highest holiness and the means of domination over the self and the world. Thus Hinduism strives to find the meaning and significance of the world and life rather than leaving such issues to a supramundane creator. Despite the opposition of the godly and the world, which did emerge in South Asia—an opposition that conditioned the systematization of life conduct in the West, namely, the "ethical personality"—Weber maintains that for the Hindu approach to knowledge and mysticism an "'inner-worldly' autonomous life methodology of Occidental character was . . . not possible."

Hinduism could never accept the notion that one could find salvation through acting to meet the "demands of the day," which Weber considers "the basis of all the specific Occidental meaning of 'personality.'" Moreover, despite the significance of life in this world for reincarnation, Asiatic thought could never associate "eternal" punishment and rewards with the transitory deeds of this world and the demands and punishments of an all-powerful God. Thus, though it could be said to have a conception of personality, Hinduism could never give to life on earth the kind of significance, and hence the kind of tension and leverage, that the West found in its own notions of the beyond. Nor could the highly ritualized and ceremonial structure of religion ever lead to the search for the unique individual self of the Occidental type.

> All Asiatic, highly developed intellectual soteriologies would reject the Occidental ideal of actively acting "personality" resting on a center, be it an other-worldly religious center, or be it inner-worldly, either as in itself ultimately contradictory or as one-sidedly philistine and specialized, or as barbaric greediness for life. Where it is not the beauty of the traditional gesture purely as such, sublimated through the refinement of the salons, as in Confucianism, then it is the realm behind the world, of salvation from the transitory, to which all the highest interests point and from which the "personality" receives its worth.

Apart from the ritualistic and ceremonial demands, however, there is, in fact, an important place in Hinduism for "identity" through work. Indeed, transmigration depends on the faithful execution of one's "vocation" within the caste system. The crafts within the system obtained a religious sanction, and its members were essentially "assigned" their special mission in life by the god or will governing the craft. According to Weber, Hindu law has an "organic, traditionalist ethic of vocation," similar to the medieval Catholic ethic but more consistent. Thus Hinduism solves the problem of the tension between its demands and the unethical powers of this world through "the relativizing and differentiating of ethics in the form of 'organic' (as opposed to ascetic) *ethics of vocation*." Hence there are no absolutely unethical callings in the world. Callings or castes are providentially ordained, and there are different ethical obligations and different functions for each. Moreover, only devotion to one's calling and remaining in it can guarantee the fulfillment of the Hindu promise of rebirth. The social theory of Hinduism thus elaborates a *dharma,* or law, for each calling, from war to prostitution, and in this it is opposed to the antispecialization of Confucianism, but it had no reason to provide principles for an ethical universalism that could raise general demands on the self and the world. "There was no universally valid ethic, but throughout only a private and social ethic separated by status," leading to different ethical codes for different status groups and hence the absolute relativizing of all ethical commandments and emphasis on adherence to the particular ethos. Moreover, what grace there is is reserved for those who perform their tasks without regard for results and without personal interest in their own acts. "Asceticism and sacrifice too are only valuable for salvation when one inwardly renounces their fruits, that is, does them for their own sake." One must do what is commanded while remaining completely detached inwardly; otherwise one becomes entangled in the world by one's desire for success and then reaps the bitter fruits of karma. Thus, such an organic ethic does not shape the self for world-transforming tasks undertaken through the strength of personality; rather, it always remains an ethic accommodating itself to the world and to the powers that be. It is, moreover, the "most important contrasting picture to the thinking on vocation of inner-worldly asceticism." An organic social ethic

> seen from the standpoint of inner-worldly asceticism lacks the inner drive toward an ethical total rationalization [*Durchrationalisierung*] of the individual life. For it lacks then a premium [*Prämie*] for the rational *methodical* formation of the life of the individual through the interest in its own personal salvation.[56]

Thus, despite the tensions with the world revealed in the structure of caste obligations and the doctrine of karma and despite the attempt to detach action from the desire for personal success, the Hindu taming of the self does not produce a center within the individual from which action and the "demands of the day" can be undertaken. One adjusts to the dharma of one's vocation within an organic cosmos of callings, obligated to ritualistic and ceremonial demands; because of the possibility of rebirth, the emphasis on the achievements of this world is played down. The self, though controlled and ascetic, is not at the same time fortified from a place within itself to impel and enable it to confront the orders of the world and to make them over in ethical service of a deity and its commands. Ultimately the path of knowledge is at best a mode of "possessing" the deity or its secret rather than of shaping a self for action and service.

Hence from the "magic garden" of Asian religion there can be no path to the "autonomous" life methodology associated with Occidental personality.

Models of Self and Personality in the Occident

Even before the Reformation, the West ought to show us the bases for the emergence of the "Occidental self" in the sixteenth and seventeenth centuries. And to an extent it does, for it is impossible to imagine the achievements of ascetic Protestantism without the contributions of Judaism and Catholicism—their revelations of a supramundane God, the emergence of prophets, the elimination of magic, the extension of Christian faith generally, the development of asceticisms of work, and so on. Whatever Weber's conclusions about the limitations of other religions in influencing economic ethics and generating a spirit of capitalism, he should not have found a fundamentally different structure of personality within the Judeo-Christian tradition generally—that is, unless the features distinguishing ascetic Protestantism and its notion of personality set it apart from all other forebears and Christian faiths. But, as we will see, even though the neo-Kantians claim that personality goes back to the Stoics and is firmly grounded by Augustine, the Weberian form of this notion cannot be dated prior to the Reformation, whatever its forebears contributed.

We would not expect Islam to have been decisive for this development, although Muslims believed in predestination, as did the Puritans, and Islam was partly modeled after Judaism. Though Weber did not live long enough to treat Islam in great depth, his evidence led him to exclude it from consideration. To Weber Islam was fundamentally the religion of world-conquering warriors, a stratum of knights who were disciplined crusaders of the faith. Later in its history contemplative Sufism appeared, changing the orientation of much popular observance, and even methodologies of orgiastics arose that greatly altered Islam's cultural orientation. But Islam was never really a religion of salvation, according to Weber, for its character was essentially political. There is no individual quest for salvation and no mysticism, for its religious promises are for this world. Even predestination concerns events in this world. Ascetic control of everyday life or any "planned procedure" is completely alien, and as a religion it flourished particularly in wars of faith. It was hence essentially feudal in its orientation toward life, work, and the world. Yet Weber does not provide enough evidence to judge his notion of Islam's orientation toward the self and personality or to determine whether there were elements that linked it to Judeo-Christian developments.[57]

Ancient Judaism presents a quite different case. The Jewish religion and its creation of the Old Testament had enormous world-historical consequences. Its only equals in historical significance, Weber argues, were Hellenic intellectual culture and three developments specific to Western Europe: first, Roman law and the Roman church built on the concept of office; second, the medieval estate order; and finally, Protestantism. Ancient Judaism was concerned with ritual correctness and segregation from the world, but it also maintained a "religious ethic of inner-worldly action that was to a high degree rational, that is, free of magic as well as of all other forms of irrational pursuit of salvation." Unlike Hinduism, Judaism did not view the world as eternal and unchangeable. Quite the contrary: it looked to the future for the appearance of God to right the imbalance of the world in politics and society. Whereas the Confucian ideal was the gentleman educated in aesthetics and literature, devoted to a life-long study of the classics, the Jewish ideal was the scholar learned in law and casuistry, the intellectual immersed in sacred writings even at the expense of his business affairs.

Further, according to Weber, though Judaism resembles Puritanism in a number of ways, it differs substantially in the relative absence of systematic asceticism. It has no doctrine of predestination, although the Book of Job comes close to it, but rather a notion of collective and joint responsibility and compensation for the Jews as a people, a view maintained particularly by the prophets. Hence, according to Weber, ancient Judaism had no idea comparable to that of the Puritans, in which individual success in business life could be regarded as a "certification" of grace, nor did it devalue the world as such, however much the prophets declaimed against corruption and straying from God's word. What mattered to the heavenly ruler was not principally external action, though Yahweh was a God of action, but unconditional obedience to the law and absolute trust. Still, Yahweh was a God of salvation and of promises, although those promises concerned principally the political situation, not personal affairs. One was to be saved from bondage, not from a senseless world of sin. The ultimate promise, of course, was not transcendent values in the beyond but dominion over Canaan. It was for this reason that the covenant was made with him.

Like the God of the Puritans, Yahweh could not be an object of mystical union through contemplation. He was a God of commandments, and individual worth and authority depended on knowledge of those commandments. Hence, Jewish law was not an "eternal Tao or dharma," a path or way, but a set of positive divine enactments. Jewish prophecy itself did not raise questions about the larger meaning of life and the world, nor was it impelled to seek God out of a need for personal salvation or redemption or even perfection of soul. The prophets influenced not so much the actual content of Jewish ethics as "the creation of systematic unification through the relation of the total life of the people and of all individuals to the observation of Yahweh's positive commandments. They eliminated further the predominance of ritual in favor of the ethical." It was this prophetic intervention, according to Weber, that enabled the religion of Israel to resist disintegration from outside. "The faith the Jewish prophets demanded was not the inner attitude [*Verhalten*] that Luther and the reformers understood by it. It actually meant only the unconditional trust that Yahweh could do everything, that his word was truly meant and would be fulfilled, all external improbabilities to the contrary."

Still, the conflict between godly promises and their actual condition led the Jews to live in a constant tension with their world, to wait in expectation, and, moreover, to pay constant attention to their fidelity to the law. Yet, despite this unification with godly imperatives, Judaism

> lacked what lent to "inner-worldly asceticism" its decisive feature: a unified relation to the "world" from the point of view of the *certitudo salutis* as a center, from which all else is nurtured. An inner-worldly ascetic treatment of the world . . . as a "task" [*Aufgabe*] and as the scene of a religious "calling," which will force this world, [and] also precisely the sins in it, under the rational norms of the revealed godly will, for God's glory and as a sign of his own election—this Calvinistic position was naturally the very last thing a traditionally pious Jew could have thought.

It is true that in one point Judaism resembled "rational ascetic principles: in the command of wakeful self-control and absolute self-domination." Yet for the ancient Jew proving one's piety in life conduct did not lie in the ascetic and rational mastery of the world; for the individual only the law and its fulfillment were essential. "There was no other holy path at all." [58]

Thus despite the antimagical and ethical character of ancient Judaism and despite faith in a supramundane God and his commandments, which put the Jews in a tension with the world and their own condition, the outcome was a scrupulous observance of law and of the self obedient to that law. It was not a domination and shaping of the natural self from an autonomous center on behalf of the search for certainty of salvation, from which could flow transformative impulses and the strength and inclination to overcome tradition and dominate and master the world according to God's commands. Whatever else the Jews accomplished, and however much they helped prepare the ground for ascetic Protestantism, we learn from Weber that they were not themselves to live in the promised land of personality.

But the consideration of Judaism has highlighted one more feature that Weber considers essential to the emergence and possibility of personality: the existence of a *certitudo salutis* that acts as a center around which the personality may unify itself. In Weber's picture only the strength created by such a certainty of salvation, focused on a goal or value transcendental in its significance, can serve as the unmovable central point for the domination and overcoming of the natural self and for the creation of the unity that is personality.

By contrast with all other Western religions, Christianity, both ancient and in its later Catholic form, presents us with the closest approach to the modern Occidental personality. Christianity began as the doctrine of itinerant artisan journeymen.[59] It was a strongly urban and civic religion in antiquity, the Middle Ages, and the Reformation, and it always had strong suspicions of intellectualism. It did not seek its way to salvation through academic education in law, through wisdom about the cosmos or the psyche, or through knowledge of the conditions of life. It had its own prophets in Jesus and Paul, who prescribed a path through faith alone to a transcendental God whose ethical demands were posed for the domination of self and the elimination of sin. Yet with Paul's stress on salvation through faith in Christ, there was little tendency in the early community for an active ethical and rational patterning of life conduct. Nevertheless, the Catholic Church in its development—finally fixed, says Weber, about the time of Gregory the Great in A.D. 600—moved toward an institutional approach to grace which denied that salvation could be achieved through the efforts of the individual alone, outside the church that dispensed grace. Still, the church has oscillated between what Weber calls a relatively "magical" and a relatively "ethical" orientation to salvation. In working out its own scriptural principles, the church was led to affirm ascetic labor as a valid calling for a human life, but it absorbed this calling into its own ranks by providing two levels for believers, one outside its churches and monasteries and one inside. Indeed, this asceticism was gradually rationalized into a disciplined method, and the monk became the "exemplary religious individual" of Catholicism, the first "man of vocation"; he lived "'methodically,' with 'subdivided time,' continuous self-control, under rejection of all spontaneous 'enjoyments' and of all employments through 'personal' obligations that did not serve the purpose of his calling." Weber says that with the fading of eschatological expectations, the monastic circles became the special province of the exemplary followers of God.

Yet, despite the exemplary work done in the monasteries and the high ethical ideals maintained there, the wider notion of the relation of man to his calling as a task, with a more general rational and methodical orientation toward activity in the world, did not emerge in Catholicism. To Weber, one need not seek far to find the reason for this, a reason that shows the unique power of ascetic Protestantism. The problem lies precisely in the reality and dominance within Catholicism of institutionally dispensed grace: sacraments, confession, and absolution provide a relief from the sense of sin and prevent religiosity from becoming totally inward. Where institutional grace operates, salvation may become universal and those other than the "aristocrats" and "virtuosi" of religion may find a home there. But in relying on ritual and confession, the individual's psychological condition leads precisely *away* from the rationalization of activity. Institutional dispensation of grace as well as ritualism lead to the weakening of ethical demands on the individual.

> It means always an inner *relief* of the one in need of salvation, therefore lightens for him the burden of guilt, and, even more, spares him, under otherwise equal conditions, the development of his own ethically systematized life method. For the sinner knows that he can always and again receive absolution from all sins through a religious action for the occasion. And above all the sins remain single actions, against which other single actions can be set as compensation or penance. It is not the complete disposition of the personality that is valued, always newly established through asceticism or contemplation or eternally wakeful self-control and verification, but the concrete single act.

Institutional grace (*Anstaltsgnade*) stresses obedience to the church—which becomes an external center of grace—as a cardinal virtue and determinant of salvation, rather than the reliance on an inner center.

> Life conduct is in this case not a systematization from within and from a center, which the individual has himself achieved, but rather it is nourished from a center that lies outside it. This cannot manifest a pressing effect for an ethical systematization for the content of life conduct in itself, but only the reverse.

Thus the church weakened the believer's psychological motivation for living everyday life as a personality, methodically and on his own responsibility. Only where there was *no* confessional or dispensation of grace by others or magical sacraments—in Judaism and ascetic Protestantism—was there "historically an unusually strong pressure in the sense of the development of an ethically rational life pattern." Only there was there no release from sin except through the efforts of self-fashioning in a way that permitted constant and wakeful self-domination and service of sacred values; even so, Judaism and Puritanism accomplished this in radically different ways and with ultimately different results. Lutheranism, though it was also a faith of the "heart" opposed to sacraments, was nonetheless so emotional and traditionalist by nature that it could not foster such rational self-control and patterns of conduct.[60] Evidently only the inner hothouse from which one cannot escape by the intervention or mediation of others can produce the inner heat that drives the self to forge a personality and to discharge its energy in rationalized action.

If we assemble, then, the different elements scattered through Weber's discussions of personality, we can conclude that the generation of personality in any context can only be conceived on the basis of four fundamental conditions. First, there must be the creation or existence of a transcendental-like ultimate goal or value that gives leverage over the world through the tension it creates between the believer and the world. Second, there must be a "witness" to action that is not social, seeing the "outer" person but transcendent, regarding the "inner." Third, there must be the possibility of salvation or redemption from death or from the meaninglessness of the world and the attainment of a sense of certainty about it. And fourth, there must be no ritual, magical, or external means for relieving one's burden, guilt, or despair. Together these four conditions anchor the sense of meaning and may later provide possibilities that life in an age without religion has otherwise lost.

The New Aristocracy

It was left principally to ascetic Protestantism to take the last step in creating a structure of personality that could serve ascetic purposes; it also created a discipline of work—the calling, or vocation—in which the systematization of life conduct and self-domination could be worked out and through which personality could be both shaped and made effective in the world. Yet, as we observed earlier, this possibility of personality and the ethic of calling are only possible for the few, for an elite gifted with exceptional powers of self-overcoming and discipline who desire to hone themselves into instruments or tools of God's will and purpose. Their "sense of self," we might say, comes from their feeling of election and from their capacity to accomplish godly purposes that re-affirm to them their grace, beginning with the subjugation of the crea-turely natural self. This "new aristocracy," whose merit derives from new capacities of self and from a high mission, differs greatly in its sense of "being" and worth from the older, more traditional representatives of aristocracy. The difference lies in the measurement and source of self-worth. When Weber came to prescribe this new path to his contempo-raries—for the generation of yet a newer kind of aristocracy, to bear the burdens of ruling and to cope with the disappearance of a commonly shared and available meaning in a world "disenchanted" by science—the "new men" were to have an altogether different orientation and understanding of self from the traditional nobility whom they were to replace. The aristocracy found its kingdom in this world, living for the present and at the same time living off its great past. "Strata in solid possession of social honor and power tend to shape their status legend in the direction of an inherent special quality: it is their (real or alleged) *being* that gives nourishment to their feeling of dignity."[61] The feeling of dignity (*Würdegefühl*), says Weber, is originally "the subjective precipi-tate of social honor and of conventional demands, which the positively privileged 'status group' [*Stand*] places on the life conduct of its adher-ents." The dignity of such groups "is naturally related to their 'being,' which does not refer beyond itself." Weber uses the classical description of the Greek nobility to express this dignity: *kalokagathia*, beauty and goodness.[62] The feeling of dignity of the most highly privileged and non-priestly strata, "specifically the nobility, their 'rank' therefore, rests on the consciousness of the 'perfection' of their life conduct as an expres-sion of their qualitative 'being,' residing in itself, not referring beyond itself."[63] In this Nietzschean portrait the older nobility judges itself not in terms of what it *does* or of a god and its demands but in terms of what it *is* and, perhaps, for the "laws" it sets for itself.

But it is quite different for the new men, the ascetics who judge their "being" to be inadequate, creaturely, sinful, and, in its natural state, hateful to God; they seek salvation from their being, and for them as-cetic action and self-transformation are the only hope. They are most likely to come from nonprivileged social strata.

> Socially repressed strata or strata whose status is negatively (or in any case: not positively) valued feed their feeling of dignity . . . most easily from the belief in a special "mission" entrusted to them: their *obligation* [*Sollen*] or

their (functional) *achievement* [*Leistung*] guarantees or constitutes their own worth, which moves into something beyond themselves, into a "task" [*Aufgabe*] placed before them by God.

This group—whose present and whose being gives them no hope and no sense of self-worth apart from their task, their God, and the laws prescribed to them—is the ground for the development of a genuine "rational religious *ethic*";[64] it looks to its God and its religion for a "guaranteed 'promise,' which is tied to a 'function,' 'mission,' 'calling' assigned to them."

> What they cannot claim to "be" they make up either through the worth of what they one day will be, are "called" to be in a future life here or beyond, or (and usually at the same time) through what they "signify" [*bedeuten*] and "achieve" [*leisten*], viewed providentially.[65]

There were, of course, the medieval knights who fought in crusades for the true faith and who therefore undertook holy work; but in general positively privileged feudal and noble strata saw only the "value of their 'being'" and could never have viewed their own existence (*Dasein*) "functionally," as "a means in the service of a 'mission,' as an 'idea' to carry through purposively."[66] But the orientation of the new men, these new Protestant "aristocrats of the faith," depends on a "this-worldly or other-worldly future lying beyond the present; it has to feed, in other words, on a providential 'mission,' on a specific honor before God as 'chosen people.'"[67]

Though these new men are oriented to salvation, to the beyond, and to religion purely, their acts and effects have resounded—and will resound—through every area and aspect of the world. They will be, and have been in many respects, the creators of the new world, or at least of its spirit. They are the appropriate heirs of the older world of the nobility. Indeed, for Weber they far surpass it in most ways. These are the soldiers of a new faith and the champions of God. They are the seekers of tasks that they are able to undertake because they have steeled themselves through self-conquest and self-domination, through absolute devotion and commitment to an ultimate holy value. They serve this value not as servants serve their master but as soldiers serve their homeland or crusaders their faith. They are far from the Islamic warriors who dominated the Near East and Africa in holy wars; but they are nonetheless warriors who make their natural self—as well as the tasks and areas of activity of everyday life—their battlefield, elevating and ennobling their every action undertaken to impose God's ways and laws upon an unruly world and an unruly self. We have in Weber's portrait what we can call the "vocational equivalent of war," even leaving aside those explicitly warlike and world-conquering saints who dominated England under Cromwell.

These religious virtuosi are knights of their faith who, unlike the ancient and medieval knights or the monastic ascetics, find their honor and their struggle everywhere on God's earth. Not only have they taken asceticism out of the monasteries and into the world, making themselves the heirs of the Christian tradition, but they have taken holy war away from the medieval aristocracy and generally (with obvious exceptions in the seventeenth century) off the battlefields of Europe and into the smallest activities of everyday life. They confront the irrational world with a personality created, remarkably, from a mere creaturely self—created through the imposition of and unification through an ultimate holy principle, which not only gives them the capacity to resist pressure and fight opposition but also impels them to make over the world in all of its aspects. Weber's picture leads us to conclude that for him they are also the heirs of the warrior tradition of the aristocracy. For Weber this world-mastering, innovating power is the essence of the Occident, the key to its success and to its uniqueness, and the object one must struggle to defend against those forces, both irrational *and* rational, destructive *and* bureaucratically controlling, that threaten to undermine or to stifle it.

CHAPTER FIVE

Mann and the
Prisonhouse of Personality

In his literary analysis of the ancestry of the artist, Mann drew on the everyday experience and understanding of personality embodied in the segment of the bourgeois class from which he came. He used that experience to construct an identity for the artist, grounding it in the same discipline and personality structure shared by the other members of his class. The personality of Mann's ancestors was not shaped principally by the direct experience of the philosophical tradition or by the ideology (and benefits) of the immersion in "culture," in *Bildung;* it was rooted more directly in the original sources of personality, in Pietism and Calvinism. In addition, the literary tradition that began with Schiller also influenced Mann's conceptions of self and artist, as did the philosophical reflections of Schopenhauer and Nietzsche and, eventually, even the tradition of *Bildung.* Still, Mann's personal experience of bourgeois life and explorations of self led to his understanding of calling and personality.

In *Buddenbrooks* Mann revealed the nature and meaning of personality as Thomas Buddenbrook exemplified it. At the same time he uncovered the roots of the collapse of personality in the bourgeoisie. When the "inner idea" that sustains personality is weakened, the personality is eaten away from within, despite evidence of its "presence" in the world outside. In Thomas's case "representation"—which is the burden and obligation of personalities that take themselves "symbolically," as Mann says Thomas does [1]—becomes difficult: it demands the performance of a role with no conviction behind it, requiring the concealment of the truth that the real center and force of personality are gone. When his calling flags and his personality begins to crumble, Thomas can find support for himself nowhere, because his vision of himself and of others is mediated purely by the bourgeois standards of his ancestors and contemporaries.

Tonio Kröger, despite his estrangement from the class he takes to be "life" in its essence, nonetheless constructs a personality for himself in the realm of art. He adopts the discipline and service of the calling, shaping it to his purposes and bending his will and self to its purposes. Yet he dwells in coldness, for his personality is constructed on the emptiness of his life. Indeed, he wins personality precisely by disowning his own life and denying the demands of self. The artist on the "true" path is able to sustain himself, in Mann's work, only through an interpretation of self and an acceptance of self-sacrifice that teach him to believe in his condition as fate and to justify his situation as the demand of art itself.

The solution found in the artist's calling, however, is not necessarily a solution for the artist alone; in principle it could be a solution and a model for all those members of the bourgeoisie estranged from the traditional bourgeois path, the descendants of declining bourgeois vitality, unable to live "normal" bourgeois lives with energy and unselfconsciousness. By this logic it would be possible to retain an important remnant of the bourgeois inheritance; if one could find again the adherence to a calling, but deployed outside the business world, one could preserve the discipline of work that was central to the self-understanding, identity, and meaning of bourgeois life. The person would take what would otherwise be experienced as wayward and make it and its laws the object of service in a self-denying and self-shaping calling. Such a person would recover the ground of personality and retain the feeling of being representative, of standing for something "higher," like Thomas Buddenbrook. But now what would be higher is the ethos of service and work itself; this is the essence and best side of bourgeois society, now no longer dependent on a particular business firm, on a particular profession in society, or even, strictly speaking, on bourgeois society itself. In this way the flagging of the calling and the personality in the bourgeois world could be reversed and the solution generalized—or so Mann's reworking of the calling might imply. The question, however, is whether this ideal can be sustained even by the artist, or whether the ideal itself does not contain flaws independent of class, profession, or national identity.

From *Tonio Kröger* to the outbreak of World War I, Mann was absorbed in continual reflection on the character of the artist as worked out in *Tonio Kröger*, and he was preoccupied with the vindication of his model of the calling and of the artistic personality that is its product.[2] Now married and with a family, Mann felt oppressed at being an artist from whom everyone continued to expect great works.[3] He wondered if the burden of his work and his personality grounded in the calling were in difficulty, if he was played out, and if the vein of his creativity had run dry.[4] In the process Mann began to fear that the problem of weariness that had undermined the bourgeois calling might now overwhelm the artistic calling as well.

Nine years separate the masterpieces *Tonio Kröger* and *Death in Venice*. The first is a defense of the artist's calling and the self as mediator; the second is a portrait of the Thomas Buddenbrook-like defeat of the calling and the person through self-deception and exhaustion in the fulfillment of duty. In between Mann developed in his shorter works a clearer conception of what the true calling was not, revealing the dangerous possibilities in art when it was lived in extremes rather than in the "middle" way. The Munich art scene in the early years of this century provided social, artistic, and cultural figures, events, and circumstances whose portrayal allowed Mann to dissect the more negative aspects of the artist.[5] It allowed him, moreover, to attack the legitimacy of these other conceptions of the artist, to brand them as negative from the point of view both of society and of the "true" artist. Thus he could fortify his own interpretation of the calling as the only viable artistic discipline and his own notion of the artistic personality as the only justifiable identity for the artist in bourgeois society. Stories like "At the Prophet's" and "Tristan," for example, reveal the personality of the artist who is poles apart from the artist with the calling rightly understood.[6] The one dwells in opposition to society, a bohemian in realms of ice and nothingness, with fantasies of power over others unmitigated by any love or touch of what Mann calls the "human." The other also dwells in opposition, an aesthete, in realms not of ice but of passion, though it is a passion for death and for decline, for a beauty born of the withdrawal from society even unto death. It is an opposition mobilizing its talents for revenge, even though "true" talent, in the person of Tonio, will always look for an escape from the decline that has created it.[7] The service of death, openly or covertly, is the trap that lies in wait for the artist unable to find a way back to bourgeois life.

But once he had worked out and validated his solution to the problem of self and identity, Mann's writing moved in a more and more restricted circle of themes, confined to vindicating his solution despite his
own sense of depletion; indeed, he was unable to find a subject that
could bring his enormous talents into play until he wrote *Death in Venice*.[8] On the surface *Death in Venice* appears to resemble Mann's earlier
stories: Mann, and the narrator in the story, read Aschenbach's fate as a
negative affirmation of an earlier lesson, a vindication of the "right
understanding" of the artistic calling, another version of dangers the
artist must avoid. But in fact this story discloses a fatal problem in the
nature of the calling Mann means to affirm. This problem is not produced by any misunderstanding of the calling, but rather lies precisely at
the heart of the calling "rightly understood." *Death in Venice* tells a
story that contradicts both the explicit lessons and the noble conclusions of Mann's earlier understanding. The true artist has to adopt the
model of the bourgeois calling and a mode of service that demands and
provides self-conquest; this model equips the self, through ascetic denial, for the "conquest" of the world. But the adherent of the calling
adopts as well, however unintentionally, the perils of the calling and the
personality constructed on it. These perils are no less real or threatening, even life-threatening, simply because they have been taken out of
the normal range of problems of the members of a single business-
oriented class. They are the perils that Thomas Buddenbrook confronted and that undermined him: inner exhaustion, self-doubt and declining feeling of success and strength in the calling, the obligation to
continue to play his role despite its burdensomeness and fruitlessness,
and the attraction to death as the only escape. But they are also perils
for artists who pursue the calling of art, including Mann himself, and
who carry on the tradition of service and of conquest of the self through
an ascetic vocation. And they are not the worst perils.

Mann's solution for Tonio was a response to the inadequacy of the
inherited "bourgeois" self; yet Mann was also critical of the oppositional questioning of that inadequate self undertaken by proponents of
what we can call the "decadent" self. To shore up his solution, Mann
developed a resolute and determined conception of the "artistic" self:
the self that could draw on the duty, the strength, and the organization
of its identity from the once-strong ethos, modes of discipline, and conception of personality rooted in the bourgeoisie. In this way Mann rescued his identity and the identity of the artist from the perils of decadence: overrefinement, lack of focus and purpose, attraction to death,

and despair. But the irony is that Mann's faith in and reliance on the calling as the saving spiritual discipline became the source of the structure of personality of the death-bound Gustav von Aschenbach. This structure, which we can call the "militarized self," is the hidden form and essence of the model of personality, and it is deadly.[9]

Mann's works before World War I reveal a number of profound continuities between the problems of Thomas Buddenbrook—which continued to resist a definitive resolution even outside normal bourgeois life—and the problems of the artist with a calling. They also reveal dimensions of identity, work, and meaning in the world of the calling "rightly understood" that help us understand the disastrous fate of Gustav von Aschenbach and the reasons why Mann could not explicitly address the deepest dangers of the calling. In this period Mann, like Tonio, tried to distance himself from the bohemian artists with their wild projects of spiritual conquest, from the morally flabby aestheticist artists who had no grasp of life or who longed to revenge themselves on life, and from the moralizing artists who hoped to dominate life by escaping the inhibiting scruples produced by "knowledge." Yet he knew that he was not completely free from such tendencies himself. One has only to read his essay "Bilse and I," written in this period, where Mann suggests that the artist has a weapon with which he can react to the appearances and experiences that are the world of his observation and that cause him pain and require coldness; this weapon is "expression," which he describes as "the sublime *revenge* of the artist on his experience."[10] For Mann, then, revenge is deeply planted even within artists with a genuine calling and reflects their rage at a life that excludes them and triumphs over them. He therefore, and not only momentarily, desires to triumph over life by means of his only remaining power, the power of words.

The aestheticist, longing for revenge, is not alone in this feeling; the only difference is that the "true" artist will have more and be more than this. He will more likely recognize it for what it is in himself and try to redeem himself from it, insofar as he can. The true artist sees the exhaustion and defeat of members of bourgeois society as a problem to be solved, especially the resulting weakness of the artistically inclined. It is solved through a conception of calling that provides artists enough distance from bourgeois society to keep what they imagine is its disappointment in them from becoming as shattering as it was for Thomas Buddenbrook, or as deadly as it was for Hanno, or as corrosive as it was for the joker. At the same time, in Mann's artistic ideology this distance

cannot become so great that artists find themselves remote and cut off
from the bourgeoisie, for they will then place themselves in deadly opposition to society, willing its undoing or willing death, as in "At the
Prophet's," or "serving death" in the guise of serving beauty, as in "Tristan." They need a conception of the calling that fortifies them and an
ideology of art that justifies them and makes it unnecessary to attack
life. They need the softening and sympathy that come from a longing
desire for the society from which they must still, because of their calling,
remain separated. They must affirm, however ironically and critically,
the values of the bourgeoisie and of the ideal nature of its normal children, even though those children reside in a state of unconsciousness
that the artist can see through and that provokes his contempt. "Yes,
what is genius?" the novelist in "At the Prophet's" asks.

> In this Daniel all the preconditions are present: the loneliness, the freedom,
> the spiritual passion, the grandiose optic, the belief in himself, even the near-
> ness of crime and madness. What is missing? Perhaps the human? A little
> feeling, longing, love? But that is a completely improvised hypothesis.[11]

Mann was critical of the self-styled aristocrats of the soul, whose self
and personality were oppositional and condescending; he sought instead an analogue to the artist in the real aristocracy: the princely ruler,
whose representation and symbolization of the self are his calling and,
unfortunately, also the seal and guarantee of his separation from life.
Yet the real artistic aristocrat—who, to Mann, creates out of suffering—can also turn himself into a hero, winning through to his work
and to acclaim by his determination and by his conviction in the redemptive power of the suffering talent.

Mann saw his own admiration of life, symbolic existence, and burden of representation as the marks of his noble calling. Yet he found that
Tonio's solution was not completely adequate after all, for he feared
that these features of his calling would still isolate him from the bourgeois life he thought he adored. Thus he sought, first, a way to wed himself to life literally and imaginatively. Second, he sought a way to sanctify his sufferings as a servant of art more completely than Tonio's
ideology of the artist could do. But, as we shall see, even this strengthened calling, renewed by the overcoming of dangers and resanctified by
the acceptance of suffering, cannot support the immense burden of identity and meaning it is meant to carry, for even its new strengths will be
revealed as weaknesses in *Death in Venice*. The bourgeois calling cannot be vindicated or preserved simply by being made less obviously

bourgeois. It is the idea and reality of the calling itself that are the problem. Its integral relation to the identity and establishment of the self, and its adherents' dependence on it for meaning, salvation, and personality, carry within them a fatal flaw, disclosed in *Death in Venice,* a flaw that explodes the idea of the calling: the personality constructed on the basis of the calling can become a prisonhouse and death trap of the self, sundering it irrevocably from the world. It is these new strengths and weaknesses, culminating in *Death in Venice,* that we must explore.

The Artist-Personality: Representation and Suffering

Representation, Redemption, and the Calling

It is not surprising that the theme of the artist's loneliness recurs in Mann's work, for even in *Tonio Kröger* it is never overcome, just "understood." It is also not surprising to find artist-characters who alternate between feeling vastly inferior to the mass of mortals and feeling vastly superior. And when he feels himself superior the artist is inclined, if only in moments of weakness, to feel himself a kind of aristocrat, at least of the spirit, lifted above the run of mankind. He turns his weakness—his icy detachment, his ineluctable drive to understand, and his need to portray the inner life of human beings—into a source of self-worth and distinction of which to be proud. Thus the artist properly understood, as Tonio Kröger understands him, is a prince of the spirit, and with spiritual royalty come the onerous burdens of royalty, especially for those who are not "born" to the aristocratic role but merely "called" to it. Yet the true artist-prince has a stronger relation to life and to the lives of the everyday members of his society than do the artists who have made themselves life's "enemies." He does not serve powers aimed against ordinary society but, on the contrary, represents and loves "his people" despite his unbridgeable distance from them and his inability to be one of them; he tries to serve their interests even when they do not recognize it.

This, then, is a further development of Mann's artist-ideology, another aspect of the self-understanding that justifies the artist to himself and to others. It is the conception of the artist as prince, symbolizing and representing the world of the everyday, but not in its everyday aspect; he symbolizes and represents—at least to himself—the world's highest part, its spiritual self. Thus, his burden of isolation and service becomes more bearable beause his estrangement is matched with superiority and is, like his icy nature, fated. But at the same time, as Mann later writes of Gustav von Aschenbach and as Tonio Kröger experiences to his horror, the artist may discover that he ultimately represents only the weak, exhausted, and defeated in society, who see in him their voice and defender and who are his only true audience. In any case such a person, like Tonio and his "father," Thomas Buddenbrook, no longer "lives": he plays a role, acts a part, presents himself as a symbol. Through this representation and symbolization the artist can accept the self-denial and emptiness of his life, that is, his possible life as an ordinary human being with an ordinary human being's passion, involvement, and possibilities. He is a sacrifice, sacrificing his life not only for art and form but for the world of "life" as well; he makes his life available as life's representative, performing duties and functions for life that it cannot do for itself.

"To stand for many in standing for oneself, to be *representative,* that too, it seems to me, is a small kind of greatness. It is the austere happiness of princes and poets," Mann wrote.[12] If life can be justified only aesthetically, as Nietzsche once remarked, then in Mann's work the artist can be justified to himself and to others only through his representative service of art and of life. "Representative vocation in any sense, whether in the Napoleonic or Klaus Heinrichian sense, whether great or small, necessarily makes one egotistic. One naturally makes much of one's personality if one sees in it a *symbol,* an incarnation, a collecting point, a microcosm."[13] Whatever the source of unity or strength of the artistic personality, its value is real for Mann only when it can be viewed as something more than itself alone, more than a personality among personalities. Its own immanent worth and the dignity of its "being" cannot sustain it, as the sense of their "being" sustained the aristocrats of old; what can is rather its special mission, service, and calling not just for art but for representation. The artist symbolizes a whole world not just as the object and task of his work but in and through his personality itself.

> Self-domination [*Selbstbeherrschung*] is certainly a good thing, and as an artist one is poorly able to renounce it. The artist is related to the prince insofar as he, like him, leads a *representative* existence. What for the prince is etiquette is for the artist the lofty obligation toward form. The artist, as I know him, is never the man who can "let himself be seen" freely and without further ado. He needs prudence in passion, idealization in self-presentation, in a word: art. That is his human weakness.[14]

The task of representation and the need for masking the self are precisely the source of the burden of real princes, as Klaus Heinrich, the hero of *Royal Highness,* discovers. Yet, interestingly, in Mann's work representation becomes the source of the *easing* of the burden of the artist; for in seeing himself as representative and presenting himself to the world in idealized form, the artist finds significance and self-acceptance through recognition of a larger meaning for his life. He derives this meaning from discovering his special role within society, that society from which he formerly felt himself estranged. Whatever his actual isolation and estrangement, the artist is not only joined through spiritual bonds to the world, as Tonio Kröger is by his love of life, but also stands for the world and is in that sense a greater figure than any other particular member of it. Yet this difference between the prince and the artist, between the role inherited and the role sought, raises the question of whether, contrary to Mann, the prince and the artist are appropriately understood as analogous. While the one must *bear* the burden and isolation of representation, the other *seeks* representation, seeks the larger role, to make the burden of his isolation and sense of worthlessness bearable. The artist needs a crown to find worth and meaning for his life. He also needs it to find a link to society, since he has given up on the role of fellow citizen; his sense of being apart can be eased only by being set above, although he feels set below. He can never see himself alongside. He can overcome inferiority only by superiority, not equality. Thus, contrary to Mann, the prince is not the true analogue of the artist; he is the expression of the artist's grandiose fantasy. Yet the burden on such an artist may be greater than he imagines or can actually bear, as Gustav von Aschenbach finds out. Still, whatever the power of this artistic ideology for the artist, it is not surprising that he continues to search for some means of rejoining life, overcoming his isolation, and being redeemed from the strain of having to exist as a symbol only. Whether redemption is truly possible for an artist with such a self-conception remains to be seen; few of Mann's characters—and none of his interesting ones—achieve it.

The idea of the uniqueness of the artist and of his unique role in society, whether as savior and educator or as its poet-conscience, has a long history in Germany, from Goethe's *Tasso* and Schiller's *Aesthetic Education of Humankind* to the revolutionary Expressionists and the world-redeeming visions of Hofmannsthal and Stefan George.[15] But no great German writer sought his worldly analogue in an allegory of an ordinary prince and the prince's routine functions, even in fairy-tale

form, until Mann's tale of Klaus Heinrich, the physically defective prince
compelled to take over the ruling position in his principality from his
sick elder brother. In his longing to escape from the isolation and burdens of his humanly empty calling and from his merely symbolic relation to life, Klaus Heinrich finds a limited but adequate amelioration of
his condition through marriage to a rich American heiress who, at the
same time, wonder of wonders, rescues the state from its declining economic and fiscal condition, thanks to the vast resources of her father.
End of fairy tale.

Yet *Royal Highness* is not merely a fairy tale but what Herman
Weigand calls a "symbolic autobiography." [16] In a letter of 1903, after
the publication of *Tonio Kröger,* Mann writes:

> No one can come nearer to me than someone who . . . is a reader of "Tonio
> Kröger," and if you found me personally reserved, it might lie in the fact that
> one loses the taste for personal communicativeness if one is accustomed to
> expressing oneself symbolically, that is, in works of art. One leads, I would
> say, a symbolic, a representative existence like that of a prince—and, you see,
> in this pathos lies the germ of a very wonderful thing [*Sache*] that I am think-
> ing of writing sometime, a story of a prince, a companion piece to "Tonio
> Kröger," which should carry the title "Royal Highness." . . . [17]

In *Royal Highness* Mann analyzed the life of royalty "as a formal, non-
objective, supra-objective existence," as he put it many years later, "in a
word, the existence of the artist." [18] When he had completed it, he began
to make plans for other works on the life of princes, including an un-
finished life of Frederick the Great—the completion of which he later
attributed to Aschenbach in *Death in Venice*—to portray what Klaus
Schröter calls "the suffering of isolation, the claim of representation,"
with which Mann was concerned during fifteen years of "secret insecurity." [19] This conception of the artist as prince was already foreshadowed, of course, not only in letters but in *Tonio Kröger* as well. As a
youth Tonio expresses his strong affinity for Schiller's *Don Carlos,* especially for the character of the king, isolated, without friends, and ultimately abandoned. "He is always so completely alone and without love,
and now he believes he has found someone, and that person betrays
him." [20] As an adult discussing with his artist friend Lisaweta his own
experience of being an artist, Tonio remarks:

> An artist, a real one, not one whose bourgeois calling is art, but a predestined
> and condemned one, you pick out of a mass of men with a minimally pierc-
> ing glance. The feeling of separation and of not belonging, of being recog-
> nized and observed, something at the same time royal and embarrassed is in

his face. In the progress of a prince, striding in plain clothes through a crowd, one can observe something similar. But no plain clothes help there, Lisaweta! Clothe yourself, disguise yourself, dress like an attaché or a lieutenant of the guards on vacation: you will hardly need to raise your eyes and speak a word, and everyone will know that you are not a person but something strange, odd, other. (297)

Tonio is already aware of the similarity of artists and princes, and the quality of being different, alone, and separated lies in the nature of their being, in their bearing, in what is revealed when the differentness of their existence is exposed in speech or in a look. The artist and the prince are seen through; their *being* is evidently remote and different, despite their efforts at concealment. And what is seen, Tonio thinks, causes humankind to recoil as if from something alien and foreign. The essence of their difference from the rest of humanity lies, of course, in their specific calling and in their self as shaped by the calling, not simply in their occupation. It is a calling to which they have been "predestined and condemned," one that unmans them, takes them away from life, and empties out their existence on behalf of something higher,[21] making the prince as much an example of decadence as the artist. In *Royal Highness* Klaus Heinrich struggles to understand a prince's "high calling" (*hohen Beruf*): "What was his calling, and in what did its highness lie?"[22] As he began to understand his situation and destiny, and what the loneliness to come would be like, "horror befell him, a shudder before this kind of determination, a fear of his 'high calling' so strong that he . . . cried with pity for himself" (63).

As he grows in "bearing," or self-possession (*Haltung*), "under the pressure of his calledness," he is able to overcome the handicap of his withered arm—a handicap shared with Kaiser Wilhelm II—which has further estranged him from the normal run of humanity by making him different and which he has learned to conceal. Mann himself spoke of the withered arm as "a moral symbol," an "inhibition," which made more difficult Klaus Heinrich's "formal-heroic service."[23] Yet while he matured, "at the same time his longing grew" (63), a longing for contact with ordinary people and with a life not transformed by an exalted calling. In a chapter entitled "The High Calling" we learn that Klaus Heinrich "had nothing to do in daily life" (171), that he left affairs of state to officials and spent his energies on "representative" functions, living "inwardly quiet, without enthusiasm or zeal for publicly disputed questions" (170). Thus "his life was without a true everyday and without true reality. . . . A strange unreality and fictitiousness ruled in the places of the exercise of his calling," confined to "representation" (159) and very tiring (163).

Despite his longing for something more from life, Klaus Heinrich is counseled to give up unrealizable hopes and look to his symbolic, or emblematic, existence (*sinnbildliche Existenz*) as the source of meaning and purpose in his life (84).

> What are you? . . . Let's say: an essence [*Inbegriff*], a kind of ideal. A vessel. An emblematic existence, Klaus Heinrich, and therewith a *formal* existence. But form and immediacy—do you not yet know that they exclude one another? You have no right to immediate intimacy, and if you sought it, you would yourself realize that it is not fit for you. . . . To represent, to stand for many, while one presents oneself, the elevated and well-bred expression of a multitude—representing is naturally more and higher than simply being, Klaus Heinrich—and that is why one calls you highness. (84, 88)

But the artist as prince is vouchsafed a victory over the emptiness of his representing, as Thomas Mann understood himself to be. Klaus Heinrich's efforts to court and win Imma Spoelmann, the rich American, strongly resemble Mann's efforts to win Katia Pringsheim; indeed, the various speeches of the prince sometimes borrow word for word from Mann's letters to Katia during their courtship. Imma confronts Klaus Heinrich with the apparent emptiness of his life and shows him the obstacles between himself and the world, revealing how problematical any possible relation between Klaus Heinrich and life would be, thanks to the innumerable difficulties posed by the calling of representation. Yet he tries to persuade her that his redemption and his only hope of joining life lie in marriage to her.[24] Imma seems to the young prince the only person with whom he can set aside and even lose his self-possession (*Haltung*), but she initially resists his efforts and purposes.

> I insist that you preserve your self-possession also with me. . . . I am not here for you to recover from your princely existence with me. . . . You came into the world for semblance [*Schein*] and now should I suddenly believe you, that there is something serious about you? . . . How could anyone trust you? No, it is not trust that you inspire, but coldness and embarrassment. (303, 306)

With tears in his eyes the prince answers: "You are right, Imma, there is much untruth in my life. But I did not make it or choose it, you must realize, but have rather done my duty" (303). He describes to her "the cold, stern, and poor existence that he had led hitherto" (308) and claims that the only cure for this existence and for the embarrassment and coldness he inspires is through her. His persistence is rewarded: she marries the young prince, her father's money rescues the ailing principality, and the prince becomes involved in the problems and the daily issues of the affairs of state, which he finds much easier to master and carry out than the tasks of representation (324). Thus he returns not only to affective life but also to a life of utility in a new kind of service, supplementing his representative calling with actual work in the service of the well-being of the state. Once again, end of fairy tale.

Klaus Heinrich comes to terms with his representative, symbolic, and isolating calling not by an immanent change in his relation to his calling but through the intervention of a saving power. This power is marriage to a woman, an outsider from another land, another world, not a Jew, whom Mann himself married, but someone almost as foreign, an American, through whom Klaus Heinrich weds life itself and at the same time becomes "useful." As Mann himself put it, he resolved the antithesis of life and art through a reconciliation of happiness and discipline and a turning from "empty form and melancholy representativity" toward "life and companionship."[25] The symbolic artist is saved. The only actual artists permitted redemption in Mann's work, apart from Tonio Kröger's limited redemption, are Schiller in "A Difficult Hour" (1905) and Goethe in Lotte in Weimar (1939). It is no accident that they are both historical figures rather than the products of pure self-symbolization. For the others the combination of the burdens of representation, icy detachment, and weariness are too much to bear.[26] Indeed, not even all the princely analogues will find a happy fate.

Mann himself continued to embody the representative bourgeois ideal of work by appropriating the form of the calling as a mode and symbol of bourgeois discipline in the service of art.[27] But the burden of representation, which weighs on Klaus Heinrich and helps to destroy Gustav von Aschenbach, was already a prison for Thomas Buddenbrook. Indeed, Mann's later interpretation of Thomas shows how strongly the experience of the bourgeois father has been retained in the self-understanding of the bourgeois artist and of the artists and artist-analogues in his novelistic work. Mann speaks of Thomas's "role in life, which he had taken symbolically and represented with bravery, but which had never satisfied his spirit, his longing for the world."[28] Thus representation has already appeared as another aspect of the original bourgeois calling, as much a symbolic existence as the existence and calling of the prince and the artist. Representation is another element appropriated by the true artist—in particular by Mann himself—from the virtues of the bourgeois class, now reborn in the person and duties of its once-wayward offspring. The wayward artist is made representative of the highest bourgeois ideals; yet at the same time his life is construed as analogous to the life of the noble prince. The failed bourgeois thus strives to be reborn as an aristocrat! Ultimately, Mann will make him a representative of German culture and Germany a representative nation.

The bourgeoisie, the prince, the artist, the nation—since they are all cast in the role of representation, even representing one another, they can be fused in an imaginative unity that makes it possible for the artist to see his special place in relation to them all. Yet Mann's extraordinary novelistic honesty did not permit him to be completely satisfied with the artist's resolution of the problem of representation or with the resolution worked out by Klaus Heinrich. Thomas Buddenbrook represents his class and bourgeois virtue; the prince represents his principality. What does the artist represent? He is a creature who remains fluid in his identities and his loyalties. He can represent the ethos of a class, a ruling nobleman, or the culture of a nation whose own existence, like the existence of his creations, must be understood symbolically. But in one of his forms he can also represent the weak, the self-repressive, and the exhausted who yet persist; they are the people bowed down by life but unwilling to admit defeat, who stay by their self-conscious callings, though their purposes are no longer clear or empowering. This representative role is part of the fate of Aschenbach, an exhausted artist who stands for all the exhausted in the world.

The Ideology of Suffering

Six years before he wrote about his experiences on the Lido, Mann wrote another story of exhaustion and struggle, but of suffering overcome and greatness achieved. It is no accident that the story is about Schiller, the analyst of the naive and the sentimental poet, written on the hundredth anniversary of his death. But it is really a story in which the personality of the artist is shored up by sanctifying his sufferings in creation.

"A Difficult Hour"—finished shortly after the completion of Mann's only play, *Fiorenza*—is an artistic portrayal of a giant of the German literary past. The particular situation Mann picked to dramatize in 1905—an imagined moment in the creative experience of Schiller writing *Wallenstein*—provides a clue to the content and difficulty of his own artistic experience as well as another element in the character of Aschenbach.[29] "A Difficult Hour" reflects in part Mann's own exhausting experience with *Fiorenza*.[30] But it is also meant to be a more general portrait of the artist, as is clear from a letter Mann wrote about the story near the end of his life: "For all that, the name of Schiller is indeed nowhere mentioned, nor that of the work with which it is concerned—which can be explained from the wish of the author to elevate it above all care for the particular and the singular and to lend to the delineation a symbolic validity for the lonely afflictions of all creativeness."[31]

The Schiller of "A Difficult Hour" is a man exhausted, whose talent brings suffering and compulsion and who strives for fame to compensate for suffering in the service of the high ideal of art. He is also an artist who thinks of his creating as a form of knowledge, and he is determined to persist despite the doubts and misgivings that come from comparing himself to the divine Goethe, whose creation is of a qualitatively different kind. Struggling to bend his material to his will, Schiller fights against a potential loss of feeling in himself while at the same time desiring distance from life to pursue his mission. He is the very portrait of the sentimental poet but with the attributes of the modern artist whose conflicts and struggles over knowledge and lack of feeling—and whose exhaustion—mark him out from the unself-conscious poet, the naive creator. His years of difficulty, Schiller reflects, now seem to have been his years of greatness. Having found his niche in the bourgeois world, with wife and children and some happiness, he feels that he is finished. He is the Thomas Buddenbrook of art, at least for the moment, exhausted and without faith in his future.

> Every time, no matter how deeply bowed down, his supple spirit bounced up, and after the hours of grief came the others of belief and of inner triumph. They came no longer, came hardly ever. . . . He was tired, barely thirty-seven years old and already at the end. Faith no longer lived, faith in the future, which was his star in distress. . . . now he was exhausted and finished.[32]

Out of this suffering the writer fashions his own moral law, not content to see Kantian wisdom, the good conscience, or the submission of the self to "cool discipline" (*Zucht*) as the only forms of morality. Morality for him is to be found in "suffering and need, passion and pain," a morality of those in distress. Indeed, for Schiller suffering is not only the key to the moral law: it is the focus of his faith and the foundation of his conception of self and of value as well. "To believe, to be able to believe in suffering . . . But he did indeed believe in suffering, so deeply, so ardently, that something that came about under suffering could be neither useless nor bad according to this belief" (375). Suffering redeems all, sanctifies all. It is the alpha and omega of his conception of artistic creativity. The Schiller of this story, like Tonio Kröger and Mann himself, has turned his condition into an ideology of art as well as a theory of self and of the artist. It is no longer the realities of the artist's life that are the foundation of his personality and the expression of his relation to life: separation, coldness, isolation. It is, rather, his *suffering* of these realities that justifies him and forms the ground of who and what he is. His identity lies not just in his service to art, the form of his calling, and the relation of that calling to the bourgeois world; rather, it is his *torment* in plying the calling that becomes his vindication, his sign of greatness, the source of his redemption. This is an experience of suffering turned into a religion of suffering. Only the aristocrats of art, the virtuosi of suffering, the heroes of creativity, could bear up under such a burden. "The will toward difficulties . . . Did one suspect how much discipline and self-overcoming a sentence, a strict thought, cost him?" (377).

> Talent itself—was it not suffering? It had never gushed forth. . . . Only with bunglers and dilettantes did it gush forth, with the quickly satisfied and the ignorant, who did not live under the pressure and the discipline of talent. For talent . . . is nothing easy, nothing trifling, it is not simply an ability [*ein Können*]. At root it is a *need* [*Bedürfnis*], a critical knowing of the ideal, an insatiability, which first creates and heightens your ability, not without torment. And to the greatest, the most insatiable, their talent is the sharpest scourge.[33] (376)

Schiller's ideology and religion of suffering mask a resentment that longs for triumph over the world, justifying itself by its mission and by the suffering that mission imposes.

> Greatness! Extraordinariness! World conquest and immortality of one's name! What was all the happiness of the eternally unknown versus this goal? To be known—known and loved by the peoples of the earth! Prattle about egotism, you who know nothing of the sweetness of this dream and drive. Everything extraordinary is egotistic, so far as it suffers. Look to yourselves, it says, you without a mission, you who have it so much easier on earth! And ambition says: Should my suffering be for nothing? It must make me great![34] (376)

Thus Schiller is a combination of suffering, ambition, and self-sacrifice in the service of art, and these define his calling, coupled with a jealousy that does not wish to see anyone advance higher who has not also suffered more deeply.

> For deeper yet than this egotism there lived still the consciousness to con-
> sume himself unselfishly and to sacrifice himself with all of this in the service
> to something higher, certainly without reward [*Verdienst*], but rather under
> a necessity. And this was his jealousy: that no one become greater than he
> who has not also suffered deeper than he for this higher thing. (376–77)

Yet this jealousy comes up against the reality of Goethe, the artist
who creates effortlessly and without suffering in creating, not burdened
with excessive consciousness and knowledge. Comparing himself with
the great Goethe leads Schiller not only to glorify his suffering and jeal-
ously to guard the "privileges" it brings him but also to define the very
nature of heroism, and of his own heroism, through pain and heavily
borne knowledge and to make himself the champion of such an art,
even superior to Goethe.

> He felt already the sting of this inevitable thought in his heart, of the thought
> of him, the other, the luminous one, blessed with feeling, sensuous, divinely
> unconscious, of *that one* there, in Weimar, whom he loved with a yearning
> hostility. . . . And again . . . he felt the task begin in himself . . . to assert and
> define his own essence and artistry against that of the other. . . . [The other
> was a] god, perhaps—a hero he was not. But it was easier to be a god than a
> hero! . . . The other had it easier! With a wiser and happier hand to separate
> knowing and creating, that may make one serene and without torment and
> gushingly fruitful. But if creating was divine, so knowledge was heroism, and
> he was both, a god and a hero, who created in knowledge. (377)

Schiller overcomes his difficult hour through these reflections and
this grandiose conception of self. He defines his art and himself in contrast to "that other" as a heroism worthy of admiration, turning his limitations into a virtue, justifying his suffering, justified *by* his suffering,
accepting the demands of his mission [*Sendung*] and the distance it
requires. To Henry Hatfield this story represents Mann's new self-
understanding, where "the artist is no longer a sort of charlatan; he is
like Dürer's knight who presses forward 'despite death and the devil.'"[35]
Schiller's resolution allows him to turn aside from the exhaustion, self-
doubt, and defeat that had overwhelmed Thomas Buddenbrook and that
will utterly shatter Gustav von Aschenbach. "Do not descend into the
chaos, or at least do not remain there! Rather, out of the chaos, which is
abundance, raise into the light whatever is fit and ripe to win form. Do
not brood: work, define, eliminate, shape, become finished" (379).

"A Difficult Hour" is meant to commemorate not only Schiller the
artist but also Thomas Mann the artist, or, better, the type of artist
whose situation is genuinely modern but who finds resonances in the

past for his difficulties, suffering, self-doubt, ambition, and persistence in the face of obstacles. This story also expresses an experience that Mann described shortly after in his essay of self-justification, "Bilse and I." There, in explaining "the appearance of the artist's *hostility* to reality," he describes himself as part of the "school of spirits" created by Nietzsche, a school that associates "the concept of the artist with that of the knower," creating a "poetic criticism." Its purposes are "to know deeply and to form beautifully [*tief erkennen und schön gestalten*]," and this task requires the bearing of pain, for artistic observation hurts. "Does one understand these pains? That all forming, creating, bringing forth is *pain*, struggle, and laboring torment. . . . Observation as emotion, as passion, martyrdom, heroism—who knows this?" Like Schiller, Mann asks, should the work "which puts the artist in pain . . . should it bring him no fame? So speaks ambition."[36]

"A Difficult Hour" takes up the problem of exhaustion and suffering transposed from the ordinary bourgeois life of Thomas Buddenbrook into the life of art. It shows that Tonio Kröger's reconciliation with his calling has not overcome the possibility of a crisis of weariness and lack of faith similar to that of his spiritual father. Further, it extends the ideologizing of art and of the artist begun in *Tonio Kröger,* but now the ideology rests not on the structural problem of the artist's calling vis-à-vis bourgeois life but on the difference between the suffering and pain of one kind of artist and the supposedly effortless creation of another. It vindicates a hero of art whose heroism derives from overcoming his inner torment and his difficulty in creating in the face of physical pain, weakness, and the burden of knowledge.

This new justification of the artist is the defense not only of a specific kind of art and of the artist in general but also of a particular kind of artistic personality, one that is steeped in suffering. This personality is not shaped principally by its separation from life, for it has been vouchsafed the normal benefits of spouse, family, success, and position, although it still desires to retain its distance from them. It is forged, instead, in the resistance to and overcoming of its own inner suffering, which it is willing to endure, even to court, to win fame and an undying reputation. Suffering has become the patent of nobility, suffering coupled with the discipline and persistence of the warrior fighting against great odds, channeling his energies into self-sacrificing service to a higher cause—in this case, to art.

But through this ideology of art and the ennoblement of suffering, the artist risks becoming trapped in an outlook and a structure of personality that threaten to isolate him from reality. He becomes rooted firmly behind a wall of isolating self-justification, a patent of suffering and triumph, and an image that he must maintain both for himself and for his public. Behind these fortifications, in which the *idea* of suffering has become a source of strength, feeling threatens to disappear, for real feeling demands vulnerability, openness, and making oneself available to the pleasures and risks of contact. But the hero of suffering, the artist who sees life only as material for forming and shaping into art, is no longer able to see reality as it is, to experience it for itself, and with that inability the wellsprings of art, as well as of life, dry up. Schiller already hints at this when, in his inner dialogue with his sleeping wife, he remarks: "I love you so. It is just that at times I cannot find my feelings, because I am often so tired from suffering and from wrestling with that task that my self has set for me" (379). This will be the fate of Gustav von Aschenbach, who will not only find his feelings fled, but will be so locked up in his artistic personality that he will be unable to see or experience the world as it is. Nor will he be able to have a passion for a real person; instead, he will transform everything into art and be able to fall in love only with the image, a symbol, of beauty. Reality and real beauty, even as they become available to him, will have disappeared. His death in Venice will finally end what has already been his death in life.

The Death in Life of the Artistic Personality: *Death in Venice*

Death in Venice is the true complement to *Tonio Kröger* and completes the portrait of the artist's personality. Mann claimed that his original inspiration was to tell a tale of "the degradation of the man with an ethic of work and achievement [*Entwürdigung des Leistungsethikers*]," the story of the old Goethe who fell in love with a young girl he had met at the baths in Marienbad and to whom he had seriously proposed marriage. It was to have been a degradation through "the passion for an exciting, innocent happiness."[37] But Mann set aside this project; instead, *Death in Venice* was the product of Mann's chance experiences on a holiday trip of his own to the aging city.[38]

Published late in 1912, *Death in Venice* tells the story of a writer whose art has begun to fail. Famous as a representative of German letters, a "classicist" in style, even ennobled, Gustav von Aschenbach travels for a much-needed vacation to Venice, hoping to renew his strength and the sources of his artistic inspiration. Instead, he becomes consumed by a passion for a young boy, only to die from a disease contracted in a city trying, like himself, to keep its illness secret from the world. On the surface the story is about the destructive power of the emergence of repressed homosexual desire in the life of a man hitherto in possession of control and dignity, leading an outwardly "normal," hence acceptable, life.[39] Further, the story is usually viewed, even by Mann himself, as an allegory of the decay and dying of an old world, a world revolted by modernity, exhausted and without direction, looking for an end.[40] But although it is true that such a passion triggers Aschenbach's collapse, and although the story is heavily laden, even overloaded, with symbols of decline and death, there is something else to be learned by considering this story from the point of view of the unique features of Aschenbach's calling and personality.

Mann makes a special point of describing the features and characteristics of Aschenbach's craft, its roots in his fictional past, and its artistic products in the present. It is no ordinary man who has this experience in Venice but a suffering soldier in the service of art. Mann chose to write about

> a modern hero, a hero of delicate type, which I had already created, full of sympathy, in earlier works, a brother of Thomas Buddenbrook and Girolamo Savonarola, a *hero of weakness* therefore, who works on the edge of exhaustion and wins for himself the utmost, in short, a hero of the stamp of him named by myself the "ethical man of work and accomplishment" [*Leistungsethiker*].[41]

Thus *Death in Venice* is the culmination of the experiences of a decade as well as the fulfillment and highest form of analysis of the aspects of the artist's existence that Mann had been chronicling since *Tonio Kröger*.[42] Its explicit intention is to deal with the enormous dangers for an artist in the calling who takes a different path from the "healthy" one that Mann discovered in *Tonio Kröger*. Mann believes he is writing about an artist who strives too strongly to become accepted as a symbol for the normal world, and he tries to distance himself from this destiny.[43] But this is a story whose true tale and meaning largely contradict the claims and interpretations of its author and reveal its narrator as well to be more than a little unreliable. For *Death in Venice* is ultimately about a man entrapped within his own personality in the prisonhouse of the calling.

Aschenbach's Calling

Gustav Aschenbach was born into a family of officials, officers, judges, and functionaries of the administration, all of whom had "lived in the service of the king, of the state," but his mother had been the daughter of a musical conductor from Bohemia. "The marriage of official, temperate conscientiousness with darker, more fiery impulses allowed an artist to arise." [44] From the first as an artist Aschenbach's "whole essence was set on fame" (450) and recognition. He hoped to show to bourgeois society the honor or dignity (*Würde*) of the artist, winning a position within society's orders and ranks and overcoming the image of the artist as illicit, distasteful, and somehow foreign. In fact he became "the master, the artist become dignified" (521); "he had won honor [*Würde*], toward which, as he maintained, a natural drive and stimulus is innate in every great talent; indeed, one can say that his whole development was a conscious and defiant [*trotziger*] ascent to honor, leaving behind all inhibitions of doubt and of irony" (454). In this description Aschenbach partially echoes Mann's self-proclaimed "secret and painful ambition continually aimed toward greatness." [45]

Impelled by his longing for honor and fame, dominated by what the world thinks of him, [46] Aschenbach continues the tradition of devoted service that his ancestors lived, but this time in a different field: he enrolls himself in "an unbending, cold, and passionate service" in art (448), for which he requires discipline "to represent from his writing table" and "to manage his fame" (450), "and discipline was fortunately his inborn inheritance from his father's side" (452). Even his precise morning ritual resembles a religious service of devotion where the strength and capacity of the self are offered up in worship, for his desk was the setting where "in two or three ardent conscientious morning hours he brought to the sacrifice the strengths he had collected in sleep" (452). Aschenbach's calling is indeed a service, a representation, and a devotion. In establishing himself as a public symbol, as the model of prose style and the champion of his age, he is in fact a kind of civil servant like his forebears, an officer and functionary in the service not only of art but also, like a prince, of the state. Furthermore, he understands his continuity and solidarity with the past, and he feels pride in being "at one" with his ancestors in his accomplishments, the descendant of men each of whom was a *Leistungsethiker* like himself. "Like every man whose natural merits inspire an aristocratic interest in his descent, he was accustomed, at the achievements and successes of his life, to think of his forebears, to assure himself of their approval, their satisfaction, their necessary respect" (503).

Yet his work is not merely routine, the plodding administration of talents and tasks, but an active and aggressive service. At the most pain-

ful moment of his self-awareness, overwhelmed by his guilty passion in
Venice, Aschenbach reflects again on his ancestors and what they might
have thought of him and reveals a profound truth about the nature of
his calling.

> He thought of them also here and now . . . thought of the principled severity,
> of the respectable masculinity of their being, and smiled dejectedly. What
> would they say? But then what would they have said to his whole life, which
> deviated from theirs to the point of degeneracy, to this life in the spell of art,
> about which he himself once, in the bourgeois spirit [*Bürgersinne*] of his fa-
> thers, had given to understand such mocking youthful judgments and which,
> at bottom, had been so similar to theirs! He too had served, he too had been
> a soldier and warrior [*Kriegsmann*] like many of them—for art was a war, a
> destructive battle, for which one was not of use for very long today. A life of
> self-overcoming and of in-spite-of [*Trotzdem*], an austere, steady, and absti-
> nent life, which he had formed into the symbol of a delicate and timely hero-
> ism—he might well call it manly, might call it brave. (503–4)

Art is war, the artist a manly soldier on the battlefield of art.[47] Despite
his misgivings about art and its waywardness, misgivings he shares with
Tonio Kröger, Aschenbach recognizes something Tonio does not: that
service in the calling is the crucial link with the past, that he has been
fundamentally like his ancestors. He is a real heir and has inherited even
more than the paternal legacy of discipline: he has inherited the calling
of the soldier, enrolled in life-and-death service, struggled against odds,
served a higher power, and differed from his forebears only in that his
service is to a different ultimate principle. This is the truth of the calling: it
is a life of battle and soldiering. Aschenbach has been all along not only a
representative figure but an exemplary one. It was not by accident that we
earlier named the calling "the vocational equivalent of war": this image of
the soldier and the combatant, of the obedient servant of king and state, is
the symbol of the times among the *Bildungsbürgertum* in Germany.

But the demands of war and of the life of the soldier are enormous.
Someone says of Aschenbach when he is ill:

> "You see, Aschenbach has always lived only like this"—and the speaker
> closed the fingers of his left hand tightly into a fist—"never like this"—and
> he let his open hand hang comfortably from the arm of his chair. It was true;
> and the gallant morality of it was that his nature from the beginning was
> something less than a robust constitution and was only called to this con-
> stant exertion, not actually born to it.[48] (451)

As we have seen, the calling is not natural. The "sentimental" modern
artist is not born to art, as was the "naive" poet, but only called to it,

and therein lies the source of heroism and ethical uprightness: the calling is a burden, taxing native capacities to the utmost. For this reason
the adherent of the calling must persist in a tight-fisted, self-commanding
way, and out of this persistence he draws self-esteem as well as empower-
ment for the performance of tasks. It is the self-esteem of those who
work beyond their means and capacities, fulfilling what they take to be
their obligations as ethical, even moral, duties. But the calling in which
the artist sacrifices himself may be too great to bear naturally. In that
case the demands on the soldier of art become more burdensome and
the virtues of the soldier more necessary, for sacrifice itself is the model
for such a life and the ultimate source of life's meaning. Aschenbach will
be defeated by his soldierly enterprise, not energized and strengthened
by it, as the Puritan saints were strengthened before him.

In exhausting the self, such a life leads Aschenbach to deception. "Indeed, he loved [that service] and also almost loved the enervating, daily
renewed battle between his tenacious and proud often-tested will and
this growing weariness, of which no one must know and which the
product must not betray in any way, through any sign of breakdown
and of weariness" (448). Like Thomas Buddenbrook, Aschenbach strives
to conceal from the world that his strength is wavering and his inspiration declining. Like Thomas, he does not take this exhaustion as a sign
that there is something the matter with the nature of the calling itself
or that there is a disharmony between his self and its needs, on the one
hand, and the requirements of the calling, on the other. Instead he hides
the weariness, warding off the possibility that others will see it and disapprove but also preventing the possibility of experiencing failure and
of radically reconsidering his service, his soldiering, and their meaning.

Yet Aschenbach has more than a glimmer of insight into the source of
his weariness and his desire to escape.

> What crippled him were the scruples of dislike, which presented itself as an
> insatiability that could not be satisfied through anything. Insatiability indeed
> had already counted to the young man as the essence and innermost nature
> of talent, and for its sake he had restrained and chilled feeling, since he knew
> that it is inclined to be satisfied with a happy approximate and with a half
> completion. Were these enslaved feelings now revenging themselves in leav-
> ing him, in refusing to carry further and to inspire his art, taking away with
> them all pleasure, all delight in form and in expression?[49] (448–49)

Having commanded his feelings to soldierly purposes by chilling them
and working against their nature, Aschenbach has harnessed them to
his will. He has overcome himself and his "heat" and transformed him-

self into a being made for art, existing only in and through his service
and its fulfillment. Like Tonio, Aschenbach has become something no
longer quite human, but unlike Tonio, Aschenbach understands that he
has chosen to *do* this to feeling and has not been fated to *be* so. On
behalf of his art Aschenbach has acted and fit himself for battle, but the
cost to him is fearful. Feeling—however unseemly, immoderate, and too
easily satisfied—is the source not only of the experience that is made
into art but also of the pleasure and delight the artist takes in his own
creating, the intoxication of his artistry. If the pleasure vanishes, then
there remains only the role, as Thomas Buddenbrook knew.

Aschenbach strives to maintain the illusion of strength and command, rather than examining the reality of his situation with his famous
cold eye to see it for what it is. Apparently committed to artistic truth,
this man actually conceals and protects a lie at the center of his life. In
this respect Aschenbach is like so many others of his time, and it is this
connection and affinity that is the source of his popularity.

> Gustav Aschenbach was the poet of all those who labor on the brink of ex-
> haustion, of the overburdened, already worn out, who still hold themselves
> upright, of all these moralists of achievement [*Leistung*], who, slight in
> growth and short of means, win for a time at least the effects of greatness
> through transports of will and wise administration. Of them there are many;
> they are the heroes of the time. And they all recognized themselves again in
> his work, they found themselves confirmed, extolled, celebrated therein, they
> were grateful to him, they proclaimed his name. (453–54)

Aschenbach's representation is now revealed: he is the representative
of the weak who, in the midst of their exhaustion, persist in their obligations and in their tasks. Indeed, Aschenbach's favorite word is
"'*Durchhalten*' . . . the essence of actively suffering virtue" (451), meaning "hold out" or "carry through." Because he will not yield his position despite his weariness, Aschenbach is able to complete works of
excellence "because their creator could hold out for years under the
pressure of one and the same work with a permanence of will and tenac-
ity" (452).

In this attitude Aschenbach resembles his own creator, who, in 1906,
describing his struggle and exhaustion in writing an essay he had promised but found difficult to complete, said: "but I had engaged myself and
obeyed my categorical imperative '*durchhalten*'!" Mann suggested that
his work method involved "clenching the teeth and slowly putting one
foot in front of the other" and that it required further "a patience—
what am I saying! an obstinacy, a stubbornness, a discipline, a self-

enslavement of the will that is hard to imagine and under which the nerves, believe me, are often stretched to screaming." Yet in this process belief in the work ceases to be automatic and natural and becomes artificial: "the greater part of one's nervous strength is expended to stimulate that faith," Mann writes, leaving the artist to wonder if the work is ultimately worth this strength and whether such energy will have been translated ultimately into a work of quality.[50]

It is in the midst of his later intoxication for the boy Tadzio that Aschenbach struggles to reaffirm a conception of himself as a man who, despite great odds, despite inner mockery and doubt, despite weariness, has been able to continue in his service: not only has he been a hero on the battlefield, but he has never before abandoned his post. Only through his attachment to his calling despite temptations, his unwavering commitment no matter what the cost, has he been able to regard himself highly in the outer world of the present and the inner world of the past. Even in Venice, where he is faced with the ultimate challenge to his dignity and persistence, he reminds himself of his heroism and so preserves a small shred of dignity based on his past "service record," though it cannot stand up for long to the onslaught of his fatal passion.

But Aschenbach believes not only that this suffering and persistence are the source of his own greatness; like the Schiller of "A Difficult Hour" and like Mann himself, he believes suffering to be the nature of all greatness. It is not only that struggling against obstacles is the strength of the great; it is also that his own achievement is won, despite his suffering, against the ultimate obstacle: the limits and weaknesses of self.

> Aschenbach had once stated directly in an inconspicuous place that nearly everything great that stands forth, stands forth as an in-spite-of [*ein Trotzdem*], has come about in spite of sorrow and suffering, poverty, destitution, physical weakness, vice, passion, and a thousand hindrances. But that was more than an observation, it was an experience, was directly the formula of his life and reputation, the key to his work; and what wonder thus if it was also the ethical character, the outward gesture of his most characteristic figures? (452–53)

As Mann wrote about himself in 1906, "Heroism is for me an 'in-spite-of' [*ein Trotzdem*], weakness overcome."[51] This is another form of the religion of suffering, in which greatness is linked to the weaknesses from which self-overcoming arises. Suffering is redeemed in the greatness achieved, the experience of service eventuating in achievement. In the midst of this suffering it is necessary to "hold on," for only so is there any chance for the achievement of great works. Schiller's self-defense against Goethe is resurrected to describe not just one form of achievement but all forms of achievement.

Aschenbach has, then, an ideological justification of the meaning and pattern of his life. Therefore it is even more necessary for him to struggle against his weaknesses and not give in, for he is not seeking a momentary accomplishment or success after which he may put down his burden. Since this ideology is the source of meaning for his life, he must struggle continuously. This is a "wakeful self-control" worthy of the Puritans. But it is, in fact, *not* a theory of persistence in the face of crises. It is a theory of permanent crisis: permanent suffering, permanent weakness, and exhaustion completely govern and determine the life of Aschenbach and of those stoical figures he creates. Weakness and suffering are the crucial and perpetual characteristics of life; for those who would achieve anything at all, the response must be a permanent war footing. Only by an institutionalized command of the impulses and weaknesses of the flesh can one's service be carried forward and one's calling preserved. Obstacles—and we are speaking now of inner obstacles—are seen only as challenges to be overcome. And if they seem overwhelming, then one must put a brave face on it and let no one else know, for Aschenbach's world is as harsh and unforgiving as Thomas Buddenbrook's. There is no relief in sight, no column of other soldiers that can support a failing warrior, for all such battles are waged alone against the elements, the elements of self and the elements of art. Doubts, hesitations, and fatigue are not questioned; they must be overcome by an effort of the will even if they are warning signals. But neither Aschenbach nor his audience and supporters care about such signals; they treasure the civilianized military virtues of the heart above all else, the determination of cripples to go on fighting.

Reading Aschenbach's works, says the narrator of the story—and Erich Heller remarks that Aschenbach has had no other life than that of a writer of works [52]—"one could doubt whether there was generally any other form of heroism [*Heroismus*] than that of weakness. What heroism [*Heldentum*], however, could be more timely after all than this one?" (453). Its model is St. Sebastian. Of this new hero an observer of Aschenbach's work writes:

> He is the conception "of an intellectual and youthful manliness who in proud shame clenches his teeth and stands there calmly, while the swords and spears go through his body." That was beautiful, ingenious and exact, despite its apparent all-too-passive stamp. For self-possession [*Haltung*] in

the face of fate, grace in the face of torture, means not only sufferance; it is an active achievement, a positive triumph, and the figure of Sebastian is the most beautiful symbol, if not for all of art, then certainly for the art under discussion. (453)

As Mann wrote in 1904: "'Happiness' is a service. Happiness, *my* happiness, is to a high degree experience, movement, knowledge, torture; it is related too little to peace and too closely to suffering."[53] Aschenbach's heroes are the analogue to the times, persistent in the midst of martyrdom despite their claims of "active" sufferance. But Sebastian suffered and died for Christ. For what do these modern Sebastians suffer and die? What faith do they profess and protect in their resistance and their death? Without a "highest value" of any kind to give content to their suffering, they must persist for the sake of persistence; they protect only their sense of themselves as soldiers who do not give in, who endure arrows on behalf of their calling, never abandoning their post. They must be satisfied with devotion to work and its achievement and completion, for they have nothing else. They are compelled to elevate their service and their accomplishments into a life-justifying, meaning-giving practice. This is their virtue and their excellence.

Aschenbach will take his virtues and persistence to Venice, ready to give up the struggle to resist his inner truth, his exhaustion and sense of defeat, and ready ultimately to give up the resistance to his passion.[54] Yet, up to this point he has been overcoming obstacles all his life. Though the greatest obstacle at present is weariness or exhaustion, it has not always been so. In his youth, the obstacles were more intellectually significant and noble, and the triumph over them more elevated and "admirable" as a consequence. They were obstacles like those Tonio Kröger encountered, the temptation of bohemianism and the life of extremes, as well as the more fatal temptation of knowledge. The obstacle most threatening to Aschenbach's life and art, we are told, was insight into the truth of human purpose and morality. His insights threatened to cripple his resolution and judgment; they set him against society and its false ideals, leading him to mock "innocent" action and the unself-consciousness of life and to become a critic, even an "enemy," of life. The young Aschenbach loved the problematical and was "absolutist." He was "a slave to intellect [*Geist*]," "discredited talent, betrayed art," addressed himself principally to "the believers," and derived his effect from "his cynicism about the questionable nature of art, of artists" (454). Had he persisted, he would have remained critical, detached, and self-conscious. Tonio found the complement, rather than the antidote, to knowledge in "love" of life, and he believed this love was necessary for a true artist. But unlike Tonio, the mature Aschenbach simply rejects these obstacles: knowledge, the disenchantment of ascetic morality, and the penetration of the pretenses and masks of life to uncover its hidden truth. He does so to make possible an ordinary life he thinks to be no longer strong and vital but rather weak and overburdened. He makes it his task to defend the morality of the weak and tired, who persist in their outer life, though their inner truth is defeat. Whereas Tonio, Mann would have us believe, knows the truth and accepts doubts, Aschenbach turns away from doubt and hides truth. Yet this means that Aschenbach takes the life of Thomas Buddenbrook as his model: in abolishing doubt, he founds his own life on self-deception and deliberate blindness.

But Mann also intends us to understand Aschenbach as an older Tonio, a Tonio who has taken a wrong turn into life and its conventionality and pretenses, and away from the critical distance given by mind, intellect, or spirit. Only distance makes the artist a mediator rather than a simple partisan; only distance gives ironic disengagement to the man who knows the truth yet still cherishes the disenchanted object. But Aschenbach leaves behind his youth, which was antiromantic, cynical, and pessimistic, and leaves behind too the knowledge that served him as sword and fire against the idols of his time. Instead, he resolved "to deny knowing [das Wissen], to reject it, to pass it by with raised head, insofar as it is suited to lame, to discourage, to degrade, in the smallest way, will, act, feeling, or even passion" (454−55). He wrote instead with "revulsion against the indecent psychologism of the time," and he proclaimed "the renunciation of all moral doubt [Zweifelsinn] and of sympathy with the abyss, the refusal of the laxity of the sympathetic principle, that to understand all means to forgive all, and what was here prepared, yes even completed, was the 'wonder of reborn ingenuousness' [Unbefangenheit]"[55] (455).

Mann purposefully chooses Unbefangenheit, which can also be translated as "naïveté" or "detachment," to signify the recapture of what Tonio Kröger believed was lost through the submission to and service of knowledge: the "enchantment," spontaneity, unself-consciousness, and naive quality of life and action that, once penetrated and understood by knowledge or mind, is "disenchanted," undermined, and destroyed. It is through the magic of the calling that Aschenbach hopes to regain the naive quality of art and overcome this disenchantment. But he can only do so at the cost of deliberate blindness, for in Tonio's calling "rightly understood," disenchantment cannot be overcome. One can only learn to live with it and recognize that life will remain enchanted for those not burdened with the artist's knowledge. The artist must live between enchantment and disenchantment, loving life but knowing that the magic is only illusion.

Thus Aschenbach's renunciation is clearly not the product of a new moral revelation or understanding but, rather, a functional resolve, a determination to free himself from the irony and criticism that have threatened to "blunt" his "noble and virtuous spirit," threatened to undermine the conviction he believes the artist requires. He has, consequently—and for the practical reason of self-protection—turned away from knowledge that disenchants and demystifies his enterprise. He has turned away from what he believes to be negativity, to cling to conviction, certainty, and a moral posture from which he is able to judge and defend and in which he is able to stand for something positive and sure. Thus he is able to write a novel, *A Wretched Man (Ein Elender)*, which "showed a whole thankful rising generation the possibility of moral resoluteness beyond the deepest knowledge" (450). Indeed, the narrator notes that Aschenbach has even written an essay on spirit and art (*Geist und Kunst*)—based on Mann's own failed attempt to write such a work—which, the narrator says, is said to rank with Schiller's essay on naive and sentimental poetry. This essay, the reader has to presume, would have worked out theoretically Aschenbach's own reborn naïveté, the salvation of the sentimental poet;[56] indeed, the narrator wonders whether it is Aschenbach's "rebirth" and departure from knowledge that have caused his works to take on a classicism of form, a "strengthening of his feeling for beauty," a "noble purity, simplicity, and symmetry of form-giving" (455).

These obstacles, then, are the ones the narrator depicts, according to his agenda, to show us the dangers that confront the artist and the times: either threatening paralysis or the need for surrender and the laying down of one's burden, neither of which is acceptable. The struggle of the aging artist who has needed to live resolutely and without doubt in a time full of doubt, without knowledge in a time when knowledge is a necessity, is a struggle that cannot come to a good end. Indeed, the narrator forecasts the dangers early in the story, dangers that lie in coupling the "morality" of artistic form with the necessary "immorality" of artistic content.

> But moral [*moralische*] resoluteness beyond knowing, beyond disintegrating and inhibiting knowledge—does that not again mean a reduction, an ethical [*sittliche*] simplification of the world and the soul and therefore also a strengthening of evil, of the forbidden, of the ethically [*sittliche*] impossible?

And does form not have two faces? Is it not moral and amoral [*sittlich und unsittlich*] at the same time—moral as a result and an expression of discipline, but amoral, and even immoral, insofar as it includes by nature a moral indifference, indeed strives essentially to bend the moral under its proud and absolute scepter? (455)

It is precisely Aschenbach's achievement in the moral realm that the narrator chooses to mock and to ironize when his prediction comes true and his forecast of danger is fulfilled. Aschenbach, who believes himself to be at one with his calling and to have surmounted the crippling of judgment, is brought low by his descent into forbidden realms, by his attraction to forbidden love, within the same sex and across the generations, even to the point of having himself made up rather grotesquely in a beauty shop to appear young and attractive.

He sat there, the master, the artist become dignified, the author of *A Wretched Man*, which had renounced the gypsy life [*Zigeunertum*] and the murky deep in such exemplary pure form, had renounced sympathy with the abyss and had rejected the rejected ones, he who had risen so high, who, overcoming his knowledge and outgrowing all irony, had accustomed himself to the obligations of public confidence, he, whose reputation was official, whose name was ennobled, and on whose style boys were encouraged to pattern [*zu bilden*] themselves. (521)

In this reversal the narrative strategy is fulfilled. Aschenbach is shown to be defeated by the powers he has defended too strongly and defeated as well by straying from the path of Tonio Kröger. The problem of moral shipwreck on the reefs of his own resolve was not the principal danger for Tonio Kröger. He faced isolation from life, emasculation by his service to art, a chilling of feeling by his use of life solely for the purposes of creation. Aschenbach too confronts similar problems, though at a much later stage of life; but the narrator of *Death in Venice* uses these problems simply as a pretext for the trip that will prove Aschenbach's undoing. Tonio's trip, in contrast, brought a confrontation with the truth and Tonio's liberation through a kind of self-acceptance. He accepted his isolation and evolved an ideology of art and the artist that justified him, but not "too much," for he remained enthralled by life while still in the service of knowledge, locked into the experience and perspective of his calling. Though Tonio lamented what knowledge had done to him, he came to a reconciliation with it and with life, never tempted to cast knowledge aside, for he believed that only the ignorant may live freely, freed of the scruples, doubts, and hesitations produced by knowledge. For those with knowledge there is no way back.

But the narrator of *Death in Venice* presents Aschenbach's case differently. Overcoming knowledge, getting too close to life, upholding persistence in the face of weakness, and defending morality are said to haunt Aschenbach and set him up for the complete destruction that the confrontation with the forbidden brings about. Mann presents this story with numerous symbols of foreboding and illness, with subtle but clear interpretations of the dilemma of Aschenbach, overloading the story and striving to draw our attention to these features of the tale. But in the gaps between these emphases and these conscious and purposeful narrative devices, we find in addition another story and a different calamity: the story of a burden and tragedy great enough to call into question both the whole meaning of art pursued as a calling and the personality constructed and enrolled in its service. This story goes unnoticed by the narrator.

Fantasy of Possession and Possession by Fantasy

Mann and his imaginary narrator take some distance from Aschenbach, interpret him, ironize him, point out what they take to be his dilemma and the source of his doom. Their interpretation is decisively and effectively summarized in the last "selection" from *Phaedrus* that Aschenbach contemplates in the midst of his exhausted hunt for his beloved Tadzio, just after he has eaten the strawberries that will kill him. The Socrates of this speech reflects on how the path of beauty is a path through the senses, which cannot lead to "wisdom and manly worth."

> Do you now see clearly that we poets cannot be either wise or dignified? That we necessarily go astray, necessarily remain dissolute and adventurers of feeling? The mastery of our style is lies and foolishness, our fame and position of honor a farce. . . . how could someone be a fit teacher who is born to an unimprovable and natural tendency to the abyss? . . . let us . . . renounce dissolving knowledge, for knowledge, Phaedrus, has no dignity and strictness. . . . Let us abandon this with decisiveness, and from now on our efforts will be applicable only to beauty, which means simplicity, greatness and new strictness, a second naïveté [*Unbefangenheit*], and form. But form and naïveté, Phaedrus, lead to intoxication and to desire . . . lead to the abyss. (521–22)

This is the fate of all poets, thinks Aschenbach's Socrates, for the path through beauty is led by Eros, and although we may be "heroes in our own way and disciplined men of war, even so we are just like women, for passion is our exaltation, and our longing must remain love—that is our desire and our shame" (522). A longing that must remain love—a notion taken directly from Lukács's discussion of the *Symposium*[57]—means in this context a longing that cannot be elevated beyond the earthly to strive for perfection and the higher ideal. To remain love means to remain earth-bound, caught in the webs of desire that cannot move beyond the traps of the senses to the higher truth. Poets, Aschenbach reflects, cannot attain wisdom; instead they are condemned to reside in the world of sense and waywardness. Here, then, is the narrator's analysis of Aschenbach's downfall: he has run from the abyss near which the poet must reside; he has hoped to fend off intoxication and desire by the renunciation of knowledge, for knowledge, to Aschenbach, "*is* the abyss"; but for him there is no escape, for it is the poet's very nature to be led astray on the path to beauty, and thus the dignity and honors sought and received are an absurdity and a deception of self and public.

But, more than this, the *Phaedrus* passage suggests that in Aschenbach's understanding the true identity of the poet is feminine, enslaved to passion, bound to give in to desire, no matter how much he struggles, no matter how great his renunciation, no matter how manly the soldierly pursuit. And now we see that in Aschenbach's mind and the narrator's interpretation, the struggle to be a soldier of the calling is a gendered struggle, a struggle to ward off identification with the feminine. Aschenbach's true identity is essentially female, construed here as the burden, embarrassment, and shame shared by all poets. The woman within every artist has her revenge over the soldier of the calling by coming back and being attracted to other men. That degrading and degraded side of the artist's self must be accepted as his fate, despite the embarrassment and disgrace it brings with it. Even if one denies it, it will still return to overwhelm and destroy the "man of war." The narrator has told a powerful story of problematical gender identity and of artistic nature that must learn to live with the sensual, the wayward, and the ambiguous as well as with the insights into this world that knowledge brings.

This interpretation of the narrator's is certainly a useful and compelling understanding of Aschenbach's problem, according to which Aschenbach cannot escape the "nature" of the artist, try as he may, but in so trying brings on his own doom.[58] Valuable as this interpretation is, however, this is not a tale whose key really lies in a "wrong" relationship to knowledge or desire, or in the consequences of an explosive homoerotic passion, which other artists have lived through with success. And it is far more than a tale of an artist too close to bourgeois life.

It is true that Aschenbach's secret homoerotic passion drives him literally to self-destruction. It is also true that Aschenbach does not wish to acknowledge the "disease" at the center of his life and that he delights, by analogy and symbol, in keeping secret his knowledge of the disease spreading in Venice. But the real key to Aschenbach's condition is found neither in his submission to illicit desires nor in his absolutist defense of bourgeois life.[59] It is found in the spreading disease of his calling, which has killed his internal life as surely as the cholera will kill his body and has made him incapable of meeting reality on its own ground.

Having made over his life and work into service, his success into a theory of persistence, the reality of his fatigue into the image of strength, Aschenbach takes his old eyes to Venice and once again turns life into something "greater" than life, though this time not only into fiction: he sees an attractive boy and turns him into a representative of Platonic beauty on earth,[60] a dream, a form, an illusion. Aschenbach's calling has become a service in which he sees, has seen, and can see nothing as it is, neither his own life nor the world. He has ceaselessly turned life into symbol and lesson, into fiction and romance. He tries in Venice to grasp and to live out as real what was, from the start of his experience of Tadzio, a wild distortion of reality. The truth of Aschenbach's passion is not mainly that it is homoerotic but that it is an all-consuming fantasy of possession and acclaim. It inspires him to seek after "beauty itself," an object of Platonic interest he had longed to conquer his whole life, whose creator he had wished to be in art, and which he now seems to see in real life.

> What a discipline, what precision of thought was expressed in this stretched-out and youthfully perfect body. Yet the strict and pure will, which, working darkly, had been able to raise this godly artwork into the light—was it not known and familiar to him, the artist? . . . in enthusiastic rapture he believed with this glance to be grasping beauty itself, form as divine thought, the single and pure perfection that lives in the mind [Geist] and from which a human replica and image was here raised up, light and lovely, for adoration. This was intoxication; and without thinking, yes eagerly, the aging artist bid it welcome. (490)

Suddenly Aschenbach's life has become a mythological drama set among the ancient Greeks,[61] drawing on Plato's *Phaedrus* as its seducer's dialogue and the vehicle of Aschenbach's reflections on beauty.[62] Mann, as narrator, has intended us to see Aschenbach as a Tonio Kröger gone astray; having turned his back on the dark forces in art and clung to the respectable side of his service, he has won honors while denying

feeling and refusing insight into hidden depths[63]—the Apollonian denying the Dionysian, which eventually takes its revenge. But at the same
time this story calls into question Aschenbach's whole relation to the
world, to fame, to calling, to feeling, to art, to symbolization, and to
self. It calls into question the whole model of personality built on self-
conquest through a calling, cherished and supported in its "true" form
by Mann as well as Weber, a model in which the self "dies to life" in
order to render life totally available for service.

It is called into question because Aschenbach never sees the real
child, the real boy—never mind the gender of the object of his passion.
Aschenbach reflects: "To rest in perfection is the longing of him who
works hard at excellence" (475), and such perfection is not found only
in the sea, which triggers this self-observation. The genuine tragedy of
Death in Venice is that Aschenbach cannot have a real passion for an
actual person in the world, male or female, because he transforms all he
sees into dream, ideal, and the artistically satisfying and desirable. It is
in fact not a real boy whom Aschenbach genuinely covets but rather a
dream child, a dream of perfection and beauty that leads to yet another,
much more powerful, dream: the fantasy of himself as master and pos-
sessor of the beautiful. That is the reason for the fatal allure that cannot
be avoided, that must be courted even unto death: how is it possible to
leave what one takes to be perfection, the idealization of all one's desires, when it seems so near to one's grasp, when one has longed for just
this conquest above all and all along? The world has other beautiful
boys, if that is what one truly desires; but embodiments of Platonic
beauty are very difficult to find. Once one has sighted, once been allowed
to view the mystery, it is hard to believe that one will ever again be able
to find it.[64] This allure does not contradict the resentment at such perfection that Aschenbach also feels when, observing Tadzio's teeth, he
experiences pleasure at the thought that the boy is sickly and will not
live to grow old (479). The ambivalence of the artist-creator toward an
embodiment of beauty he has not created is here revealed, a testimony
to the limitations of his own art and life's work, triggering an even more
intense desire for possession.

Tadzio is in fact a creation of the artist who has totally displaced the
man; just as feeling has fled after its too stringent domination by art, so
too has the life of the man. Aschenbach has himself "died to life," as
Tonio said one must, but he has done so too fully: he is now only an
artist, only a soldier in the calling, struggling through the darkness and
the mist after the fantasy objective of conquest. He has to this point sac-

rificed everything for the calling: feeling, truth, internal divisions, and doubts. Now there is nothing else left. What Mann has actually revealed is the nature of the calling as a way of life, visible in its total powerlessness when truly confronted with life. Aschenbach is the only artist Mann ever created with a passion, and even he is incapable of real passion, that is, passion for something real. He is so locked into art that even his passion is mediated by it and by the devotion to the abstract ideal of beauty. As Mann once put it in an essay (1906): "'The artist,' a poet and thinker has said, 'who does not abandon [preisgeben] his whole self, is a useless slave.' That is undyingly true." But Mann's next sentence is even more telling and full of foreboding when read in the context of this story, and it reveals the dilemma that the choice for self-sacrifice creates: "Yet how can I abandon my whole self without at the same time abandoning the world, which is my representation [Vorstellung]?" [65]

T. J. Reed suggests that Aschenbach's passion starts out as self-deceiving: Aschenbach takes his strong interest to be a merely aesthetic interest in the boy as an image of beauty, as a statue, as an embodiment of perfection, and only afterward is he overcome by the real interest, which is passionate, physical, and homoerotic. Moreover, Reed suggests, remarking on Tadzio's bad teeth and his flirtatiousness: "Tadzio is here far from the ideal, not a mere perfect statue, nor a miraculous epiphany. . . . His beauty is skin-deep." Of course, as Reed notes, the narrator does not have "a positive view of Aschenbach's passion." [66] But Aschenbach's passion from beginning to end is actually a love of the myth, of the statuesque, of the beautiful—never a love of the *real* boy but only of his fantasy of the boy. The difference between the early observation and the later longing lies in the development of the uncontrollable desire for possession of the fantasized object, *not* in the changing nature or appearance of the actual object. Aschenbach has looked at everything—and lived his own life—as a symbol. He has finally come to *love* only symbols. The tragedy is that *Aschenbach now lives completely in symbols.* This is the outcome and consequence of the calling that has forced feeling to its knees, denied real life, and dwelled in coldness, rendering everything else cold as well. His personality is entrapped by the conquest of the self purely for the higher ideal of art and by its transformation for service in the calling. The higher ideal or cause—art, beauty, whatever—has taken his whole substance for itself and has left the man a shell.

Death in Venice is in many ways a tale of what René Girard calls "triangular" or "mediated desire," desire for an object that has been elevated through perception of it as an embodiment of the ideal.[67] Thomas Mann has shown here, in fact, what can happen to the personality "immoderately" given over to the icy service of the ideal. *Death in Venice* is not principally about the return of repressed life; it is about the *inability* of "dead" life to return, and about the revenge of the real self and inner man that have been conquered and killed. They are revenged on the Kantian and Schopenhauerian aesthetic ideal, according to which one must "disown for some time his own personality" in order to produce the object of art. It is revenge because the personality, the reborn self of art, is now a coffin for the soul and nothing more. The "aristocrat of the spirit" has, first, died to life completely, then, second, been degraded, which is another death in life, and only then does he finally die. It is the *first* death, which Mann does not recognize as such, that is the key to the other deaths: the death in life of the life in the calling, where the self is remade and equipped for service and the purposes of art and *can do nothing other* than serve, can no longer really live. The religion of suffering, which compensates for the fact of suffering, is the hope of the weak, exhausted, and tired. This heroism of suffering does not recognize that the suffering is the product of the choice for the death of life among the living, but believes in this death as the source of its heroism, as a form of nobility, as the meaning of its life. Hence it can no longer gain access to life, no matter how understood. Aschenbach has always lived his life as the clenched fist. Now the hand cannot open.[68]

In a sensitive interpretation of the work, Hans Vaget suggests that "in the argument with the Aschenbach within him" Mann was able to distance himself from the model of "neoclassical" writing to which he had recently been drawn. Moreover, Vaget argues, the story must be seen as a "critique of Wilhelminianism," for Aschenbach shares the qualities of the "ruling powers" in Germany. "He is unequivocally constructed as an embodiment of the puritanical-soldierly heritage in Wilhelmine Germany. Insofar as Thomas Mann conveys the intellectual and moral aporia of this heritage, he provides the diagnosis of the state that appeals to this heritage."[69] Subtle and profound as this argument is, it is not in fact what the story's narrator tries to convey, nor is it what Thomas Mann initially felt about the story, for shortly after the outbreak of war Mann passionately defended precisely this soldierly conception of the artist. Vaget is right, however, in pointing to this theme as the central lesson to be learned about such a conception of the calling, even though this conclusion must be teased out of the story *against* the purposes of both the narrator and the author. The model of the self-sacrificing soldier, whose life is put up for his cause and who can no longer return to "civilian" life even if he physically survives, is the heart and essence of the calling.

Mann has revealed here, whatever his explicit intentions, the potential truth of the calling as a way of life and the cost to its practitioners. It has been a form of self-conquest and conquest of others that sunders the man from life itself and undercuts the ability to have real relationships. Controlling relations to the world by struggling after fame, persisting despite his exhaustion, controlling the real inner man by resisting all desires and all misgivings, refusing to reveal himself as he truly is, Aschenbach has no other possibilities of relating save domination, possession, resistance, and control.[70] Still, his strongest desire in Venice is to give up struggling, to cease resisting, to leave aside self-analysis, and to yield to impulse and feeling. When he achieves his desire it is, of course, suicidal, for it is out of all proportion to reality. To pursue his fantasy object he even courts death by remaining in a city plagued with cholera, and he has himself covered with makeup in a beauty shop in an effort to appear attractive to youth. Having covered up so much in his inner, spiritual, life until then and transformed everything in the outer world into symbol and emblem, Aschenbach now conceals his real external appearance so that his own physical life and body now deny their truth and cover themselves up.

The narrator of the story has said that the calling was against Aschenbach's nature. The calling is in fact an elaborate contrivance to overcome nature. It overcomes natural limits of strength as well as doubts about living and art. It overcomes others' negative judgments about oneself and one's own images of oneself as unsoldierly and unfaithful to one's ancestors or one's task. Finally, it overcomes the reality of the world in its everyday existence: others are remade as well as oneself. Aschenbach carries out a fantasy of possession through devoted service in which he is shaped, inwardly and outwardly, for transforming the world into an object of his creation and for achieving success despite natural limitations. His project is to win strength and unself-consciousness and to be able to carry on in service. But he never pauses to examine the calling for its worth, meaning, function, and effect on the self and the world or for its real purposes.

The calling is, at bottom, a form of magic, elevating work into a totem of redemption when transformed into service and devotion to a high ideal in the calling. Hanno Buddenbrook died for lack of a calling, either in life or in art. But even for the survivors and those strong enough to endure the calling, it may still end up killing the person, either for life or actually in life. It can render real relationships with others impossible, for others have been transformed beyond reality into idealizations of life or good or beauty or evil. Tonio Kröger's vision of Hans and Inge, the embodiments of idealized life, was no less fanciful than Aschenbach's of Tadzio. The difference is that Tonio "spiritualizes" and sublimates his love. In either case the real man is still displaced by art and must be supported by ideology. Identity becomes dependent on the death of the self and its rebirth for the purpose of work. Art does not use the self for only a time, for purposes other than those of desire and feeling, after which the self may feel again; it traps the self behind impenetrable walls. Reality is reified into essences and hypostatized qualities; everything is transformed into art and symbol. The calling prevents the called person from facing others and self truly and equips him with a mask, a persona, that protects the personality and conceals the truth. But disappointments overcome by mystifications of calling, destiny, art, and life are disappointments unfaced and unresolved.

The life of the artist in the calling may, of course, be viable. Look at Mann himself; not everyone need end like Aschenbach, for it is still possible to diagnose the sickness within oneself and to combat it. Yet the possibility of such a degeneration of life in the calling remains a constant threat, for it is a threat too close to the heart and nature of the calling to be completely and definitively overcome. Aschenbach's life has brought him to a position of exhaustion and weakness, as has Schiller's in "A Difficult Hour," but its resolution in Venice is complete defeat and death, not self-overcoming and the resumption of work. Such a life is not lived honestly and truthfully, not while it is in thrall to an art that claims to be interested in truth but will not acknowledge the truth about itself. *Death in Venice* reveals and inadvertently explodes a crucial aspect of the ideology of the calling—the calling as the life of a soldier— not only in the guise of a critique of a degenerated calling but, more important, in its defense of the calling "rightly understood." This revelation of the truth will have important consequences for Max Weber's later attempt to generalize the calling as a solution for Germany.

As Vaget suggests, "to the degree that *Tonio Kröger* wants to persuade us to the belief in a successful overcoming of decadence, *Death in Venice* signals its revocation."[71] Yet in *Death in Venice,* which Mann claimed was "actually *Tonio Kröger* told again at a higher stage of life,"[72] the fate of the bourgeois personality becomes the fate of the artist's personality as well. Aschenbach is another Thomas Buddenbrook, as Mann suggested, endowed with many of Mann's own characteristics along with some of Goethe's.[73] Having tried to master the world through his calling, Aschenbach collapses inwardly, yet persists. Eventually he collapses outwardly as well. Mann even spoke of him later as his "dead friend."[74] Ultimately Aschenbach finds no refuge of any kind in life, despite his defense of it and his overwhelming and successful drive to win its approval. All he has left is his art, and it is cold. His art—or, rather, his way of serving his art in the calling—estranges him from life and in an even more dramatic and frightful way than it does Tonio Kröger: his personality, constructed in the service of art, is a prison of the soul preventing him from seeing anything in life with the eyes of a real human being unmediated by the fictionalizing, symbolizing, and elevating tendencies of his art.

The Crisis of Personality

In Mann's work after *Tonio Kröger,* the calling is recognized more explicitly for the suffering it is part of. Yet although the life of service-as-justification is a principal cause of suffering, it remains the source of redemption in the minds of its adherents. It transforms the mere worker into a soldier, hero, and champion of art and ennobles him by teaching him the princely and representative role he plays. Hence the personality of the artist in the calling is elevated and built on the identical forms of self-conquest and self-denial that have always been part of its meaning.

But underneath these developments a serious crisis is brewing, revealed in *Death in Venice,* where the self-absorption of the artist and his transformation into a soldier have led to a more total estrangement from life than even Tonio Kröger experienced. It is the crisis of the artist no longer able to penetrate the world, frozen within the icy realms of his artistry, unable to see anything more significant in the world than what his imagination creates or his artistic self desires. Without the sense of proportion brought by a more constructive relation to the world, he projects his inner fantasies strongly and irresistibly onto the outer world so that all life is finally negated—not only the inner life of the artist but the reality of life outside as well. Since Mann saw himself in Thomas Buddenbrook, Tonio Kröger, and Aschenbach, decline and collapse in some form and at some point must have been a possible danger for him.

But though Aschenbach sinks, Mann not only survives: he triumphs. His artistic nature, as he says in a letter, forced him to objectify his own experience, to detach himself from it, and thus to turn it into art, a symbolic version of his own experience. Thus Mann's art can be identified with Aschenbach's only partially, for it marks a form of overcoming. Only the outside intervention of war, however, rescued Mann definitively from these threats.

Conclusion to Part II and Prospect: The Redemption of the Self

Our task has been to reveal Weber's and Mann's notion of the calling, in its origins and development, as a mode of asceticism for legitimating and accepting the self by using it to build and shape a new and higher self and mobilizing it on behalf of an ultimate value. For both men it was important to recover the calling from its routinization and its failures in order to appropriate it for contemporary use. Ultimately they strove to adapt the calling for the regeneration of the self and the reformation of the identity of the sons of the modern bourgeoisie.

Weber and Mann confronted the problem of identity through a consideration of their personal experience of the self and their rejection of it in its natural form. The self is initially experienced as unacceptable to the "witness" within the bourgeois class and to the internalized bourgeois witness within the self. Weber and Mann then construct an acceptable or redeemed self by discovering a new and higher validating witness in the form of a more ultimate value. For them only the use of the self, not its being, can make it valuable, or at least acceptable; only its capacity to live in service redeems it. In its own terms the natural self is not only without value to Weber and Mann but is an obstacle to the discovery and service of value and to the forging of identity as well. In subjecting the self to a discipline that makes it acceptable, however, they do not investigate the nature of the self as it is given. In place of an "open" attitude toward self-understanding and self-discovery, Weber and Mann "close" the self by making the ascetic self the supreme self and only "strong" self and by making service to higher values the only legitimate form of life conduct. By transforming the self into a personality they redeem the self from itself, from its loss of social recognition, and from helplessness. But in so doing they can never fully discover or accept the self as it truly is or may be, with its strengths, weaknesses, and needs, or understand the personal and social reasons why they believe the self must be fashioned thus or redeemed at all. Instead, in their examinations of history and of their own experience, they rely on an inherited ascetic self-discipline whose roots are in religion and the bourgeois class. This resolution certainly protects them from the loss of direction and self-certainty that the cultural and social crisis of modern Europe threatened. But it does not allow them to understand the deeper nature of Europe's crisis or of their own.

Though they began from very different places, Weber's and Mann's work converged on these questions of self, identity, and meaning. Weber, on the one hand, began with an investigation into certain components of the capitalist cultural order but ended up identifying one of the most powerful disciplines of self-justification and self-empowerment that the West had ever seen. Mann, on the other hand, started from the inner experience of a capitalist family in crisis but ended up identifying a discipline for self-redemption that derives from that family and from the same cultural order that Weber analyzed. The "Occidental self" of Weber's work and the artist's calling of Mann's are devices of self-transformation with enormous ramifications, both historical and personal. A few words are in order about where these discoveries lead them.

In his analysis of the crisis of meaning in the modern world and in his proposed solutions to the crisis of the political order in Germany, Weber brought to bear what he had learned about calling and personality from his scholarly studies: he attempted the reconsideration and revival of a personal ethos and a pattern for the self, now degraded or lost, and a mode of shaping political character that had no precedent in the German past. Apart from the significant historical "discovery" in *The Protestant Ethic* of a unique spirit linked to ascetic Protestantism and its role in the development of capitalism, Weber discovered not just a new self that appeared in the West in the sixteenth century, but a new "overcoming" of self: a self that is understood, in its natural form, to be creaturely, vain, and even damned. Yet it is a self that can be—indeed, must be—used to create a personality, achieved through the commitment to serve an ultimate ideal through *Beruf*. At the same time Weber wished to salvage personality from the degradation of vulgar interpreters and the wreckage of religious traditions to inject it more systematically and clearly into secular life, especially in the realms of intellectual inquiry, or "science," and politics. The Puritan conception of personality ultimately served him, in a secular form and a secular world, as a prescription for the illness of the times and of his nation. It was intended as a corrective to the false paths he thought his fellow countrymen were treading in private and public life and in intellectual and political struggles. It was also intended as a substitute for failed models of the self and the self's relation to society, no longer sustainable by the traditional but now-problematical German ideals of *Kultur* and *Bildung,* or by any viable religious conception that could be supported in an age disenchanted by science.

The calling and the personality were intended to serve neither as a source of innovation against tradition, which had been their pre-dominant seventeenth- and eighteenth-century role, nor as a vehicle of self-perfection and moral elevation, which had been their nineteenth-century role. Instead they were to serve in the twentieth century, first, as a means for the mastery, by transformed individuals and selves, of the various rationalized "spheres of life" that threatened to become autono-mous, resist control, and dominate humankind. Second, they were to be a bulwark against the "demagification" [*Entzauberung*] of the world and the emptying-out of meaning from life. This meaning was threat-ened by both the rationality and the irrationality of Weber's time; his contemporaries and his students, in their experience of defeat, in their impatience and false understanding, hoped to escape by the desperate search for personal masters to follow and to serve. But Weber himself thought the only hope to be the service in a calling of impersonal values, goals, and objects.

For Weber the modern world confronts the wholesale disappearance of the older sources of the strength and personality that made it what it is. For that world to continue to subsist, to find the strength to meet its new challenges, to remain vital in every sense of the term, it has to find new sources of strength. For Weber the Puritans were not just another historical contributor to the modern West and its vitality; they brought a new spirit, a new spiritual discipline, a new self. In "Science as a Voca-tion" Weber realized how it was possible to go back to Puritan roots, strip the calling and personality of their specifically religious coloration, combat the degeneration in their meaning, and make them available for the creation of "newer men." These men would be rooted in secular life, a life not only free of magical religion but also seemingly free of all faith and of any other spiritual disciplines capable of shaping the self for the difficult tasks ahead.

Germany was confronted with the exhaustion of its hopes for creating personality through *Bildung,* with the decline of faith in the value of all *Wissenschaft,* and with the crisis of the nation's identity experienced in battle and in the struggle for economic and political control and development in a competitive world. Weber reexamined German and Western spiritual history and the advance of rationalization in the light of World War I, and with his understanding of the calling and personality he was ready to provide a response.

Mann too drew into cultural and political analysis terms that in his work had focused more narrowly on his personal situation as an artist. World War I rescued Mann from an increasingly sterile creative universe—the war and his determined defense of himself and Germany, of himself *as* Germany. It led him to see as a single issue the issues of his own identity and self-doubt and those of Germany's identity, insecurity, and destiny. Ultimately Mann resolved the problem of the relation of the artist to bourgeois society by supplanting bourgeois identity and by making the identity of the artist-as-mediator the key to the identity of Germany. He went beyond his class to a higher entity by absorbing Germany and experiencing its doubts and problems as his own. The nation shares the situation of the artist: Germany becomes the artist writ large. With this fusion of self and nation, this identification of ego and other, this appropriation of the national other by the self, Mann broke out of his isolation from mere bourgeois society; he was the nation writ small. This permitted him to rise above concern for the fate of his class and above concern for himself, his personal culture, and his self-development. The connection with Germany enlarged his self-understanding and provided him with an altogether new inspiration for the completion of *The Magic Mountain,* which he had begun before the war.

The personality of the artist, produced not by all-around development but by the sense of duty and service that are part and parcel of the calling, had been a valuable product of the struggle for identity. Ultimately, however, Mann depicted the personality undermined by the recalcitrance of self and world; worse, it was a form of identity that could become rigid and even threaten existence. The calling devoted to an art pure of social purpose could not inspire Mann's artistry any further. But when Mann's purpose became Germany, when he could explore the self,

understood as identical with the nation, then his literary possibilities revived: the calling of the artist, and the calling in general, regained vitality and became the key to the nation itself as well as to the private
self. The personality and the calling now found support in a connection
with others and in an encounter with ideas about the nature of society,
freedom, and order no longer mediated by material success or bourgeois
function but by common membership in a nation and a culture under
fire. The two greatest works of his maturity, *The Magic Mountain* and
Doctor Faustus, both draw their inspiration and their power from this
new source.

Mann reevaluated his past and his work and re-appropriated his cultural ancestors in the process of positioning himself in the cultural war
of Germany against its enemies and of himself against his brother. But
the *Reflections of an Unpolitical Man* also marks a temporary step backward, from which Mann only freed himself a few years after the war.
He had provided a prophetic picture of the *Leistungsethiker* in the figure of Aschenbach and had shown the disastrous consequences of so
soldierly a life and so strong a desire to bind oneself to decisiveness in
moral matters.[1] Nevertheless, on the path to his new identity Mann re-
turned to the search for an "inner tyranny" to bring certainty to a decadent age, and he put up a convulsive and insistent defense of just such
soldierly qualities and of the "soldier in art." By 1922, as Hans Vaget
argues, Mann was already distancing himself again from this conception of the artist.[2] Yet the passion he displayed in the wartime argument
suggests the difficulty of going beyond it. Indeed, this conception and
the struggle for an "absolute table of values" and for "constraint" (*Ge-
bundenheit*) and meaning in *The Magic Mountain* raise once again the
question of Mann's relation to asceticism, the calling, and personality.

The contradiction within the artist between his sense of dissipation
and his desire for representation was not completely resolved until
much later.[3] Only with the rise of National Socialism did the artist finally become for Mann something even more important than the symbol of the nation: he became the supreme embodiment of Western
ideals, and, more than that, of the idea of humanity in general. The artist, then, was no longer an outcast—quite the contrary, though it is no
accident that *Doctor Faustus,* Mann's allegory of the rise of Nazi Germany, has an artist as its hero and symbol of the nation gone mad. But
this transformation from outcast to representative is not as great as it
seems at first. Mann's prototypical artist, even in his early formulations,
always keeps himself firmly within accepted social traditions and pat-

terns of work and respectability, however much he sees the content and form of his life as problematical and however much he views society with a critical eye. Especially in *Doctor Faustus* Mann remained deeply committed to the necessity and value of justification through a right understanding of the calling. The calling always governs the action, successful and unsuccessful, of his characters, even when he himself attributes their downfall to other causes.

Thus, when Weber and Mann approached the social and political crisis of their time, they were armed with intellectual and spiritual weapons to do battle against the malaise, the failure, and the loss of direction and strength that their time and nation experienced. But their responses to these crises were to reveal not only the power but also the hidden meanings and dangers of the analyses and resolutions they had discovered elsewhere in their intellectual careers.

Notes

All notes to works of Weber and Mann refer to the German originals, and all translations are my own. The major editions of the works are cited in abbreviated form, as indicated below. However, for the convenience of the general reader, titles of works are usually given in English in the text. If there exists an English translation of a cited book, story, or essay, an English title, though not an English edition, is provided in the notes; where no such translation is known to me, the titles have been left in German. For example, "Die protestantische Ethik und der Geist des Kapitalismus" is cited as: Weber, "Protestant Ethic," in *GRS* 1. (This work should not be confused with *Die protestantische Ethik* [vol. 2, *Kritiken und Antikritiken*], which is a collection of early criticism of Weber and his responses.) *Betrachtungen eines Unpolitischen* is cited as: Mann, *Reflections*, in *GW* 12. But "Bilse and I" is cited as: Mann, "Bilse und Ich," in *GW* 11.

Although many of Weber's principal works appear in larger collected volumes in German, a number of these same works were published as separate volumes in translation in English. Because English-speaking readers will be most familiar with the English titles of the individual volumes, these works (for example, *The Protestant Ethic*) will be cited in text discussion as book titles, although note citations will refer to the German editions.

Because of the size and diversity of Weber's *Economy and Society,* and because a good English edition is readily available, notes to that work specify the sections from which the reference is taken, as, for example: Weber, "Sociology of Religion," in *WG.*

GRS   Max Weber. *Gesammelte Aufsätze zur Religionssoziologie.* 3 vols. Tübingen: J. C. B. Mohr (Paul Siebeck), 1920–23.

GW   Thomas Mann. *Gesammelte Werke in zwölf Bände.* Edited by Hans Bürgin. Frankfurt am Main: S. Fischer Verlag, 1960.

WG   Max Weber. *Wirtschaft und Gesellschaft.* 5th ed. Tübingen: J. C. B.
        Mohr (Paul Siebeck), 1976.

WL   Max Weber. *Gesammelte Aufsätze zur Wissenschaftslehre.* 5th ed.
        Edited by Johannes Winckelmann. Tübingen: J. C. B. Mohr (Paul
        Siebeck), 1982.

THE PROBLEM OF WORK AND IDENTITY

1. For biographical material on Weber, see Marianne Weber, *Max Weber: Ein Lebensbild* (Tübingen: J. C. B. Mohr [Paul Siebeck], 1926), now translated by Harry Zohn as *Max Weber: A Biography* (New York: Wiley, 1975). See also Arthur Mitzman, *The Iron Cage: An Historical Interpretation of Max Weber* (New York: Knopf, 1970); Martin Green, *The von Richthofen Sisters* (New York: Basic Books, 1974), chap. 2; and, most recently, Hans Norbert Fügen, *Max Weber mit Selbstzeugnissen und Bilddokumenten* (Reinbeck bei Hamburg: Rowohlt, 1985).

2. For the life and background of Thomas Mann, see Klaus Schröter, *Thomas Mann in Selbstzeugnissen und Bilddokumenten* (Reinbeck bei Hamburg: Rowohlt, 1964); and Nigel Hamilton, *The Brothers Mann* (New Haven: Yale University Press, 1979). There is also Hans Bürgin and Hans-Otto Mayer, *Thomas Mann: A Chronicle of His Life,* trans. Eugene Dobson (University, Ala.: University of Alabama Press, 1969).

3. Weber and Mann met at least twice, in Munich, after the end of World War I. See Thomas Mann, *Tagebücher: 1918–1921,* ed. Peter de Mendelssohn (Frankfurt am Main: S. Fischer Verlag, 1979). Weber is mentioned six times, beginning with the entry for 5 Nov. 1918, mostly in connection with newspaper articles or discussions of Weber's well-publicized political activities. These entries include 6 June 1919, 21 Jan. 1920, and 22 June 1920, where Weber's death is mentioned. Mann met Weber briefly for the first time on 9 Nov. 1919 at a crowded *Hochzeitsthee.* Their most intimate meeting took place 28 Dec. 1919, when only a few couples met for tea, and Mann says of that occasion: "Weber polemicized against Spengler and proved himself the good, clever, and lively speaker that he is regarded as" (352). So far as I can determine, there is no reference to Mann in Weber's published work or in his wife's biography of him, though there are probably some details in Weber's *Nachlass* or unpublished letters.

Mann also made comments in his writings about Weber and Weber's work, principally about *The Protestant Ethic.* See Mann, *Reflections of an Unpolitical Man,* in *GW* 12:145–47, in the section entitled "Bürgerlichkeit."

4. Mann began *Buddenbrooks* in 1897, and Weber claimed that his work on Protestantism went back "in all of its decisive points of view" to around 1897. See Max Weber, "Antikritisches zum 'Geist' des Kapitalismus" (1910), in *Die protestantische Ethik,* vol. 2, *Kritiken und Antikritiken,* ed. Johannes Winckelmann (Hamburg: Siebenstern Taschenbuch Verlag, 1972), 150. See also Weber, "The Protestant Ethic," in *GRS* 1:43n.2.

INTRODUCTION TO PART I

1. Czeslaw Milosz, "The Nobel Lecture, 1980," in *New York Review of Books* 28, no. 3 (5 Mar. 1981): 12.

2. Jean-Paul Sartre, *Sartre by Himself* (New York: Urizen Books, 1978), 28.

3. See Hannah Arendt, *The Human Condition* (Chicago: University of Chicago Press, 1957).

4. The best overviews of the history of the concept of the calling are Werner Conze, "Beruf," in Otto Brunner, Werner Conze, and Reinhart Koselleck, eds., *Geschichtliche Grundbegriffe: Historisches Lexikon zur politisch-sozialen Sprache in Deutschland* (Stuttgart: Ernst Klett Verlag, 1972), 1:490–507; and Karl Holl, "Die Geschichte des Worts Beruf," in *Gesammelte Aufsätze zur Kirchengeschichte* (Tübingen: J. C. B. Mohr [Paul Siebeck], 1928), 3:189–219. See also Arthur Salz, "Zur Geschichte der Berufsidee," *Archiv für Sozialwissenschaft und Sozialpolitik* 37 (1913): 380–423. On the Lutheran work ethic alone and its history, see Klara Vontobel, *Das Arbeitsethos des deutschen Protestantismus von der nachreformatorischen Zeit bis zur Aufklärung* (Bern: Francke Verlag, 1946).

5. See Perry Miller, "The Protestant Ethic," chap. 3 in *The New England Mind: From Colony to Province* (Cambridge: Harvard University Press, 1953; Boston: Beacon Press, 1961). See also William Haller, "The Calling of the Saints," chap. 3 in *The Rise of Puritanism* (New York: Columbia University Press, 1938; Harper Torchbooks, 1957).

6. Michael Walzer, "The New World of Discipline and Work" and "Puritanism and the Gentry: Politics as a Vocation," chaps. 6 and 7 in *The Revolution of the Saints: A Study in the Origins of Radical Politics* (Cambridge: Harvard University Press, 1965; New York: Atheneum, 1970). John Dunn, "The Calling: Tradition and Change," chap. 18 in *The Political Thought of John Locke: An Historical Account of the Argument of the "Two Treatises of Government"* (Cambridge: Cambridge University Press, 1969).

7. Karl Löwith, *From Hegel to Nietzsche: The Revolution in Nineteenth-Century Thought*, trans. David E. Green (New York: Holt, Rinehart, & Winston, 1964; Garden City, N.Y.: Anchor Books, 1967), 285. See also pt. 2, chap. 2, "The Problem of Work." Löwith argues that with the concept of calling, a new "ethical" component entered the world of work (268).

8. On the concept of the bourgeoisie generally, see Manfred Riedel, "Bürger, Staatsbürger, Bürgertum," in Brunner, Conze, and Koselleck, eds., *Geschichtliche Grundbegriffe* 1:672–727. For Weber's discussion of the concept, see Max Weber, *Wirtschaftsgeschichte: Abriss der universalen Sozial- und Wirtschafts-Geschichte*, 2d. ed., ed. S. Hellmann and M. Palyi (Munich and Leipzig: Duncker & Humblot, 1924), 270–71, 280, 288–89; and "The City," in *WG*, 765.

Among the many usages that he points to, Weber describes a "*status* (or estate) [*ständische*]" meaning, in which we include the people of "property and culture [*Bildung*]," the *Bildungsbürgertum*, or even "property or culture." This group is distinguished as a stratum both from the proletariat and from the bureaucratic strata, which are mainly from the nobility. It may include entrepreneurs, rentiers, and, particularly in the German context, "all personalities who possess academic culture [*Bildung*] and with it a certain status standard, a social prestige." This status, in the sense of positive privileges, is unique to the modern Occident and extremely important for German experience. According to Weber, it is in modern times that "out of the alliance of the state and capital, created by necessity, there developed the national burgher estate [*nationale Bürgerstand*], the bourgeoisie in the modern sense of the word." This "national *Bürgerstand*" developed first in medieval English towns and is the carrier and developer of capitalism.

According to Roy Pascal, following the usage of Werner Sombart, *bourgeois* tends to denote "entrepreneur" in German, whereas *Bürger* denotes the "staid middle class." That there is an important kind of historical relation between them is shown by Thomas Mann's remark, in his *Reflections*, that he had "overslept" the evolution of the *Bürger* into the bourgeois. Pascal remarks that Mann is one of "the rare authors to show sympathy with, even nostalgia for, the simple, orderly, conventional *Bürger*," though not for the ruthless conquering bourgeois. See Roy Pascal, *From Naturalism to Expressionism: German Literature and Society, 1890–1918* (New York: Basic Books, 1973), 33, 34. Reference to Mann's *Reflections* is in ibid., 35; see also Pascal's remarks on Sombart, ibid., 30.

Mann spoke later of *Buddenbrooks*, his *Bürger* novel, as "a piece of the history of the soul of the German *Bürgertum*" whose success revealed that it was also "a piece of the history of the soul of the European *Bürgertum*." See Mann, "Lübeck as a Spiritual Form of Life," in *GW* 11:383.

9. On the *Bildungsbürgertum* as a part of the *Bürgertum*, but not to be confused with the "big" bourgeoisie of industry and wealth, see the fine work on the academic elite by Fritz Ringer, *The Decline of the German Mandarins, 1890–1933* (Cambridge: Harvard University Press, 1969); Klaus Vondung, "Zur Lage der Gebildeten in der wilhelminischen Zeit," in Klaus Vondung, ed., *Das Wilhelminische Bildungsbürgertum: Zur Sozialgeschichte seiner Ideen* (Göttingen: Vandenhoeck & Ruprecht, 1976), 20–33; and Karl Mannheim, *Ideology and Utopia* (New York: Harcourt, Brace & World, 1936), 154–58. Whereas the industrial bourgeoisie in Wilhelmine Germany became part of the ruling elite and thus had a share in power through its alliances with and mimicry of the aristocracy, the *Bildungsbürgertum*, though it also struggled for recognition, saw its importance and its cultural influence wane during this period.

10. See Eckart Kehr, "Zur Genesis des Königlich Preussischen Reserveoffiziers" and "Das soziale System der Reaktion in Preussen unter dem Ministerium Puttkamer," in *Der Primat der Innenpolitik*, ed. Hans-Ulrich Wehler (Berlin: Walter de Gruyter, 1965; Frankfurt am Main: Ullstein Verlag, 1970), 53–86. See also Hans Rosenberg, "Die Pseudodemokratisierung der Rittergutsbesitzerklasse," in Hans-Ulrich Wehler, ed., *Moderne deutsche Sozialgeschichte* (Cologne: Kiepenhauer & Witsch, 1976), 287–308; Karl Erich Born, "Structural Changes in German Social and Economic Development at the End of the Nineteenth Century," in James Sheehan, ed., *Imperial Germany* (New York: New Viewpoints [Franklin Watts], 1976), 16–38, esp. 24–27, and the

German version of this essay in Wehler, ed., *Moderne deutsche Sozialgeschichte*, 282–83; Gordon Craig, *The Politics of the Prussian Army, 1640–1945* (New York: Oxford University Press, 1964), 232–38. For a reconsideration of this subject, see David Blackbourn and Geoff Eley, *The Peculiarities of German History* (New York: Oxford University Press, 1984), 228–37. On the literary expression of the bourgeois relation to aristocracy, see E. K. Bramsted, *Aristocracy and the Middle-Classes in Germany: Social Types in German Literature, 1830–1900* (London: P. S. King & Son, 1937; Chicago: University of Chicago Press, 1964), 183, 197–98, 228–32, 333–34.

11. For Weber's references to the feudalization of the bourgeoisie, see "The Protestant Ethic," in *GRS* 1:54–55, 193–95; on the effects of Puritanism on political possibilities, see ibid., 98–99n.1, 167n.2. For a comment on this problem in his lecture at the World's Fair in 1904, see Weber, "Capitalism and Rural Society in Germany," in H. H. Gerth and C. Wright Mills, trans. and eds., *From Max Weber: Essays in Sociology* (New York: Oxford University Press, 1946), 383. See also Wolfgang Mommsen, *Max Weber und die deutsche Politik, 1890–1920*, 2d ed. (Tübingen: J. C. B. Mohr [Paul Siebeck], 1974), 97–107, where Mommsen says: "Weber projected the capitalist economic ethos deriving from the Puritan spirit into the realm of philosophy of history." See Robert Bellah, "Reflections on the Protestant Ethic Analogy in Asia," in S. N. Eisenstadt, ed., *The Protestant Ethic and Modernization: A Comparative View* (New York: Basic Books, 1968), 247, 248. Bellah says that Weber was led to the problem of the Protestant ethic by his awareness of "the failure of structural transformation in important sectors of German society."

CHAPTER ONE

1. Weber, *Die protestantische Ethik*, vol. 2, contains the early criticisms of Fischer and Rachfahl and Weber's responses to them. See the footnotes to the revised edition of "The Protestant Ethic," published in *GRS*, vol. 1. See also Gordon Marshall, *In Search of the Spirit of Capitalism* (New York: Columbia University Press, 1982); David Little, *Religion, Order, and Law: A Study in Pre-Revolutionary England* (New York: Harper & Row, 1969); Ephraim Fischoff, "The Protestant Ethic and the Spirit of Capitalism: The History of a Controversy," in Eisenstadt, ed., *Protestant Ethic and Modernization*, 67–86; and Anthony Giddens's 1976 introduction to Max Weber, *The Protestant Ethic and the Spirit of Capitalism*, trans. Talcott Parsons (New York: Scribner's, 1958), 1–12b.

2. For earlier observers, see Weber, "Protestant Ethic," in *GRS* 1:22n.2, 23n.1, 28, 28n.3, 29, 195n.2, 196n.2; idem, "Antikritisches Schlusswort zum 'Geist des Kapitalismus,'" in *Die protestantische Ethik* 2:320–21, 344n.27. See also Reinhard Bendix, "The Protestant Ethic—Revisited," in Reinhard Bendix and Guenther Roth, *Scholarship and Partisanship: Essays on Max Weber* (Berkeley and Los Angeles: University of California Press, 1971), 299–310.

3. On other works on Protestantism and capitalism, see Bendix, "Protestant Ethic—Revisited," 299–310. Curiously the one figure Bendix does not mention is Eduard Bernstein, whose work Weber suggested was the first "to indicate these important connections" between asceticism and bourgeois virtue, although it is

not certain that Weber read it when it first appeared. Weber was quick to suggest, however, that the implications of asceticism were wider and more consequential than Bernstein had imagined. See Weber, "Protestant Ethic," in *GRS* 1:88n.1, 160n.1, 192–93n.2.

4. See Guenther Roth, introduction to Max Weber, *Economy and Society*, ed. Guenther Roth and Claus Wittich (Berkeley and Los Angeles: University of California Press, 1978), lxxvii; and idem, "The Historical Relationship to Marxism," in Bendix and Roth, *Scholarship and Partisanship*, 244.

Whether Weber was also engaged in debating Marx's positions is subject to dispute. We know that he was assigning all three volumes of *Capital* to his students in the late 1890s. This information comes to me from Dr. Martin Riesebrodt, based on the research of Prof. Rainer Lepsius. Parsons maintained in his early articles that *The Protestant Ethic* was meant as a refutation of Marx; see Talcott Parsons, "Capitalism in Recent German Literature," pt. 2, *Journal of Political Economy* 37 (1929): 40; and idem, *The Structure of Social Action* (New York: McGraw-Hill, 1937; New York: Free Press, 1949), vol. 2. Marshall's views are in *Spirit of Capitalism*, 19–33. In contrast, Gerhart von Schulze-Gävernitz, one of Weber's friends, said in his eulogy for Weber: "Max Weber further develops here the central ideas of the Marxian theoretical construction [*Lehrgebäude*]. He links up with Marx, where he describes the spirit of capitalism; but he rejects the one-sidedness of the Marxian theory, which derives from the Hegelian dialectic" ("Max Weber als Nationalökonom und Politiker," introduction to Melchior Palyi, ed., *Erinnerungsgabe für Max Weber* [Munich and Leipzig: Duncker & Humblot, 1923], 1:xv).

5. See details in Marianne Weber, *Max Weber: A Biography*, 259–60, 277–79, 306–7, 325–26, 356.

6. The significance of the calling is also affirmed by Maurice Weyembergh, although in a way that inaccurately characterizes Weber's thesis: "If Western capitalism has for its origin ascetic Protestantism and the notion of 'calling,' produced by Puritanism, the thought of the sociologist culminates in the philosophy of 'calling.'" See his *Le Voluntarisme rationnel de Max Weber*, Mémoires de la Classe des Lettres, 2d series, vol. 61, no. 1 (Brussels: Académie Royale de Belgique, 1972), xxi. Chap. 5 is entitled "The Philosophy of Calling."

7. Quoted in Marianne Weber, *Max Weber: Ein Lebensbild*, 274.

8. Karl Löwith, "Max Weber und Karl Marx," in *Gesammelte Abhandlungen* (Stuttgart: W. Kohlhammer Verlag, 1960), 27.

9. Quoted in Marianne Weber, *Max Weber: Ein Lebensbild*, 359.

10. Weber, "Antikritisches zum 'Geist,'" *Die Protestantische Ethik* 2:167, 168.

11. Weber, "Protestant Ethic," in *GRS* 1:36. See also Ernst Troeltsch, *The Social Teaching of the Christian Churches*, trans. Olive Wyon (London: Allen & Unwin, 1931), 2:609.

12. Weber, "Protestant Ethic," in *GRS* 1:36, 62, 204, 203.

13. Ibid., 49, 50n.1, 43.

14. The notion of spirit used in this way probably goes back to Herder and to the romantics' notions of *Volksgeist* and may even have derived from Hegel's notions of *Zeitgeist* or of the spirit of a nation. The historical school of econom-

ics strove to find the unique aspects and spirit of a particular national economy rather than of an economic system in general (see List, Schmoller, etc.) It seems most likely that concern with such a concept developed out of the tradition of the historical school.

On Herder and the notion of *Zeitgeist,* see Löwith, *From Hegel to Nietzsche,* 200–207; and Georg G. Iggers, *The German Conception of History,* rev. ed. (Middletown, Conn.: Wesleyan University Press, 1983), 34–40. On the German Historical School, see Joseph Schumpeter, *A History of Economic Analysis* (New York: Oxford University Press, 1955), 800–824; W. B. Cherin, "The German School of Economics" (Ph.D. diss., University of California, Berkeley, 1933); Werner Cahnman, "Max Weber and the Methodological Controversy in the Social Sciences," in Werner J. Cahnman and Alvin Boskoff, eds., *Sociology and History* (New York: Free Press, 1964), 103–27; and Iggers, *German Conception of History,* 131–33.

15. Weber, "Protestant Ethic," in *GRS* 1:33, 35, 40n.1.

16. Ibid., 35–36.

17. Ibid., 33–34. On Jacob Fugger and his attitude, see Richard Ehrenburg, *Capital and Finance in the Age of the Renaissance: A Study of the Fuggers and Their Connections,* trans. H. M. Lucas (London: Jonathan Cape, 1928).

18. Weber, "Protestant Ethic," in *GRS* 1:49. Vontobel, *Das Arbeitsethos,* is a misleading guide to the problem of the spirit of capitalism. However well the author characterizes Lutheran teaching, she totally misunderstands Weber's work as well as the relation of Protestantism and the calling to capitalism.

19. Weber, "Protestant Ethic," in *GRS* 1:37, 55, 56.

20. Ibid., 37, 55, 56, 201n.4. Marx agrees with this in his *Grundrisse: Foundations of the Critique of Political Economy,* trans. Martin Nicolaus (New York: Vintage, 1973), 252, 459ff., on the history of the formation of capital. He asserts that the historic presuppositions of capital are part of the history of capital's formation but not part of capital's *present* history. Once capital is established, *it* creates its own presuppositions, which now appear "*not as conditions of its arising, but as results of its presence.*"

21. Weber, "Protestant Ethic," in *GRS* 1:53. Amintore Fanfani does not agree with Weber in identifying the origins of capitalism or its connection with Protestantism (*Catholicism, Protestantism, and Capitalism* [London: Sheed & Ward, 1938]). Indeed, he believes that the link with Protestantism is through the release of acquisitiveness by the separation of any connection between worldly behavior and salvation (ibid., 205), which means that "the restrictions imposed by religious morality on the acquisition of wealth cease to exist" (ibid., 22–23). Charles H. George and Katherine George call his view "a standard Catholic misunderstanding of the Protestant doctrine" in *The Protestant Mind of the English Reformation, 1570–1640* (Princeton: Princeton University Press, 1961), 145n.4.

22. Weber, "Protestant Ethic," in *GRS* 1:56. But see Georg Brodnitz, *Englische Wirtschaftsgeschichte* (Jena: Verlag von Gustav Fischer, 1918), 283, where he argues that the capitalist spirit was not at all new, though it changed quantitatively later. Even so, the Reformation was not the key to this change.

23. Weber, "Protestant Ethic," in *GRS* 1:37–38, 60, 195n.1. On New England, see the confirming work of Bernard Bailyn, *The New England Merchants*

of the Seventeenth Century (Cambridge: Harvard University Press, 1955), esp. chap. 2, where Bailyn describes the Puritan merchants' conception of the calling and its effects on business conduct. He also discusses the conflicts between magistrates and merchants in the disputes between the defenders of the purity of doctrine and the practitioners of business. Curiously C. H. Wilson claims that Bailyn's evidence casts doubt on Weber's thesis, which it does not; see E. E. Rich and C. H. Wilson, eds., *The Cambridge Economic History of Europe* (Cambridge: Cambridge University Press, 1967), 4:488.

24. Weber, "Protestant Ethic," in *GRS* 1:38, 43.

25. Ibid., 43. See also Reinhard Bendix, *Work and Authority in Industry,* rev. ed. (Berkeley and Los Angeles: University of California Press, 1974), 4–5.

26. Weber, "Protestant Ethic," in *GRS* 1:49, 50, 51–52; idem, "Kritische Bemerkungen zu den Vorstehenden 'Kritische Beitragen,'" in *Die protestantische Ethik* 2:29. On the effects of feudalism in preserving the power of traditionalism, see idem, "Feudalism, Ständestaat, and Patrimonialism," in *WG,* 642–43, 648.

27. Weber, "Protestant Ethic," in *GRS* 1:47, 44–45, 46, 45n.1.

28. Ibid., 42, 43, 50, 53, 195n.3. See also "Preface," in ibid., 4, 7, 8n.1; idem, "The Protestant Sects and the Spirit of Capitalism," in *GRS* 1:214; idem, *Wirtschaftsgeschichte,* 302–303.

29. Weber, "Protestant Ethic," in *GRS* 1:52–53; idem, "Antikritisches Schlusswort," in *Die protestantische Ethik* 2:342n.20.

30. Weber, "Protestant Ethic," in *GRS* 1:53–54; emphasis added, except for last instances of "*kind*" and "*temperate and constant.*"

31. Ibid., 55. The entrepreneur was not only able to overcome tradition in business but was precisely the type who was later impervious to the "snobs" (*Protzentum*) who fled into the haven of "entailed estates and patented nobility" (*Fideikommissbesitzes und Briefadels*), who sent their sons to the university and into the reserve officer corps to erase the memory of their social origin, and who were all too typical among German "parvenue families." On the contrary, the "ideal type of the entrepreneur" displayed an ascetic quality in all his worldly dealings.

32. Ibid., 40–41n.1.

33. But see Weber's "Introduction" to "Economic Ethics of the World Religions," in *GRS* 1:238. "No economic ethic has ever been determined only religiously. . . . But certainly: to the determinants of the economic ethic there belongs as one—note well: only one—also the religious determination of life conduct." Still, Weber considered "the influence of economic development on the fate of religious conceptions [*Gedankenbildungen*]" very important, along with the significance of political developments for the fate of capitalism and economic life generally. See Weber, "Protestant Ethic," in *GRS* 1:192n.1, and "Antikritisches Schlusswort," in *Die protestantische Ethik* 2:324.

For Weber religious conceptions remain central to the understanding of the origin of this ethic, and neither the Reformation nor the specific religious ideas it engendered can be deduced from or reduced to economic conditions. See "Protestant Ethic," in *GRS* 1:82–83, 192n.1. This is what Weber considers the hardest issue to grasp: "the limitation of the origin of an 'economic attitude,' of the 'ethos,' of an economic form through the contents of specifically religious beliefs" ("Preface," in *GRS* 1:12). See also his comments on the Reformation in "Political and Hierocratic Domination," in *WG*, 716–17.

34. Weber, "Protestant Ethic," in *GRS* 1:151–52n.1.

35. Ibid., 60. At this point Weber still speaks of ideas (*Gedanken*) as crucial, whereas later he speaks of "ideal interests." See "Introduction" to "Economic Ethics," in *GRS* 1:252.

36. Weber, "The Economy and the Social Orders," in *WG*, 188.

37. Weber, "Protestant Ethic," in *GRS* 1:38–41n.1.

38. Ibid., 203. On Weber's relation to Goethe, see Chapter 3, below.

39. On charisma, see Weber, "Charismatic Domination" and "Charismatic Domination and Its Transformation," in *WG*, 140–42, 654–87. In a discussion of salvation through faith alone, Weber speaks of faith "as a specific charisma of an extraordinary *trust* in God's totally personal providence, which the shepherds of souls and the heroes of faith must have" ("Sociology of Religion," *WG*, 343). I might add that the first great entrepreneurs had to have it as well. Rudolph Sohm was the first scholar to make general use of the concept of charisma. See Peter Haley, "Rudolph Sohm on Charisma," *Journal of Religion* 60 (1980): 185–97.

40. Indeed, Dieter Lindenlaub argues that Weber was *unable* to provide a single example of a person who was simultaneously a capitalist entrepreneur and an adherent of ascetic Calvinism and that "inner-worldly asceticism . . . was much more an agonizing norm that the descendant of French Huguenots settled on himself and the bourgeoisie" than the real attribute of concrete individuals; see *Richtungskämpfe im Verein für Sozialpolitik*, in *Vierteljahrschrift für Sozial- und Wirtschaftsgeschichte*, supplement 53, pt. 2 (Wiesbaden: Franz Steiner Verlag, 1967), 297.

But see the work of David Landes on the industrial revolution and the significance of the "attitude" that helped separate Britain from the Continent and contributed to making the breakthrough in Britain: *The Unbound Prometheus* (Cambridge: Cambridge University Press, 1969), esp. introduction and chap. 2. See also idem, "The Industrial Revolution," in *Chapters in Western Civilization*, 3d ed. (New York: Columbia University Press, 1962), 140–93, esp. 165, 167, 179, 180.

41. For his discussion of ideal types, see Weber, "The 'Objectivity' of Social Scientific and Social Political Knowledge," in *WL*, 146–214.

42. On Weber's standpoint, see "Protestant Ethic" in *GRS* 1:30–31. Actually both H. M. Robertson, *Aspects of the Rise of Economic Individualism: A Criticism of Max Weber and His School* (Cambridge: Cambridge University Press, 1935), xi–xii, and George and George, *Protestant Mind*, 145–47, insist on the antihistorical bias of the ideal-type method as Weber used it and claim that only by overcoming it can the truth be found. But such assertions cannot substitute for a genuine analysis of the operation of these types in his work, nor can simple empirical evidence make such types superfluous. George and George accuse Weber's whole argument of being "less anti-Marxist than anti-empirical"

(ibid., 146), and they maintain that his system of creating ideal types builds a priori terms into his definitions, which make his conclusions about a Protestant ethic tautologies (see ibid., chap. 4).

43. Weber, "Protestant Ethic," in *GRS* 1:62.

44. Weber does not intend to identify such an ascetic motive with the spirit of capitalism, but he does claim that it is "*one* constitutive component of this 'spirit' (and furthermore, expressly of still *further* modern cultural characteristics!) alongside others." His purpose was to make clear the role of "religious motifs" in shaping modern culture, understanding culture as the product of "innumerable single historical motifs," profoundly political as well as economic. He did not argue "that the 'capitalist spirit' (always in the provisional sense here applied) *could* have originated *only* as an outflow of specific influences of the Reformation, or indeed, that capitalism as an *economic system* was a product of the Reformation." The question is only to what extent religious influences "have *shared* in the qualitative stamping [*Prägung*] and the quantitative expansion of that 'spirit' over the world." See ibid., 82–83. See also ibid., 205–6n.3, on the absurdity of attributing too much weight to Protestantism; idem, "Sociology of Religion," in *WG,* 292–93; idem, "Antikritisches zum 'Geist,'" in *Die protestantische Ethik* 2:164–65; and idem, "Kritische Bemerkungen," in ibid., 30, where he says that one cannot attribute to him the position that "the naked fact of confessional adherence could conjure up out of the ground a specific economic kind of development."

45. Richard M. Douglas, "Talent and Vocation in Humanist and Protestant Thought," in Theodore K. Rabb and Jerrold Siegel, eds., *Action and Conviction in Early Modern Europe: Essays in Memory of E. H. Harbison* (Princeton: Princeton University Press, 1969), 261–98. I am indebted to Allan Silver for bringing this article to my attention.

46. Douglas, "Talent and Vocation," 276.

47. Weber, "Protestant Ethic," in *GRS* 1:63, 63n.1. Robertson disputes Weber's philological claim (*Economic Individualism,* 2–4), relying on Lujo Brentano, *Die Anfänge des modernen Kapitalismus* (Munich: Verlag der K. B. Akademie der Wissenschaften, 1916), 136ff. Most of Robertson's versions of Weber's positions are colossal distortions, when he does not simply ignore crucial issues like predestination, and his own arguments rarely go to the heart of the issue. For a stinging critique, see Talcott Parsons, "H. M. Robertson on Max Weber and His School," *Journal of Political Economy* 43 (1935): 688–97.

48. Weber, "Political and Hierocratic Domination," in *WG,* 709, 699, 707.

49. Vontobel, *Das Arbeitsethos,* 4. See also George and George, *Protestant Mind,* 122: "For the Protestant, sainthood is the vocation of everyman. There are not two ways to go to God, there is only one. . . . And the world is neutral."

50. Weber, "Protestant Ethic," in *GRS* 1:65–69n.2, 63–65n.1; "Sociology of Religion," in *WG,* 344. Douglas says that Luther first used *Beruf* to mean occupation, class, or office even earlier—in the *Kirchenpostille* of 1522—in the sense that, insofar as one belongs to a class or profession, one must feel oneself "called" to it ("Talent and Vocation," 287).

51. Douglas, "Talent and Vocation," 287–92. See also George and George, *Protestant Mind,* 126–27, and "Protestantism and Capitalism in Pre-Revolu-

tionary England," in Eisenstadt, ed., *Protestant Ethic and Modernization,* 165–66.

52. Weber, "Protestant Ethic," in *GRS* 1:69. See also Vontobel, *Das Arbeitsethos,* 6, 9, 11; Troeltsch, *Social Teaching,* 2:561–69, on Luther's social ideals; and George and George, *Protestant Mind,* 122, 129.

53. Indeed, according to George and George the doctrine of the calling represents a profound break "from the social theory of medieval Roman Catholicism." In the calling "we find as in no other single concept perhaps the ideological watershed between the ancient medieval and the modern mind" ("Protestantism and Capitalism," 174).

54. Weber, "Protestant Ethic," in *GRS* 1:76, 77–78, 78n.1, 77n.2.

55. Weber, "Sociology of Religion," in *WG,* 345; "Protestant Ethic," in *GRS* 1:72, 77, 81–82, 86.

56. Weber, "Protestant Ethic," in *GRS* 1:79, 74, 80.

57. Ibid., 84, 87–88. For a good short essay on the Puritan calling, see Arnold Eisen, "Called to Order: The Role of the Puritan *Berufsmensch* in Weberian Sociology," *Sociology* 13 (1979): 203–18.

58. Richard Douglas claims that Calvin's position on the calling "was essentially the same as Luther's in every important assumption," although Robert Michaelson suggests that Calvin was more systematic and put more emphasis on "obligation and strenuousness." Werner Conze agrees with Douglas, though he points out that the French translation of *Beruf, "vocation,"* could not lead to a distinction like that between *Beruf* and *Berufung,* a distinction that was later so important for Germany. Still, for Conze as for Weber, Calvin adapted the Lutheran notion of the calling according to "the strict consistency of his predestination theory," thus making possible the later intensification of work under its influence. Douglas, "Talent and Vocation," 261, 262, 263, 292, 293, 294; Conze, "Beruf," 496; Robert S. Michaelson, "Changes in the Puritan Concept of Calling or Vocation," *New England Quarterly* 26 (1953): 315–36, esp. 317; William Haller, *Rise of Puritanism,* 384n.1; and Robert Martin Krapp, "A Note on the Puritan 'Calling,'" *Review of Religion* 7 (1943): 242–51.

59. Weber, "Protestant Ethic," in *GRS* 1:89, 93. For Weber's later discussions of Calvinism, see "Political and Hierocratic Domination," in *WG,* 717–19, and "Sociology of Religion," in *WG,* 317, 346–48.

60. Weber, "Protestant Ethic," in *GRS* 1:93–94.

61. Ibid., 94–95.

62. Ibid., 96. See also ibid., 144n.1, on the effects of the confessional on believers.

63. Ibid., 98–99, 100–101. On charity, see also "Sociology of Religion," in *WG,* 355, where Weber argues that charity became a rationalized "enterprise"; and Troeltsch, *Social Teaching,* 2:809. In "Political and Hierocratic Domination," in *WG,* 718, Weber even speaks of the purposes of church and sect, in working for the glory of God exclusively, as "a kind of cold godly *Staatsraison*"! George and George dispute Weber's picture of Calvinist charity in *Protestant Mind,* 154–59, where they speak of Protestantism's "welfare-state approach" to charity.

64. Weber, "Protestant Ethic," in *GRS* 1:104–5, 103n.2; Douglas, "Talent

and Vocation," 295. For an interesting later statement, see Weber's "Introduction" to "Economic Ethics," in *GRS* 1:249–50.

65. Weber, "Protestant Ethic," in *GRS* 1:105–6; Douglas, "Talent and Vocation," 295.

66. Weber, "Protestant Ethic," in *GRS* 1:108, 110.

67. George and George, "Protestantism and Capitalism," 167; see also idem, *Protestant Mind*, 129.

68. Weber, "Protestant Ethic," in *GRS* 1:108–9, 111, 124–26. As Robert Martin Krapp says of the preachers: "They have a system; they describe a method, a discipline" ("Puritan 'Calling,'" 247).

69. Weber, "Protestant Ethic," in *GRS* 1:114–15, 117.

70. Ibid., 188. See also idem, "Confucianism and Taoism," in *GRS* 1:525–27.

71. Weber, "Protestant Ethic," in *GRS* 1:116–17. For Weber's later treatment of this theme, see "Political and Hierocratic Domination," in *WG*, 696, 699, 707, 709.

72. Weber, "Protestant Ethic," in *GRS* 1:113–16, 114n.3, 120. On Catholicism, asceticism, and the confessional, see ibid., 58n.1; "Political and Hierocratic Domination," in *WG*, 694, 712–13; and "Sociology of Religion," in *WG*, 354. See also Troeltsch, *Social Teaching*, 2:604–5.

73. Weber, "Protestant Ethic," in *GRS* 1:162–63. In "Sociology of Religion" Weber later writes: "Ethical behavior can never have the meaning here of improving one's chances in the beyond or in the world, but rather the other practical-psychological one, in certain conditions working still stronger, of being a *symptom* of one's own state of grace established through God's decree" (*WG*, 317). Michaelson notes: "Thus one is not called first of all to the particular work, but is called to respond to God in the whole of life" ("Puritan Concept of Calling," 323). See also George and George, "Protestantism and Capitalism," 156–58.

74. These other movements provide "impulses" to asceticism different from Calvinist predestination, although they are weaker than the "inner consistency" of Calvinism. See Weber, "Protestant Ethic," in *GRS* 1:128. On Pietism, see ibid., 128–45; on Methodism, ibid., 145–50; on Baptism and the Quakers, ibid., 150–62. For the quotes, see ibid., 158, 160, 161. For testimony on the Quakers confirming Weber's analysis, see David Ogg, *England in the Reigns of James II and William III* (Oxford: Clarendon Press, 1955), 43–44. Interestingly, Weber notes that despite their support of formal legality, the Calvinists were more ruthless (*gewissenslos*) than honest (see "Protestant Ethic," in *GRS* 1:160–61).

75. Weber, "Introduction" to "Economic Ethics," in *GRS* 1:263–64; "Protestant Ethic," in *GRS* 1:112–13. Weber later speaks of rational ethical conduct in the world as the means to prove one's religious *charisma* ("Sociology of Religion," in *WG*, 329). John Dunn stresses the Calvinists' need "for the rediscovery of some palpable index of salvation," in which hard labor provided "the power to allay their anxieties" and allowed them "to discipline their entire lives so that they felt totally subordinated to the fulfillments of this purpose" (see *John Locke*, pts. 4 and 5, esp. 213, 217, 218, 220, 224, 225–26).

76. Weber, "Protestant Ethic," in *GRS* 1:172, 174–75, 105–6n.5, 110, 115, 142, 98–99n.1; see also "Introduction" to "Economic Ethics," in ibid., 263.

77. Weber, "Intermediate Reflection," in ibid., 539. See also Troeltsch, *Social Teaching* 2:609–12.

78. Weber, "Protestant Ethic," in *GRS* 1:165n.3, 192, 202. Here the focus is on "not exclusively but as much as possible the ascetic movement of the second half of the seventeenth century immediately before the turn to utilitarianism" (ibid., 165n.2). As he writes in "Antikritisches zum 'Geist,'" in *Die protestantische Ethik* 2:163: "it is not my intention to suppose *more* than indeed the presence [*Vorhandensein*] of this 'driving force' [*Triebkraft*]."

79. Weber, "Bemerkungen zu den vorstehenden Replik," in *Die protestantische Ethik* 2:46, 47; "Antikritisches Schlusswort," in ibid., 322; "Charismatic Domination and Its Transformation," in *WG*, 659.

80. Weber, "Protestant Ethic," in *GRS* 1:183, 190, 98–99n.1, 175, 176, 192, 166–67. On pp. 176–77n.3, Weber says that "the Protestant idea of the calling set precisely the *most serious* adherents of ascetic life after success in the service of the capitalist life of acquisition." See also "Bemerkungen zu der vorstehenden Replik," in *Die protestantische Ethik* 2:46–47. See also Troeltsch, *Social Teaching* 2:605, 607, 611, for a compelling description of the Calvinist "method."

81. Weber, "Protestant Ethic," in *GRS* 1:192; see also "Sociology of Religion," in *WG*, 347.

82. Weber, "Protestant Ethic," in *GRS* 1:198, 201; see also ibid., 46–47n.1 and 200n.3.

83. Weber, "The Protestant Sects and the Spirit of Capitalism," in *GRS* 1:236.

84. Weber, "Protestant Ethic," in *GRS* 1:200–201. For further features, see ibid., 187–88, 189; idem, "Political and Hierocratic Domination," in *WG*, 719; Douglas, "Talent and Vocation," 295–98. See also George and George, *Protestant Mind,* 127; Weber, "Sociology of Religion," in *WG*, 370; Krapp, "Puritan 'Calling,'" 246.

85. Indeed, George and George claim that the calling "is not so much a bourgeois as an antifeudal" ethic, though they also believe it is "not so much a capitalistic as an industrial" ethic; see "Protestantism and Capitalism," 174. See also Weber, "Protestant Ethic," in *GRS* 1:185–86, 186–87n.1, 192–95, 193n.2, 194n.1. On pp. 25 and 29 Weber refers to the real Calvinists as people without a feeling for enjoyment or joy of life (*Weltfreude*). See the comments of Klara Vontobel, *Das Arbeitsethos,* 78–79. See also Weber, "Antikritisches Schlusswort," in *Die protestantische Ethik* 2:320–21.

86. See Weber, *Wirtschaftsgeschichte,* 314.

87. Weber, "Protestant Ethic," in *GRS* 1:195; "Sociology of Religion," in *WG,* 337; "Political and Hierocratic Domination," in *WG,* 719. See also Michaelson, "Puritan Concept of Calling," 333; and R. Schlatter, *Social Ideas of the Religious Leaders, 1660–1688* (London: Oxford University Press, 1940).

88. Weber, "Protestant Ethic," in *GRS* 1:178, 190n.1, 203, 197, 54, 55, 56, 204, 105. In "Sociology of Religion," in *WG,* 348, and in *Wirtschaftsgeschichte,* 314, Weber calls the idea of the calling a "*caput mortuum.*" See also Michaelson,

"Puritan Concept of Calling," 324, on how the later, utilitarian, view forgot the larger frame of the early Puritans.

89. Weber, "Antikritisches zum 'Geist,'" in *Die protestantische Ethik* 2:167.
90. Weber, "Protestant Ethic," in *GRS* 1:204.
91. Weber, "Sociology of Religion," in *WG,* 343.

CHAPTER TWO

1. For context, see Hans Speier, "Zur Soziologie der bürgerlichen Intelligenz in Deutschland," in Gert Mattenklott and Klaus R. Scherpe, eds., *Positionen der literarischen Intelligenz zwischen bürgerliche Reaktion und Imperialismus* (Kronberg: Scriptor Verlag, 1973).

2. On naturalism, see Pascal, *From Naturalism to Expressionism,* 18–21, 37, 59; Arnold Hauser, *The Social History of Art* (New York: Vintage, 1951), 4:5, 26, 64–72, 177; Jean Pierrot, *The Decadent Imagination, 1880–1900,* trans. Derek Coltman (Chicago: University of Chicago Press, 1981), 4. On the crisis of positivism generally, see H. Stuart Hughes, *Consciousness and Society: The Reorientation of European Social Thought, 1890–1930* (New York: Vintage, 1958), esp. chaps. 1 and 2; and on other aspects of European development in this period, see Gerhard Masur, *Prophets of Yesterday: Studies in European Culture, 1890–1914* (New York: Harper & Row, 1961). On the relation of socialism and naturalism, see Vernon L. Lidtke, "Naturalism and Socialism in Germany," *American Historical Review* 79 (1974): 14–37.

3. In Germany naturalism dissolved in disillusion in the 1890s because of the disappointment of its social-reformist hopes. It was succeeded by an even more introverted aestheticism than in France, exclusive and unconcerned with everyday social issues, yet unable to produce "a bourgeois culture of psychological intimacy" and hence unable to establish a new relation to its traditional audience.

On impressionism, see Pascal, *From Naturalism to Expressionism,* 60, 61; Pierrot, *Decadent Imagination,* 4; Hauser, *Social History of Art,* 4:170, 177–89; Peter Jelavich, "Art and Mammon in Wilhelmine Germany: The Case of Frank Wedekind," *Central European History* 12 (1979): 203–36, esp. 223–24; idem, "'Die Elf Scharfrichter,'" in Gerald Chapple and Hans H. Schulte, eds., *The Turn of the Century: German Literature and Art, 1890–1915* (Bonn: Bouvier Verlag Herbert Grundmann, 1981), 520. On Germany in general, see Wolfdietrich Rasch, *Zur deutschen Literatur seit der Jahrhundertwende: Gesammelte Aufsätze* (Stuttgart: J. B. Metzlersche Verlagsbuchhandlung, 1967), 1–48. On Austria and elsewhere, see Hermann Broch, *Hugo von Hofmannsthal and His Time: The European Imagination, 1860–1920,* trans. and ed. Michael P. Steinberg (Chicago: University of Chicago Press, 1984). On aestheticism in Britain, see Raymond Williams, *Culture and Society, 1780–1950* (London: Chatto & Windus, 1958; Harmondsworth: Penguin Books, 1963), 169–75.

4. Mann, "Meine Zeit," in *GW* 11:311.

5. Hauser, *Social History of Art,* 4:185, 193; Pierrot, *Decadent Imagination,* 5–11, 45, 47, 48. See also Edmund Wilson, *Axel's Castle: A Study in the Imaginative Literature of 1870–1930* (New York: Scribner's, 1931), chaps. 1 and 7.

6. The quotes from Paul Bourget are from *Essais de psychologie contemporaine* (Paris: Plon, 1883; augmented ed., 1899), 1:18–25. On Mann's reading of Bourget, see Thomas Mann, *Briefe an Otto Grautoff, 1894–1901, und Ida Boy-Ed, 1903–1928* (Frankfurt am Main: S. Fischer Verlag, 1975), 30, 62; Richard Winston, *Thomas Mann: The Making of an Artist, 1871–1911* (New York: Knopf, 1981), 50–51; and Schröter, *Thomas Mann*, 31, 34–44. It is almost certainly from Bourget that Mann learned the concept of decadence, not from Nietzsche, whom he cites above. On Bourget, see Pierrot, *Decadent Imagination*, 11–16, and on decadence, 47–50; Micheline Tison-Braun, *La Crise de l'humanisme: Le Conflit de l'individu et de la société dans la littérature française moderne*, vol. 1, *1890–1914* (Paris: Librairie Nizet, 1958), 98–104; Victor Brombert, *The Intellectual Hero: Studies in the French Novel, 1880–1955* (Philadelphia and New York: J. B. Lippincott, 1960), 20–40, 52–67; and Michel Mansuy, *Un Moderne, Paul Bourget: De l'enfance au disciple*, Annales Littéraires de l'Université de Besançon (Paris: Belles Lettres, 1960). On the generational problem of decadence, see Robert Wohl, *The Generation of 1914* (Cambridge: Harvard University Press, 1979).

7. "Der Bajazzo" ("The Buffoon" or "The Joker") was published in 1897 and probably takes its title from Leoncavallo's opera *I Pagliacci*, performed in Germany in 1892 under the title *Der Bajazzo*. See the useful background information in Hans Rudolf Vaget, *Thomas-Mann-Kommentar: Zu sämtlichen Erzählungen* (Munich: Winkler Verlag, 1984), 65–70; and in Peter de Mendelssohn, *Nachbemerkungen zu Thomas Mann* (Frankfurt am Main: Fischer Taschenbuch Verlag, 1982), 2:13–14, 19–21.

8. Mann, *Otto Grautoff und Ida Boy-Ed*, 47, 50.

9. See Hans Rudolf Vaget, "Thomas Mann und Oskar Panizza: Zwei Splitter zu *Buddenbrooks* und *Doktor Faustus*," *Germanisch-Romanische Monatsschrift* 56 (1975): 231–37. One of the principal claims Mann makes is in "Meine Zeit," in *GW* 11:311, as quoted by Vaget. On the influence of impressionism and of other writers on Mann, see T. J. Reed, *Thomas Mann: The Uses of Tradition* (Oxford: Oxford University Press, 1974), 12n.7, 21, 22n.35.

10. Mann, "The Joker," in *GW* 8:106, 113, 115–16.

11. Ibid., 122, 123.

12. Ibid., 122, 123, 125, 118–19.

13. Ibid., 136–37, 138.

14. Schröter, *Thomas Mann*, 38, 36. See also Pascal, *From Naturalism to Expressionism*, 61, where he shows how the characters of the new psychological novels of decadence lack any ethical impulse, feel they are role playing, and are subject to "an irresistible process that disintegrates the will and personality and evokes in them only grief, suffering and the longing for death." See also Winston, *Thomas Mann*, 80.

15. Schröter, *Thomas Mann*, 38; Winston, *Thomas Mann*, 77–81; Vaget, *Thomas-Mann-Kommentar*, 69–70; Mendelssohn, *Nachbemerkungen* 2:19–20.

16. Helmut Haug, *Erkenntnisekel: Zum frühen Werk Thomas Manns* (Tübingen: Max Niemeyer Verlag, 1969), 18, 16; see also ibid., 19, 22. The expression "*Willen zum Werk*" is from Mann's autobiographical "Süsser Schlaf," in *GW* 11:338.

17. Schröter, *Thomas Mann*, 36.

18. Mann, "Lübeck as a Spiritual Form of Life," in *GW* 11:554.

19. Reed, *Thomas Mann*, 45, 46.

20. Mann, "Lübeck as a Spiritual Form of Life," in *GW* 11:554; Reed, *Thomas Mann*, 47.

21. Fritz Kaufmann, *Thomas Mann: The World as Will and Representation* (Boston: Beacon Press, 1957; New York: Cooper Square Publishers, 1973), 89.

22. Mann, quoted from marginalia in Reed, *Thomas Mann*, 44.

23. Mann, "Lübeck as a Spiritual Form of Life," in *GW* 11:379; see also "Zu einem Kapitel aus 'Buddenbrooks,'" in *GW* 11:554, 556.

Reed suggests that Nietzsche was behind Mann's notions of decadence and inherited weakness, though Schröter adds that Bourget too was crucial here. Toward the end of the work the whole issue of decline was "heightened" through Mann's reading of Schopenhauer and its incorporation into the work. Generally Nietzsche and Schopenhauer changed the terms and understanding of decadence for Mann, so that *Buddenbrooks* escaped from the more narrow influence Bourget had previously exercised. See Reed, *Thomas Mann*, 48, 18nn.21 and 22, 19, 72, 73; Schröter, *Thomas Mann*, 60, 61; Mann, "Lübeck as a Spiritual Form of Life," in *GW* 11:381. Schröter points out that although Bourget's influence is visible in the character of Christian and in the "nervous" quality of Thomas and Gerda, the three key themes for Bourget—religion, love of fatherland, and the role of the family—are overthrown in Mann's novel. Schröter says these changes are all "effects of Nietzsche's critique of the time." See also Mendelssohn, *Nachbemerkungen* 1:10, 13–15, 23–24.

24. Schröter, *Thomas Mann*, 46, 47. For the references in Mann, see "Lübeck as a Spiritual Form of Life," in *GW* 11:379–80, 381. The most thorough work on this subject is Heinz Peter Pütz, *Kunst und Künstlerexistenz bei Nietzsche und Thomas Mann: Zum Problem des ästhetischen Perspektivismus in der Moderne*, Bonner Arbeiten zur deutschen Literatur, vol. 6, ed. Benno von Wiese (Bonn: H. Bouvier & Co. Verlag, 1963).

25. Reed, *Thomas Mann*, 70.

26. Wolfgang Martens, *Lyrik Kommerziell: Das Kartell lyrischer Autoren, 1902–1933* (Munich: Wilhelm Fink Verlag, 1974), 16.

27. See Schröter, *Thomas Mann*, 55; Reed, *Thomas Mann*, 39. On the economic history of Lübeck, see Jochen Vogt, *Thomas Mann: "Buddenbrooks"* (Munich: Wilhelm Fink Verlag, 1983), esp. 54–63; and Pierre-Paul Sagave, *Réalité sociale et idéologie religieuse dans les romans de Thomas Mann*, Faculté des Lettres de l'Université de Strasbourg, no. 124 (Paris: Belles Lettres, 1954). On the depression of 1873–96 and its effects, see Hans Rosenberg, "Political and Social Consequences of the Great Depression of 1873–1896 in Central Europe," *Economic History Review* 13 (1943): 58–73; idem, *Grosse Depression und Bismarckzeit: Wirtschaftsablauf, Gesellschaft und Politik in Mitteleuropa* (Berlin: Walter de Gruyter, 1967; Frankfurt am Main: Ullstein Verlag, 1976). See also Martin Kitchen, *The Political Economy of Germany, 1815–1914* (London: Croom Helm, 1978), 161–79.

28. Mann, "Lübeck as a Spiritual Form of Life," in *GW* 11:386.

29. Mann, "Hundert Jahre Reclam," in *GW* 10:239–40.

30. Mann, "Lübeck as a Spiritual Form of Life," in *GW* 11:387. See also idem, "Lebensabriss," in *GW* 11:98–104; and Sagave, *Réalité sociale*, 30, 31, 32. Sagave recognizes not only Mann's strong feeling for the *Bürger* but also the importance of the continuity of "service" in a calling and the role of service in self-justification. He says quite incisively: "The literary work that he undertakes in a bourgeois spirit and through which he gives an account of his bourgeois origins is the result of a work that rehabilitates the author, a fallen bourgeois. . . . The affinity between the author and his characters is such that one can say: The effort in the service of the literary work justifies the writer Thomas Mann in his own eyes, by the same right that the effort in the service of the Buddenbrook enterprise justifies the heroes of the novel to themselves."

31. Mann, *Reflections*, in *GW* 12:72, quoted in Reed, *Thomas Mann*, 49.

32. Mann, "Lübeck as a Spiritual Form of Life," in *GW* 11:384.

33. Rainer Maria Rilke, "Thomas Mann's *Buddenbrooks*," in Henry Hatfield, ed., *Thomas Mann: A Collection of Critical Essays* (Englewood Cliffs, N.J.: Prentice-Hall, 1964), 8–9.

34. *GW* 1:14. Quotations from *Buddenbrooks* in this chapter will hereafter be cited by page number in the text.

35. For an excellent discussion of the differences between old Johann and his son, see Larry David Nachman and Albert S. Braverman, "Thomas Mann's *Buddenbrooks*: Bourgeois Society and the Inner Life," *Germanic Review* 45 (1970): 201–25.

36. Erich Heller, *Thomas Mann: The Ironic German* (New York: Little, Brown, 1958; Cleveland: World, 1961), 41.

37. Nachman and Braverman, "Thomas Mann's *Buddenbrooks*," 209.

38. See Paul Weigand, "Thomas Mann's 'Tonio Kröger' and Kleist's 'Über das Marionettentheater,'" *Symposium* 12 (1958): 133–38.

39. In describing Thomas's relation to work, Vogt makes the brilliant comment that "his devotion [*Hingebung*] remains this-worldly [*diesseitig*], directed solely to the demands that are placed on the present chief of the firm by the family tradition." Furthermore, the "meaning and goal of the calling's 'pains and work' are no longer transcendentally warranted, as they still were in the Protestant ethic of his father, but are rather decisionistically maintained. Thus Thomas Buddenbrook's principles of duty and achievement express the almost violent attempt to *posit* a meaning for existence, which is no longer given without question; ultimately [this attempt] manages to resist the threatening feeling of meaninglessness through 'self-control' [*Haltung*]" (*Thomas Mann: Buddenbrooks*, 64, 67).

40. Nachman and Braverman maintain that Thomas's "self-consciousness did not weaken his will merely by its presence. It was rather that his denial and terror of his own impulses and aspirations poisoned his life and made willing futile" ("Thomas Mann's *Buddenbrooks*," 215). They suggest, further, that in giving up the development of himself he is forging his own destruction. "*His* sacrifice did not merely mean the self-discipline necessary to play an active role in the world. It meant a total rejection of self-consciousness for life. . . . he had vitiated what were precisely the well-springs of his life—creative personality and originality" (ibid.).

41. This injection of Schopenhauer into the novel reveals more than Mann's eccentric and idiosyncratic affection for the philosopher. Indeed, Erich Heller maintains that Schopenhauer provides the "intellectual plot" of the whole novel, though Nachman and Braverman, as well as T. J. Reed, effectively counter Heller's argument. See Heller, *Thomas Mann,* 31; Nachman and Braverman, "Thomas Mann's *Buddenbrooks,*" 201, 203–4; Reed, *Thomas Mann,* 80, 82.

42. See Rasch, *Zur deutschen Literatur,* 41, 42. Rasch says that when we encounter Thomas reading Schopenhauer in the novel, we can see it "as a description of a process that offers nothing surprising" (43). See Hauser, *Social History of Art* 4:181.

Moreover, the whole of French literature at the end of the nineteenth century was impregnated with gloomy pessimism about the possibilities of happiness and vitality in life. Schopenhauer's influence coincided with this fashion and provided "a philosophical foundation for the profound melancholy and discouragement" by which the decadents felt themselves burdened. This influence spread widely from at least the time of Schopenhauer's first translation into French in 1886, although his name appears slightly earlier in the work of Bourget. Bourget considered Schopenhauer the expression of German disillusion, parallel to Slavic nihilism and to the "solitary and bizarre neuroses" in France. He even appears in works of Rémy de Gourmont, Joris-Karl Huysmans, and Guy de Maupassant. See Pierrot, *Decadent Imagination,* 45–46, 56–60, 15.

43. Mann, "Schopenhauer," in *GW* 9:559.

44. Mann calls this pessimism "the spiritual life breath of the second half of the nineteenth century" and says Schopenhauer gave to his readers the "feeling of triumph" through the power of the "magnificent word" over the unhappiness and suffering that life inflicts. See ibid., 558–59, 542.

45. Heller, *Thomas Mann,* 60–63.

46. Kaufmann says of Schopenhauer's influence on Thomas that "it is Schopenhauer's doctrine without Schopenhauer's asceticism; it is Schopenhauer in a Nietzschean interpretation" (*Thomas Mann,* 90). On Mann's reading of Nietzsche, see Reed, *Thomas Mann,* 18, 80.

47. Contrary to this view, Nachman and Braverman ("Thomas Mann's *Buddenbrooks,*" 215) maintain that "Gerda's quite unworldly culture . . stood forth as the only healthy, the only real and vital activity in the Buddenbrook house"!

48. Kaufmann, *Thomas Mann,* 94.

49. I am indebted to George Shulman for this formulation.

50. Nachman and Braverman suggest that at this point in his career Mann still takes "life" to mean the commercial life of the bourgeoisie and that therefore "the needs of the personality which could not be satisfied" in such a life must seem illegitimate ("Thomas Mann's *Buddenbrooks,*" 224).

51. For details, see Hans Wysling, "Dokumente zur Entstehung des 'Tonio Kröger': Archivalisches aus der Nach-*Buddenbrooks*-Zeit," in Paul Scherrer and Hans Wysling, eds., *Thomas-Mann-Studien,* vol. 1, *Quellenkritische Studien zum Werk Thomas Manns* (Bern and Munich: Francke Verlag, 1967), 48–63. See also Vaget, *Thomas-Mann-Kommentar,* 108–16. Reed refers to the "experience of insubstantiality" that is the lot of the artist cut off from reality, and he suggests that this actually leaves little else as a theme of literature

but the experience of this attenuated reality itself (*Thomas Mann*, 92, 93–94).

52. On Flaubert's understanding of art and the artist, see Hauser, *Social History of Art* 4 : 66, 71–75, 77–80; Geneviève Bollème, *La Leçon de Flaubert* (Paris: Lettres Nouvelles, 1964), 60–100; Benjamin Bart, *Flaubert* (Syracuse, N.Y.: Syracuse University Press, 1967), 119–20, 328–53; Enid Starkie, *Flaubert: The Making of the Master* (New York: Atheneum, 1967), 277–88, 334–62; René Dumesnil, *La Vocation de Gustave Flaubert* (Paris: Gallimard, 1961), 203–14. The best source on Flaubert's views is his letters. See Charles Carlut's guide, *La Correspondance de Flaubert: Étude et répertoire critique* (Columbus, Ohio: Ohio University Press, 1968), esp. 257–59, 270–73, 311–25, 461–68, 475–515. See also Paul Bourget, *Essais de psychologie contemporaine* 1: 151–64.

53. Heller, *Thomas Mann*, 77, 83.

54. For Mann's discussion of his career, see "Lebensabriss," in *GW* 11: 98–144.

55. Mendelssohn, *Nachbemerkungen* 2 : 31. See also Thomas Mann and Heinrich Mann, *Briefwechsel, 1900–1949*, rev. ed., ed. Hans Wysling (Frankfurt am Main: Fischer Taschenbuch Verlag, 1975), 73; and *Thomas Mann*, ed. Hans Wysling and Marianne Fischer, pt. 1: *1889–1917*, vol. 14 of *Dichter über ihre Dichtungen* (Munich: Ernst Heimeran Verlag, 1975), 176.

56. Vaget, *Thomas-Mann-Kommentar*, 150.

57. *GW* 8 : 27. Quotations from "The Hungry" and *Tonio Kröger* in this chapter will hereafter be cited by page number in the text.

58. See Vaget, *Thomas-Mann-Kommentar*, 114–16, which gives *Tonio Kröger* as an example of European decadence literature in which decadence and dilettantism are overcome.

59. See Thomas Anz, *Literatur der Existenz: Literarische Psychopathographie und ihre soziale Bedeutung im Frühexpressionismus* (Stuttgart: J. B. Metzlersche Verlagsbuchhandlung, 1977), 86. He maintains that for oppositional artists like the Expressionists, the "bourgeois calling became a 'distinctive sign'" separating the individual integrated into society from the outsider. But on the right as well, artists like Hofmannsthal and George defended "an art free from all service," the concern of aristocrats of the soul who repudiated the claims of bourgeois society. See Pascal, *From Naturalism to Expressionism*, 61. Mann and Tonio overcome this need for escaping service in the calling; thus they are not really outsiders after all.

60. Heller maintains that in this story, which he calls a tale of "a man's separation from ordinary existence," "no other being, apart from himself, comes to life. . . . Hans Hansen is a mere creature of Tonio's youthful eros, a blond and blue-eyed apparition invoked by an erotic craving the burghers would be anxious to disown" (*Thomas Mann*, 73).

61. Flaubert is the first artist to announce this ethos, but he does not renounce involvement in life only as a limited technical principle of artistic production, to protect artistic vision. Rather, he defends a form of renunciation of life itself. "We [artists] are made for saying it, not for having it." Zola remarked that Flaubert "had entered literature as formerly one entered a religious order," and Mauriac claimed Flaubert had "substituted Art for God." See Starkie, *Flaubert*, 340–41, 349, and her references to Flaubert's letters of 5–6 Dec.

1866 to George Sand, in Gustave Flaubert, *Correspondance*, rev. ed., 9 vols. (Paris: Louis Conard, 1926–33), 5:253. In ibid. see also letters of 8 Feb. 1852 to Louise Colet, 2:365; 6 Feb. 1876 to George Sand, 7:285; 22 Apr. 1854 to Louise Colet, 4:61–62; 1 Sept. 1852 to Louise Colet, 3:7. See also Bart, *Flaubert*, 333, 339, 114.

As Bart says, Flaubert began to live a "life for art's sake" rather than create an art for art's sake; he became a "monk of letters" and the "priest of a special cult accomplishing a duty and obeying a higher fate." See Bart, *Flaubert*, 119–20, 329, 327, 337, 137. Hauser maintains that Flaubert's "self-surrender of life to art" became much more than "a mere service and a mere sacrifice": it became quasi-religious and mystical, "an anti-social and life-negating nihilism." See Hauser, *Social History of Art* 4:79–80. Yet Hauser is not sufficiently aware of the inherently religious nature of all service in a bourgeois calling.

62. See Heller, *Thomas Mann*, 75, who says that Tonio "submits to the 'curse' of literature as one accepting a mission."

63. Peter Pütz speaks of the transformation of Nietzsche's "blond beast" in the *Genealogy of Morals* into the "spiritless but lovable representative of normality" in *Tonio Kröger* ("Thomas Mann und Nietzsche," in Peter Pütz, ed., *Thomas Mann und die Tradition* [Frankfurt am Main: Atheneum Verlag, 1971], 238). Quoted in Vaget, *Thomas-Mann-Kommentar*, 119.

64. Describing his relation to art, Mann refers to the "*revenge* of the artist on his experience" ("Bilse und Ich," in *GW* 10:9–22).

65. See Pascal, *From Naturalism to Expressionism*, 286–87, 289–90, 291–92, 61. See also Jelavich, "Art and Mammon," 223, 224; idem, "Munich as Cultural Center: Politics and the Arts," in *Kandinsky in Munich: 1896–1914* (New York: Guggenheim Museum, n.d.), 23–25; and idem, "'Die Elf Scharfrichter,'" 520.

66. See Bramsted, *Aristocracy and the Middle-Classes*, 278, 288–89, 333, 335. See also Martens, *Lyrik Kommerziell*, 164–68.

67. See Robin Lenman, "Art, Society, and the Law in Wilhelmine Germany: The Lex Heinze," *Oxford German Studies* 8 (1973): 86–113; idem, "Politics and Culture: The State and the Avant-Garde in Munich, 1886–1914," in Richard J. Evans, ed., *Society and Politics in Wilhelmine Germany* (London: Croom Helm, 1978), 90–111; Jelavich, "'Die Elf Scharfrichter,'" 508–9; idem, "Munich as Cultural Center," 22, where the author persuasively maintains that Mann's "Gladius Dei" was inspired by a legal case concerning blasphemy; and Pascal, *From Naturalism to Expressionism*, 256–76. See also the papers and comments delivered at the German Studies Association annual meeting, Washington, D.C., Oct. 1985, in the panel "Outcasts, Victims, Martyrs: Literary Alienation in Imperial Germany." On France, see Hauser, *Social History of Art* 4:66, 71, 72; and Dominick LaCapra, *"Madame Bovary" on Trial* (Ithaca, N.Y.: Cornell University Press, 1982).

68. Tonio does have philosophical defenders. Kant and Schopenhauer, among others, insist on the conflict between "objectivity," art, intellect, and detachment, on the one hand, and life, engagement, and feeling, on the other. Though Tonio may curse the coldness of his calling, both Kant and Schopenhauer insist on the "pure objectivity" of the aesthetic vision. Furthermore, they argue that to produce genuine art the artist must "disown for some time his

whole personality" and separate artistic vision from the "real person" (Heller, *Thomas Mann*, 77, 78).

69. The advent of *Lebensphilosophie*, shaped by Nietzsche, Dilthey, Bergson, Klages, and Simmel, revealed the unity of what Wolfdietrich Rasch calls the central concept of the epoch: "bonding with life" (*Bindung an das Leben*). Moreover, in this concept of life made into an absolute—life in all its aspects, not just as vitality or strength—all the tendencies of the time converge (Rasch, *Zur deutschen Literatur*, 17–18, 26). He quotes Karl Löwith on Nietzsche that "the governing locus of Nietzsche's complete teachings is specified with the word 'life.'" Rasch points out, however, that despite Nietzsche's critique, Schopenhauer was a key figure in mediating the reception of the concept of life (ibid., 41). Still, the younger generation, moved by their reading of Nietzsche, saw the weakness of Christianity, and "it sought within a this-worldly orientation in the mysticism of life refuge from the isolation of the self. This is the decisive motif for the acceptance of this mysticism of life" (ibid., 43).

70. Heller says Mann was right to say that in *Tonio Kröger* "Nietzsche's philosophy of life gains the upper hand over Schopenhauer's denial of it" (*Thomas Mann*, 75, 80, 81). Heller refers especially to Nietzsche's *Birth of Tragedy*, chap. 5, and *Genealogy of Morals*. Schröter says that both *Tonio Kröger* and *Fiorenza* come from conceptions that emerged in the *Buddenbrooks* period but that are truly the spiritual consequences of reading Nietzsche (*Thomas Mann*, 68). He also observes that before Mann had read Nietzsche in 1896, he treated the problem of the artist purely as a sociological problem, not as the psychological problem of his later novels. After 1896 Nietzsche's work "confirmed his own experience" (ibid., 42). Wysling notes that the problem of the artist as Tonio describes it is based on chap. 7 of Nietzsche's *Birth of Tragedy*, which discusses Hamlet's disgust with knowledge (*Erkenntnisekel*) and his resulting paralysis (Scherrer and Wysling, *Thomas-Mann-Studien*, 330n.6).

Pascal says that Mann's treatment of the "more subtle distinction between artist and bourgeois, that runs through all his pre-1918 work" is "of purer Nietzschean origin" than the treatment of those authors who identified with the image of the artist in a "crude" Nietzschean sense, using it as a challenge to the bourgeoisie (*From Naturalism to Expressionism*, 58). Schröter denies that Nietzsche is the origin of this distinction between artist and bourgeois, which he claims Nietzsche never makes in the form in which Mann appropriates it. He says that both Mann and Nietzsche learned this from Bourget (Schröter, *Thomas Mann*, 43). Vaget quotes Mann's *Reflections* (in *GW* 12:91), which says that with *Tonio Kröger* "the Nietzschean cultural element [*Bildungselement*] came to its breakthrough and from then on it was to remain dominant" (*Thomas-Mann-Kommentar*, 113).

71. On Nietzsche's role in the development of *Lebensphilosophie*, see Herbert Schnädelbach, *Philosophy in Germany, 1831–1933* (Cambridge: Cambridge University Press, 1984), 144–46. As Pierrot points out, the rising tide of interest in Nietzsche shows the change in the public's mood in the last years of the nineteenth century and the shift in the focus of artists as well, marking a return, although in widely varying forms, to action and the celebration of energy. See Pierrot, *Decadent Imagination*, 248, 250, 251.

72. Rasch speaks of the desire of the turn-of-the-century generation to be

"consciously unconscious," to achieve unself-consciousness through the contrivances of the mind (*Zur deutschen Literatur*, 28–29).

73. Pierrot, *Decadent Imagination*, 50–52, 60–63. The Maupassant quotations are from *Sur l'eau* (1888).

74. Pierrot, *Decadent Imagination*, 52–55, 60. Feeling their isolation as necessary but painful, the decadents sought "scientific justification" for their plight in contemporary analyses of the psychology of the artist such as those produced by Cesare Lombroso (whose name appears in Mann's notes for his discourse on literature and for *Tonio Kröger*) and by Max Nordau. See Scherrer and Wysling, *Thomas-Mann-Studien*, 57. On Nordau, see Pierrot, *Decadent Imagination*, 52–55, 60; and Pascal, *From Naturalism to Expressionism*, 22–23.

75. In "Lebensabriss" Mann says that Tonio's word *Erkenntnisekel* "describes quite accurately that sickness of my youth" (*GW* 11:110–11). Vaget points out that the word *Erkenntnisekel* comes from chap. 7 of Nietzsche's *Birth of Tragedy* (*Thomas-Mann-Kommentar*, 107). On the desire among the Expressionists "to escape the inhibiting and disenchanting consequences" of intellect, see Walter Sokel, *The Writer in Extremis: Expressionism in Twentieth-Century German Literature* (Stanford: Stanford University Press, 1959; New York: McGraw-Hill, 1964), 102–4.

76. Vaget observes that the artist's problem of being caught between art and life and of being unmanned "is not specifically Thomas Mannish, but appears similarly in Flaubert, Maupassant, Nietzsche, Hauptmann, and Ibsen, among others" (*Thomas-Mann-Kommentar*, 115). Kaufmann says that Mann makes the dualism somewhat new by building into the relation between life and intellect "the idea of a mutual longing between them" (*Thomas Mann*, 27). Heller maintains that with "the romantic agony, through Flaubert, Rimbaud, Ibsen, to Valéry, Rilke, and indeed Thomas Mann, the feud between art and life has never ceased, demanding great sacrifices of 'real entity' and 'identical self'" (*Thomas Mann*, 79).

77. See Lida Kirchberger, "Popularity as a Technique: Notes on 'Tonio Kröger,'" *Monatschefte* 63, no. 4 (1971): 333; she suggests that Mann's own desire for fame inspired the form of the story.

78. See Gunter Reiss, "Herrenrecht: Bemerkungen zum Syndrom des Autoritären in Thomas Manns frühen Erzählungen," in Rolf Wiecker, ed., *Gedenkschrift für Thomas Mann, 1875–1955* (Copenhagen: Verlag Text und Kontext, 1975), 85–86. Reiss suggests that Tonio's inner conflicts "are embedded in the authoritarian relationship between him and his father." He explains Tonio's problem of standing "between two worlds" as "an expression of the uncompleted emancipation from the world of Consul Kröger."

79. See Mann, *Otto Grautoff und Ida Boy-Ed*, passim. See also Herbert Lehnert, "Die Künstler-Bürger-Brüder," in Pütz, ed., *Thomas Mann und die Tradition*, 14–51, on Mann's brother as the secret opponent in *Tonio Kröger*.

80. See L. Furst, "Thomas Mann's 'Tonio Kröger': A Critique Reconsidered," *Revue des Langues Vivantes* 27 (1961): 232–40, on the unconvincing ending of the story, as referred to in Vaget, *Thomas-Mann-Kommentar*, 120. Burton Pike says of Tonio, Leverkühn, and other of Mann's artists that "for

these serious artists art amounts to a religious calling, and service to it demands, in more than one sense, their lives" ("Thomas Mann and the Problematic Self," in Elizabeth M. Wilkinson, B. A. Rowley, and Ann C. Weaver, eds., *Publications of the English Goethe Society: Papers Read Before the Society, 1966–67* [Leeds: Maney & Son, 1967], 125).

81. Speier speaks of the "dualisms" in Mann and others as an ideology "that has validity only for an isolated intelligentsia." He argues for a view in which "artistry" is a "calling [*Beruf*] like that of the worker, diplomat, farmer, or engineer." Here Speier means to demystify and discard the older meaning of calling and replace it with "occupation" or "profession"; see "Soziologie der bürgerlichen Intelligenz," 23–24.

82. Indeed, Haug says that Tonio turns Nietzsche upside down, making the calling of the artist not a consequence of the impoverishment of modern life but its cause (*Erkenntnisekel*, 59).

83. Mann, "Lübeck as a Spiritual Form of Life," in *GW* 11:398.

84. Paul Weigand, "Thomas Mann's 'Tonio Kröger,'" 145.

85. Mann, *Reflections*, in *GW* 12:573–74.

86. Mann, "Lebensabriss," in *GW* 11:113–14.

87. Letter of 13 Feb. 1901 to Heinrich Mann, in Thomas Mann, *Briefe*, vol. 1, *1889–1936*, ed. Erika Mann (Frankfurt am Main: S. Fischer Verlag, 1961; Fischer Taschenbuch Verlag, 1979), 25; also in Thomas Mann and Heinrich Mann, *Briefwechsel*, 13–14.

88. See letters of 7 Mar. and 1 Apr. 1901 to brother Heinrich, in Mann, *Briefe* 1:26–27, 28.

89. Letter to Heinrich, 23 Dec. 1904, in Thomas Mann and Heinrich Mann, *Briefwechsel*, 31.

90. Letter of 1 Apr. 1901 to Heinrich, in Mann, *Briefe*, 1:28.

91. Letter of early June 1904 to Katia Pringsheim, in ibid., 45–46.

92. Letter to Katia, end of August 1904, in ibid., 53. See also Jean Finck, *Thomas Mann und die Psychoanalyse*, Bibliothèque de la Faculté de Philosophie et Lettres de l'Université de Liège (Paris: Belles Lettres, 1973), 108. Finck speaks of Mann's "problematic," as revealed in these letters, as "ambivalence."

93. Letter to Ida Boy-Ed, 19 Aug. 1904, in Mann, *Otto Grautoff und Ida Boy-Ed*, 150.

94. Günter de Bruyn insists that *Tonio Kröger* "is autobiographical in detail and theme" ("Der Künstler und die Andern," *Sinn und Form* 27 [1975]: 173).

95. This interpretation is supported by Inge Diersen (*Thomas Mann: Episches Werk, Weltanschauung, Leben* [Berlin: Aufbau Verlag, 1975], 65, 74), as referred to in Vaget (*Thomas-Mann-Kommentar*, 119). She speaks of Mann's "idealistic generalization of the basic experience of the hostility to art of the bourgeoisie into an "abstract, 'eternal' contradiction between artist and burgher, art and life." In contrast, Heller maintains that "the historical truth of Tonio Kröger's vision of life, art, and artists seems indisputable." Yet he also says that acceptance by the world of "a perverted doctrine of the human person" was required before this vision could be accepted by artists (*Thomas Mann*, 82, 83).

96. Kaufmann, *Thomas Mann*, 8, 9, 10, 11.

97. Nachman and Braverman, "Thomas Mann's *Buddenbrooks*," 216.

98. This is why Lukács's brilliant discussion of the calling in his 1909 essay "Theodor Storm oder die Bürgerlichkeit und l'art pour l'art" is an extraordinary characterization of the bourgeois calling carried over into art, although he does not fully recognize the extent to which the calling may be turned to more "romantically" ascetic purposes and still remain bourgeois. Lukács does suggest, however, that *Bürgerlichkeit* is a "whip that drives the life-denying man to work without cease," and "only the works which it brings forth confer value upon a life lived in such a framework." An asceticism based on the pursuit of a *Beruf* was not a mere occupation but a "life-form," and in such a form it was essentially "ethical," "the rule of order over mood." In "Lübeck as a Spiritual Form of Life," Mann may even have drawn on this essay, as his title suggests. See Georg Lukács, *Soul and Form*, trans. Anna Bostock (Cambridge: MIT Press, 1974), 55–78. See also Andrew Arato and Paul Breines, *The Young Lukács and the Origins of Western Marxism* (New York: Seabury Press, 1979), 33–43, where they also briefly consider Weber's analysis of the Protestant ethic.

CONCLUSION TO PART I

1. Löwith, *From Hegel to Nietzsche*, 331.

INTRODUCTION TO PART II

1. See Søren Kierkegaard, "Equilibrium between the Aesthetical and the Ethical in the Composition of Personality," in *Either/Or*, vol. 2, trans. Walter Lowrie (Princeton: Princeton University Press, 1959). On the Kierkegaard revival, see Allan Janik and Stephen Toulmin, *Wittgenstein's Vienna* (New York: Simon & Schuster, 1973), 161, 164–65, 177–78; and Georg Lukács's 1962 preface to *The Theory of the Novel*, trans. Anna Bostock (Cambridge: MIT Press, 1971), 18–19.

2. In 1912 Durkheim published *The Elementary Forms of the Religious Life*, trans. Joseph Ward Swain (New York: Free Press, 1965); book 2, chap. 8, raises the question of the nature of personality in a discussion of the origin of the soul. On Durkheim's interest in the personality and the soul, see Steven Collins, "Categories, Concepts or Predicaments? Remarks on Mauss's Use of Philosophical Terminology," in Michael Carrithers, Steven Collins, and Steven Lukes, eds., *The Category of the Person* (Cambridge: Cambridge University Press, 1985), 46–82, esp. 62–63.

3. On French developments, see Jerrold Seigel, "Cults of the Self," chap. 10 in *Bohemian Paris: Culture, Politics, and the Boundaries of Bourgeois Life, 1830–1930* (New York: Viking, 1986). Stefan George, whom Weber knew and members of whose circle Mann knew, tried to develop explicitly and purposefully a cult of personality around himself and his work. See Arvid Broderson, "Stefan George und sein Kreis: Eine Deutung aus der Sicht Max Webers," *Castrum Peregrini* 91 (1970): 5–24; Edgar Salin, *Um Stefan George*, 2d ed. (Munich: Helmut Küpper, vormals Georg Bondi, 1954); and Friedrich Wolters,

Stefan George und die Blätter für die Kunst (Berlin: Georg Bondi, 1930). Rilke, Hofmannsthal, Simmel, and Rathenau are other important figures.

4. See Friedrich Nietzsche, *The Will to Power*, trans. Walter Kaufmann and R. J. Hollingdale, ed. Walter Kaufmann (New York: Vintage, 1968), 522, aphorism 1009: "Points of view for *my* values: . . . whether one is *genuine* or merely an *actor* . . . whether one is a 'representative' or that which is represented? whether a 'personality' or merely a rendezvous of personalities . . . whether one is still capable of a 'duty'? (—there are those who would lose their whole joy in living if their duty were taken from them—especially the womanly, the born subjects)." Georg Simmel says: "For Nietzsche, it is the qualitative *being* of the personality which marks the stage that the development of mankind has reached." Moreover, we have to distinguish the personal qualities of individuals within the social process, judged in terms of their effects or usefulness, from the other side of their "significance," which is "the intrinsic fact of their existence in the personality," and this is the side that Nietzsche regards. See Georg Simmel, *The Sociology of Georg Simmel*, trans. and ed. Kurt H. Wolff (New York: Free Press, 1950), 62–63.

5. See R. Hinton Thomas, *Nietzsche in German Politics and Society, 1890–1918* (LaSalle, Ill.: Open Court, 1983), 96–111.

CHAPTER THREE

1. See Marcel Mauss, "A Category of the Human Mind: The Notion of Person; the Notion of Self," in Carrithers, Collins, and Lukes, eds., *Category of the Person*, 1–25. The term *Persönlichkeit* appears among the German mystics of the late fourteenth century, and in Meister Eckhart it is shown in the contrast between *persönlicheit* [*sic*] and *wesenheit*, personality and essence, suggesting that personality was understood in terms of mask or impersonation. See Jacob Grimm and Wilhelm Grimm, *Deutsches Wörterbuch* (Leipzig: Verlag von S. Hirzel, 1889), vol. 7, cols. 1561–65, 1567–68; see also *Trübner's Deutsches Wörterbuch* (Berlin: Walter de Gruyter, 1954), under the heading *personal*. The principal Protestant lexicon of the eighteenth century has no entry for *Persönlichkeit*, using only the word *Personalitas* for the "subsistence" or essence of *Person*. See *Grosses Vollständiges Universal-Lexikon aller Wissenschaften und Künste* (Leipzig and Halle: Verlegt Johann Heinrich Zedler, 1741), vol. 27, known as Zedler's Lexikon.

I am grateful to Reinhart Koselleck for advice on sources and help in clarifying concepts.

2. Weber, "Protestant Ethic," in *GRS* 1 : 181–82n.2.

3. Immanuel Kant, *Kritik der praktischen Vernunft*, vol. 5 of *Kants gesammelte Schriften* (Berlin: Preussische Akademie der Wissenschaften, 1900–1942), 86–88.

4. Ibid., 161–62. Simmel, one of Weber's contemporaries, says: "Kant and his epoch make abstract man, the individuality that is freed from all ties and specificities and is therefore always identical, the ultimate substance of personality and, thereby, the ultimate *value* of personality" (*Sociology of Georg Sim-*

mel, 70). For the importance of *Willkür* (rather than *Wille*) for Kant, see John R. Silber, "The Ethical Significance of Kant's *Religion*," introduction to Immanuel Kant, *Religion within the Limits of Reason Alone*, trans. Theodore M. Greene and Hoyt H. Hudson (New York: Harper & Row, 1960).

5. Kant, *Kritik*, 65–67. Simmel observes: "Within the natural-social cosmos, 'being-for-oneself' or 'personality' do [*sic*] not exist. Only when we are rooted in absolute freedom (the metaphysical counterpart of *laissez-faire*) do we gain both personality and the dignity of the moral" ₍*Sociology of Georg Simmel*, 72). Otto von Gierke remarks that Kant limited "the conception of personality entirely to the individual in his capacity of a free rational being," but that Kant nevertheless depersonalized the individual into an "abstract rational being"; see *Natural Law and the Theory of Society, 1500 to 1800*, trans. Ernest Barker (1913; reprint, Cambridge: Cambridge University Press, 1950), 134–35.

6. Kant, *Kritik*, 88.

7. Immanuel Kant, *Die Religion innerhalb der Grenzen der blossen Vernunft*, vol. 6 of *Immanuel Kants Werke*, ed. Ernst Cassirer (Berlin: Bruno Cassirer, 1914), 163.

8. Ibid., 164–67.

9. Ibid., 187–88.

10. See Silber, "Kant's *Religion*," cxvi, cxvii.

11. The relevant passages of Augustine are found in *The City of God* XIV.9.

12. Kant, *Religion*, 197–98.

13. Ibid., 226–27. Silber says that "the ground of evil is found in man's tendency or disposition to will the rejection of himself as a self-determining personality, as a free being, for the sake of himself as a creature of nature" ("Kant's *Religion*," cxiv).

14. Ernst Cassirer, *Kant's Life and Thought*, trans. James Haden (New Haven: Yale University Press, 1981), 333; see also ibid., 243.

15. Simmel says of Kant's conception: "The absolutely self-dependent and self-responsible personality is precisely the personality whose action is ethically justified by the identical claim to this action on the part of all others" (*Sociology of Georg Simmel*, 72).

16. Hans Rosenberg, *Bureaucracy, Aristocracy, Autocracy: The Prussian Experience, 1660–1815* (Cambridge: Harvard University Press, 1958; Boston: Beacon Press, 1966), 182. See also Ringer, *German Mandarins*, 86; and Rudolf Vierhaus, "Bildung," in Otto Brunner, Werner Conze, and Reinhart Koselleck, eds., *Geschichtliche Grundbegriffe: Historisches Lexikon zur politisch-sozialen Sprache in Deutschland* (Stuttgart: Ernst Klett Verlag, 1972), 1:534–36.

17. See W. H. Bruford, *The German Tradition of Self-Cultivation: 'Bildung' from Humboldt to Thomas Mann* (Cambridge: Cambridge University Press, 1975), 19; see also his quotation from Thomas Mann on *Bildung*, ibid., vii.

18. Humboldt, quoted in Vierhaus ("Bildung," 521), who then observes: "The universal historical meaning of *Bildung* could not be elevated higher."

19. Herbert Schnädelbach, *Philosophie in Deutschland, 1831–1933* (Frankfurt am Main: Suhrkamp Verlag, 1983), 43.

20. See Konrad Jarausch, *Students, Society, and Politics in Imperial Germany: The Rise of Academic Illiberalism* (Princeton: Princeton University Press,

1982), 9. See also Hans-Georg Gadamer, *Truth and Method* (New York: Seabury Press, 1975), 10, 11.

According to Vierhaus, the meaning of *Bildung* and its "elevation over other concepts like 'education' [*Erziehung*] and 'training' [*Ausbildung*]" can only be understood in relation to the "governmental-social development of Germany." Vierhaus even finds that the development of *Bildung* parallels the "qualitative distinction between 'culture' and 'civilization' in Germany." See Vierhaus, "Bildung," 508–9, 511, 515. According to Lichtenstein, "the secularization, humanization, and pedagogization of the *Bildung* concept in the eighteenth century is connected with the emancipation of the emotional in German Pietism and with the eminent influence of Shaftesbury on German spiritual life." See E. Lichtenstein, "Bildung," in Joachim Ritter, ed., *Historisches Wörterbuch der Philosophie* (Basel and Stuttgart: Schwabe & Co. Verlag, 1971), vol. 1, cols. 922–23.

21. Humboldt, quoted in Lichtenstein, "Bildung," 926, and in Vierhaus, "Bildung," 520. See also Paul R. Sweet, *Wilhelm von Humboldt: A Biography* (Columbus, Ohio: Ohio State University Press, 1978), 1:88, 99. Humboldt even defends war, because risking "everything for a high goal" is something he considers essential for *Bildung* (ibid., 111). Fritz Stern says that after the strengthening of the universities following the defeat of Napoleon, "the moral indispensability of education became an article of faith: the self-fulfillment of the individual required the humanistic cultivation of the mind" (*The Failure of Illiberalism* [New York: Knopf, 1972], 7).

22. Humboldt, quoted in Bruford, *Self-Cultivation*, 24.

23. Stern, *Failure of Illiberalism*, 9.

24. See Roy Pascal, "The Concept of 'Bildung' and the Division of Labour: Wilhelm von Humboldt, Fichte, Schiller, Goethe," in *Culture and the Division of Labour: Three Essays on Literary Culture in Germany*, University of Warwick Occasional Papers (Coventry: University of Warwick, 1974), 5, 10–11, 12, 13. Pascal points out that for the figures of the *Sturm und Drang* period the division of labor was a problem not for its social and political effects, which had been the concern of the Scottish Enlightenment, but for its effects on personal life and the fragmentation of the personality.

25. Humboldt, quoted in Bruford, *Self-Cultivation*, 19. For details of his withdrawal from the Prussian civil service and his "search for an intellectual vocation," see Sweet, *Humboldt*, 83–150. Friedrich Meinecke says that for Humboldt "strength" (*Kraft*) was always connected in life with "one-sidedness" ("Schiller und der Individualitätsgedanke," in Meinecke, *Werke* [Stuttgart: K. F. Koehler Verlag, 1965] 4:310).

26. Humboldt, quoted in Sweet, *Humboldt*, 1:84. See also Friedrich Meinecke, *The Age of German Liberation, 1795–1815*, trans. Peter Paret (Berkeley and Los Angeles: University of California Press, 1977), 21.

27. Bruford, *Self-Cultivation*, 28.

28. Meinecke says that Humboldt became a politician because of "his recognition that working for the community afforded men new opportunities for personal development and effectiveness" (*German Liberation*, 55–56).

29. Humboldt, quoted in Bruford, *Self-Cultivation*, 123. Schleiermacher is the most important figure in the tradition of *Bildung* after Humboldt and may

have been even more influential. See ibid., 26, 80–83; Simmel, *Sociology of Georg Simmel*, 80, 81; Meinecke, *German Liberation*, 29–30. On Hegel and *Bildung*, see Gadamer, *Truth and Method*, 13–17.

30. Lichtenstein, "Bildung," 924.

31. Schiller too was concerned with this. See Pascal, "Division of Labor," 16, 21; Bruford, *Self-Cultivation*, 57; and Meinecke, "Schiller," 313. On Fichte, see Pascal, "Division of Labor," 13, 14. On Fichte and the ideal of humanity, see Meinecke, *German Liberation*, 44, 45; and Jarausch, *Students, Society, and Politics*, 161.

32. See Manfred Riedel, "Bürger," 699–700; Roy Pascal, *The German Novel* (Manchester: Manchester University Press, 1956), 3–29; Georg Lukács, *Goethe and His Age*, trans. Robert Anchor (New York: Grosset & Dunlap, 1969), 35–67; Leo Lowenthal, *Literature and the Image of Man* (Boston: Beacon Press, 1957), 136–65; Werner Kohlschmidt, *A History of German Literature, 1760–1805*, trans. Ian Hilton (New York: Holmes & Meier, 1975), 295–336. Friedrich Paulsen, one of Heinrich Rickert's teachers, confirms the larger significance of Goethe's world when he says that the ideal of enlightenment and the revolution in moral philosophy from Kant were superseded, in the midst of a change in the "German conception of life," by an ideal of Goethe's age, namely, the "perfection of the personality" (*A System of Ethics*, 4th ed., trans. Frank Tilly [New York: Charles Scribner's Sons, 1899], 201–3).

33. Johann Wolfgang von Goethe, *Goethes Werke*, Hamburger Ausgabe, ed. Erich Trunz (Hamburg: Christian Wegner Verlag, 1950), 7 : 290–91.

34. Ibid., 291.

35. Pascal, *German Novel*, 11, 22. Pascal points out that this novel reveals Goethe's appreciation of the distinctiveness of each personality and his understanding that there is no single ideal of humankind. See ibid., 12.

36. Riedel, "Bürger," 700.

37. Weber, "Protestant Ethic," in *GRS* 1 : 111n.2.

38. Lukács, *Goethe and His Age*, 57, 41. It is not possible to take up here the subject of Schiller and his relation to both Kant and Goethe. See Friedrich von Schiller, *Über Anmut und Würde*, in *Schillers Werke*, Nationalausgabe, ed. Benno von Wiese (Weimar: Hermann Böhlaus Nachfolger, 1962), vol. 20, pt. 1. Kant responded to this work in the second edition of *Religion*, 161–62, second footnote. See also Kohlschmidt, *German Literature*, 295–302; Roy Pascal, "The Creative Personality," chap. 5 in *The German Sturm und Drang* (Manchester: Manchester University Press, 1953), 133–69.

39. The idea of personality is important for the romantics as well, influenced both by Goethe and Herder and by Pietism, and romantic inwardness as the mysterious core of personality was attractive to Mann but criticized by Weber. I plan to deal with the romantics' *Seinsethik*, as opposed to Kant's *Sollensethik*, in a later study.

40. Pascal, "Division of Labor," 20, 23, 24. Pascal further observes that in Goethe's novel class distinctions are the grounds both of the necessity of one-sidedness and of the fantasy of its overcoming, the "dream of all-sided and un-committed 'Bildung'" (ibid., 25).

41. Kurt May, quoted in Bruford, *Self-Cultivation*, 56. Bruford points out

that in the course of writing the two parts of *Wilhelm Meister,* Goethe "shifted the aim of 'Bildung' from the extension and elaboration of one's own mental life, the conversion of as much as possible of the world outside into inner experience and the molding nearer to perfection of one's own personality—the kind of effort we have studied in Wilhelm von Humboldt—to work for the material and spiritual good of a specific group of one's fellow-men."

Lichtenstein says that even in *Wilhelm Meister, Bildung* "meant essentially not spiritual *Bildung* but rather the genesis of the persona, the elaboration of individuality into the ripe personality in an active environment" ("Bildung," 924).

42. Pascal, "Division of Labor", 27. Vierhaus says that if "Goethe was persuaded, on the one hand, that one's own will toward *Bildung* was valuable and useful . . . he was aware, on the other hand, of the external, above all the social, conditions of *Bildung*" ("Bildung," 517, 518).

Simmel says of Goethe's *Wanderjahre* that specialization is not about the personality in itself but only about the personality for society: "The individualistic requirement of specificity does not make for the valuation of total personality within society, but for the personality's objective achievement for the benefit of society." He quotes Goethe: "Any man's task is to do *something* extraordinarily well, as no other man in his immediate environment can" (*Sociology of Georg Simmel,* 80).

CHAPTER FOUR

1. There have been a few attempts to discuss Weber's concept of personality. See E. B. Portis, "Max Weber's Theory of Personality," *Sociological Inquiry* 48 (1978): 113–20; Dieter Henrich, *Die Einheit Max Webers Wissenschaftslehre* (Tübingen: J. C. B. Mohr [Paul Siebeck], 1952), esp. pt. 2; Wolfgang Schluchter, *Rationalismus der Weltbeherrschung: Studien zu Max Weber* (Frankfurt am Main: Suhrkamp Verlag, 1980), 35, 47, 56, 247n.57; Johannes Weiss, *Max Webers Grundlegung der Soziologie: Eine Einführung* (Munich: Uni-Taschenbücher, Verlag Dokumentation, 1975), esp. 144–52; and Wilhelm Hennis, "Max Webers Thema: 'Die Persönlichkeit und die Lebensordnungen,'" *Zeitschrift für Politik* 31 (1984): 11–52.

2. See R. Hinton Thomas, "The Uses of 'Bildung,'" *German Language and Literature,* n.s. 30 (1977): 177–86; George Mosse, *The Crisis of German Ideology: Intellectual Origins of the Third Reich* (New York: Grosset & Dunlap, 1964); and Fritz Stern, *The Politics of Cultural Despair: A Study in the Rise of the Germanic Ideology* (Berkeley and Los Angeles: University of California Press, 1961; reprint, Garden City, N.Y.: Doubleday, 1965).

3. On Windelband and the Baden neo-Kantians, see Thomas E. Willey, *Back to Kant: The Revival of Kantianism in German Social and Historical Thought, 1860–1914* (Detroit: Wayne State University Press, 1978), 131–52; and Iggers, *German Conception of History,* 124–33, 144–59. Weber refers to both Windelband and Rickert in his earliest methodological essays of 1903, and to Windelband several times in *The Protestant Ethic.*

4. Wilhelm Windelband, *Lehrbuch der Geschichte der Philosophie,* 4th ed.

(Tübingen: J. C. B. Mohr [Paul Siebeck], 1907), 283, 139–41, 146, 182, 185, 193ff., 199. Italics in original.

5. Ibid., 232. For confirmation of this view of Augustine as the central figure in the origin of the Christian, and hence Western, conception of personality, see Charles N. Cochrane, "Nostra Philosophia: The Discovery of Personality," chap. 11 in *Christianity and Classical Culture* (New York: Oxford University Press, 1957), esp. 401, 426, 432, 446, 454, 455.

6. On "the Augustinian influence, which held fast to the self-experience of the *personality* as the highest principle," see Windelband, *Lehrbuch*, 284, 285–86, 288, 340–41.

7. See Windelband, *Über Willensfreiheit* (Tübingen: J. C. B. Mohr [Paul Siebeck], 1904), 78. In his discussion of the role and importance of the primacy of the will, Windelband refers to W. Kahl's *Die Lehre vom Primat des Willens bei Augustinus, Duns Scotus, und Descartes* (1886), which Weber uses in *The Protestant Ethic* along with Windelband's *Über Willensfreiheit* (see Windelband, *Lehrbuch*, 274). Both works are important for Weber's understanding of the enduring will as the essence of personality, which then acts on its "constant motives." Weber notes that the "primacy of the will is common" to Luther, the Calvinists, and the Pietists. For references to Windelband and Kahl, see Weber, "Protestant Ethic," in *GRS* 1:116n.1, 117n.3, 141–42n.5, 203n.1.

8. The main sources used here are Manfred Schick, *Kulturprotestantismus und soziale Frage: Versuche zur Begründung der Sozialethik, vornehmlich in der Zeit um der Gründung des Evangelisch-Sozialen Kongresses bis zum Ausbruch des 1. Weltkrieges (1890–1914)* (Tübingen: J. C. B. Mohr [Paul Siebeck], 1970); Werner Elert, *Der Kampf um das Christentum: Geschichte der Beziehungen zwischen dem evangelischen Christentum in Deutschland und dem allgemeinen Denken seit Schleiermacher und Hegel* (Munich: C. H. Beck'sche Verlagsbuchhandlung, 1921), esp. 334–39, 344–50, 360–65, 420–29, 443–47; and Gordon Rupp, *Culture-Protestantism: German Liberal Theology at the Turn of the Century*, American Academy of Religion, Studies in Religion Series, no. 15 (Missoula, Montana: Scholars Press, 1977). See also Friedrich Naumann's pamphlet, *Die Erziehung zur Persönlichkeit im Zeitalter des Grossbetriebs* (Berlin-Schöneberg: Buchverlag der "Hilfe," 1907).

9. Schick, *Kulturprotestantismus*, 22–26.

10. The principal figures in this debate were Kaftan, Naumann, and Harnack. See Rupp, *Culture-Protestantism*, 47–48; also Troeltsch, *Social Teaching* 2:985n.504.

11. Schick, *Kulturprotestantismus*, 26.

12. For a fine presentation of Weber's views on the East Elbian land question, see Martin Riesebrodt, "Vom Patriarchalismus zum Kapitalismus: Max Webers Analyse der Transformation der ostelbischen Agrarverhältnisse im Kontext zeitgenössischer Theorien," *Kölner Zeitschrift für Soziologie und Sozialpsychologie* 37 (1985): 546–67. See also Vernon Dibble, "Social Science and Political Commitments in the Young Max Weber," *Archives Européenes de Sociologie* 9–10 (1968–69): 92–110; and Keith Tribe, "Prussian Agriculture—German Politics: Max Weber, 1892–7," *Economy and Society* 12 (1983): 181–226.

13. Schick, *Kulturprotestantismus,* 97–99, 111–112. According to Rupp, Naumann maintained in 1911 that if the Evangelisch-Soziale Kongress were to be founded again, it would have to be named Protestantisch-Ideal, marking the shift he believed had taken place in the organization from issues of the social relevance of the Gospel to the Reformation and Kantian preoccupation with "the cultivation of the individual, the personality" (*Culture-Protestantism,* 49).

14. Schick, *Kulturprotestantismus,* 100–102, 114. Troeltsch also wrote on this subject as early as 1904. See ibid., 101.

15. Ibid., 109–10. Even Naumann begins his *Die Erziehung zur Persön-lichkeit* with Kant.

16. On Troeltsch in the Evangelisch-Soziale Kongress, see Schick, *Kulturprotestantismus,* 30–32; see also the introduction and the editors' essays on Troeltsch in *Ernst Troeltsch: Writings on Theology and Religion,* trans. and ed. Robert Morgan and Michael Pye (Atlanta: John Knox Press, 1977), 1–51, 208–52. His works are collected principally in the four volumes of *Gesammelte Schriften,* 2d ed. (Tübingen: J. C. B. Mohr [Paul Siebeck], 1922). Troeltsch claimed that his work on the sects did not start from Weber's but goes back at least to 1901, though Weber claimed that his own work began in the late 1890s. See Troeltsch, *Social Teaching* 2:987n.510.

17. Troeltsch, *Social Teaching* 1:89.

18. Ernst Troeltsch, *Protestantism and Progress: A Historical Study of the Relation of Protestantism to the Modern World,* trans. W. Montgomery (Boston: Beacon Press, 1958), 207, 36. This is a translation of lectures published in 1906, enlarged in 1911, and published in English in 1912. See also Troeltsch's "Renaissance und Reformation" (1913), in *Gesammelte Schriften* 4:261–96.

19. Troeltsch, *Social Teaching* 1:328, 326, 202. He says further that the medieval church "united the fellowship in absolute spiritual values, and through the very share of the individual in these personal values gave to the individual his own independent value" (ibid., 325).

20. Ibid., 2:1004–6.

21. Troeltsch, "Luther, der Protestantismus, und die moderne Welt," in *Gesammelte Schriften* 4:202–54, esp. 223. The concept of *Gesinnungsethik* means "the working out of a unified conviction [*Gesinnung*] in a unified life conduct [*Lebenshaltung*] and a unified life work" (ibid., 222).

22. Ernst Troeltsch, *Christian Thought: Its History and Application,* edited, introduced, and indexed by Baron F. von Hügel (London: University of London Press, 1923), 51–52. This is a translation of *Der Historismus und seine Überwindung.*

23. Troeltsch, "Das Wesen des modernen Geistes," in *Gesammelte Schriften* 4:326. Troeltsch says there that "ruling are the features of an *autonomous, inwardly grounded morality of persuasion [Ueberzeugungsmoral],* with the goal of the elaboration of one's own personality to a work of moral freedom. . . . But this is also the whole of the modern world's individualism, yet harnessed through the ideal of personality, which no one is from nature, and everyone may only become through freedom" (Troeltsch's italics).

24. Troeltsch, *Christian Thought,* 79–80, 52.

25. Troeltsch, *Social Teaching* 1:30, 76, 65. Troeltsch maintains that the

Stoic conception leads to the theory of individualism, "expressed in terms of the idea of religious and ethical personality," and that it is analogous with the social thought of Christianity and its focus on "moral personalities."

26. Ibid., 1: 68.

27. Ibid., 2:591, 502, 588, 617.

28. Ibid., 2:583–84, 589–90, 603, 607, 617–18, 608, 794–95. See also Troeltsch, "The Ideas of Natural Law and Humanity in World Politics," in Gierke, *Natural Law,* 201–22.

29. Along with this emphasis is a conception of fellowship that is "an entirely new form of the Christian sociological idea," founded on "the predestinating will of God itself" and built on a conception of "national community." For Troeltsch, this combination of individuality and solidarity has unique significance and consequences for the destiny of the West. "Down to the present day the peculiar nature of this structure stamps the life of the Calvinistic peoples with a unique emphasis on the cultivation of independent personality, which leads to a power of initiative and a sense of responsibility for action, combined also with a very strong sense of unity for common, positive ends and values, which are invulnerable on account of their religious character." See Troeltsch, *Social Teaching* 2:618, 623–624, 619. For a discussion of how Calvinism became so influential, see Troeltsch, "Calvinismus und Luthertum" (1909), in *Gesammelte Schriften* 4:254–61.

30. There are a number of instances of Weber's use of personality outside his substantive writings. See Marianne Weber, *Max Weber: Ein Lebensbild,* 90, 92, 94, 96. In a letter to his sister of 20 Sept. 1910 introducing a collection of Rilke's poetry, he says: "Rilke is a mystic. . . . He is on the whole no formed personality, *from* which poetry as its product might break forth; 'he' does not write poetry, but rather 'it' is written in him. Therein lies his limitation, but also his peculiarity" (ibid., 464). Notice, though, that this concept of personality is different from the Puritan concept, where the personality is a tool of higher powers. It is used, rather, to mean fullness and completeness, out of whose richness initiative and action result. Here Weber is using a concept of personality more like that of the original tradition of *Bildung.* See also Otto Kohlmeyer, *Stefan George und die Persönlichkeitsgestalt als Erziehungsziel in Deutschlands Zeitenwende* (Magdeburg: Lichtenberg & Bühling, 1930). But see also Michael Ermarth, *Wilhelm Dilthey: The Critique of Historical Reason* (Chicago: University of Chicago Press, 1978), 121; and Stanley Corngold, *The Fate of the Self: German Writers and French Theory* (New York: Columbia University Press, 1986), 55–93.

31. See Weber, "Roscher and Knies and the Logical Problems of Historical National Economics," in *WL,* 132. Weber claims that Treitschke, in his notion of the riddle (*Rätsel*) of the personality, uses a romantic concept of personality and that Meinecke does as well when he speaks of the "irrational 'residue' [*Rest*]" of the personality as the personality's "inner sanctum [*Heiligtum*]." See ibid., 46n.1. Weber also criticizes Knies's concept of personality, which begins reasonably in the notion of personality as a unity (*Einheit*), but which Knies then transforms into a uniformity or homogeneity (*Einheitlichkeit*), free of all inner contradiction and combining disparate elements. Knies's concept, Weber

argues, cannot comprehend that most important of personalities, the Puritan. Moreover, Knies extends the concept to describe the unity or essence of a people (*Volk*), and what gives personality or character to either an individual or a people has the character of a "substance," which in Weber's view is a metaphysical residue, nothing but an expression of the "spirit of romanticism" and its concept of the *Volksseele*. See ibid., 138–39, 142–43. On Roscher, Hildebrand, and Knies, see Gottfried Eisermann, *Die Grundlagen des Historismus in der deutschen Nationalökonomie* (Stuttgart: Ferdinand Enke Verlag, 1956). On the problems with Meyer's interpretations of personality, see Weber, "Critical Studies in the Logic of the Cultural Sciences," in *WL*, 218, 222–23, 239–40.

32. Weber, "The 'Objectivity' of Social-scientific and Social-political Knowledge," in *WL*, 152.

33. Weber, "Protestant Ethic," in *GRS* 1:117. This capacity of Calvinism was found as well in Catholic monasticism, of course, and accounts, in Weber's opinion, for the expansiveness of both: the methodical control of the whole man made certain kinds of effective rational action possible. It is at this point that Weber refers to Windelband. See also Weyembergh, *Volontarisme rationnel*, 147. Simmel says, in a purely Nietzschean vein: "Certain extremely individualized persons and collectivities do not have the strength to preserve their individualization in the face of suppressive or leveling forces. The *strong* personality, on the other hand, usually intensifies its formation precisely through opposition, through the fight for its particular character and against all temptation to blend and intermix" (*Sociology of Georg Simmel*, 137).

34. In *History and Class Consciousness* (trans. Rodney Livingstone [Cambridge: MIT Press, 1971], 220n.54), Georg Lukács observes that "the same structure of ethics and existence [that exists in Calvinism] is still active in the Kantian system." He observes, furthermore, that there are passages in the *Kritik* "which sound wholly in line with Franklin's acquisitive ethics."

35. Weber, "Sociology of Religion," in *WG*, 339–40; "Confucianism and Taoism," in *GRS* 1:521, 518; "Hinduism and Buddhism," in *GRS* 2:371. Norbert Elias offers a critique of what he calls the "closed personality," proposing an "open personality . . . fundamentally oriented toward and dependent on other people throughout his life" (*The Civilizing Process*, trans. Edmund Jephcott [New York: Urizen Books, 1978], 245–63).

For a similar conception of personality, see Paulsen, *System of Ethics*, 468–69: The faculty of regulating and determining the particular functions of life by an "idea of one's life" is "precisely what we mean by free will." Thus the human being emancipates himself from the course of nature; "he rises above nature and opposes it as a self, he determines it and employs it, is not determined by it: man becomes a *personality*. As such he is able to put his whole self, his ego, into every phase of his life, and therefore he is *responsible* for it."

36. Weber, "Hinduism and Buddhism," in *GRS* 2:373–74, 377–78, 371, 345. The question of universal versus particular in defining the personality appears in Émile Durkheim as well; see *The Elementary Forms of the Religious Life*, trans. Joseph Ward Swain (New York: Free Press, 1965), book 2, chap. 8, 305–8. In the tradition of Leibniz and Kant, Durkheim argues that the notion of person derives from two factors, an impersonal principle that is the soul of

the group and a principle of individuation that derives from the body. Yet, he argues, we do not become more "personal" as we become more individualized: "individuation is not the essential characteristic of the personality." For Kant the sense and the body, "all that individualizes is . . . considered as the antagonist of the personality." "Passion individualizes, yet it also enslaves. Our sensations are essentially individual; yet we are more personal the more we are freed from our senses and able to think and act with concepts." Thus, agreeing with Kant, Durkheim suggests that personality should not be confused with individuality.

37. Weber, "Sociology of Religion," in WG, 372.

38. Ibid., 320–21.

39. Weber, "Confucianism and Taoism," in GRS 1:526; "Sociology of Religion," in WG, 346.

40. For an outstanding brief summary of Calvinism, see Weber, "Political and Hierocratic Domination," in WG, 717–19. Weber says that in Calvinism it was a question of "the valuation of the total personality [Gesamtpersönlichkeit] as graced or condemned," in contrast to Catholic practice, and that neither confession and absolution nor "individual 'good' deeds" could compensate for committed sins or change one's relation to God. Thus, to be convinced of grace the Calvinist needed to be convinced that his "total behavior [Gesamtverhalten]," his "'methodical' principle of life conduct," was on the single right path, working for God's glory (ibid., 718–19).

41. Weber, "Sociology of Religion," in WG 348.

42. Ibid., 323–24.

43. Ibid., 324.

44. The most compact discussion of salvation religions in Weber's work is in the "Introduction" to "Economic Ethics," in GRS 1:237–75. Comparative material, including more on the origins of such religions, is in "Sociology of Religion," in WG, 245–381, esp. 306–7. Weber also devotes attention to Nietzsche's postulate of "ressentiment" and the "slave revolt in morals," which he criticizes selectively. See "Sociology of Religion," in WG, 300–304, 357; "Political Communities," in WG, 536–37; and "Introduction" to "Economic Ethics," in GRS 1:241–42.

45. Weber, "Sociology of Religion," in WG, 378–79; "Confucianism and Taoism," in GRS 1:449–50.

46. For a summary of these features, see Weber, "Sociology of Religion," in WG 334–37. On the importance of the specific stratum that is the "carrier" (Träger) of the religion for the development of the religious ethos and hence its conception of self, see Weber's "Preface," in GRS 1:15; "Introduction" to "Economic Ethics," in GRS 1:242, 251, 253–57; and "Sociology of Religion," in WG, 285–314, esp. 263, 288, 293–94, 299–30, 311.

47. On religions of intellectuals, see Weber, "Sociology of Religion," in WG, 304–6; "Hinduism and Buddhism," in GRS 2:136n.1, 362, 377–78n.1.

48. Weber, "Confucianism and Taoism," in GRS 1:473; "Sociology of Religion," in WG, 325. In "Religious Rejections" (GRS 1:538), Weber points out that the conception of a supramundane God has not by itself determined the direction of Occidental asceticism but must be considered along with the specific religious promises of a religion and the paths to salvation they determined.

49. Weber, "Sociology of Religion," in *WG*, 328–30, 332, 333; "Religious Rejections," in *GRS* 1:538–40; "Confucianism and Taoism," in *GRS* 1:526; "Introduction" to "Economic Ethics," in *GRS* 1:257.

50. Weber, "Sociology of Religion," in *WG*, 326–28; "Religious Rejections," in *GRS* 1:545–46.

51. Weber, "Sociology of Religion," in *WG*, 273.

52. Weber, "Confucianism and Taoism," in *GRS* 1:521; "Introduction" to "Economic Ethics," in *GRS* 1:257–58.

53. Weber, "Sociology of Religion," in *WG*, 275, 285; "Religious Rejections," in *GRS* 1:540.

54. The above discussion of Confucianism draws on Weber, "Introduction" to "Economic Ethics," in *GRS* 1:239; "Sociology of Religion," in *WG*, 371; "Patriarchal and Patrimonial Domination," in *WG*, 610; "Confucianism and Taoism," in *GRS* 1:307, 430, 441, 444, 448, 449, 451, 492, 493, 495–96, 503, 511, 514–15, 516, 518, 521, 522–23, 530–31, 532, 534. According to Benjamin Nelson ("On Orient and Occident in Max Weber," *Social Research* 43 (1976): 114–29), Weber believed that China lacked only two orientations to spark the "fraternization" and "universalization" that Nelson believes so crucial for modern development: "an ontological commitment to a trans-mundane reality and a charismatic opening to prophecy" (ibid., 118).

Thomas Metzger's inquiry into the neo-Confucian self has raised doubts about Weber's approach to the Confucian concept of self, although Metzger bases his criticism principally on the view that Weber did not have available to him the sources and materials that we have today. Thus, he does not undertake an "immanent" critique of Weber's concepts. He urges us to see China not primarily from the point of view of its limitations versus the Occidental "personality" but in terms of what, in a *positive* sense, the Confucian self was capable of (*Escape from Predicament: Neo-Confucianism and China's Evolving Political Culture* [New York: Columbia University Press, 1977], 3–4, 18–19, 39, 45, 49–60, 108, 113, 198, 200–201, 203–4, 234–35, 237–38n.4).

See also Metzger's "Selfhood and Authority in Neo-Confucian Political Culture," in Arthur Kleinman and Tsung-Yi Lin, eds., *Normal and Abnormal Behavior in Chinese Culture* (Dordrecht: D. Reidel, 1981), 7–27. See also William Theodore de Bary, introduction and "Neo-Confucian Cultivation and the Seventeenth-Century Enlightenment," in William Theodore de Bary et al., *The Unfolding of Neo-Confucianism* (New York: Columbia University Press, 1975), 1–36, 141–214; de Bary, *The Liberal Tradition in China* (New York: Columbia University Press, 1983); Mark Elvin, "Between the Earth and Heaven: Conceptions of Self in China," in Carrithers, Collins, and Lukes, eds., *Category of the Person*, 156–89; Wolfgang Schluchter, ed., *Max Webers Studie über Konfuzianismus und Taoismus: Interpretation und Kritik* (Frankfurt am Main: Suhrkamp Verlag, 1983); Mark Elvin, "Why China Failed to Create an Endogenous Industrial Capitalism: A Critique of Max Weber's Explanation," *Theory and Society* 13 (1984): 379–91; and Stephen Molloy, "Max Weber and the Religions of China: Any Way out of the Maze?" *British Journal of Sociology* 31 (1980): 377–400.

55. Weber, "Introduction" to "Economic Ethics," in *GRS* 1:239; "Sociol-

ogy of Religion," in *WG*, 377–78; "Hinduism and Buddhism," 2:220, 221, 222–23, 230.

56. The above discussion of Hinduism draws on Weber, "Introduction" to "Economic Ethics," in *GRS* 1:239; "Sociology of Religion," in *WG*, 266–67, 318–19, 360–61, 379; "Hinduism and Buddhism," in *GRS* 2:24, 26, 117–18, 121, 134–37, 142, 146–47, 174–75, 193–94, 196, 199–200, 345, 359–63, 364–65, 365–66, 366–67, 369, 371, 373–74, 377–78; "Religious Rejections," in *GRS* 1:551–52. For a reevaluation of certain elements of Weber's analysis of Hinduism and Buddhism, see Wolfgang Schluchter, ed., *Max Webers Studie über Hinduismus und Buddhismus: Interpretation und Kritik* (Frankfurt am Main: Suhrkamp Verlag, 1984).

57. Weber, "Introduction" to "Economic Ethics," in *GRS* 1:239–40; "Sociology of Religion," in *WG*, 347, 375–76. See also Bryan Turner, *Weber and Islam: A Critical Study* (London: Routledge & Kegan Paul, 1974).

58. The above discussion of ancient Judaism draws on Weber, "Introduction," to "Economic Ethics," in *GRS* 1:240; "Sociology of Religion," in *WG*, 267, 302, 303, 368, 371, 372, 373, 374; "Political and Hierocratic Domination," in *WG*, 719; "Ancient Judaism," in *GRS* 3:6, 7, 136, 140, 142, 231, 239, 250–51, 271, 303, 312, 319–20, 326, 328–29, 330, 333, 357–58, 360, 417–18, 421. See also Wolfgang Schluchter, ed., *Max Webers Studie über das antike Judentum: Interpretation und Kritik* (Frankfurt am Main: Suhrkamp Verlag, 1981).

59. See Wolfgang Schluchter, ed., *Max Webers Sicht des antiken Christentums: Interpretation und Kritik* (Frankfurt am Main: Suhrkamp Verlag, 1985). See also Claude Mossé, *The Ancient World at Work*, trans. Janet Lloyd (New York: Norton, 1969), 25–30, 112–13.

60. The above discussion of Catholicism draws on Weber, "Introduction" to "Economic Ethics," in *GRS* 1:240; "Sociology of Religion," in *WG*, 293, 311, 322, 338–39, 339–40, 344; "Political and Hierocratic Domination," in *WG*, 694, 696, 699, 707, 709, 712–13; "Protestant Ethic," in *GRS* 1:61.

61. Weber, "Introduction" to "Economic Ethics," in *GRS* 1:248.

62. Weber, "Political Communities," in *WG*, 536. On the concept of *kalos kai agathos* in the Greek world, see Werner Jaeger, *Paideia: The Ideals of Greek Culture* (New York: Oxford University Press, 1965), vol. 1, chap. 1 and p. 416n.4.

63. Weber, "Sociology of Religion," in *WG*, 298–99.

64. Weber, "Introduction" to "Economic Ethics," in *GRS* 1:248.

65. Weber, "Sociology of Religion," in *WG*, 299.

66. Weber, "Feudalism, 'Ständestaat,' and Patrimonialism," in *WG*, 651. See also "Political and Hierocratic Domination," in *WG*, 703–4; and "Feudalism," in *WG*, 651–52.

67. Weber, "Sociology of Religion," in *WG*, 536–37. Here Weber maintains that it is this need, not Nietzsche's *ressentiment*, that accounts for the character of "pariah" religions like Judaism.

CHAPTER FIVE

1. Mann, "Schopenhauer," in *GW* 9:559.
2. T. J. Reed observes: "Fictional and direct statements from *Tonio Krö-*

ger onwards make up a single argument culminating in *Der Tod in Venedig*" (*Thomas Mann*, 119).

3. In a letter of 5 Dec. 1903 to W. Opitz, Mann speaks of how the responsibility of using his talents has grown much greater now that he has been unwise enough to reveal them to the world (*Briefe* 1:39).

4. The sense of exhaustion and defeat reached its peak in a letter of 8 Nov. 1913 to his brother Heinrich, in which he sounds like a combination of Thomas Buddenbrook and Gustav von Aschenbach: "If only strength to work and desire to work were proportionate. But the inner: the always threatening exhaustion, scruple, tiredness, doubt, a soreness and weakness, so that every attack shakes me to the foundations . . . a growing sympathy with death. . . . My whole interest was always in 'decline' [*Verfall*]. . . . I am worn out, I think, and apparently should not have become a writer" (Thomas Mann and Heinrich Mann, *Briefwechsel*, 103–4).

Reed points out that "Thomas Mann's work in the first decade of the century was in general in a transitional phase, and failure arguably outweighed success" (*Thomas Mann*, 149–50).

5. For Munich as a cultural center, see Gerdi Huber, *Das klassische Schwabing: München als Zentrum der intellektuellen Zeit- und Gesellschaftskritik an der Wende des 19. zum 20. Jahrhundert*, Miscellanea Bavarica Monacensia, vol. 37 (Munich: Stadtsarchiv München, 1973). See also Jelavich, "Munich as Cultural Center," 17–26; and idem, *Munich and Theatrical Modernism: Politics, Playwriting, and Performance, 1890–1914* (Cambridge: Harvard University Press, 1985), 1–52.

6. Despite his later praise of the "deep austerity and dignity of a phenomenon like Stefan George," Mann used the occasion of an encounter with Ludwig Derleth's work as the subject of "At the Prophet's," which recounts the events at a reading (letter of 4 July 1920 to Carl Maria Weber, in Mann, *Briefe* 1:178). See also Wolfgang F. Michael, "Thomas Mann—Ludwig Derleth—Stefan George," *Modern Language Forum* 35 (1950): 35–38. On the origin of the story, see Mendelssohn, *Nachbemerkungen* 2:39–41; see also Vaget, *Thomas-Mann-Kommentar*, 133. On Derleth, see Dominick Jost, *Ludwig Derleth: Gestalt und Leistung* (Stuttgart: W. Kohlhammer Verlag, 1965), who speaks of Mann's encounter on pp. 52–54. On the George Circle, see Michael Winkler, *George-Kreis* (Stuttgart: Metzlersche Verlagsbuchhandlung, 1972), who refers to Mann on p. 36; and Wolters, *Stefan George*. See also Lukács, *Soul and Form*, 79–90.

Hans Vaget maintains that with "Tristan," written before *Tonio Kröger*, Mann actually cleared the ground for the new understanding of artistry he was soon to present. See Vaget, *Thomas-Mann-Kommentar*, 87. See also Lida Kirchberger, "Thomas Mann's 'Tristan,'" *Germanic Review* 36 (1961): 282–97. Though Mann clearly modeled Detlev Spinell's physical appearance and some of his decadent literary characteristics after a writer friend, he later claimed: "I chastised myself in this form," and "held a 'judgment day' over this bad part of myself, aestheticism, this expired artificiality, in which I see the danger of dangers." See the quote from "Bilse und Ich" (1906) in Vaget, *Thomas-Mann-Kommentar*, 86. See also Rasch, "Thomas Manns *Tristan*," in *Zur deutschen Literatur*, 162ff.

7. Yet Rasch maintains that "Tristan" is also a challenge to the defense of unthinking life: "If one wants to understand the story as Thomas Mann's settle-

ment of accounts with his own and with German decadence, one must also point out that it is at the same time . . . the vindication of this decadence: its vindication against the pretension of an all-too-robust vitality" (*Zur deutschen Literatur*, 184).

8. Mann composed another work about weakness before *Death in Venice*, and he later called its hero a "brother" of Gustav von Aschenbach. *Fiorenza*, Mann's only attempt at a play, was first conceived during the period of *Buddenbrooks* but not completed until 1905. It dramatizes an imagined encounter between Lorenzo de Medici and Savonarola at Lorenzo's court on the day of his death. The hesitations, doubts, and uncertainties of the artistic calling (dramatized in Lorenzo) are overwhelmed by the certainties and determination of the spiritual calling, a power that judges, blames, and casts out (Savonarola). Any hesitations of the spiritual calling are completely overcome by its conviction of the absoluteness of the cause it defends, even though it knows its own motives to be more complicated, base, self-serving, and resentful. These two aspects, here separated and at war, will be combined, though still at war, in the same character in Aschenbach. Mann characterized the play, which he originally intended to entitle *The King of Florence*, in the following way: "The ambiguity of the title is of course intentional. Christ and Fra Girolamo are one: weakness become genius succeeding at the domination of life." See the letter of Thomas Mann to Heinrich Mann in 1900, in Thomas Mann and Heinrich Mann, *Briefwechsel*, 6. For more on *Fiorenza*'s origin, see Mendelssohn, *Nachbemerkungen* 2 : 44–47. Walter Stewart discusses the affinities between this play and *Death in Venice;* he considers both Lorenzo's capacity to live "despite himself", similar to Aschenbach's, and the Platonic aspect of *Fiorenza;* see "*Der Tod in Venedig:* The Path to Insight," *Germanic Review* 53 (1978): 50–54.

9. For an interesting way of talking about the "psychic structure" of Wilhelmine Prussia, see Michael Rogin, "Max Weber and Woodrow Wilson: The Iron Cage in Germany and America," *Polity* 3 (1971): 557–75.

10. Mann, "Bilse und Ich," in *GW* 10 : 20.

11. Mann, "At the Prophet's," in *GW* 8 : 370.

12. Mann, "Bilse und Ich," in *GW* 10 : 11. On the subject of representation, see Hinrich Siefken, "Thomas Mann and the Concept of 'Repräsentation': *Königliche Hoheit*," *Modern Language Review* 73 (1978): 22–50.

13. Quoted from a Thomas Mann notebook in Winston, *Thomas Mann*, 214. Winston quotes from Volkmar Hansen, *Thomas Manns Heine-Rezeption* (Hamburg: Hoffmann & Campe, 1975), 116.

14. Letter of 14 Nov. 1906 to Hilde Distel, in Mann, *Briefe* 1 : 67.

15. See Pascal, "Writers as a Social Class," chap. 11 in *From Naturalism to Expressionism*, esp. 286–92.

16. Hermann J. Weigand, "Thomas Mann's *Royal Highness* as Symbolic Autobiography," in Henry Hatfield, ed., *Thomas Mann: A Collection of Critical Essays* (Englewood Cliffs, N.J.: Prentice-Hall, 1964), 35–45. He says it is "the representative calling and the lofty task of the creative writer . . . of which Mann gives an accounting here" (ibid., 43).

17. Letter of 5 Dec. 1903 to Walter Opitz, in Mann, *Briefe* 1 : 40. On 29 Oct. 1903 Mann wrote to his publisher, S. Fischer, of the disappointments people would experience in meeting him: "Perhaps I compensate them even further

through the diligently forged symbols of my life, which is less uninteresting than my mustachioed personality" (*Briefe* 1:39).

18. Mann, "Vorwort zu einer amerikanischen Ausgabe von 'Königliche Hoheit,'" in *GW* 11:575.

Mann wrote *Royal Highness* between 1906 and 1909, after his marriage to Katia Pringsheim, and in her memoirs Katia Mann says that "the prince's story is also the novel of the early days of our marriage. . . . not in every detail but in a more general sense." See Katia Mann, *Unwritten Memories*, ed. Elisabeth Plessner and Michael Mann, trans. Hunter Hannum and Hildegarde Hannum (New York: Knopf, 1975), 58. On the origins of *Königliche Hoheit*, see Hans Wysling, "Die Fragmente zu Thomas Manns 'Fürsten-Novelle,'" in Scherrer and Wysling, *Thomas-Mann-Studien* 1:64–105. Mann defended this work against its critics, especially an aristocratic critic, in his short essay "Über 'Königliche Hoheit,'" in *GW* 11:567–71. He argues there that the work is not really about the life of the nobility but rather about the life of the artist, namely, himself, and that the work is thereby also representative, for he lives symbolically. "The analysis, full of allusions, of princely existence as a formal, non-objective, supra-objective, in a word, artistic, existence and the redemption of highness through love: that is the content of my novel." It is not an accurate picture of life at court but "an instructive fairy tale." Finally, "What is a poet? He whose life is symbolic" (ibid., 570, 571).

19. Schröter, *Thomas Mann*, 69.

20. *GW* 8:277. Quotations from *Tonio Kröger* in this chapter will hereafter be cited by page numbers in the text.

21. Weigand says: "Related in its severe, ascetic fulfillment of duty to the ethic of the categorical imperative, and owing much both in ascetic severity and in the lofty, confident sense of being chosen to Nietzsche's inspiration, the existence of the sovereign and of the artist is of markedly aristocratic nature; with proud contempt it puts the merely human in its place" ("Thomas Mann's *Royal Highness*," 39).

22. *GW* 2:56. Quotations from *Royal Highness* in this chapter will hereafter be cited by page number in the text.

23. Mann, "Vorwort zu 'Königliche Hoheit,'" in *GW* 11:575.

24. Weigand says that Mann the artist, having slain emotion, must then "find again the road to ingenuous emotion," although it is not clear how he is to do that ("Thomas Mann's *Royal Highness*," 41).

25. Mann, "Vorwort zu 'Königliche Hoheit,'" in *GW* 11:574–75.

26. Weigand suggests that something else is going on here. First, the artist as representative is forced to abandon "a purely individualistic attitude," the notion of "autonomous genius à la Nietzsche," and to replace it with "the idea of obligation to the whole and responsibility towards the cultural community." Second, "there must be a living sense of kinship and reciprocal affinity between the people and the poet." These, says Weigand surprisingly, are summed up in Mann's love for the bourgeoisie ("Thomas Mann's *Royal Highness*," 43–44).

27. Pascal maintains that the image of the uniqueness of the artist and his representativeness occurs "in a more sober form . . . in many of the pre-1914 stories of Thomas Mann." Yet, he suggests, "Mann does not, in this pre-war period, find a consistent formulation, and it was only after the war that he came

to recognize that the poet combines separateness with representativeness" (*From Naturalism to Expressionism,* 289). This is a surprising conclusion in the light of Mann's prewar letters and of *Royal Highness* as an allegory of the poet's life and existence.

28. Mann, "Schopenhauer," in *GW* 9 : 559.

29. This relation to Aschenbach is also supported by Vaget (*Thomas-Mann-Kommentar,* 130), who says, "With the self-assurance that suffering in the work and in one's own spiritual-soulful constitution is the precondition of a quiet heroic greatness, this portrait of Schiller reveals itself as a prefiguration of Aschenbach"; and by Mendelssohn (*Nachbemerkungen* 2 : 43), who says, "Thomas Mann's conception of heroism, which his work during the next years essentially confirms until it receives its definitive stamp in *Death in Venice,* is outlined for the first time in the study of Schiller."

30. See Mendelssohn, *Nachbemerkungen* 2 : 41; and Vaget, *Thomas-Mann-Kommentar,* 130. In a letter to his brother Mann speaks of his efforts in writing *Fiorenza* as a *Solness-Absturz,* echoing the sudden fall to his death of Ibsen's architect Solness in *The Master Builder,* striving beyond his capacities to reattain earlier greatness.

31. Letter of 19 Feb. 1955 to the editor of *Sonntag,* in Mann, *Briefe,* vol. 3, *1948–1955,* ed. Erika Mann (Frankfurt am Main: S. Fischer Verlag, 1965; Fischer Taschenbuch Verlag, 1979), 379–80. See also Mendelssohn (*Nachbemerkungen* 2 : 43), who says of Savonarola in *Fiorenza* and of Schiller that "it is both times Thomas Mann who is speaking here for himself. It is his personal disposition of life, his conception of his own life and work."

32. *GW* 8 : 373–74. Quotations from "A Difficult Hour" in this chapter will henceforth be cited by page number in the text.

33. Mendelssohn points out that the discussion of talent as pain comes word for word from a letter of Mann's to Katia at the end of August 1904 (*Nachbemerkungen* 2 : 42). See Mann, *Briefe* 1 : 53.

34. Here Schiller echoes the sentiments of the character of Savonarola in *Fiorenza.* In the midst of his debate with Lorenzo about art, purpose, and weakness, Savonarola reveals himself, the monk, to be an admirer of Caesar and tells of his ambition to rise: "Why should I not have [ambition]—since I have suffered so? Ambition says: The suffering should not have been for nothing. It must bring me fame" (*GW* 8 : 1064). See Mendelssohn, *Nachbemerkungen* 2 : 43.

35. Henry Hatfield, *Thomas Mann: An Introduction to His Fiction,* rev. ed. (Norfolk, Conn.: New Directions, 1962), 56–57, quoted in Vaget, *Thomas-Mann-Kommentar,* 131.

36. See Mann, "Bilse und Ich," in *GW* 10 : 18–19, 21.

37. Mann, "On Myself," quoted in *Thomas Mann,* pt. 1, 439. See also the quotes from Thomas Mann in Mendelssohn, *Nachbemerkungen* 2 : 54. On Mann's interest in the Goethe story, see Stewart, *"Tod in Venedig,"* 50–54.

38. See the excellent piece by Erich Heller, "Thomas Mann in Venice," in *The Poet's Self and the Poem: Essays on Goethe, Nietzsche, Rilke, and Thomas Mann* (London: Athlone Press, 1976), 73–91. According to Mann's letters, Heller asserts, "not one of the story's features and incidents had to be invented, because everything in it was offered to him 'by reality.'"

See also the fascinating discussion of Mann's letter of 1920 to Carl Maria Weber in Reed, *Thomas Mann*, 152–54. Reed persuasively argues that the letter describes Mann's original intention to take his homoerotic experience on the trip to Venice and turn it into something positive and affirmative, not critical, cold, and sober. Yet Mann's explicit declaration of personal mistrust of passion, which, Reed says, "counteracted any 'Greek' view of homosexual love," must be considered doubtful, given Ignace Feuerlicht's startling discussion in "Thomas Mann and Homoeroticism," *Germanic Review* 57 (1982): 89–97, a remarkable portrait of Mann's homoerotic feelings.

39. See, e.g., Heinz Kohut, "'Death in Venice' by Thomas Mann: A Story about the Disintegration of Artistic Sublimation," *Psychoanalytic Quarterly* 26 (1957): 206–28. See also J. R. McWilliams, "The Failure of a Repression: Thomas Mann's *Tod in Venedig*," *German Life and Letters*, n.s. 20 (1967): 233–41. See also Feuerlicht, "Thomas Mann and Homoeroticism."

40. See, e.g., Jelavich, "Munich as Cultural Center," 23. See the reference to this "end" in Mann, "On Myself," in *Thomas Mann*, pt. 1, 441; and in *GW* 13:147–49. For brief examples of Mann's changing views of this work, see Vaget, *Thomas-Mann-Kommentar*, 181–84.

41. Mann, "On Myself," in *GW* 13:148–49, quoted in idem, *Thomas Mann*, pt. 1, 439. Winston confirms Mann's interest in *Leistungsethik* (*Thomas Mann*, 224).

42. Heller maintains that "*Death in Venice*, like *Tonio Kröger*, is a highly autobiographical tale, reflecting important developments in Thomas Mann's emotional *and* intellectual life" ("Thomas Mann in Venice," 83–84). Weigand says that Aschenbach's collapse "implies an anticipation of tragic possibilities which are inherent in the artist of . . . [Mann's] own type. Aschenbach's fate signifies a projection summoned up by the author as a warning to himself" ("Thomas Mann's *Royal Highness*," 45).

43. Reed remarks that "Mann dissociates himself from Aschenbach more obviously than from any of his other protagonists" (*Thomas Mann*, 148).

44. *GW* 8:450. Quotations from *Death in Venice* in this chapter will hereafter be cited by page number in the text.

45. Mann, quoted in Schröter, *Thomas Mann*, 62.

46. Pike believes, inaccurately, that this desire for fame distinguishes Aschenbach from the true artist, for the true artist "can only hope to be understood by a few of his contemporaries; widespread acclaim is left to posterity" ("Problematic Self," 129–30).

47. Idris Parry says that Mann, "in a disapproving reference to Wagner's satin dressing-gowns," had suggested "the costume of a soldier or a monk as more suitable to the stern service of art"; see "Thomas Mann, 1875–1955," *German Language and Letters* 9 (1955–56): 15–16.

48. The image of the artist as the closed fist comes from Goethe. See Schröter, *Thomas Mann*, 71; and Vaget, *Thomas-Mann-Kommentar*, 171–72.

49. In "Failure of a Repression," 234, McWilliams says: "Like Tonio, Aschenbach has been living in an emotional vacuum. He has put Tonio Kröger's programme to the fullest test, exhausting himself in dedication to his calling."

50. Mann, "Mitteilung an die Literaturhistorische Gesellschaft in Bonn," in

GW 11:714–15, 716–17. I am grateful to Winston (*Thomas Mann*, 227, 230) for drawing my attention to this essay and these passages.

51. Letter of 28 Mar. 1906 to Kurt Martens, in Mann, *Briefe* 1:63. See also Jean Finck, *Thomas Mann und die Psychoanalyse*, 326. As Heller says, not only are these words from Mann himself, but "we learn nothing of Aschenbach's writings that does not confirm the literary identity of Gustav von Aschenbach and Thomas Mann" ("Thomas Mann in Venice," 76–77).

52. Heller, "Thomas Mann in Venice," 75.

53. Letter of 23 Dec. 1904 to Heinrich Mann, in Thomas Mann and Heinrich Mann, *Briefwechsel*, 31.

54. Frank Baron, "Sensuality and Morality in Thomas Mann's *Tod in Venedig*," *Germanic Review* 45 (1970): 115–25. Baron interprets Aschenbach's problem in terms from Schopenhauer and *Buddenbrooks:* "Aschenbach's decision to interrupt his work . . . reflects what is primarily a crisis of the will" (ibid., 121).

55. Savonarola, the hero of *Fiorenza*, was the first of Mann's heroes to recover this unreservedness, naïveté, and moral innocence. His regained moral resolve was a product of absolutist faith and absolute devotion to his task. When Lorenzo asks, "Are you not ashamed to win . . such power since you know through what you win it?" Savonarola replies, "I do not want to know that. . . . I am chosen. I may know and still want. For I must be strong. God works miracles. You see the miracle of ingenuousness [*Unbefangenheit*] reborn" (*GW* 8:1064). But when Savonarola claims to have achieved this rebirth, he is clearly hypocritical and self-serving. Mann remarks of his exhaustion with the efforts at writing this play, "About face! Back to Buddenbrook naïveté" (Thomas Mann and Heinrich Mann, *Briefwechsel*, 34–35). Yet knowledge cannot be overcome simply by willing its opposite—by negation and willful ignorance—but only by genuinely overcoming the "sentimental" personality.

56. See Eva Brann, "The Venetian Phaedrus," *The College* (St. John's College) 24, no. 2 (1972): 1–9. Brann says of Aschenbach and his relation to Tadzio: "For the master of classical form sees a live work of art which is the realization of his own efforts to become a 'naive' artist."

57. Vaget refers to excerpts in Mann's work notes for *Death in Venice* from Lukács's discourse on Socratic longing and love in his essay on Charles-Louis Philippe, in *Soul and Form*, 91–106 (see Vaget, *Thomas-Mann-Kommentar*, 175). See also Michael Löwy, *Georg Lukács: From Romanticism to Bolshevism*, trans. Patrick Camiller (London: New Left Books, 1979), 100.

58. In contrast, Reed believes that it is "possible to detach Mann from the emphatic condemnations of the later pages. These formulations, despite the more critical view the author is by now taking of his character, are Mann's concession to more confident moralists than himself." Moreover, Reed claims that "in what it implies about the Artist, the story constitutes a moral victory . . . a decision to reject the values by which he had so far lived and worked" (*Thomas Mann*, 173).

59. Heller puts the issue this way: "*Death in Venice* . . . is the story of an artist's frozen feelings destructively released by a sudden thaw that makes them flood the soul and annihilate the person" ("Thomas Mann in Venice," 79).

60. See Reed (*Thomas Mann*, 156–71) for a discussion of the use of Platonic

material in Mann's work notes and their transformation in the story. See also Stewart ("*Tod in Venedig,*" 53–54), who is critical of Reed.

61. See André von Gronicka, "Myth plus Psychology: A Stylistic Analysis of *Death in Venice,*" in Hatfield, ed., *Thomas Mann,* 46–61; see also Manfred Dierks, "Untersuchungen zum *Tod in Venedig,*" in *Thomas-Mann-Studien,* vol. 3, *Studien zu Mythos und Psychologie bei Thomas Mann* (Bern and Munich: Francke Verlag, 1972), 13–59.

See also James Northcote-Bade, *Die Wagner-Mythen im Frühwerk Thomas Manns* (Bonn: Bouvier Verlag Herbert Grundmann, 1975), 87. Northcote-Bade maintains that the story reflects Mann's "Wagner crisis": the rejection of Wagner's Germanic mythology in favor of Goethe and classicism. He quotes a letter from Mann to Julius Bab of 20 Sept. 1911: "One should give the Germans a choice. Goethe or Wagner. The two do not go together." But see Vaget (*Thomas-Mann-Kommentar,* 186–87) on Mann's *overcoming* of the tendency to classicism in the process of writing this work. For more on Wagner and Aschenbach, and on Wagner's influence on Mann elsewhere, see Erwin Koppen, *Dekadenter Wagnerismus: Studien zur europäischen Literatur des Fin de siècle* (Berlin: Walter de Gruyter, 1973), 225–33, 184–94, 197–205, 265–77.

Feuerlicht says that although "Mann once contended that the Greek backdrop was just an auxiliary means and a spiritual refuge of the man whose experience was narrated," in fact it was a refuge for Mann himself, who tried to veil his real-life experience to make it palatable for the public ("Thomas Mann and Homoeroticism," 93–94). Heller even suggests that "Thomas Mann first tried to cover the all too autobiographical with the mantle of Goethe, and failed" ("Thomas Mann in Venice," 89).

62. In her extremely profound essay Eva Brann says that "Tadzio, on whom the use of myth centers, is, so to speak, not a person at all but a living statue, so that the use of myth is, as it were, bolder than in later works. . . . In a word, the novella is about the decadent artist's confrontation with a living work of art" ("Venetian Phaedrus," 6, 8). Her view is largely true, but neither art nor "the artist" is at fault. Rather, the problem is with the relation of this particular artist to art and to life. Indeed, *Death in Venice* is about an *anti*decadent artist's confrontation with something living that he must *make over* into a living artwork out of the emptiness of his life, proving that he cannot overcome decadence after all. The transformation of life is the expression of his decadence. Brann concludes with a misguided and unfortunately hypostatized critique of art from the point of view of philosophy: Mann ultimately condemned the artist "as a man of form, and his form, or rather formalism, has a false relation to the passions" (ibid., 9).

63. McWilliams says: "Though Aschenbach's kinship with Tonio Kröger is extremely close, his need for chastisement sets him apart, and in this he represents a kind of culmination of his artistic precursors" ("Failure of a Repression," 235, 237).

64. For one of the best remarks ever made on this story, see Harry Slochower, "Thomas Mann's *Death in Venice,*" *American Imago* 26 (1969): 106–7: "Another leading imagery of the story is *looking* and *watching.* Aschenbach engages in a kind of voyeurism with Tadzio as the object. What he sees may be

characterized as mirror-images, and his 'creativity' may be said to be an esthetic onanism, and the famous author ceases to write in Venice. Our pleasure tends to turn into sadness as we become aware of Aschenbach's central self-deception, namely that Tadzio can be an object of his love. In essence, *the boy is Aschenbach's 'double.'* In his yearning for Tadzio, Aschenbach is reaching out for that which lies beyond his grasp. We realize that Tadzio has no independent existence, that Aschenbach is creating the boy and his beauty out of his phantasy. This gives the story a mythico-tragic character." Stewart says that "the Platonic ideal of beauty, its creation, imitation, and enjoyment, is the single consuming obsession of those about Lorenzo, just as it becomes Aschenbach's obsession" ("Tod in Venedig," 54). See also McWilliams, "Failure of a Repression," 240; and Albert Braverman and Larry David Nachman, "The Dialectic of Decadence: An Analysis of Thomas Mann's *Death in Venice*," *Germanic Review* 45 (1970): 293.

65. Mann, "Bilse und Ich," in *GW* 10:22.

66. Reed, *Thomas Mann*, 146–49, 163–64. Reed says: "*Der Tod in Venedig* is about psychological decay finding in the outside world pretext and occasion for its fulfillment. Aschenbach's creative discipline is essentially broken at the very outset" (ibid., 171).

67. René Girard, *Deceit, Desire, and the Novel: Self and Other in Literary Structure* (Baltimore: Johns Hopkins University Press, 1965), chap. 1.

68. Braverman and Nachman maintain: "Aschenbach's regained detachment from all mankind was permanent; he could not overcome his distance.... But he never, in his most fevered dream, imagined the one other alternative to detached individuality or orgiastic immersion in the sensual: to lose himself in the real and independent existence of another human being" ("Dialectic of Decadence," 293). But in fact this is *not* a problem of Aschenbach's failed imagination but of his deadened life in the calling, which puts other human beings completely out of reach.

69. Vaget, *Thomas-Mann-Kommentar*, 187.

70. Braverman and Nachman write: "In his early period, Mann could find no worldly context for gifted personality.... Developed personality could be achieved only over and against the world; its only context was the inner life" ("Dialectic of Decadence," 295). This is the source, they argue, of Aschenbach's inability to overcome his distance. But they fail to recognize that personality, in its classical sense, is always achieved thus, according to Kant, Goethe, and Weber.

Stewart notes that "Gustav Aschenbach never becomes an integrated personality, simply because he fails to keep the spiritual and sensual aspects of his nature in balance" ("Tod in Venedig," 54). For Stewart a lack of balance prevents the "integration" of the sides of the self. Yet all of Mann's earlier work on the calling, along with Weber's, suggests that Stewart has an incorrect understanding of the ideal of personality. The tradition of personality requires self-conquest and self-overcoming on behalf of one ideal, *not* balance, even according to Goethe.

71. Vaget, *Thomas-Mann-Kommentar*, 187. Reed believes that *Death in*

Venice is the breakthrough work for Mann in which he turned on his earlier views and created an "ambivalent art" (*Thomas Mann,* 178).

72. Letter of 1 Mar. 1923 to Felix Bertaux, in Mann, *Briefe* 1:206.

73. See Schröter, *Thomas Mann,* 71. Heller quotes Goethe's letter to Frau von Stein (1777): "You know how symbolic my existence is" ("Thomas Mann in Venice," 74).

74. Schröter, *Thomas Mann,* 69.

CONCLUSION TO PART II AND PROSPECT

1. See Reinhard Baumgart, *Das Ironische und die Ironie in den Werken Thomas Manns* (Munich: Carl Hanser Verlag, 1964; Frankfurt am Main: Ullstein Verlag, 1974), 123. Baumgart says that in *Death in Venice* "ironic consciousness overcomes the pathos of the ascetic ideal." Mann spoke much later of the crucial turning point that *Death in Venice* had played in his inner life as well as in the life of Europe, since it meant a "conclusion": "it was the moral and formally sharpest and most collected portrait of the decadence and artist problem, under whose sign my production had stood since 'Buddenbrooks,' and whose form, with 'Death in Venice,' was indeed played out. . . . On the personal path that had led to 'Death in Venice,' there was nothing further, no way out" (quoted in Mendelssohn, *Nachbemerkungen* 2:60–61).

2. See Vaget's outstanding discussion of *Death in Venice* in *Thomas-Mann-Kommentar,* esp. 181–88.

3. On Mann's later development in this respect, see Nachman and Braverman, "Thomas Mann's *Buddenbrooks,*" 224–25.

Bibliography

WORKS OF MAX WEBER

From Max Weber: Essays in Sociology. Edited and translated by H. H. Gerth and C. Wright Mills. New York: Oxford University Press, 1946.

Gesammelte Aufsätze zur Religionssoziologie. 3 vols. Tübingen: J. C. B. Mohr (Paul Siebeck), 1920–23.

Gesammelte Aufsätze zur Wissenschaftslehre. 5th ed. Edited by Johannes Winckelmann. Tübingen: J. C. B. Mohr (Paul Siebeck), 1982.

Die protestantische Ethik. Vol. 2, *Kritiken und Antikritiken.* 2d ed. Edited by Johannes Winckelmann. Hamburg: Siebenstern Taschenbuch Verlag, 1972.

Wirtschaftsgeschichte: Abriss der universalen Sozial- und Wirtschaftsgeschichte (General economic history). 2d ed. Edited by S. Hellman and M. Palyi. Munich and Leipzig: Duncker & Humblot, 1924.

Wirtschaft und Gesellschaft (Economy and society). 5th ed. Tübingen: J. C. B. Mohr (Paul Siebeck), 1976.

WORKS OF THOMAS MANN

Briefe. Vol. 1, *1889–1936.* Edited by Erika Mann. Frankfurt am Main: S. Fischer Verlag, 1961. Reprint. Frankfurt am Main: Fischer Taschenbuch Verlag, 1979.

Briefe. Vol. 3, *1948–1955.* Edited by Erika Mann. Frankfurt am Main: S. Fischer Verlag, 1965. Reprint. Frankfurt am Main: Fischer Taschenbuch Verlag, 1979.

Briefe an Otto Grautoff, 1894–1901, und Ida Boy-Ed, 1903–1928. Frankfurt am Main: S. Fischer Verlag, 1975.

Gesammelte Werke in zwölf Bänden. Edited by Hans Bürgin. Frankfurt am Main: S. Fischer Verlag, 1960.

Tagebücher. 1918–1921. Edited by Peter de Mendelssohn. Frankfurt am Main: S. Fischer Verlag, 1979.

Thomas Mann. Edited by Hans Wysling and Marianne Fischer. Part 1, *1889–1917.* Vol. 14 of *Dichter über ihre Dichtungen.* Munich: Ernst Heimeran Verlag, 1975.

Thomas Mann and Heinrich Mann. *Briefwechsel, 1900–1949.* Rev. ed. Edited by Hans Wysling. Frankfurt am Main: Fischer Taschenbuch Verlag, 1975.

OTHER WORKS

Anz, Thomas. *Literatur der Existenz: Literarische Psychopathographie und ihre soziale Bedeutung im Frühexpressionismus.* Stuttgart: J. B. Metzlersche Verlagsbuchhandlung, 1977.

Arato, Andrew, and Paul Breines. *The Young Lukács and the Origins of Western Marxism.* New York: Seabury Press, 1979.

Arendt, Hannah. *The Human Condition.* Chicago: University of Chicago Press, 1957.

Bailyn, Bernard. *The New England Merchants of the Seventeenth Century.* Cambridge: Harvard University Press, 1955.

Barkin, Kenneth. *The Controversy over German Industrialization, 1890–1902.* Chicago: University of Chicago Press, 1970.

Baron, Frank. "Sensuality and Morality in Thomas Mann's *Tod in Venedig.*" *Germanic Review* 45 (1970): 115–25.

Bart, Benjamin. *Flaubert.* Syracuse, N.Y.: Syracuse University Press, 1967.

Baumgart, Reinhard. *Das Ironische und die Ironie in den Werken Thomas Manns.* Munich: Carl Hanser Verlag, 1964. Reprint. Frankfurt am Main: Ullstein Verlag, 1974.

Bendix, Reinhard. *Work and Authority in Industry.* New York: Wiley, 1956. Reprint. Berkeley and Los Angeles: University of California Press, 1974.

Bendix, Reinhard, and Guenther Roth. *Scholarship and Partisanship: Essays on Max Weber.* Berkeley and Los Angeles: University of California Press, 1971.

Bercovitch, Sacvan. *The Puritan Origins of the American Self.* New Haven: Yale University Press, 1975.

Berendsohn, Walter A. "Ein Blick in die Werkstatt." *Die Neue Rundschau: Sonderausgabe zu Thomas Manns 70. Geburtstag.* 6 June 1945: 177–70.

Blackbourn, David, and Geoff Eley. *The Peculiarities of German History.* New York: Oxford University Press, 1984.

Bollème, Geneviève. *La Leçon de Flaubert.* Paris: Lettres Nouvelles, 1964.

Bourget, Paul. *Essais de psychologie contemporaine.* Vol. 1. Paris: Plon, 1883. Augmented ed., 1899.

Bramsted, E. K. *Aristocracy and the Middle-Classes in Germany: Social Types in German Literature, 1830–1900.* London: P. S. King & Son, 1937. Reprint. Chicago: University of Chicago Press, 1964.

Brann, Eva. "The Venetian Phaedrus." *The College* (St. John's College) 24, no. 2 (1972): 1–9.

Braverman, Albert, and Larry David Nachman. "The Dialectic of Decadence:

An Analysis of Thomas Mann's *Death in Venice.*" *Germanic Review* 45 (1970): 289–98.

Brentano, Lujo. *Die Anfänge des modernen Kapitalismus.* Munich: Verlag der K. B. Akademie der Wissenschaften, 1916.

Broch, Hermann. *Hugo von Hofmannsthal and His Time: The European Imagination, 1860–1920.* Translated, edited, and introduced by Michael P. Steinberg. Chicago: University of Chicago Press, 1984.

Broderson, Arvid. "Stefan George und sein Kreis: Eine Deutung aus der Sicht Max Webers." *Castrum Peregrini* 91 (1970): 5–24.

Brodnitz, Georg. *Englische Wirtschaftsgeschichte.* Jena: Verlag von Gustav Fischer, 1918.

Brombert, Victor. *The Intellectual Hero: Studies in the French Novel, 1880–1955.* Philadelphia and New York: J. B. Lippincott, 1960.

Bruford, W. H. *The German Tradition of Self-Cultivation: 'Bildung' from Humboldt to Thomas Mann.* Cambridge: Cambridge University Press, 1975.

Bruyn, Günter de. "Der Künstler und die Andern." *Sinn und Form* 27 (1975): 171–78.

Bürgin, Hans, and Hans-Otto Mayer. *Thomas Mann: A Chronicle of His Life.* Translated by Eugene Dobson. University, Ala.: University of Alabama Press, 1969.

Cahnman, Werner. "Max Weber and the Methodological Controversy in the Social Sciences." In *Sociology and History,* edited by Werner Cahnman and Alvin Boskoff. New York: Free Press, 1964.

Carlut, Charles. *La Correspondance de Flaubert: Étude et répertoire critique.* Columbus, Ohio: Ohio University Press, 1968.

Carrithers, Michael, Steven Collins, and Steven Lukes, eds. *The Category of the Person.* Cambridge: Cambridge University Press, 1985.

Cassirer, Ernst. *Kant's Life and Thought.* Translated by James Haden. New Haven: Yale University Press, 1981.

Cherin, W. B. "The German School of Economics." Ph.D. diss., University of California, Berkeley, 1933.

Cochrane, Charles N. *Christianity and Classical Culture.* New York: Oxford University Press, 1957.

Conze, Werner. "Beruf." In *Geschichtliche Grundbegriffe: Historisches Lexikon zur politisch-sozialen Sprache in Deutschland,* edited by Otto Brunner, Werner Conze, and Reinhart Koselleck. Vol. 1. Stuttgart: Ernst Klett Verlag, 1972.

Corngold, Stanley. *The Fate of the Self: German Writers and French Theory.* New York: Columbia University Press, 1986.

Craig, Gordon. *Germany, 1866–1945.* Oxford: Oxford University Press, 1978.

———. *The Politics of the Prussian Army, 1640–1945.* New York: Oxford University Press, 1964.

de Bary, William Theodore. *The Liberal Tradition in China.* New York: Columbia University Press, 1983.

de Bary, William Theodore, et al. *The Unfolding of Neo-Confucianism.* New York: Columbia University Press, 1975.

Dibble, Vernon. "Social Science and Political Commitments in the Young Max Weber." *Archives Européenes de Sociologie* 9–10 (1968–69): 92–110.

Dierks, Manfred. "Untersuchungen zum *Tod in Venedig*." In *Thomas-Mann-Studien*. Vol. 3, *Studien zu Mythos und Psychologie bei Thomas Mann*. Bern and Munich: Francke Verlag, 1972.

Diersen, Inge. *Thomas Mann: Episches Werk, Weltanschauung, Leben*. Berlin: Aufbau Verlag, 1975.

Douglas, Richard M. "Talent and Vocation in Humanist and Protestant Thought." In *Action and Conviction in Early Modern Europe: Essays in Memory of E. H. Harbison*, edited by Theodore K. Rabb and Jerrold Siegel. Princeton: Princeton University Press, 1969.

Dumesnil, René. *La Vocation de Gustave Flaubert*. Paris: Gallimard, 1961.

Dunn, John. *The Political Thought of John Locke: An Historical Account of the Argument of the "Two Treatises of Government."* Cambridge: Cambridge University Press, 1969.

Durkheim, Émile. *The Elementary Forms of the Religious Life*. Translated by Joseph Ward Swain. New York: Free Press, 1965.

Edwards, Brian F. M. "Kafka and Kierkegaard: A Reassessment." *German Life and Letters*, n.s. 20 (1967): 218–25.

Ehrenburg, Richard. *Capital and Finance in the Age of the Renaissance: A Study of the Fuggers and Their Connections*. Translated by H. M. Lucas. London: Jonathan Cape, 1928.

Eisen, Arnold. "Called to Order: The Role of the Puritan *Berufsmensch* in Weberian Sociology." *Sociology* 13 (1979): 203–18.

Eisenstadt, S. N., ed. *The Protestant Ethic and Modernization: A Comparative View*. New York: Basic Books, 1968.

Eisermann, Gottfried. *Die Grundlagen des Historismus in der deutschen Nationalökonomie*. Stuttgart: Ferdinand Enke Verlag, 1956.

Elert, Werner. *Der Kampf um das Christentum: Geschichte der Beziehungen zwischen dem evangelischen Christentum in Deutschland und dem allgemeinen Denken bei Schleiermacher und Hegel*. Munich: C. H. Beck'sche Verlagsbuchhandlung, 1921.

Elias, Norbert. *The Civilizing Process*. Translated by Edmund Jephcott. New York: Urizen Books, 1978.

Elvin, Mark. "Between the Earth and Heaven: Conceptions of Self in China." In *The Category of the Person*, edited by Michael Carrithers, Steven Collins, and Steven Lukes. Cambridge: Cambridge University Press, 1985.

———. "Why China Failed to Create an Endogenous Industrial Capitalism: A Critique of Max Weber's Explanation." *Theory and Society* 13 (1984): 379–91.

Ermarth, Michael. *Wilhelm Dilthey: The Critique of Historical Reason*. Chicago: University of Chicago Press, 1978.

Ezergailis, Inta. "Spinell's Letter: An Approach to Thomas Mann's *Tristan*." *German Life and Letters* 25 (1971–72): 377–82.

Fanfani, Amintore. *Catholicism, Protestantism, and Capitalism*. London: Sheed & Ward, 1938.

Feuerlicht, Ignace. "Thomas Mann and Homoeroticism." *Germanic Review* 57 (1982): 89–97.

Finck, Jean. *Thomas Mann und die Psychoanalyse.* Bibliothèque de la Faculté de Philosophie et Lettres de l'Université de Liège. Paris: Belles Lettres, 1973.

Flaubert, Gustave. *Correspondance.* Rev. ed. 9 vols. Paris: Louis Conard, 1926–33.

Francke, Kuno. *Personality in German Literature before Luther.* Cambridge: Harvard University Press, 1916. Reprint. Westport, Conn.: Greenwood Press, 1973.

Fügen, Hans Norbert. *Max Weber mit Selbstzeugnissen und Bilddokumenten.* Reinbeck bei Hamburg: Rowohlt, 1985.

Fürst, L. "Thomas Mann's 'Tonio Kröger': A Critique Reconsidered." *Revue des Langues Vivantes* 27 (1961): 232–40.

Gadamer, Hans-Georg. *Truth and Method.* New York: Seabury Press, 1975.

George, Charles H., and Katherine George. "Protestantism and Capitalism in Pre-Revolutionary England." In *The Protestant Ethic and Modernization: A Comparative View,* edited by S. N. Eisenstadt. New York: Basic Books, 1968.

———. *The Protestant Mind of the English Reformation, 1570–1640.* Princeton: Princeton University Press, 1961.

Giddens, Anthony. Introduction to Max Weber, *The Protestant Ethic and the Spirit of Capitalism,* translated by Talcott Parsons. New York: Scribner's, 1958.

Gierke, Otto von. *Natural Law and the Theory of Society, 1500 to 1800.* Translated by Ernest Barker. Cambridge: Cambridge University Press, 1913. Reprint, 1950.

Girard, René. *Deceit, Desire, and the Novel: Self and Other in Literary Structure.* Baltimore: Johns Hopkins University Press, 1965.

Goethe, Johann Wolfgang von. *Goethes Werke.* Vol. 7. Hamburger Ausgabe. Edited by Erich Trunz. Hamburg: Christian Wegner Verlag, 1950.

Green, Martin. *The von Richthofen Sisters.* New York: Basic Books, 1974.

Grimm, Jacob, and Wilhelm Grimm. *Deutsches Wörterbuch.* Leipzig: Verlag von S. Hirzel, 1889.

Gronicka, André von. "Myth plus Psychology: A Stylistic Analysis of *Death in Venice.*" In *Thomas Mann: A Collection of Critical Essays,* edited by Henry Hatfield. Englewood Cliffs, N.J.: Prentice-Hall, 1964.

Grosses Vollständiges Universal-Lexikon aller Wissenschaften und Künste. Leipzig and Halle: Verlegt Johann Heinrich Zedler, 1741.

Haley, Peter. "Rudolph Sohm on Charisma." *Journal of Religion* 60 (1980): 185–97.

Haller, William. *The Rise of Puritanism.* New York: Columbia University Press, 1938. Reprint. New York: Harper Torchbooks, 1957.

Hamilton, Nigel. *The Brothers Mann.* New Haven: Yale University Press, 1979.

Hansen, Volkmar. *Thomas Manns Heine-Rezeption.* Hamburg: Hoffmann & Campe, 1975.

Hatfield, Henry, ed. *Thomas Mann: A Collection of Critical Essays.* Englewood Cliffs, N.J.: Prentice-Hall, 1964.

————. *Thomas Mann: An Introduction to His Fiction*. Norfolk, Conn.: New Directions, 1951. Rev. ed., 1962.

————. "Two Notes on Thomas Mann's *Doktor Faustus*." *Modern Language Forum* 34 (1949): 11–13.

Haug, Helmut. *Erkenntnisekel: Zum frühen Werk Thomas Manns*. Tübingen: Max Niemeyer Verlag, 1969.

Hauser, Arnold. *The Social History of Art*. Vol. 4. New York: Vintage, 1951.

Heidegger, Martin. "Plato's Doctrine of Truth." In *Philosophy in the Twentieth Century*, edited by Henry Aiken and William Barrett. Vol. 3. New York: Random House, 1962.

Heller, Erich. *Thomas Mann: The Ironic German*. New York: Little, Brown, 1958. Reprint. Cleveland: World, 1961.

————. "Thomas Mann in Venice." In *The Poet's Self and the Poem: Essays on Goethe, Nietzsche, Rilke, and Thomas Mann*. London: Athlone Press, 1976.

Hennis, Wilhelm. "Max Webers Thema: 'Die Persönlichkeit und die Lebens-ordnungen.'" *Zeitschrift für Politik* 31 (1984): 11–52.

Henrich, Dieter. *Die Einheit Max Webers Wissenschaftslehre*. Tübingen: J. C. B. Mohr (Paul Siebeck), 1952.

Hinton, Thomas R. *Nietzsche in German Politics and Society, 1890–1918*. La Salle, Ill.: Open Court, 1983.

————. *Thomas Mann: The Mediation of Art*. Oxford: Oxford University Press, 1956.

————. "The Uses of 'Bildung.'" *German Language and Literature*, n.s. 30 (1977): 177–86.

Holl, Karl. "Die Geschichte des Worts Beruf." In *Gesammelte Aufsätze zur Kirchengeschichte*. Vol. 3. Tübingen: J. C. B. Mohr (Paul Siebeck), 1928.

Huber, Gerdi. *Das klassische Schwabing: München als Zentrum der intellek-tuellen Zeit- und Gesellschaftskritik an der Wende des 19. zum 20. Jahrhun-dert*. Miscellanea Bavarica Monacensia, vol. 37. Munich: Stadtsarchiv München, 1973.

Hughes, H. Stuart. *Consciousness and Society: The Reorientation of European Social Thought, 1890–1930*. New York: Vintage, 1958.

Iggers, Georg G. *The German Conception of History*. Rev. ed. Middletown, Conn.: Wesleyan University Press, 1983.

Jaeger, Werner. *Paideia: The Ideals of Greek Culture*. New York: Oxford University Press, 1965.

Janik, Allan, and Stephen Toulmin. *Wittgenstein's Vienna*. New York: Simon & Schuster, 1973.

Jarausch, Konrad. *Students, Society, and Politics in Imperial Germany: The Rise of Academic Illiberalism*. Princeton: Princeton University Press, 1982.

Jelavich, Peter. "Art and Mammon in Wilhelmine Germany: The Case of Frank Wedekind." *Central European History* 12 (1979): 203–36.

————. Comment on papers in panel, "Outcasts, Victims, Martyrs: Literary Alienation in Imperial Germany." Annual meeting of the German Studies Association, Washington, D.C., October 1985.

————. "'Die Elf Scharfrichter.'" In *The Turn of the Century: German Litera-*

ture and Art, 1890–1915, edited by Gerald Chapple and Hans H. Schulte. Bonn: Bouvier Verlag Herbert Grundmann, 1981.

———. *Munich and Theatrical Modernism: Politics, Playwriting, and Performance, 1890–1914*. Cambridge: Harvard University Press, 1985.

———. "Munich as Cultural Center: Politics and the Arts." In *Kandinsky in Munich: 1896–1914*. New York: Guggenheim Museum, n.d.

Jost, Dominick. *Ludwig Derleth: Gestalt und Leistung*. Stuttgart: W. Kohlhammer Verlag, 1965.

Kant, Immanuel. *Immanuel Kants Werke*. Vol. 6, *Die Religion innerhalb der Grenzen der blossen Vernunft*. Edited by Ernst Cassirer. Berlin: Bruno Cassirer, 1914.

———. *Kants gesammelte Schriften*. Vol. 5, *Kritik der praktischen Vernunft*. Berlin: Preussische Akademie der Wissenschaften, 1900–1942.

Kaufmann, Fritz. *Thomas Mann: The World as Will and Representation*. Boston: Beacon Press, 1957. Reprint. New York: Cooper Square, 1973.

Kehr, Eckart. *Der Primat der Innenpolitik*. Edited by Hans-Ulrich Wehler. Berlin: Walter de Gruyter, 1965. Reprint. Frankfurt am Main: Ullstein Verlag, 1970.

Kierkegaard, Søren. *Either/Or*. Vol. 2. Translated by Walter Lowrie, with revisions and a foreword by Howard A. Johnson. Princeton: Princeton University Press, 1959.

Kirchberger, Lida. "Popularity as a Technique: Notes on 'Tonio Kröger.'" *Monatshefte* 63 (1971): 321–34.

———. "Thomas Mann's 'Tristan.'" *Germanic Review* 36 (1961): 282–97.

Kitchen, Martin. *The Political Economy of Germany, 1815–1914*. London: Croom Helm, 1978.

Kluckhohn, Paul. *Das Ideengut der deutschen Romantik*. 4th ed. Tübingen: Max Niemeyer Verlag, 1961.

———. *Persönlichkeit und Gemeinschaft: Studien zur Stastsauffassung der deutschen Romantik*. Halle: Max Niemeyer Verlag, 1925.

Kohlmeyer, Otto. *Stefan George und die Persönlichkeitsgestalt als Erziehungsziel in Deutschlands Zeitenwende*. Magdeburg: Lichtenberg & Bühling, 1930.

Kohlschmidt, Werner. *A History of German Literature, 1760–1805*. Translated by Ian Hilton. New York: Holmes & Meier, 1975.

Kohut, Heinz. "'Death in Venice' by Thomas Mann: A Story about the Disintegration of Artistic Sublimation." *Psychoanalytic Quarterly* 26 (1957): 206–28.

Koppen, Erwin. *Dekadenter Wagnerismus: Studien zur europäischen Literatur des Fin de siècle*. Berlin: Walter de Gruyter, 1973.

———. "Vom Décadent zum Proto-Hitler: Wagner-Bilder Thomas Manns." In *Thomas Mann und die Tradition*, edited by Peter Pütz. Frankfurt am Main: Athenäum Verlag, 1971.

Krapp, Robert Martin. "A Note on the Puritan 'Calling.'" *Review of Religion* 7 (1943): 242–51.

LaCapra, Dominick. *"Madame Bovary" on Trial*. Ithaca: Cornell University Press, 1982.

Landes, David. "The Industrial Revolution." In *Chapters in Western Civilization.* 3d ed. New York: Columbia University Press, 1948. Reprint, 1962.

———. *The Unbound Prometheus.* Cambridge: Cambridge University Press, 1969.

Lehnert, Herbert. "Die Künstler-Bürger-Brüder." In *Thomas Mann und die Tradition,* edited by Peter Pütz. Frankfurt am Main: Athenäum Verlag, 1971.

Lenman, Robin. "Art, Society, and the Law in Wilhelmine Germany: The Lex Heinze." *Oxford German Studies* 8 (1973): 86–113.

———. "Politics and Culture: The State and the Avant-Garde in Munich, 1886–1914." In *Society and Politics in Wilhelmine Germany,* edited by Richard J. Evans. London: Croom Helm, 1978.

Lichtenstein, E. "Bildung." In *Historisches Wörterbuch der Philosophie,* edited by Joachim Ritter. Vol. 1. Basel and Stuttgart: Schwabe & Co. Verlag, 1971.

Lidtke, Vernon. "Naturalism and Socialism in Germany." *American Historical Review* 79 (1974): 14–37.

Lindenlaub, Dieter. *Richtungskämpfe im Verein für Sozialpolitik.* In *Vierteljahrschrift für Sozial- und Wirtschaftsgeschichte,* supplement 53, pt. 2. Wiesbaden: Franz Steiner Verlag, 1967.

Little, David. *Religion, Order, and Law: A Study of Pre-Revolutionary England.* New York: Harper & Row, 1969.

Lowenthal, Leo. *Literature and the Image of Man.* Boston: Beacon Press, 1957.

Löwith, Karl. *From Hegel to Nietzsche: The Revolution in Nineteenth-Century Thought.* Translated by David E. Green. New York: Holt, Rinehart, & Winston, 1964. Reprint. Garden City, N.Y.: Anchor Books, 1967.

———. *Gesammelte Abhandlungen.* Stuttgart: W. Kohlhammer Verlag, 1960.

Löwy, Michael. *Georg Lukács: From Romanticism to Bolshevism.* Translated by Patrick Cammiller. London: New Left Books, 1979.

Lukács, Georg. *Goethe and His Age.* Translated by Robert Anchor. New York: Grosset & Dunlap, 1969.

———. *History and Class Consciousness.* Translated by Rodney Livingstone. Cambridge: MIT Press, 1971.

———. *Soul and Form.* Translated by Anna Bostock. Cambridge: MIT Press, 1974.

———. *The Theory of the Novel.* Translated by Anna Bostock. Cambridge: MIT Press, 1971.

McWilliams, J. R. "The Failure of a Repression: Thomas Mann's *Tod in Venedig.*" *German Life and Letters,* n.s. 20 (1967): 233–41.

Mann, Katia. *Unwritten Memories.* Edited by Elisabeth Plessner and Michael Mann. Translated by Hunter Hannum and Hildegarde Hannum. New York: Knopf, 1975.

Mann, Otto, and Wolfgang Rothe, eds. *Deutsche Literatur im 20. Jahrhundert: Strukturen und Gestalten.* Vol. 1. 5th ed. Bern and Munich: Francke Verlag, 1967.

Mannheim, Karl. *Ideology and Utopia.* New York: Harcourt, Brace & World, 1936.

Mansuy, Michel. *Un Moderne, Paul Bourget: De l'enfance au disciple.* Annales Littéraires de l'Université de Besançon, vol. 39. Paris: Belles Lettres, 1960.

Marshall, Gordon. *In Search of the Spirit of Capitalism*. New York: Columbia University Press, 1982.

Martens, Wolfgang. *Lyrik Kommerziell: Das Kartell lyrischer Autoren, 1902–1933*. Munich: Wilhelm Fink Verlag, 1974.

Marx, Karl. *Grundrisse: Foundations of the Critique of Political Economy*. Translated by Martin Nicolaus. New York: Vintage, 1973.

Masur, Gerhard. *Prophets of Yesterday: Studies in European Culture, 1890–1914*. New York: Harper & Row, 1961.

Meinecke, Friedrich. *The Age of German Liberation, 1795–1815*. Translated with an introduction by Peter Paret. Berkeley and Los Angeles: University of California Press, 1977.

———. *Werke*. 4 vols. Stuttgart: K. F. Koehler Verlag, 1965.

Mendelssohn, Peter de. *Nachbemerkungen zu Thomas Mann*. 2 vols. Frankfurt am Main: Fischer Taschenbuch Verlag, 1982.

Metzger, Thomas. *Escape from Predicament: Neo-Confucianism and China's Evolving Political Culture*. New York: Columbia University Press, 1977.

———. "Selfhood and Authority in Neo-Confucian Political Culture." In *Normal and Abnormal Behavior in Chinese Culture*, edited by Arthur Kleinman and Tsung-Yi Lin. Dordrecht: D. Reidel, 1981.

Michael, Wolfgang F. "Thomas Mann—Ludwig Derleth—Stefan George." *Modern Language Forum* 35 (1950): 35–38.

Michaelson, Robert S. "Changes in the Puritan Concept of Calling or Vocation." *New England Quarterly* 26 (1953): 315–36.

Miller, Perry. *The New England Mind: From Colony to Province*. Cambridge: Harvard University Press, 1953. Reprint. Boston: Beacon Press, 1961.

Milosz, Czeslaw. "The Nobel Lecture, 1980." *New York Review of Books* 28, no. 3 (5 Mar. 1981): 11–15.

Mitzman, Arthur. *The Iron Cage: An Historical Interpretation of Max Weber*. New York: Knopf, 1970.

Molloy, Stephen. "Max Weber and the Religions of China: Any Way out of the Maze?" *British Journal of Sociology* 31 (1980): 377–400.

Mommsen, Wolfgang. *The Age of Bureaucracy: Perspectives on the Political Sociology of Max Weber*. Oxford: Basil Blackwell, 1974. Reprint. New York: Harper Torchbooks, 1977.

———. *Max Weber und die deutsche Politik, 1890–1920*. 2d ed. Tübingen: J. C. B. Mohr (Paul Siebeck), 1974.

Mossé, Claude. *The Ancient World at Work*. Translated by Janet Lloyd. New York: Norton, 1969.

Mosse, George. *The Crisis of German Ideology: Intellectual Origins of the Third Reich*. New York: Grosset & Dunlap, 1964.

Nachman, Larry David, and Albert S. Braverman. "Thomas Mann's *Buddenbrooks*: Bourgeois Society and the Inner Life." *Germanic Review* 45 (1970): 201–25.

Naumann, Friedrich. *Die Erziehung zur Persönlichkeit im Zeitalter des Grossbetriebs*. Berlin-Schöneberg: Buchverlag der "Hilfe," 1907.

Nelson, Benjamin. "On Orient and Occident in Max Weber." *Social Research* 43 (1976): 114–29.

Nicholls, R. A. *Nietzsche in the Early Work of Thomas Mann*. Berkeley and Los Angeles: University of California Press, 1955.

Nietzsche, Friedrich. *The Will to Power*. Translated by Walter Kaufmann and R. J. Hollingdale. Edited by Walter Kaufmann. New York: Vintage, 1968.

Northcote-Bade, James. "'Hingabe zusammen mit Erkenntnis': Thomas Mann's Wagnererlebnis Reflected in the Early Novellen." Ph.D. diss., University of Wellington, British Columbia, 1971.

―――. *Die Wagner-Mythen im Frühwerk Thomas Manns*. Bonn: Bouvier Verlag Herbert Grundmann, 1975.

Ogg, David. *England in the Reigns of James II and William III*. Oxford: Clarendon Press, 1955.

Palyi, Melchior, ed. *Erinnerungsgabe für Max Weber*. Vol. 1. Munich and Leipzig: Duncker & Humblot, 1923.

Parry, Idris. "Thomas Mann, 1875–1955." *German Language and Letters* 9 (1955–56): 15–19.

Parsons, Talcott. "Capitalism in Recent German Literature." Part 2. *Journal of Political Economy* 37 (1929): 31–51.

―――. "H. M. Robertson on Max Weber and His School." *Journal of Political Economy* 43 (1935): 688–97.

―――. *The Structure of Social Action*. Vol. 2, *Weber*. New York: McGraw-Hill, 1937. Reprint. New York: The Free Press, 1949.

Pascal, Roy. "The Concept of 'Bildung' and the Division of Labour: Wilhelm von Humboldt, Fichte, Schiller, Goethe." In *Culture and the Division of Labour: Three Essays on Literary Culture in Germany*. University of Warwick Occasional Papers. Coventry: University of Warwick, 1974.

―――. *From Naturalism to Expressionism: German Literature and Society, 1890–1918*. New York: Basic Books, 1973.

―――. *The German Novel*. Manchester: Manchester University Press, 1956.

―――. *The German Sturm und Drang*. Manchester: Manchester University Press, 1953.

Paulsen, Friedrich. *A System of Ethics*. 4th ed. Translated by Frank Tilly. New York: Scribner's, 1899.

Pierrot, Jean. *The Decadent Imagination, 1880–1900*. Translated by Derek Coltman. Chicago: University of Chicago Press, 1981.

Pike, Burton. "Thomas Mann and the Problematic Self." In *Publications of the English Goethe Society: Papers Read before the Society, 1966–67*, edited by Elizabeth M. Wilkinson, B. A. Rowley, and Ann C. Weaver. London: Maney, 1967.

Portis, E. B. "Max Weber's Theory of Personality." *Sociological Inquiry* 48 (1978): 113–20.

Pütz, Peter. *Kunst und Künstlerexistenz bei Nietzsche und Thomas Mann: Zum Problem des ästhetischen Perspektivismus in der Moderne*. Bonner Arbeiten zur deutschen Literatur, vol. 6. Edited by Benno von Wiese. Bonn: H. Bouvier & Co. Verlag, 1963.

―――, ed. *Thomas Mann und die Tradition*. Frankfurt am Main: Athenäum Verlag, 1971.

Rasch, Wolfdietrich. *Zur deutschen Literatur seit der Jahrhundertwende: Gesammelte Aufsätze.* Stuttgart: J. B. Metzlersche Verlagsbuchhandlung, 1967.

Reed, T. J. *Thomas Mann: The Uses of Tradition.* Oxford: Oxford University Press, 1974.

Reiss, Gunter. "Herrenrecht: Bemerkungen zum Syndrom des Autoritären in Thomas Manns frühen Erzählungen." In *Gedenkschrift für Thomas Mann, 1875–1955,* edited by Rolf Wiecker. Copenhagen: Verlag Text und Kontext, 1975.

Rich, E. E., and C. H. Wilson, eds. *The Cambridge Economic History of Europe.* Vol. 4. Cambridge: Cambridge University Press, 1967.

Riedel, Manfred. "Bürger, Staatsbürger, Bürgertum." In *Geschichtliche Grundbegriffe: Historisches Lexikon zur politisch-sozialen Sprache in Deutschland,* edited by Otto Brunner, Werner Conze, and Reinhart Koselleck. Vol. 1. Stuttgart: Ernst Klett Verlag, 1972.

Riesebrodt, Martin. "Vom Patriarchalismus zum Kapitalismus: Max Webers Analyse der Transformation der ostelbischen Agrarverhältnisse im Kontext zeitgenossischer Theorien." *Kölner Zeitschrift für Soziologie und Sozialpsychologie* 37 (1985): 546–67.

Ringer, Fritz. *The Decline of the German Mandarins, 1890–1933.* Cambridge: Harvard University Press, 1969.

Robertson, H. M. *Aspects of the Rise of Economic Individualism: A Criticism of Max Weber and His School.* Cambridge: Cambridge University Press, 1935.

Rogin, Michael. "Max Weber and Woodrow Wilson: The Iron Cage in Germany and America." *Polity* 3 (1971): 557–75.

Rosenberg, Hans. *Bureaucracy, Aristocracy, Autocracy: The Prussian Experience, 1660–1815.* Cambridge: Harvard University Press, 1958. Reprint. Boston: Beacon Press, 1966.

———. *Grosse Depression und Bismarckzeit: Wirtschaftsablauf, Gesellschaft und Politik in Mitteleuropa.* Berlin: Walter de Gruyter, 1967. Reprint. Frankfurt am Main: Ullstein Verlag, 1976.

———. "Political and Social Consequences of the Great Depression of 1873–1896 in Central Europe." *Economic History Review* 13 (1943): 58–73.

Roth, Guenther. Introduction to Max Weber, *Economy and Society.* Edited by Guenther Roth and Claus Wittich. Berkeley and Los Angeles: University of California Press, 1978.

Rupp, Gordon. *Culture-Protestantism: German Liberal Theology at the Turn of the Century.* American Academy of Religion, Studies in Religion Series, no. 15. Missoula, Montana: Scholars Press, 1977.

Sagave, Pierre-Paul. *Réalité sociale et idéologie religieuse dans les romans de Thomas Mann.* Faculté des Lettres de l'Université de Strasbourg, no. 124. Paris: Belles Lettres, 1954.

Salin, Edgar. *Um Stefan George.* 2d ed. Munich: Helmut Küpper, vormals Georg Bondi, 1954.

Salz, Arthur. "Zur Geschichte der Berufsidee." *Archiv für Sozialwissenschaft und Sozialpolitik* 37 (1913): 380–423.

Samuelsson, Kurt. *Religion and Economic Action: A Critique of Max Weber.* New York: Harper & Row, 1961.

Sartre, Jean-Paul. *Sartre by Himself*. New York: Urizen Books, 1978.

Sauer, Wolfgang. "Weimar Culture: Experiments in Modernism." *Social Research* 39 (1972): 254–84.

Scherrer, Paul, and Hans Wysling, eds. *Thomas-Mann-Studien*. Vol. 1, *Quellenkritische Studien zum Werk Thomas Manns*. Bern and Munich: Francke Verlag, 1967.

Schick, Manfred. *Kulturprotestantismus und soziale Frage: Versuche zur Begründung der Sozialethik, vornehmlich in der Zeit um der Gründung des Evangelisch-Sozialen Kongresses bis zum Ausbruch des 1. Weltkrieges (1890–1914)*. Tübingen: J. C. B. Mohr (Paul Siebeck), 1970.

Schiller, Friedrich von. *Schillers Werke*. Nationalausgabe. Edited by Benno von Wiese. Vol. 20. Weimar: Hermann Böhlaus Nachfolger, 1962.

Schlatter, R. *Social Ideas of the Religious Leaders, 1660–1688*. London: Oxford University Press, 1940.

Schluchter, Wolfgang, ed. *Max Webers Sicht des antiken Christentums: Interpretation und Kritik*. Frankfurt am Main: Suhrkamp Verlag, 1985.

———, ed. *Max Webers Studie über das antike Judentum: Interpretation und Kritik*. Frankfurt am Main: Suhrkamp Verlag, 1981.

———, ed. *Max Webers Studie über Hinduismus und Buddhismus: Interpretation und Kritik*. Frankfurt am Main: Suhrkamp Verlag, 1984.

———, ed. *Max Webers Studie über Konfuzianismus und Taoismus: Interpretation und Kritik*. Frankfurt am Main: Suhrkamp Verlag, 1983.

———. *Rationalismus der Weltbeherrschung: Studien zu Max Weber*. Frankfurt am Main: Suhrkamp Verlag, 1980.

Schnädelbach, Herbert. *Philosophie in Deutschland, 1831–1933*. Frankfurt am Main: Suhrkamp Verlag, 1983.

———. *Philosophy in Germany, 1831–1933*. Cambridge: Cambridge University Press, 1984.

Schröter, Klaus. *Thomas Mann in Selbstzeugnissen und Bilddokumenten*. Reinbeck bei Hamburg: Rowohlt, 1964.

Schumpeter, Joseph. *A History of Economic Analysis*. New York: Oxford University Press, 1955.

Seigel, Jerrold. *Bohemian Paris: Culture, Politics, and the Boundaries of Bourgeois Life, 1830–1930*. New York: Viking, 1986.

Shanahan, William O. "Friedrich Naumann: A Mirror of Wilhelmian Germany." *Review of Politics* 13 (1951): 267–301.

Sheehan, James, ed. *Imperial Germany*. New York: New Viewpoints (Franklin Watts), 1976.

Siefken, Hinrich. "Thomas Mann and the Concept of 'Repräsentation': *Königliche Hoheit*." *Modern Language Review* 73 (1978): 22–50.

Silber, John R. "The Ethical Significance of Kant's *Religion*." Introduction to *Religion within the Limits of Reason Alone*, by Immanuel Kant. Translated by Theodore M. Greene and Hoyt H. Hudson. New York: Harper & Row, 1960.

Simmel, Georg. *The Sociology of Georg Simmel*. Translated and edited by Kurt H. Wolff. New York: Free Press, 1950.

Slochower, Harry. "Thomas Mann's *Death in Venice.*" *American Imago* 26 (1969): 99–122.

Sokel, Walter. *The Writer in Extremis: Expressionism in Twentieth-Century German Literature.* Stanford: Stanford University Press, 1959. Reprint. New York: McGraw-Hill, 1964.

Speier, Hans. "Zur Soziologie der bürgerlichen Intelligenz in Deutschland." In *Positionen der literarischen Intelligenz zwischen bürgerliche Reaktion und Imperialismus,* edited by Gert Mattenklott and Klaus R. Scherpe. Kronberg: Scriptor Verlag, 1973.

Stark, Gary. "Trials and Tribulations: Authors' Responses to Censorship in Imperial Germany, 1885–1914." Paper presented in panel, "Outcasts, Victims, Martyrs: Literary Alienation in Imperial Germany." Annual meeting of the German Studies Association, Washington, D.C., October 1985.

Starkie, Enid. *Flaubert: The Making of the Master.* New York: Atheneum, 1967.

Steegmuller, Francis, ed. *The Letters of Gustave Flaubert, 1830–1857.* Cambridge: Harvard University Press, 1980.

Stern, Fritz. *The Failure of Illiberalism.* New York: Knopf, 1972.

———. *The Politics of Cultural Despair: A Study in the Rise of the Germanic Ideology.* Berkeley and Los Angeles: University of California Press, 1961. Reprint. Garden City, N.Y.: Doubleday, 1965.

Stewart, Walter. "*Der Tod in Venedig:* The Path to Insight." *Germanic Review* 53 (1978): 50–54.

Swanson, Guy. *Religion and Regime: A Sociological Account of the Reformation.* Ann Arbor: University of Michigan Press, 1967.

Sweet, Paul. *Wilhelm von Humboldt: A Biography.* Vol. 1. Columbus, Ohio: Ohio State University Press, 1978.

Tison-Braun, Micheline. *La Crise de l'humanisme: Le Conflit de l'individu et de la société dans la littérature française moderne.* Vol. 1, 1890–1914. Paris: Librairie Nizet, 1958.

Tribe, Keith. "Prussian Agriculture—German Politics: Max Weber, 1892–7." *Economy and Society* 12 (1983): 181–226.

Troeltsch, Ernst. *Christian Thought: Its History and Application.* Edited, introduced, and indexed by Baron F. von Hügel. London: University of London Press, 1923.

———. *Ernst Troeltsch: Writings on Theology and Religion.* Translated and edited by Robert Morgan and Michael Pye. Atlanta: John Knox Press, 1977.

———. *Gesammelte Schriften.* 4 vols. 2d ed. Tübingen: J. C. B. Mohr (Paul Siebeck), 1922.

———. *Protestantism and Progress: A Historical Study of the Relation of Protestantism to the Modern World.* Translated by W. Montgomery. Boston: Beacon Press, 1958.

———. *The Social Teaching of the Christian Churches.* 2 vols. Translated by Olive Wyon. London: Allen & Unwin, 1931.

Trübner's Deutsches Wörterbuch. Berlin: Walter de Gruyter, 1954.

Turner, Bryan. *Weber and Islam: A Critical Study.* London: Routledge & Kegan Paul, 1974.

Vaget, Hans Rudolf. *Thomas-Mann-Kommentar: Zu sämtlichen Erzählungen.* Munich: Winkler Verlag, 1984.

———. "Thomas Mann und Oskar Panizza: Zwei Splitter zu *Buddenbrooks* und *Doktor Faustus.*" *Germanisch-Romanische Monatsschrift* 56 (1975): 231–37.

Vierhaus, Rudolf. "Bildung." In *Geschichtliche Grundbegriffe: Historisches Lexikon zur politisch-sozialen Sprache in Deutschland,* edited by Otto Brunner, Werner Conze, and Reinhart Koselleck. Vol. 1. Stuttgart: Ernst Klett Verlag, 1972.

Vogt, Jochen. *Thomas Mann: "Buddenbrooks."* Munich: Wilhelm Fink Verlag, 1983.

Vondung, Klaus, ed. *Das Wilhelminische Bildungsbürgertum: Zur Sozialgeschichte seiner Ideen.* Göttingen: Vandenhoeck & Ruprecht, 1976.

Vontobel, Klara. *Das Arbeitsethos des deutschen Protestantismus von der nachreformatorischen Zeit bis zur Aufklärung.* Bern: Francke Verlag, 1946.

Walzer, Michael. *The Revolution of the Saints: A Study in the Origins of Radical Politics.* Cambridge: Harvard University Press, 1965. Reprint. New York: Atheneum, 1970.

Wax, Murray. "Ancient Judaism and the Protestant Ethic." *American Journal of Sociology* 65 (1959–60): 449–55.

Weber, Marianne. *Max Weber: Ein Lebensbild.* Tübingen: J. C. B. Mohr (Paul Siebeck), 1926.

———. *Max Weber: A Biography.* Translated by Harry Zohn. New York: Wiley, 1975.

Wehler, Hans-Ulrich. *Das Deutsche Kaiserreich, 1871–1918.* 5th ed. Göttingen: Vandenhoeck & Ruprecht, 1983.

———, ed. *Moderne deutsche Sozialgeschichte.* Cologne: Kiepenhauer & Witsch, 1976.

Weigand, Hermann J. "Thomas Mann's *Royal Highness* as Symbolic Autobiography." In *Thomas Mann: A Collection of Critical Essays,* edited by Henry Hatfield. Englewood Cliffs, N.J.: Prentice-Hall, 1964.

Weigand, Paul. "Thomas Mann's 'Tonio Kröger' and Kleist's 'Über das Marionettentheater.'" *Symposium* 12 (1958): 133–38.

Weiss, Johannes. *Max Webers Grundlegung der Soziologie: Eine Einführung.* Munich: Uni-Taschenbücher, Verlag Dokumentation, 1975.

Weyembergh, Maurice. *Le Voluntarisme rationnel de Max Weber.* Mémoires de la Classe des Lettres, 2d series, vol. 61, no. 1. Brussels: Académie Royale de Belgique, 1972.

Willey, Thomas E. *Back to Kant: The Revival of Kantianism in German Social and Historical Thought, 1860–1914.* Detroit: Wayne State University Press, 1978.

Williams, Raymond. *Culture and Society, 1780–1950.* London: Chatto & Windus, 1958. Reprint. Harmondsworth: Penguin Books, 1963.

Wilson, Charles. *England's Apprenticeship, 1603–1763.* New York: St. Martin's Press, 1965.

Wilson, Edmund. *Axel's Castle: A Study in the Imaginative Literature of 1870–1930.* New York: Scribner's, 1931.

Windelband, Wilhelm. *A History of Philosophy*. Vol. 2. Rev. ed. New York: Macmillan, 1893. Reprint, 1901.

————. *Lehrbuch der Geschichte der Philosophie*. 4th ed. Tübingen: J. C. B. Mohr (Paul Siebeck), 1907.

————. *Über Willensfreiheit*. Tübingen: J. C. B. Mohr (Paul Siebeck), 1904.

Winkler, Michael. *George-Kreis*. Stuttgart: Metzlersche Verlagsbuchhandlung, 1972.

Winston, Richard. *Thomas Mann: The Making of an Artist, 1871–1911*. New York: Knopf, 1981.

Wohl, Robert. *The Generation of 1914*. Cambridge: Harvard University Press, 1979.

Wolters, Friedrich. *Stefan George und die Blätter für die Kunst*. Berlin: Georg Bondi, 1930.

Young, Frank W. *Montage and Motif in Thomas Mann's 'Tristan.'* Bonn: Bouvier Verlag Herbert Grundmann, 1975.

Zmegac, Viktor, ed. *Deutsche Literatur der Jahrhundertwende*. Neue Wissenschaftliche Bibliothek, no. 133. Königstein im Taunus: Verlagsgruppe Athenäum, Hain, Scriptor, Hanstein, 1981.

Index

Compositor: G & S Typesetters, Inc.
   Printer: Braun-Brumfield, Inc.
   Binder: Braun-Brumfield, Inc.
     Text: 10/13 Sabon
  Display: Sabon